ULRLS ITEM BARCODE

19 1803885 3

European Studies in English Literature

The Rise of the English Street Ballad, 1550–1650

This study of the street ballad is the first to investigate both the rise and the period of flourishing of a specific genre of popular literature which has so far been vastly neglected. Attention is focused on the social and cultural conditions which accompanied its development: the relative position of authors and printers, the marketing and distribution of texts, the nature of the balladmonger and his audience. The contemporary reputation of the street ballad is examined, as is the importance of the genre for the history of ideas. The street ballad is also looked at as a literary form, and its various types and the literary devices they employed are described in detail and richly illustrated in order to convey a general notion of the genre and of the features which were relevant to its subsequent development in the eighteenth and nineteenth centuries.

In the period from 1550 to 1650 the street ballad was a widespread and well-known type of ephemeral literature which, both from the point of view of content and that of form, met the literary needs of the middle and lower classes of the time, and the broadsheets on which it was printed were singularly well suited to the conditions that street and marketplace imposed on performance and sale. The development of the street ballad in this period also mirrors a change from religious dogmatism and a world view orientated towards redemption and salvation to one that is secular in attitude, worldly-wise, and a reflection of a modern individualism.

The street ballad is of literary interest because of the wide range of subjects it touches upon as well as its capacity for giving literary expression to everyday human experience from a variety of points of view – pious, sentimental, humorous, sensational. It is also of interest to the literary historian since it decisively influenced the subsequent development of the ballad as a medium of entertainment and instruction. Such diverse forms as the popular songs and political ballads of the seventeenth and eighteenth centuries, the ballad opera, the *chanson*, the cabaret song, the pop song and some types of literary ballad all belong to a tradition reaching back to the street ballad.

Natascha Würzbach's study, appearing now for the first time in English, will be of value to scholars and students of sixteenth- and seventeenth-century English literature, balladry, folklore, street literature, cultural studies, and the history of journalism.

D1388448

European Studies in English Literature

SERIES EDITORS
Ulrich Broich, Professor of English, University of Munich
Herbert Grabes, Professor of English, University of Giessen
Dieter Mehl, Professor of English, University of Bonn

Roger Asselineau, Professor Emeritus of American Literature, University of Paris–Sorbonne
Paul-Gabriel Boucé, Professor of English, University of Sorbonne–Nouvelle
Robert Ellrodt, Professor of English, University of Sorbonne–Nouvelle
Sylvère Monod, Professor Emeritus of English, University of Sorbonne–Nouvelle

This series is devoted to publishing translations into English of the best works written in European languages on English and American literature. These may be first-rate books recently published in their original versions, or they may be classic studies which have influenced the course of scholarship in their field while never having been available in English before.

To begin with, the series has concentrated on works translated from the German; but its range will expand to cover other languages.

TRANSLATIONS PUBLISHED
Walter Pater: The aesthetic moment by Wolfgang Iser
The Theory and Analysis of Drama by Manfred Pfister
The Symbolist Tradition in English Literature: A study of pre-Raphaelitism and 'fin de siècle' by Lothar Hönnighausen
Oscar Wilde by Norbert Kohl
The Rise of the English Street Ballad 1550–1650 by Natascha Würzbach

TITLES UNDER CONTRACT FOR TRANSLATION
Studien zum komischen Epos by Ulrich Broich
Redeformen des englischen Mysterienspiels by Hans-Jürgen Diller
Die romantische Verserzählung in England by Hermann Fischer
Studien zur Dramenform vor Shakespeare: Moralität, Interlude, romaneskes Drama by Werner Habicht
Die Frauenklage: Studien zur elegischen Verserzählung in der englischen Literatur des Spätmittelalters und der Renaissance by Götz Schmitz
Das englische Theater der Gegenwart by Christian Werner Thomsen
La Dupe Elisabéthaine by Christiane Gallenca
Shakespeare et La Fête: Essai d'archéologie du spectacle dans l'Angleterre Elisabéthaine by François Laroque

The Rise of the English
Street Ballad, 1550–1650

Natascha Würzbach

Translated from the German by Gayna Walls

The right of the
University of Cambridge
to print and sell
all manner of books
was granted by
Henry VIII in 1534.
The University has printed
and published continuously
since 1584.

CAMBRIDGE UNIVERSITY PRESS

Cambridge
New York   Port Chester
Melbourne   Sydney

BIBL.
LONDIN.
UNIV.

CAMBRIDGE UNIVERSITY PRESS
Cambridge, New York, Melbourne, Madrid, Cape Town,
Singapore, São Paulo, Delhi, Tokyo, Mexico City

Cambridge University Press
The Edinburgh Building, Cambridge CB2 8RU, UK

Published in the United States of America by Cambridge University Press, New York

www.cambridge.org
Information on this title: www.cambridge.org/9780521177443

Originally published in German as Die englische Strassenballade 1550–1650
by Wilhelm Fink Verlag, Munich, 1981
and © Wilhelm Fink Verlag, Munich
First published in English by Cambridge University Press 1990 as
The Rise of the English Street Ballad, 1550–1650

English translation © Cambridge University Press 1990

This publication is in copyright. Subject to statutory exception
and to the provisions of relevant collective licensing agreements,
no reproduction of any part may take place without the written
permission of Cambridge University Press.

First paperback edition 2011

A catalogue record for this publication is available from the British Library

Library of Congress Cataloguing in Publication data
[Anfänge und gattungstypische Ausformung der englischen
Strassenballade 1550–1650. English]
The rise of the English street ballad, 1550–1650 / Natascha
Würzbach; translated from the German by Gayna Walls.
    p.   cm. – (European studies in English literature)
Translation of Anfänge und gattungstypische Ausformung der
englischen Strassenballade 1550–1650.
Bibliography.
ISBN 0 521 32061 5
1. Ballads. English – History and criticism. 2. English poetry –
Early modern, 1500–1700 – History and criticism. 3. Street
literature – England – History and criticism. 4. Broadsides – England –
History. 5. England – Popular culture. I. Title. II. Series.
PR976.W813 1990
821'.04409 – dc20   89–7315   CIP

ISBN 978-0-521-32061-0 Hardback
ISBN 978-0-521-17744-3 Paperback

Cambridge University Press has no responsibility for the persistence or
accuracy of URLs for external or third-party internet websites referred to in
this publication, and does not guarantee that any content on such websites is,
or will remain, accurate or appropriate.

A Ballet, a ballet! let every Poet,
     A ballet make with speed:
And he that has wit, now let him shew it;
     For never was greater need:
And I that never made a ballet befor;
Will make one now, though never make more.
                              (1658)

Who makes a ballet for an ale-house doore,
Shall liue in future times for euer more.
                    (between 1597 and 1601)

Contents

Contents

Preface

Popular literature has generally been considered the province of folklore studies. In the present work I have attempted to do justice to the English street ballad as a valid literary form from the standpoint of literary criticism. The English street ballad emerged out of specific social and cultural conditions in the sixteenth century and in the first half of the seventeenth century, when the genre was at its height; it was capable of giving literary expression to everyday human experience. It was a literary genre which corresponded in both form and content to the literary requirements of the lower and middle classes of the time, and which singularly fulfilled the conditions for performance and sale in the street and the marketplace. The street ballad used simple, clear, descriptive means, and made use of presenters' devices commonly found in the popular entertainment of the time. With this, the element of fictional self-presentation was introduced into the literature, pointing up the subjective mediating function of a textual speaker. The speaker's sole responsibility for his textual message corresponded to the plurality of opinion, secular in nature, which was evident in the transition from the Middle Ages to modern times. The literary-historical innovations of the street ballad decisively influenced the further development of the ballad within the area of entertainment and instruction: the popular song and political ballad of the seventeenth and eighteenth centuries, ballad opera, the drawing-room ballad, music-hall song, *chanson*, cabaret song and pop song, and not least some types of literary ballad, all belong to the same genre tradition as the street ballad.

The present study, which was published in German in 1981, has been revised and abridged for the English version. My particular thanks are due to the translator, Dr Gayna Walls, who has shown perception and a fine understanding in her English rendering of the text. Working with Gayna Walls was for me a most pleasurable and profitable experience.

Abbreviations

Titles are given in shortened form

AB	*Ancient Ballads and Broadsides*, H. Huth, ed. (London 1867)
BB	*Ballads and Broadsides*, H. L. Collmann, ed. (Oxford 1912)
BBBM	*The British Broadside Ballad and Its Music*, C. M. Simpson, ed. (New Brunswick 1966)
BBLB	*Broadside Black-letter Ballads*, J. P. Collier, ed. (published privately, 1868)
CM	*The Common Muse*, V. de Sola Pinto, ed. (London 1957)
CP	*Cavalier and Puritan*, H. E. Rollins, ed. (New York 1923)
OB	*Old Ballads from Early Printed Copies*, J. P. Collier, ed. (London 1840)
OEB	*Old English Ballads: 1553–1625*, H. E. Rollins, ed. (Cambridge 1920)
POA	*The Pack of Autolycus*, H. E. Rollins, ed. (Cambridge, Mass. 1927)
PB	*The Pepys Ballads*, 8 vols., H. E. Rollins, ed. (Cambridge, Mass. 1929–32)
PG	*A Pepysian Garland*, H. E. Rollins, ed. (Cambridge 1922)
PMO	*Popular Music of the Olden Time*, 2 vols., W. Chappell, ed. (London 1855–9)
RB	*The Roxburghe Ballads*, 9 vols., W. Chappell and J. W. Ebsworth, eds. (London, Hertford 1869–99)
SB	*Songs and Ballads*, T. Wright, ed. (London 1860)
SHB	*The Shirburn Ballads*, A. Clark, ed. (Oxford 1907)

System of quotation from the above ballad editions: reference to sources in these editions is by abbreviation, the number of the text (in so far as the texts are numbered in the particular edition), volume number in roman numerals (if there is more than one volume), and page number in arabic numerals. For example: *PB*, no. 84, II, pp. 224–8; *PG*, no. 8, pp. 49–53; *RB*, III, pp. 556–9. For reasons of consistency the verse number is given in every case, even if in the edition itself the verses are not numbered (in the case of *RB* the *line* number is also given). Where there is no division into verses, only the line number is given, even if lines are not numbered in the editions. For example: *PG*, no. 44, v. 10, pp. 52–3; ibid. 10, 1–3, p. 52; *RB*, II, vv. 3–5, lines 17–40, p. 263; *AB*, no. 22, lines 10–32, p. 125.

1 *The cunning Northerne Begger* (between 1626 and 1681); Roxburghe
Collection, vol. I

2 *The Cooper of Norfolke* (between 1625 and 1660); Roxburghe Collection, vol. I

3 *The Cruell Shrow* (between 1601 and 1640); Roxburghe Collection, vol. I

Introduction: survey of research to date and delineation of study area

> Shakespeare's picture of Autolycus and Earle's character of the pot-poet relieve the historian from a vain effort to describe a vast amount of heterogeneous material, though a lively and instructive chapter might be made of a mere list of titles.

Such was Douglas Bush's assessment, in 1945, of the state of research and extent of intellectual interest in the English street ballad. He repeats this judgement in the volume of the *Oxford History of English Literature* ([1962], p. 48) dealing with the years 1600–60, the period, as Bush informs us with reference to the specialist H. E. Rollins, of the flowering of the street ballad. This short, concise and necessarily simplified dictum admirably describes the state of research on the subject. The reference to the comic figure of the low-class balladmonger in *The Winter's Tale*, and to the frequently cited caricature of a drunken hack writer whose main income derived from ballads, has become a convention in historical literary scholarship, and shows the extent to which the study of the street ballad has always been hampered by prejudice. This is a traditional prejudice, which originated in the age of the street ballad itself and is directed against both the 'inferior' quality of the actual ballads and also against the genre *per se*, which is regarded as having low- to middle-class social and literary status.

The description and classification of street ballads has up till now been confined to content, together with bibliographical, cultural–historical and some textual aspects. No attempt has been made systematically to bring these together into a cohesive picture, and it is the construction of the texts which has here been most neglected. It is immediately noticeable that the texts have a metric and verse pattern, with rhyming couplets or alternate rhyme scheme. The length (80–120 lines) was determined by the fact that street ballads were printed on a single sheet (broadside) or on both sides (broadsheet),[1] usually illustrated with a woodcut. This form of publication was also used for prose texts, and for other purposes than entertainment and instruction, so that a distinction can be discerned here which is important though not always obvious.[2] 'Black-letter' type, in general use only until the middle of the sixteenth century when 'white-letter' type became the rule, was retained for street ballads and for prose of popular entertain-

1

ment and instruction for over a century longer than for more 'highbrow' material.[3] This typographical indication of the low literary status of the street ballad was not abandoned until the turn of the seventeenth century.[4] The text of the ballad was sung or recited as the printed copy was being sold, and this distribution in the street, marketplace, public house or at the fair, instead of through the usual channels for books, is a further distinguishing factor of the street ballad. The relevance of this for a socio-literary genre definition has not, however, been investigated so far.

The predominantly bibliographical and editorial interest in the street ballad continued the seventeenth- and eighteenth-century tradition of antiquarian collecting. The editions, published between the nineteenth century and the 1930s, have provided an excellent basis for further research. These editions contain a major proportion of the printed copies of ballads surviving in amateur collections.

Texts from the so-called Suffolk Collection,[5] which for the most part contains ballads from 1560 to 1570, were published by H. Huth in *Ancient Ballads and Broadsides* (1867)[6] and by H. L. Collmann in *Ballads and Broadsides* (1912). The texts edited by Huth comprise mainly ballads showing those street-ballad features which were to become characteristic of the genre in the seventeenth century. Their relatively wide thematic variety can be seen as representative of the second half of the sixteenth century. The texts in Collmann's selection show more the fluctuation between the street ballad and other forms of verse of this early period. Similarly, J. P. Collier's *Broadside Black-letter Ballads* (1868) contains a large number of early ballads, some from H. Huth's collection.[7] Some texts overlap with the volume published by Collier in 1840, *Old Ballads from Early Printed Copies*. T. Wright provided access to the MS. Ashmole 48 with his publication *Songs and Ballads* (1860). This is a collection of verses presumed to have been put together by the itinerant singer Richard Sheale in the mid-sixteenth century. There is disagreement as to whether it preceded the corresponding printed copies.[8] From the point of view of the textual make-up, the verses in this collection represent more or less a transitional stage leading to the street ballad proper.

The transition from early street ballads to textual material from the seventeenth century is illustrated by H. E. Rollins in his first editions. *Old English Ballads: 1553–1625* (1920) contains texts from various printed copies and from MSS in the British Library, and also from the Rawlinson MS. (Bodleian), most of which are religious in content. *A Pepysian Garland* (1922) comprises a selection from the largest ballad collection, the Pepys Collection.[9] Rollins chose here texts between 1595 and 1639 for the first volume of the collection, evidently selected from the standpoint of quality,[10] in order to awaken interest in this literary form among a wider public. A. Clark had already published texts from the transition period in his *The Shirburn Ballads 1585–1616* (1907). This is a collection from the beginning of the seventeenth century[11] of handwritten copies of printed copies of varying provenance. Over a third of these have been published following the printed copy, in other editions (especially in *RB*).

The most comprehensive editions are W. Chappell and J. W. Ebsworth's *Roxburghe Ballads* (1869–99) and Rollins's *Pepys Ballads* (1929–32). The Roxburghe Collection[12] contains 1,466 ballads, mainly from the seventeenth century, of which 176 are duplicates. It is in four volumes, of which the third contains numerous eighteenth-century texts. The edition comprises nine volumes. The first three, edited by Chappell, follow exactly the order of the collection, whereas Ebsworth in the subsequent volumes arranged the texts, which he dated, in thematically related groups. Most relevant to our period of investigation are volumes I and II.[13] The Pepys Collection also contains mainly seventeenth-century ballads,[14] which Rollins arranged in chronological order. The first two volumes span the period from 1610 to 1640, and the third begins in 1666.[15] His commentary on the individual texts is, compared with other editors', particularly detailed and informative, and always includes a chronological reference. A further edition by Rollins contains exclusively news and sensational ballads from the seventeenth century: *The Pack of Autolycus or Strange and Terrible News* (1927).[16] With all these taken together, a fair proportion of sixteenth- and seventeenth-century street ballads had been made available.[17]

The dating of street ballads presents relatively few problems in the majority of cases.[18] If the publication date is not given in the title of the text, it can be deduced from the name of the printer on the statutory imprint which is normally to be found: the period of activity of most of the printers has been established.[19] Further, the entries in the Stationers' Register[20] for the period 1557–1709, compiled by Rollins, provide a set of precise dates. Finally, references to or treatment of contemporary events, together with the use of tunes to earlier street ballads as announced in the title, enable us approximately to date the ballads. Frequent reprintings or imitations of previously published texts present a particular bibliographical problem, appearing as they do without any indication that they are not the original. These become more common in the second half of the seventeenth century. We can, however, establish a relatively precise chronological framework, according to which the texts can be arranged and which enables us to build up a description of the historical development of the various types of ballad.[21] The reverse process, that is, deducing the date of origin from the thematic material, style, and structure type, produces imprecise results. This is because popular literature, with its functional nature and consequent rigidity of form, allows of gradual change only, while similarly the tradition-bound character of the street ballad inclined authors towards outmoded styles. Further, borrowings from other literary genres often appeared long after the original.

The history of the term 'ballad' was elucidated by A. B. Friedmann ([1958], pp. 95–110; [1961], pp. 35–9). He proved convincingly that the English word 'ballad' was taken over, not from the Italian *ballata* ('dance'), but from the French *balade*, a type of verse-form which became established in England in the fourteenth century. The form of the *balade* differs so markedly from the verse-form of the street ballad that the evolution of the term only becomes clear with the discovery of the missing link in the chain of development: the 'pseudo-ballade'. Right up to the early eighteenth century, the English version of the term 'ballad' referred exclusively to street ballads printed on broadsheets.[22] It was only with the reawakening of interest in folk ballads that the reference of the term was extended to include these too. No distinction was made between the terms 'traditional ballad' and 'broadside ballad' until the first editions of street ballads appeared. The name 'street ballad', as used by V. de Sola Pinto (1947; 1957), has the advantage of being a socio-cultural (cf. 'street literature', R. Collison [1973]) as well as a biographical definition of the genre. The German translation of the work as '*Strassenballade*' signals the difference between the street ballad and the German *Bänkelsang*.[23]

The reasons for the marked neglect in academic research of the street ballad as opposed to the folk ballad, in spite of the many available editions of the former, are rooted in the history of ideas and of literary scholarship. This can be deduced both from the extensive research work produced on the folk ballad in contrast with the sparse material relating to the street ballad,[24] and from explicit comments on the subject. The folk ballad, with its high tragedy and lofty ideals, archaic techniques, and supposedly age-old texts[25] fitted in more easily with accepted poetic norms and with the sense of historical pride[26] than the street ballad. As long as the latter was measured against the folk ballad in terms of its literary-historical placing, structure and function, there could be no prospect of an unbiased view or a more thorough study of the street ballad.[27] In addition there was, even during its heyday, a predominantly negative evaluation of the street ballad from the point of view of orthodox literature. This attitude persisted, despite possible differences in quality in the text corpus and despite the popularity and widespread influence of the street ballad and its own internal literary development which was of long-term significance. Irregular verse-formation, inelegance of style, incredible and fantastic content, obscenity and dubious morality,[28] together with a general lack of 'poetry', 'culture', and 'taste', are the criticisms levelled at the street ballad.[29] Such judgements, usually brief generalizations, indicate a lack of more precise interpretational perception of the texts on the part of the ballad specialists

Rollins, Chappell and Ebsworth, in spite of their undoubted contribution by way of a preliminary classification of the material.

The study of the street ballad has up till now been characterized by attempts at justification which stem from traditional literary and aesthetic value judgements, and also by a predominant interest in content. Rollins's doubtless literary interest in the texts is often expressed through an emphasis on qualities which are orientated towards the norm of orthodox literature:

'A pleasant wooing song' (*PB*, I, p. 72), 'this graceful ballad' (*PB*, I, p. 186), 'The ballad is worthy of its distinguished tune: it is a fine love-song, the composition either of an extraordinarily gifted ballad-writer or of a real poet' (*PB*, II, p. 3), 'Certainly this is a pretty ballad, even though its language and ideas always border on indecency' (*PB*, II, p. 8).

And:

This charming love-song is an illustration of what a broadside ballad could become when a real poet turned to that medium of expression. There are few poems in the Elizabethan miscellanies more delightful than this. It is commended to the attention of those – if there be such – who believe all ballads to be trash.   (*PB*, II, p. 249)

A. B. Friedmann ([1961], pp. 49–53), too, clearly evaluates what he calls the 'literary ballad' as opposed to the 'journalistic ballad' according to content and the presence or absence of 'high poetry'. Rollins does however recognize the poetic achievement of the street ballad on its own literary level:

When the authors and the audience for which the songs were intended are considered, the poetry seems especially good. Frankly writing for money, the balladists nevertheless often had a lyric gift that made their ditties superior to the average American ragtime songs. The words of the most popular 'lyrics' of recent days seem all the more contemptible when compared with these ballads, and their music is hardly superior to the ballad tunes. The common people of the seventeenth century who admired ballads had, it appears, better taste than have the mass of people in the twentieth-century England and America. Accordingly, it is not hard to understand why they flocked to see and hear the great poetic drama of their time.
(*PB*, II, p. xiii)

Interest in the content of the street ballad was at first historical.[30] The texts proved to be dubious source material, however, since they were more concerned to sensationalize than to give an accurate account of events. The change to a mainly cultural–historical and anthropological consideration of the street ballad from the end of the nineteenth century onwards not only produced the valuable information given in commentaries on single texts:[31] it also corresponded more closely to the nature of the street ballad as both realistic presentation of life and provider of entertaining and practical instruction in the ways of the world for an audience unaccustomed to literature of any kind. Ebsworth mentions, in 1878 (I, p. xv), the import-ance of the texts 'to the student of human nature and of English history' and admires the 'Touches of genuine humour, genuine pathos . . . Only the dainty and discontented reader can possibly find these ballads valueless' (ibid., p. xiv). Rollins goes further:

> The ballads here reproduced give pictures of a many-sided age. Their quaintness and melody and humor should appeal to the general reader, while the historian and the student of literature will find in them value of another sort.[32]

Attempts at classifying according to content[33] have mentioned the journalistic aspects of the street ballad[34] and pointed out the marketplace methods of advertising and selling religious and secular instruction: 'Wis-dom crying aloud in the Streets' (Ebsworth, RB, pp. viii, xxvii) together with the variety of topical themes, in the widest sense: 'All Sorts and Conditions of Men' (ibid., p. xxxvi). It has been shown that love is the pre-dominant theme,[35] as is usual in literature, and that 'low life' (ibid.) is preferred as a setting. The differing levels of fictionalization have also been noted.[36]

Recurrent assertions that the street ballad reflects low- to middle-class customs and attitudes signalled the development of a new objectivity of perspective in street-ballad research. This new sociological side of the literary study of the street ballad was formulated in 1935 by its adherent L. B. Wright:

> The unity of aristocratic tone in Elizabethan literature has been greatly emphasized by literary historians. 'One can hardly exaggerate the aristocratic nature of Elizabethan literature', one writer asserts. So complete has been the preoccupation of students with the aristocratic tradition that they have almost forgotten the existence of any other point of view. If one means by 'literature' the works that have stood the test of time and are still regarded as worth reading for their own sakes, then it is true that most literature was aristocratic; but if one considers the books that delighted the mass of Elizabethans, much will be found which does not show the touch of gentleman or scholar.   ([1935], pp. 90–1f.)

Even if Wright discounts the 'test of time' variable, which probably depends on general public approval, he does take audience reaction and the practical purpose of the texts as a basic criterion for investigation and assessment in his *Middle Class Culture in Elizabethan England*. He stres-ses the significance of the street ballad as one of the most important read-ing media, ranking with chapbooks, tracts and prose pieces, educational and didactic texts of the time. The cultural justification and selling success of street-ballad texts had its origin in their practical moral instruction and advice on social behaviour, in their information, entertainment and social protest and in the development of the sense of identity of the middle classes.

In order to place the actual texts culturally and historically, and elucidate the relationship between author, text and audience, it is necessary to look at more than just content. It is only by examining the textual procedures of the text that an insight can be gained into the conditions for and possibilities of communicating a textual item, and into the closely related receptive capacity and changing taste of the audience. The first – and only – scholar to characterize the street ballad on aesthetic grounds was V. de Sola Pinto, who published a high-quality selection in his anthology *The Common Muse* in 1957. From a specifically social and class-orientated standpoint of literary criticism he stresses the distinctive worth of the street ballad in comparison with what he calls 'hall-marked' literature. In describing the particular qualities of the street ballad, he refers in his introduction to 'common sense', an 'unsentimental, uncourtly and irreverent' attitude to love, knowledge of the 'simple life', the penetrating directness of the colloquial language ('racy homely English'), and clarity of meaning without the sacrifice of complexity. He also mentions harmony of intention and execution, that is, the street ballad does not go beyond the possibilities of a literature of instruction and entertainment for a low- to middle-class urban audience but often puts these possibilities to excellent use.[37] Pinto is, however, quite objective when it comes to a comparative literary evaluation of the street ballad:

it has to be admitted that the Common Muse at her best falls a good deal short of the Olympian sublime. Her characteristic virtues are those of the middle way: directness, simplicity and honest earthly realism.   (ibid., p. 12)

Pinto notes with regret the lack of scholarly research on the street ballad, both as a subject in its own right and as a genre which influenced the poetry of the eighteenth and nineteenth centuries, which he describes in brief as a research problem, in an earlier essay:[38]

My contention is that here we have a vast body of popular poetry which has hitherto been grossly neglected and undervalued by the academic critics and historians of English literature. One of the great tasks which lies before English scholarship is the exploration and revaluation of this popular art, which expressed so admirably for three centuries the spirit of the common English people. Another task of equal importance is to examine the relationship between this popular poetry and the work of the great English poets, from Shakespeare down to the nineteenth century.

In formulating these two tasks Pinto, an authority in literary scholarship, is clearly distancing himself from the prejudices which had up till then prevailed among historians. Of the two tasks he describes, the first is a prerequisite for the second. Aspects of historical literary relationships can only be explored on the basis of a more precise description of the text corpus. It therefore proved convenient to limit the period of this study to the years 1550–1650, for reasons which are socio-literary, bibliographical, and inherent in the texts themselves. Extant printed copies very rarely date from before the mid-sixteenth century.[39] It was only in the second half of the sixteenth century that the circulation of the street ballad gradually increased owing to the larger printings and a more organized method of distribution. Although broadsides were used for state proclamations and church edicts they were not used for literary texts, and certainly not for ballads of any kind, until around the middle of the sixteenth century.[40] From this time onwards certain characteristics of the street ballad begin to develop, evident also in the texts themselves. This early phase in the history of the street ballad, when textual composition, function, and method of distribution were not yet established,[41] forms one of the historical bases for the accumulation and combination of genre-specific features. For the purposes of genre description and definition, this part of the text corpus is better seen as a contrastive background, while the main interest will be focused on the period when the street ballad came into its own as a genre type. The diversity and quality of the street ballad at this the apex of its development was due to a wider circulation and greater effectiveness, within its own limitations. At the end of the sixteenth century this development can be observed together with a striking change from religious to secular thematic content. There is a clear hiatus during the Civil War years, when street ballads were suppressed and for a time banned completely. From then on they show a significant narrowing on both the thematic and functional sides which was accompanied by a downward trend in quality. The period I have chosen for my investigation spans thus the origins and rise of the street ballad and the years of its greatest flowering as an independent genre. With the definition of specific genre characteristics and their function, a basis for further diachronic research has been established even where the street ballad lacks complexity of characteristics and literary message and where it is effective as a model for other literary forms.[42]

Out of approximately 1,000 edited ballads[43] of our period of study, a selection of about 200 examples will be interpreted from different standpoints. I have chosen this limited number because the themes and procedures in the text corpus recur relatively frequently, due to the powerful constraints of tradition and what we can almost call 'low-brow' consumer pressure. I have selected texts of special quality in the sense that they illustrate convincingly genre-specific features which serve to convey a literary message of contemporary relevance which is orientated towards the audience. One of my main purposes in doing this is to counteract somewhat the low prestige of the street ballad. This concept of quality is not determined by one-sided, specifically literary values, such as are often applied, either explicitly or implicitly, through a traditional ranking of genres and types of content. The texts are 'literary' in so far as the entertaining and instructional aspects of their message differ from the purely practical purpose of factual and 'useful' literature. It is for this reason that the texts are preferably, though not necessarily, fictional in content. Ballads with a political or historical content are not included in this study, since their essential historicity would require a close historical analysis which is not possible within the framework of this investigation. Furthermore, texts of this kind frequently appear in the earlier period in a song form which was not yet typical of the street ballad, and again in the second half of the seventeenth century. Ample quotations are provided to compensate for the fact that the texts are not easily accessible otherwise.

The iconographic and musical dimensions of the street ballad cannot be dealt with in this study, for reasons connected with both the material in hand and the space available. The woodcut illustration on the broadside, increasingly common in the seventeenth century, was a crude affair and had little actual illustrative function with regard to the text.[44] Since there were usually only one or two figures involved it was possible to use an idea several times over, which resulted not infrequently in a crass incongruence between illustration and text.[45] The woodcut, therefore, offers little scope for research within the context of this study, though its principal function of helping to sell the product should not be underestimated.

It was common practice to use the same tunes for several street-ballad texts.[46] This allowed the use of popular tunes in the introduction and spreading of new texts, so there was no definite functional interrelation. The coordination of melody and text was certainly easier because at that time musical performance was far freer in its relation to musical content than is the case today. Tempo and rhythm were not fixed, and missing notes could be added to texts as necessary. Musical notation is very seldom found on the printed sheets, however. The naming of the tune in the subtitle – 'To the tune of *Fortune my Foe*'[47] – is clearly a resort to the familiar, which is reactivated by the singing or reciting of the performer. The quality of the tunes, which extend into the area of folk-song, dance music, and contemporary song tradition, is higher than one would assume from contemporary opinion of street ballads.[48] Apart from its mnemonic function, the tune doubtless had an emotive and sometimes illuminating effect which should be examined from the psychological and musical point of view to supplement the analysis of the texts. The consistently simple structure and easy comprehensibility of the texts guaranteed a form of verbal communication which was relatively independent of the music.

The main concern of this study is to describe the texts systematically, a process which will lead to the establishing of essential and recurrent textual characteristics. The aim is to discover the differential criteria which mark the English street ballad as a genre which comprised the mass of broadsides. The bibliographical form of publication of the street ballad in close relation to its distribution by means of performance and sale at the same time, and the strikingly communicative structure of the texts as an obvious consequence of this, require a pragmatic approach to the texts, bearing in mind the present stage of methodology. Since this method of investigation takes into account the fact that utterances – also literary ones – are dependent on both situation and action, a textual description and interpretation based on literary and social aspects is indeed possible. In Elizabethan and Stuart times, the street ballad was integrated into the social activities of the lower and middle classes, as has been shown in socio-historical research. This invites the question as to the relationship between textual construction and non-textual determinant components. We have to remember the special nature of the communicative relationship between performer and listener and its effect on the textual procedures and successful distribution. It will be necessary to define more precisely the topicality value, that is, the relevance to the outside world, of a literary form which is often described as the forerunner of journalism.

The literary and sociological framework within which a literary form of substantial independence and diversity developed will prove to be an important contributory determinant in explaining the genre characteristic of a particular communication structure. For a further categorization of the various forms of publication of the street ballad, the traditional genre-theory distinctions according to the speech criterion will hold; they can be systematically applied through the communication-theory approach. Here the communication levels of the street-ballad texts which will be established constitute an important coherence factor. In addition, there are further principles of coherence which denote a particular sub-category of genre, which must be examined by the tentative use of linguistic category analysis. It will be seen that the undeniable but until now overemphasized heterogeneity of the text corpus is, from the point of view of structure, only slight and can be reduced to the predominance of a few characteristic textual procedures. But the main feature of the street ballad, the 'story',[49] frequently cited in the few references to the genre in works of literary criticism, must be considered as in no way valid for all texts.

Because of the size of the text corpus and the priorities of this study, the first classificatory genre description and definition based on socio-literary considerations, the analysis has to be limited to mainly systematic and macrostructural aspects. For this, speech-act theory has been applied as a model for the principal connection between textual procedures and non-textual components, although a complete analysis according to the criteria of speech-act theory is not possible for each individual text. Similarly, investigations of linguistic style, an important area on which little research has so far been produced, have to be left out of consideration, as does the phono-aesthetic dimension of presentation with its musical and textual significance. The basic function of sound and prosody in the segmentation and construction of an argument or fictional plot can be presumed, though it would only be possible to examine this individually if comparison were made with prose texts having similar subject-matter. The amount and diversity of themes and types of content, especially the plurality of opinion which characterized the street ballad in the first half of the seventeenth century, will be illustrated more clearly than has been the case previously. This is made possible by the number and selection of examples for interpretation, together with an analysis of their terms of reference, which up till now has necessarily been outside the scope of generalizing judgements and individual commentaries. At the same time, there can only be an analysis of single examples of links with traditional motifs, types of content, and genre, as this would involve an expansion into separate and extensive areas such as late medieval carols and folk drama, prose tales, and song lyrics of the time, together with literature of the supernatural, pamphlets, and the like. The unique, innovative position of the street ballad within the whole spectrum of literary history will first of all be established with reference to the structure of single, particular, forms of publication, and to their cultural and social functions. This needs, however, to be supplemented and possibly modified by further studies, above all in the area of historical development. Diachronic changes in the street ballad within our period of study can be demonstrated on the basis of a systematic genre description.

From this brief delineation of the area of our necessarily limited study and method of approach suited to it, the following investigative procedure will have emerged: a comprehensive description of the economic, social, and cultural conditions directly affecting the production and distribution of the street ballad forms the basis of a socio-literary enquiry into the possible connections between textual construction and non-textual determining factors (chapter 1). This requires first of all an explanation of the methodological procedures adopted, together with the modifications which arise from the application of communication- and speech-act theories to literary and fictional texts (chapter 2). The distinction between different communication levels in a literary text makes it possible analytically to isolate the 'communicatory level of performance' and to describe the speech acts evident there in terms of their relation to reality, that is, the actual act of performance (chapter 3). With this, the most important genre characteristic of the street ballad is established – that the speech situation is quite obviously taken into consideration and the close relationship between text and socio-cultural environment is clearly recognizable. The conformity of further communication levels in the street-ballad text to genre-theory categories according to the speech criterion leads to the definition of sub-genres of the street ballad, which can again be sub-divided into individual ballad types. Their interpretation will show the spectrum of themes and textual procedures in the street ballad of our period of study (chapter 4). To sum up, it is possible to define pragmatically the street-ballad genre as a literary and journalistic medium of its time (chapter 5). Finally, contemporary opinion of the street ballad has been reconstructed with the help of the relevant documents (chapter 6), whereby, on the basis of the understanding acquired in the course of this study, it can be safely said that the street ballad was in some respects better than its reputation.

A study of the street ballad is of interest in the areas of literary history, genre history, and in its own right. In histories of literature up till now the street ballad has been either silently passed over[50] or dismissed with references to 'popular' and 'ephemeral literature'.[51] The narrative prose of Elizabethan and Stuart times, however, which can equally be described, if not as 'trivial literature', at least as entertainment within the literary and social framework of the time, has been given considerable prominence regarding its role in the history of the novel. Further, countless literary historians, spurred on by the superior quality of Shakespeare's dramas, have researched into the mass of contemporary plays. The study of the street ballad serves not only to close a gap in the whole spectrum of literary-historical knowledge, but also throws light on the history of the development of the ballad as such. Features common to the folk ballad and the street ballad, and above all the seldom recognized differences between them which emerge on closer analysis, have hardly been acknowledged by literary historians. They form the basis for a corresponding description of the history of the literary ballad,[52] which is orientated towards the genre structure and thematic content of either the folk ballad or the street ballad. The interpretation and evaluation of the literary ballad is only possible if the extent of imitation and originality is taken into account.[53] Finally, the functional nature of the street ballad, which can be positively established and which shares an ambivalence of practical objective and literary message with other sub-genres such as the public speech, commissioned poem, cabaret song, *chanson*, advertising slogan, and the like, is of immense value in our understanding of literary texts.

1 Literary and social conditions for the rise, distribution and textual structure of the street ballad

1.1 Performance and rendition

The text of the street ballad, available to us in broadsides and in edited collections, some of which are annotated, was usually sung and sometimes read to the audience of the time as part of the selling process. Performance and sale were closely linked, and it is only later analyses which artificially separated these two integral aspects of the street ballad.

'Performance' and 'rendition' are extremes of possible textual realization. They denote on the one hand dramatic role-play, which is evidently required in many of the texts, and simple rendition on the other. The latter follows the text and the tune, rendering the ballad without any special gesturing, mime, or varied voice inflection. In practice, the tendency towards simple rendition probably predominated, though a textual rendering in the manner of a performance after Richard Tarlton, as an 'afterpiece'in the theatre or by an ambitions balladmonger, cannot be ruled out. Whatever the case, the performance and rendition of the street ballad had the function of communicating the text in as lively a way as possible and of catching and holding the attention of the audience.

Starting out with his arms and his pack full of broadsides, the singer would go to the doors of theaters, to markets, fairs, bear baitings, taverns, ale-houses, wakes or any other places where a crowd could gather, and begin his song.

(Rollins [1919a], pp. 308–9)

Such is the list which the street-ballad expert gives of the places where the balladmonger hawked his wares. The performance and distribution of the street ballad took place on the periphery of certain, mainly popular, festivities but was not integrated into them to the same extent as were the songs of the minstrel into court occasions, Lord Mayors' processions, May games, weddings or christenings. It was the printer and the publisher who commissioned the ballad-singer, not a festival organizer. The singer would go along independently to places where crowds were expected, since it was his responsibility to distribute the printed copies he had been commissioned to sell. So the balladmonger, who had only his performance and the copies themselves to attract an audience and potential customers and hold their attention, was dependent on the success of his rendition. He would make use of any possible raised position, a bench or simple stall, for

instance, though he could also attract an audience without such aids.[1]
Unlike the German *Bänkelsänger*, the balladmonger did not have the use
of a series of pictures on a board with a pointing-stick, as both eyecatcher
and text illustration. The woodcut on the broadside was of only limited
illustrative use as it usually depicted single figures and not scenes, far less
a series of scenes. In addition, the illustrations were often hackneyed and
had little or no connection with the actual text.[2] Apart from the fact that
the balladmonger was his own manager and dependent on his performance of the ballad for success (with the help of the tune), he also had to contend with very fierce competition. There was a large and diverse selection
of ballads on offer,[3] especially in London, and this required of him the high
degree of persuasive power and skill of a present-day salesman in order to
arouse people's interest and attract their attention. The means to do this
lie, as we shall see, in the text itself, and only had to be put into practice in
the performance. In small towns and rural areas the pedlar[4] selling his
wares would often function as ballad-seller and performer as well, or the
ballads might be performed as part of the entertainment offered at a fair.
The urban performance of ballads had to compete with many other
diversions and amusements, however.

The street-ballad texts themselves give some explicit references to the
performance situation. The frequent request for attention (see chapter 3.3)
was meant to keep the passer-by standing at the balladmonger's pitch or,
in a public house, to keep the focus of interest solely on the ballad-singer,
or again, to beat the showman at the fair at his own game. The exhortation
to stop and gather round emphasizes this:

> Good people all to me draw neer,
> and to my Song a while attend,[5]
>
> I Pray good People all draw near,
> and mark these lines that here are pen'd,[6]
>
> Give eare, my loving countrey-men,
>   that still desire newes,
> Nor passe not while you heare it sung,
>   or else the song peruse;
> For, ere you heare it, I must tell,
>   my newes it is not common;
> But Ile unfold a trueth betwixt.[7]

Frequent references to both the oral and written transmission of a ballad
text appear juxtaposed in the text itself. This makes quite explicit the
duality of text rendition on the one hand, and the sale of copies as back-up
to the performance and opportunity for private perusal on the other. The
printing of street ballads brought about the transition from purely oral
tradition to duplication, distribution of written copies and a consequent

fixing of the text. Although this also holds true for the development of book printing, we cannot overlook the close link between the writing of the street ballad and its performance, and the resulting more complex process of initial reception. Terms such as 'written' and 'lines penned' are often interchangeable with 'Ile tell' and 'song', without any distortion of meaning. There is always an invitation to listen implied, whereby the (past tense) allusion to the writing of the ballad often, significantly, referred to the process of writing which preceded the performance, so giving priority to the actual performance itself. This is also seen in the textual procedures which involve direct communication with the audience.

> Let no body grudge,
> Nor ill of me iudge
>   because I haue *pend* this same *ditty*.[8]

> O whoe can *wryte with pen*, or yet what *tongue* can showe,
> What loue these blessèd men did to their maker owe?[9]

> All you which sober minded are,
>   come listen and Ile *tell*,
> The saddest story Ile declare,
>   which in our dayes befell:
> Therefore 'tis for example sake,
>   the business *written is* . . . [10]

> Be silent, therefore, and stand still!
>   marke what proceedeth from *my quill*;
>   I *speake* of tokens good and ill,[11]

> Give eare, my loving countrey-men,
>   that still desire newes,
> Nor passe not while you heare it *sung*,
>   or else the *song peruse*;[12]

> *Round boyes indeed.*
>   *Or*
> *The Shoomakers Holy-day.*
> *Being a very pleasant new Ditty,*
> *To fit both Country, Towne and Citie,*
> *Delightfull to peruse in every degree.*[13]

The balladmonger performing and selling his wares was such a common component of everyday life in the seventeenth century that many allusions to this figure can be found (see chapter 6). There are several literary depictions of balladmongers, of which the best known is the character Autolycus in Shakespeare's *The Winter's Tale*,[14] although Nightingale's scene in Ben Jonson's *Bartholomew Fair* (1614)[15] is more informative on the subject of performance practices. The balladmonger formed part of the whole pattern of the fair, where ballads, as well as other items from mouse-traps to gingerbread, were offered for sale. Nightingale is the same kind of showman as a market-crier, and tries to entice his audience by describing and praising his wares (naming of themes). Although he has difficulty in making himself heard among the visitors to the fair he does find a ballad fan in Cokes, who is immediately ready both to listen and to buy. The rendition is prefaced by an address to the audience and a request to gather round; the fascination thus established is so strong that the pickpocket Edgeworth succeeds in relieving the listener Cokes of his purse while Nightingale is just delivering a warning about such practices. The ballad-monger keeps the interest of the audience constantly on the boil by means of his addresses, explanations, and responses to heckling. His success is confirmed by the sale of copies which then follows.

Similarly, the showmanlike and market-crier aspect of ballad perform-ance is illustrated in *A Song for Autolycus* (c. 1620, see appendix B 50). The name 'Autolycus' as an allusion to Shakespeare's balladmonger shows the almost proverbial renown of the figure of the balladmonger under that name. Here also, the ballad itself is not given, but instead the typical behaviour of the balladmonger is reproduced. The same goes for a ser-vants' scene in William Cavendish's *The Triumphant Widow* (1677, see appendix B 83), where the pedlar and balladmonger Footpad offers the rendition of a ballad as the high point of his selection of wares. He skilfully arouses the curiosity of his audience by giving a general description of theme and content, a typical procedure of the balladmonger. The docu-mentary value of this literary treatment of the phenomenon of street-ballad performance and sale lies not only in the portrayal of the typical behaviour of balladmonger and audience. It is also of interest for the fact that knowledge of street-ballad texts and performance practice was taken for granted to such an extent that quoting the ballad texts themselves was found to be unnecessary for an albeit rudimentary portrayal of the process on stage. The mainly negative evaluation of ballad literature and ballad selling is biased, being based on the tenets of 'orthodox' literature.[16]

The musical quality of the ballad rendition was judged inferior by con-temporaries.[17] The coarseness of the tunes was deplored,[18] and the untrained croaking or sentimental whining of the singers dismissed with contempt.[19] Here too the decided rejection, already entrenched at the time, by men of letters of ballad literature and its enormous and enviable success was probably instrumental in distorting the reality of the situation. In fact those tunes which have survived, if in some cases altered by time, prove to be of better quality than contemporary commentators would have had us believe (see also Rollins [1919a], p. 312). Rollins accords them higher status than the popular hits of his time,[20] describing them as 'attractive' and clearly distancing himself from seventeenth-century opinion (ibid., p. 314). In any event the tune had an important phatic and mnemonic function, and it was one of the balladmonger's tasks to teach it to those who bought his printed copies (ibid., p. 312).

The transmission and distribution of the street-ballad text is characterized by its public nature, and the personal element in the phatic relationship between balladmonger and audience. This relationship was based partly on economic considerations, but also developed as a result of the showmanship involved in the performance of street ballads, which were instruments of amusement or of instruction. They were hawked and performed in places familiar to the public at which they were aimed: markets, street corners, public houses, and fairs. The absence of any elitist cultural nimbus makes these texts of the lower stratum of the populace particularly accessible. They involve no psychological block in relation to printed texts, no claims on the intellect, and no contact with the unfamiliar. The popular nature of the street ballad is evident in the affinity between audience and text in theme, language, straightforwardness of textual procedure, and ease of reception due to certain communication factors. It becomes even clearer when comparison is made with some analogous aspects of late medieval popular drama. The showmanlike demeanour of the balladmonger, which has its expression in the text itself, has characteristics in common with the presenter in popular drama. The latter stands at the edge of the stage or walks round it, thereby indicating a certain distance between himself and the action, which makes him an ideal go-between and commentator. His position near the audience on the *platea*, that part of the stage reserved for action representing ordinary life and the common people as opposed to the *locus*, confirms his close association with the audience and especially with those of the lower classes (R. Weinmann [1967], pp. 55, 164). This presenter, together with low-class characters only, addresses the audience directly from the *plateau* (ibid., pp. 39–40, 174–5, 181, 249). R. Weimann and H.-J. Diller have shown that the audience relationship as an explicit constituent of the text and dramaturgy is a device limited to popular drama only.[21] It became a distinctive feature of the type of drama which evolved in the vernacular, while liturgical drama contains no genuine address to the audience which would interrupt the solemnity of the closed ritual (see Diller [1973], p. 148, *passim*). The orientation of the ballad performance towards the audience is even more obvious in the street ballad than in popular drama.

1.2 Position of the street ballad within the contemporary sphere of literary activity

It is the coupling of the performance of street ballads with the sale of copies that gives this literary form, in very large measure, the character of 'wares'.

The institutional reasons for this lie in special features relating to the printing of the street ballad and to its distributors. The position of the street ballad within the literary sphere of the time is of interest to us from the point of view of both social history and literary scholarship. Here also there is reciprocal influence between the social, literary, and economic environments on the one hand, and the form of the text on the other.

1.2.1 Printing production, and street ballads as 'wares'

The position of the street ballad in the contemporary sphere of literary activity, as with other printed matter of the time, can be understood from two main aspects. These are on the one hand trade controls, after the establishing of the Stationers' Company in 1557 from which time entries in the Stationers' Register are to be found, and state decrees on the other. From the outset there are numerous ballad entries to be found (see Rollins [1924]) and as early as 1559 'ballates' are expressly mentioned together with plays and prose works in the *Injunctions given by the Queen's Majesty* against 'publicatyon of vnfrutefull, vayne and infamous bokes and papers . . . nothinge therein should be either heretical, seditious, or vnsemely for Christian eares'.[22] Queen Elizabeth was particularly concerned, together with the church, to retain influence over at least the most important and successful printers such as John Day, Richard Tottel, and John Jugge. This was achieved through the use of patronage, the conferring of privileges, and special commissions.[23] Although the role of the street ballad in this system of feudally controlled business competition has not yet been examined, there are indications that owing to certain circumstances the ballad became free from this constraint more rapidly than most of the other printed works of the time.

The business of the literature of entertainment, the cheap chapbooks and the ballads, must have flourished increasingly[24] alongside the bestsellers of the time. These were the Bible, the catechism, the ABC, Foxe's *Martyrs*, Sternhold and Hopkins's *Singing Psalms*, legal works and state proclamations, and they provided the main source of income for the leading printers in the Company. As early as 1557 there was a printer who specialized in the production and distribution of ballads: William Pickering, a founder member of the Stationers' Company, who had a shop at London Bridge (see F. A. Mumby [1956], p. 94). In the last two decades of the sixteenth century, the fierce competition between the printers, together with high printing costs, led to a gradual separation of printing and selling (ibid., p. 69). After that the booksellers, as a separate marketing group, began to gain influence over the printers. The demand for printed works – the needs of a public which also expected to be offered entertainment and moral instruction in an interesting form – in turn influenced the production of printed material. It was therefore possible to achieve success in the business outside the sphere of royal privilege. At the same time, this influence of public taste on what was printed was only possible in a social context where author and seller were dependent solely on financial profit, and not relatively protected from that necessity by membership of a rich and respectable social class, enjoying the patronage that went with it.[25]

When the Stationers' Company became something similar to a joint-stock company in 1603 and was reorganized by James I into five sections, ballad literature was clearly such an important component that as Ballad Stock it was given its own defined area alongside Bible Stock, Irish Stock, Latin Stock, and English Stock.[26] Ballad production was thus drawn into the aegis of the Stationers' Company, whose monopoly position was becoming increasingly established. It can be assumed that the street ballad thus acquired a special financial back-up and a certain literary legitimacy. There are other indications, however, that the producers of street ballads were despised by the higher-status Company printers and tried to leave the monopoly, thus showing a greater willingness to take financial risks.[27]

The broadside should be assigned, bibliographically and institutionally, to the periodical press rather than the book trade. Although it did not appear with an exact date nor in a series published periodically, it was a fly-sheet, like the first newsletters in the second half of the sixteenth century and the later news-sheets of the seventeenth century, and was sold under the same conditions.[28] Those who dealt with the sale of ballads on a large scale were often also involved in the publication of news-sheets and cheap, small-scale popular literature: printers and booksellers such as Bernard Alsop (1617–53?), Francis Coles (1626–81), Henry Gosson (1601–40), Francis Grove (1623–61), Thomas Pavier (1600–25), Thomas Symcock (1619–29), and John Wright (1605–58).[29] This cheap and popular material was not printed by the rich and influential members of the Company but most frequently by printers on the periphery of that institution. We do know of some printers, such as Henry Gosson, John Grismand (1618–38), Thomas Pavier, John Wright, and Edward Wright (1642–48), who were presumably shareholders in the Ballad Stock (see McKerrow [1910], pp. 302–3) and others, like Francis Coles, William Gilbertson (1640–65), and Thomas Vere (1646–80), who had business connections with them. But there seem to be no indications that any ballad-printer ever belonged to the higher echelons of the Company as warden or assistant, able to share in policy decisions. We know that the better-known ballad-printers were accepted as freemen, so they were certainly members. Whether this was as livery-men, with some communal influence on policy, or as mere yeomen, is not clear.[30] A large number of ballad-printers, whose activity can often be established only for a short period, were not members of the Company. These printers would probably dabble only occasionally in ballads and ephemera, dependent as they were on immediate profit.[31]

For any printer, whether a specialist in the genre or only an occasional producer, the ballad trade would, at the very least, have been profitable enough for them to do without privileges (monopoly), patronage, and subsidies.[32] The popularity of the texts,[33] the low price of a broadside, and a comparatively effective distribution, where the product was taken directly to the buyer,[34] resulted in relatively high sales.[35] The price of a ballad copy (one halfpenny) was the same as the cost of half a loaf of bread; standing room in the stalls of the public theatre cost a penny, seats in the gallery tuppence, and comfortable chairs in the stalls threepence (see H. Castrop [1972], p. 120). Popular literature in book form could be had from a penny upwards, but more serious books cost a shilling, which was beyond the means of members of a class earning £10 a year (see E. H. Miller [1959], pp. 41–2).

Like the newspaper today, the broadside was so cheap that any apprentice could soon accumulate a collection, which had for the Elizabethan somewhat more permanency than present-day papers hold for their readers.

(L. B. Wright [1964], p. 419)

The ballad business was mostly fairly profitable for both printer and author.[36] Indeed it could be lucrative enough to enable a printer to start up on his own. The ballad producers' urge to make a profit even outweighed the fear of censorship and punishment during the Cromwell dictatorship. The large number of broadsides printed at that time was not only due to the need for news and political invective (see Rollins, *CP*, p. 14). Rollins calculated that the ballad-writer sometimes earned more than a playwright.[37]

The importance of street ballads – as shown by the large quantity printed – contrasts with the low status of street-ballad publishers in the guild. At the same time there is a consequent independence of street-ballad publishers as an enterprise, as they were in receipt of absolutely no support through privilege or subsidy. All these are determinant components in the production of street ballads which contribute to the character of this literary form as one of 'wares'. The method of distribution emphasized this aspect which was especially obvious when one considers that copies of a ballad were handed round at a low price like fruit and vegetables, as soon as there was a need for them. The printed copy was highly desirable both as an illustrated reminder of the performance experience and as a means of privately repeating it. The wide circulation of this printed product made it profitable for the printer/publisher and author in spite of its low price; nothing is known of the size of the balladmonger's cut.

The street ballad can be described as an early type of bestseller. Its production and distribution correspond to the increasingly capitalist economic system of the seventeenth century, where the spirit of enterprise and calculated risk held out the promise of success (see A. L. Rowse [1964], pp. 109–12), a motivation which no doubt had its effect in the field of literature. The Company's contempt for the street ballad, in spite of its incorporation in the Stock, is probably based not only on its trivial and ephemeral character but also on a certain competitive envy, which is often evident in other criticism of the ballad (see below, pp. 243–4).

1.2.2 Social and economic status of the ballad writer and singer/seller

The ballad writer stood completely outside the feudal system of patronage. This was a specifically medieval component of cultural life which was already diminishing in importance after 1600.[38] Only one or two authors of recognized serious literature still had noble patrons with whom they were in personal contact and who offered them permanent support and encouragement. In popular literature circles it was customary, even for insignificant hack writers who would not normally have come up to the cultural and aesthetic standards required by noble patrons, to try to establish an apparent connection with and extract money from a rich and socially well-placed gentleman, by means of flattering dedications. The ballad-writer dispensed with this, whether from a sense of financial independence or a realistic assessment of the success of such an attempt. Advancement through patronage or the conferring of public or private offices was similarly closed to him. Most ballad writers probably shared the proverbial poverty of Elizabethan writers,[39] unless writing was not their main source of income. It was the printers and publishers who made the money.

Like the street-ballad trade, which did not belong to a feudalistically organized printing 'guild', the balladmonger was under no corporate or social obligation. A comparison with the actor, with whom he shared the role of performer, makes this quite clear. The actor was a member of a troupe which enjoyed the patronage of a nobleman or the Master of the Revels of the royal court. He had a contract of service and his social status was determined by his rights and obligations. He could be fairly sure that his clothing and keep would be provided, as long as the theatres did not close for any length of time owing to the threat of plague. For its part the troupe had to put on the agreed number of performances, eliminate any subversive or seditious political opinion from the texts of their plays, and take preventive measures against theft or other immoral activities during their performance.[40] In contrast, the balladmonger's activity was merely included in the printing licence which the publisher had to obtain for each new ballad. The balladmonger could sell the ballads wherever and whenever he liked, thus supplementing his income. He needed no licence to trade or perform, and he as an individual was defined only by his ability or inability to perform the text and sell the broadsheets. Thus his value, or lack of it, as a member of society derived primarily from his individual standing and not from a fixed social position. As a result, the author of a ballad could risk expressing subversive opinions through the balladmonger, thereby slipping through the censor's net. Similarly, it was not uncommon for a balladmonger, while performing, to work sucessfully in collusion with a pickpocket.[41]

The financial success[42] of the balladmonger, a certain legitimizing of his performance, and the popularity of his 'wares' also derived from the tradition of the minstrel.[43] The late medieval figure of the minstrel in his role of entertainer with various functions is certainly similar to that of the balladmonger. In contrast to the minstrel, however, with his diverse talents and functions – musician, actor, acrobat, story-teller, reciter, poet, singer, dancer, and comedian – the balladmonger was a specialist. At its widest, his range included very occasionally textual construction, but for the most part his job was to perform and sell. Performance did imply some acting and musical ability, however, and selling involved a certain amount of showmanship and salesmanship. The diversification of the balladmonger's tasks derived from the relatively large number of possibilities for textual shaping allowed the performer in that genre. We may also assume that wandering minstrels sometimes took over the balladmonger's business,[44] and that itinerant actors, too, would try their hand at the job.[45] We should keep in mind, however, that ballad production was a specifically urban activity which was dependent on the printers in and around London. On the other hand there would be fewer failed actors in London, and the activity of down-at-heel minstrels would be confined to the provinces. Other occasional writers and performers of ballads would probably have been the general unemployed, the work-shy, and cripples (see Rollins [1919a], pp. 306–10). In the provinces the ballads were marketed mainly by itinerant traders, whose assortment of cures, cosmetics, haberdashery, and calendars would sometimes include thin, often loosely bound, chapbooks and broadsides (see appendix B 3, 23, 24, 45, 61, 68).

The figures of the ballad writer and the balladmonger of Elizabethan and Stuart times are difficult to define clearly. They belonged to the literary *demi-monde* but also to the vague no-man's-land between hack writer, itinerant trader, vagabond, and cony-catcher. If the texts were by more or less professional ballad authors such as William Elderton (d. 1592?), Thomas Deloney (1543?–1600?), Laurence Price (1628–80?), and Martin Parker,[46] and handled by booksellers and proficient ballad-singers, one could expect a relatively high quality of ballad and a performance which did justice to the text. The products of occasional writers, and the marketing of them by traders and dubious individuals, tended to result in ballads and performances of inferior quality. The increasing mobility of the lower classes of the populace and especially of the vagabonds, due to social reshuffling and unemployment, made possible a larger-scale distribution of ballads. The author's and balladmonger's lack of social ties stems not least from this circumstance. The relationship between performer and audience can similarly be described as fluctuating. The 'no obligation' element of the performance was matched by the ready availability and ease of transportation of the broadsides, and in general the texts and tunes were simple and easily retained. There is therefore a correspondence between author status, performance and sales methods, reception, bibliographical format, and text construction, which can be summed up as mobility, independence, and availability.

1.2.3 Censorship and public taste

The extent of the ballad producers' and distributors' free hand was limited by two essential factors: censorship and public taste. Both were components of contemporary literary activity which represented links with social reality and could influence textual content and strategy only indirectly. Influence was exerted by means of directives, institutional measures, and sanctions on the one hand, and through the market mechanism of supply and demand on the other. In the case of the ballad, literary criticism as a possible regulator of literary production played only a marginal role. Evidence of the practicalities and functioning of censorship is sparse.[47] Censorship decrees have for the most part survived, but only isolated cases of their enforcement have come down to us.

Censorship was directed against seditious, politically or religiously inopportune, immoral, and obscene publications, and affected therefore in the first instance the content of texts and their vocabulary. The power and effect of censorship in our period of study is difficult to assess, especially as so little research has been done on the subject. The aim and the severity of censorship changed according to the political situation and the circumstances of the day. The strictness or laxity of its enforcement depended not least on the occupancy of the relevant posts, which were in the hands of the state and church. Before 1576 the censor's role was presumably performed by the Master and the wardens of the Stationers' Company, who were not infrequently represented by a clerk who kept the Register. In addition there were the Archbishop of Canterbury and the Bishop of London, who could delegate the job to other clerics,[48] and of course there were censors appointed in their own right.[49] There are very few references to, or records of, rejected publications,[50] although Rollins ([1919a], p. 285) estimates that half of the extant ballads were never recorded in the Register in the first place. Evidence of the punishment of individual printers or authors does not prove anything with regard to the general operation and effectiveness of the censorship system.[51]

From the middle of the sixteenth century onwards there was no lack of government edicts on the licensing and control of printed matter.[52] In 1559 a royal edict decreed that ballads, together with plays and shorter printed texts, could only be published with a licence from minor officials of the church and state. Control over the publication of more serious books was in the hands of higher-ranking officials (see F. S. Siebert [1952], p. 56). The Star Chamber Decree of 1586 reinforced the compulsory licensing of ballads (ibid., pp. 72–3). We know little of the individual operation of the controls. The issue of licences was mainly the responsibility of the Company, which tended towards a milder enforcement of controls, perhaps because of the in-fighting over monopolies (ibid., p. 59). E. H. Miller attributes to Elizabethan censorship nominal rather than actual success, surmising on the other hand that pressure of public opinion, which was predominantly loyal to the government and morally conservative, would have exerted a considerable controlling effect. Miller maintains that political criticism was more harshly dealt with than offences of a moral nature. He comes to the conclusion that 'most authors were not seriously affected by the edicts and proclamations' (see E. H. Miller [1959], p. 199).

During the first period of Stuart rule up to 1640, the system of censorship remained the same, but as the power of the crown diminished and political opinion became more differentiated it lost its effectiveness.[53] At the same time business interests, both of the members of the Company and of the journeymen, who were printing in secret, began to outweigh the interests of church and state. Everywhere, ways and means were being found to circumvent censorship controls.[54] Since ballads were checked less stringently than books, a typical ballad title would often serve as cover for the registering of a book (see F. S. Siebert [1952], pp. 143–4). There was generally less risk of being caught and punished for publishing without a licence than in the Elizabethan era, in spite of more stringent government measures (see H. S. Bennett [1970], pp. 45–8). The rapid burgeoning of print production made censorship doubly difficult (ibid., pp. 78–86). H. S. Bennett describes the situation as follows: 'From the evidence available it would seem that the trade took a very liberal view of what it might publish, always remembering that the risks of meddling with matters of Church or State were considerable, so that other kind of business was desirable could it be obtained' (ibid., p. 58).

It is the period 1640–60 which yields most information on censorship and its effectiveness (see Rollins, *CP*, pp. 3–29). Nearly every year Parliament passed new, stricter laws against any form of criticism of its policies, and against itinerant traders and balladmongers. At first the effect was only slight: 'Hawkers and ballad singers flourished in spite of occasional mishaps' (ibid., p. 29). But gradually the number of ballads and prose texts decreased, especially those of a royalist tendency; they were only sold clandestinely. In 1649 ballad-singers and sellers of broadsheets were no longer to be seen in the streets. Royalist news-books also disappeared. Ballads continued to be published: secretly in anthologies, in the royalist *drolleries*, and as insertions in prose texts. Between 1643 and 1656 no ballads were recorded in the Stationers' Register. After Cromwell's death in 1658 the censorship of ballads ceased and ballad production started up again with renewed vigour.

It is just as difficult to establish the influence of public taste on ballad production and textual form as it is to assess the effects of censorship. Author and seller were dependent on the profit from the sale of broadsides, the supply was large, and competition fierce.[55] It is tempting to assume here concessions to public taste and a backwash effect of public expectation on textual form. This is difficult to prove, however, as apart from the literary texts we have hardly any evidence of what that taste was. Investigations of the topic have always moved in the methodological circle of literary supply and the public taste which derived from it.[56] For popular literature, especially the street ballad, this is justified in so far as the sales success confirms a certain conformity between literary 'consumer goods' and 'consumer needs'. The question remains, however, as to how far this consumer pattern, which derived from the methods of distribution described above, in turn generated certain public needs which it then proceeded to reinforce. It is only in isolated cases that we can observe a backwash effect of non-literary factors on the text. For the rest, we can only describe the tendencies of public taste in very general terms.

We must first establish the type and composition of the ballad public. If 'public' in this sense is defined as a group of persons characterized by a 'common interest in some specific kind of social behaviour such as music, literature or sport' (see A. Silbermann [1969], p. 11), it is necessary to make the difficult distinction between the regular ballad audience and customers, and occasional listeners. Certainly it can be assumed that there was a large regular public for whom the author wrote and the printer/publisher made his selection, although business interests must have encouraged them to try to extend the range of customers; the wide variation of form and content in the ballads supports this assumption.

The interest shown by the public in the ballad – a very small part of an individual's whole spectrum of behaviour – was not dependent on the nature of the ballad alone. There were certain preconditions which affected public reaction, involving the audience's own experience and cultural background as well as the social origins of the individual.[57] The mass of the ballad public belonged to the urban bourgeoisie – merchants and crafts-men and the servants of their household – and secondly to the urban and agricultural working classes.[58] There are various reasons for assuming this to be the case. For one thing the low price of the street ballad would bring it within the means of the poorer classes. Another important point is that the method of sale – market-crier and showman tactics – would tend to reduce built-in prejudices and inhibitions regarding a 'culture' which ordi-narily would have been inaccessible to the common man. The middle-class audience brought with them not only their literacy – acquired in order to cope with the practical demands of business and further their knowledge and understanding of religion and the Bible (see L. B. Wright [1964], pp. 43–80) – but also curiosity, open-mindedness, and a need for infor-mation and entertainment, as can be generally deduced from the substan-tial and diverse selection of printed works on offer (ibid., pp. 81–200).

Since the primary reading interests of such a public were in works which were useful for their practical advice, and given their meagre literary back-ground, very limited leisure and general lack of means, they were likely to have been passive rather than otherwise with regard to purchasing printed texts or influencing their content. It was in these circumstances that the street ballad came into its own, saving the potential customer the journey to the bookstalls near St Paul's[59] and providing short, manageable, straightforward listening and reading material. The ballad catered for a mainly lower-class, relatively uncultured, practically minded public with simple needs in the way of entertainment.

In the absence of more solid evidence we will assume a broad corre-spondence between public taste and ballad production. Cautious deduc-tions concerning the needs of the ballad public will emerge during the course of this study when themes and textual procedures in the ballad are investigated. The uncomplicated nature of the entertainment and instruc-tion, combined with strategies for simplifying reception, point to a certain element of audience expectation.

1.3 Relationship of texts to social and cultural context

Transmission of the street-ballad text was characterized by improvisation – of a given text – by a 'no obligation' situation with the likelihood of interruptions, and a fluctuating audience. It must be assumed that this necessitated special techniques both for attracting and keeping the public's attention and also for ease of reception. Indeed these techniques can be found in the texts in both implicit and explicit form. The predominantly lower-class audiences and the atmosphere surrounding the performance would require an accommodation of both language and topic to the taste of the public. The on-the-spot mercantilism of the street-ballad trade demanded effective advertising strategies, which are similarly incorporated into the text. The balladmonger was under severe pressure from competition, and moreover he had to rely absolutely on his own performance techniques for financial success. He would therefore do his utmost to impress himself, and press his 'wares', as literary products, upon his audience, a factor that is also allowed for in the text. We know little about the actual vocal and mimetic interpretation of the 'textual score'. The accounts we do have of street-ballad performances, although they are polemical in tone, indicate little exploitation of the possibilities inherent in the text. We must merely conjecture about the histrionic shaping of the text on the basis of the theatrical connections. The use of the street ballad as an 'afterpiece' in the theatre, the similarity of the dialogue ballad to the short 'jig' – a play interpolated with songs[60] – which was performed both in the theatre and at popular festivities and dance (see C. R. Baskerville [1929], pp. 32, 35, 164), and the possible coming together of the ballad-singer and unemployed actor in one person, imply an occasional very competent ballad performance which did justice to the text. The possibility of itinerant trader or market-crier doubling as ballad-singer also presupposes at least some mastery of the art of showmanship.

The assumption that textual composition was influenced by literary and social considerations,[61] that is, that the author bore in mind the context of performance and sale at the time of writing, is reinforced by the fact that the ballad writer was paid once, in a lump sum (see Rollins [1919a], pp. 296–300). It was therefore in his interest, if he wanted further commissions from the printer/publisher, to ensure sales by bolstering up the function of the singer as salesman and producing a performer-friendly text. The effects of these conditioning factors on the nature of the texts performed should not be underestimated, especially as the genre, being in an early phase of development, was still fairly flexible.

2 Preliminary investigation of the interrelation between street-ballad text and socio-cultural environment; description of textual structure

Our further investigation will be based on the assumption that the special conditions surrounding the performance, together with the concomitant sale of broadsides, played an essential part in determining the textual make-up of the street ballad.

2.1 A literary and sociological communication model for the socio-cultural placing of the street ballad

During the last twenty years, sociological aspects of literary study have become increasingly prominent in literary scholarship. Scholars have constantly emphasized the complicated relationship between socio-cultural environment and text, especially a text of some literary sophistication, as two distinct areas of reality. Ever since they began to consider this problem scholars have from time to time confessed themselves to be at a loss. The methodological core of the problem lies in the fact that a description has to be found for the relationship between text and cultural environment. In order to do this, the diversity and variety of influences of a social, political, historical and philosophical, scientific, cultural and political, and economic nature have to be considered. A textual approach which sees these not as isolated phenomena but as components of a communication act, whatever its nature, will establish not only a plausible connection between 'literature and society' but also one capable of scholarly analysis. Communication theory offers an appropriate and at the same time systematically comprehensive literary and sociological starting-point for an investigation of this kind. The communication model serves as a descriptive model conveying information through language. Consequently it can also be applied to literary spoken information. Like every model, it is an abstract formulation of a certain area of reality. For the purposes of analysis, its principal components are divided into segments whose functional relationships are formulated. The components of the communication model are those which are necessary for conveying information, and they are interdependent. For spoken communication it is necessary[1] to have a speaker (transmitter), who communicates an item of information (sends a message) to a listener (receiver) via a channel. He forms the message using the speech signs of a given speech system (code) which have

28

reference to reality (referent). It can be assumed that author (speaker) and audience (listeners) share a common language and socio-cultural environment. On the basis of a common stock of linguistic signs, the author formulates a message which has, through the use of specific literary procedures, aesthetically conveyed reality reference. The channel by which this message is transmitted is primarily composed of the actual concrete text: printed material (optical channel) or oral transmission (acoustic and usually also optical channel, cf. also electronic media); secondary conditions for transmission are the stages of production and distribution (printer, publisher, retailers, the institutions of radio and television etc.) which may be understood as secondary channels.

This socio-literary starting-point for our investigation, based on communication theory, will in the following be developed as a model which will refer to the specific features of the street ballad. The socio-literary communication model, constructed in order to place the street ballad in its socio-cultural environment, will later have to be refined and modified, with the help of speech-act theory, for the purposes of textual analysis. As a basis we have taken K. Bühler's organon model (Bühler [1965], pp. 24–33) and the communicative network developed by T. Sebeok.[2] In the centre of our general model (p. 31) is the text corpus 'street ballad', symbolized by an up-ended triangle. The speech functions of the 'reference to self' contained in the text in relation to the speaker, the 'appeal to listener/reader' with regard to the addressee and the 'reference to the outside world' relating to the reality described, constitute a close correspondence inherent in the text between speaker, listener, and the referent which is conveyed by means of the code and the message.[3] These categories enable us to examine individual texts with regard to their communicative strategies of reference to self, appeals to listener/reader and reference to the outside world in conveying their thematic message, and at the same time help us to establish a systematic genre description. These communicative strategies are especially important in determining the structure of the street ballad.[4]

The outer triangle in the model represents the area of actual realization of street-ballad communication. Its special feature lies in the fact that with the balladmonger an extra transmitter is introduced between author and audience, an actual speaker, who in contrast to the author is in direct contact with his listeners. Secondly, the primary channel is not restricted to the printed material (broadside) but is considerably reinforced, both optically and acoustically, by the recital of the text. The balladmonger's function as seller must also be considered as one of the secondary conditions of transmission comprising the stages of production and distribution. The triangular representation reproduces the functional interrelation of the various components of the communication process and their relative positions more clearly than horizontal models. The balladmonger is *vis-à-vis* the audience in the performance situation, and the special conditions surrounding this confrontation, including the sale of ballads, are taken into account by the author in his textual construction. Here they appear as techniques orientated towards self-expression, appeals to the audience, and presentation of the outside world referred to in the text, as will be shown during the course of this investigation. The street-ballad message, transmitted on the level of actual realization (outer triangle), is presentation-orientated, being formulated by means of the stock of linguistic signs available as a common code to author and audience. Whatever way the message is transmitted, it always relates to a common experience of socio-cultural reality. The term 'interpreting agent'[5] implies that this reality is subject to historical conditions and change and is made a topic of current interest for the audience by the respective street ballad. The street ballad with its particular sets of references presents us with historically conditioned interpretations of reality.

With the inner and outer triangles of the figure, textual reality[6] and historical reality are brought into a relationship which is regulated in a communicative way. The genre-specific rules of the street ballad, which we shall be investigating, should therefore be understood as 'street-ballad competence', common to both the producer and the recipient of the text, whereby at the same time individual differences in quality and awareness according to 'ballad experience' have to be allowed. It should be possible to reduce strategies of textual composition in the street ballad to a number of basic rules according to which the individual text is produced and received on the performance level. The balladmonger must also have some street-ballad competence, in order to carry out his part of the performance correspondingly well or badly. Street-ballad competence in a wider sense would include, over and above specific kinds of text, a knowledge of literary styles and genres, fictionalization procedures, popular myths, and literary themes and techniques. A scientific reconstruction of street-ballad competence starts out from the performance level of the texts available; as to the competence and performance on the part of the audience, we can only make deductions.

Street-ballad communication is discernible on two levels, which can in theory be separated but in practice merge into one another, and which must be approached using different methods. The factual level of execution and performance lies at a historical distance of almost three hundred years and must be investigated with scientific and historical methods. What is available as a concrete subject of investigation is the 'street-ballad sign complex' in a wealth of individual texts which can be analysed using the methods of literary and linguistic scholarship. During such investigations it will be seen that social and cultural environmental

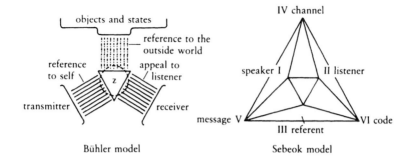

Bühler model   Sebeok model

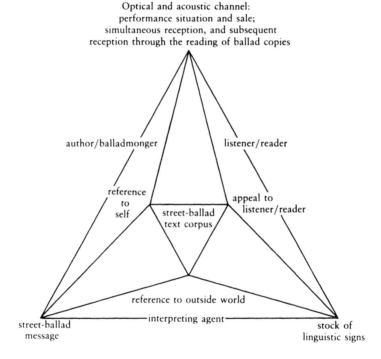

Fig. 1. Communication model for the production and reception of the street ballad in its socio-cultural context

conditions, especially those involved in the context of street-ballad performance, substantially determined textual construction. Over and above this, historical and philosophical processes in a wider sense are reflected in subject-matter and types of procedure. This can be explained with recourse to the communication process and its conditional components. In the case of the street ballad their special features can be understood as markers of specific types of text.

2.2 Speech-act theory and the interrelation between street-ballad text, situational context and components relating to socio-cultural conditions: textual structure and functional role

Speech-act theory provides analytical categories which can be used to establish a more precise understanding of the communicative conditions and instructions contained in a text.[7] These are particularly suited to our purposes because they take account of the interrelation between linguistic and non-linguistic components of the speech act and the speech situation, the relationship between textual speech situation and situational context. The speech-act categories thus enable us to establish precisely the correlation between the positions of the inner triangle (street-ballad text corpus) and those of the outer triangle (reality of performance) in our model of communication for the production and reception of the street ballad in its socio-cultural context.

When applying the linguistic method of analysis of speech-act theory to literary texts, their particular conditions of communication have to be borne in mind. These are conceived as a model in which five (for narrative text) or four (for dramatic text) different levels of communication overlay each other (R. Fieguth [1973], also D. Janik [1973]). The first level of communication is that between the fictional characters as dialogue partners. In the narrative text these are conveyed by a narrator to a fictional addressee[8] who is seldom explicitly represented, or occasionally through the comments of an explicit narrator. This level of communication does not apply in a dramatic text, where the characters speak for themselves. It is here that this model is relevant to genre theory.[9] Of special importance for interpretational perception is the third layer of communication in a complex message of the text as a whole whose ramifications can never be completely exhausted. It is on this level that a speaker cannot be specified, as Fieguth's term 'subject of the work as a whole' might imply, and that the correlative is also an 'implicit' addressee, a reader who similarly should be understood, not as having any concrete personal reference, but as symbolizing the receptive capacity of the empirical reader. In the non-textual empirical sphere, two levels of communication can be distinguished: empirical author and listener/reader as members of society (with various social roles) and their roles relating specifically to the text as producer (street-ballad author) and receiver of the work (street-ballad recipient).

The roles of the producer and the recipient are regulated by literary convention and historical socio-literary stereotypes. As far as the street ballad is concerned, the area of 'social roles' cannot be dealt with in detail, as the texts were usually published anonymously. Furthermore, we have only scant information on the few authors known to us, and individual readers cannot be dealt with at all. Historical literary conventions and stereotypes can if necessary be deduced from the interrelation between textual procedures and the audience's taste, whereas they appear distorted in the documents pertaining to reception (cf. chapter 6).

In a literary text, information of varying exactness is given concerning the person of a speaker and the place and time of his speech situation, that is, giving personal, local, and temporal reference. Most detail is given for the characters on communication level 1; we are given far less precise information on the explicit narrator of communication level 2. At the same time it must be understood that the speech situations in these fictional texts are contained within themselves and do not correspond to the speaker, listener, and context of the actual speech situation in which such texts are spoken, read, or performed. This is a characteristic of their fictional nature. While in everyday speech communication considerable knowledge of the partner can be mutually assumed – the same goes for letter-writing – the fictional text must provide this information itself. Its imaginary world remains removed from the real world. But there are also cases of 'functional' texts, such as the commissioned poem, advertising text, or cabaret song, where the constitutive speech situation is contrived and indeed specified in such a way that it can be transferred on to a real communication situation. But the text should have just the amount of deictic indicators and references to speaker and listener as is compatible with the components which would be expected of the non-textual communication situation. A specific and characteristic communication level of this kind is often found in the street ballad, with such congruent elements already formed in the text. A speaker–listener correlation which is geared towards the performance and sale situation takes precedence over the relevant genre-specific (narrative, dramatic, or discursive) speech situation and is distinguishable from it through particular deictic features and speech acts. I shall term the speaker concerned the 'presenter' and 'showman' in keeping with his functions which can be transferred onto the balladmonger (cf. chapter 3). Because his textual speech situation can in principle be transposed on to the concrete communication situation of the street ballad, only a slight degree of fictionality can be ascribed to this speaker as entertainer, in contrast to the narrator, dramatic role-player, or discursive speaker, who are also found in different types of street ballad.

The normal speech situation can be defined as a speaker and listener relating to each other in a certain time and space by means of speech acts, with a purpose involving some kind of communication or action (cf. D. Wunderlich [1969], especially pp. 270–1). These components of the speech situation are divided among the spoken text and the situational context in ways that differ from and complement each other. Information on such components is contained in many street-ballad texts, which is

compatible with the situation of public performance and which characterizes and enlivens the latter, fulfilling the conditions required.

The speaker, realized by the balladmonger, attracts attention through
his use of the personal pronoun and through his functions as presenter:
self-presentation, imparter of a textual message, advertiser of his wares,
and provider of amusement and instruction. These functions are incorporated in the text as indications of communication and action, to be more
or less explicitly understood as illocutionary acts,[10] often relating more
directly to reality than the declarations of intent of the fictional speakers in
a text. At the same time these illocutions of the presenter are usually closely
concerned with the topic of the fictional object of communication, thus
showing the presenter to be the transmitter of a literary textual message
which has imaginative, cognitive, and emotional intent.

The relationship to the listener in the speech situation of the street
ballad, that is, to the ballad audience, is already clearly and manifoldly preformed in the text through the general types of address or naming of target
groups. There are also many and various requests to behave in a certain
way, both implicit and explicit. Whether these requests had any effect on
the listeners, as was obviously one of the aims included in the illocutionary
activity of the presenter, is impossible to establish. The effectiveness of the
requests to come nearer, listen, join in the song and buy is in the main
confirmed by what we know of street-ballad practice. How far the proven
sales success was due to the advertising strategies inherent in the text must
remain open. Changes of attitude and behaviour because of the textual
content, suggested to the audience through warnings and pieces of advice
from the presenter, we can assume to have been infinitesimal, as with any
other form of literature. The most that we can be certain of is the entertainment element in the street ballads, which the performer would have
exploited fully.

The time and the place of street-ballad performance and the related sale
of broadsides are indicated in the text by requests to come up, listen, and
buy, and by the use of adverbs of place and of the present tense, as well as
by the presence of speaker and listener. The conditions of performance and
immediate sale are – from the point of view of speech-act theory – pre-
requisites of the showman elements of the text as experienced in the speech
situation.[11] Performance and sale as a separate empirical situation are for
their part embedded in that sector of the socio-cultural environment in
which author, printer/publisher, balladmonger, and audience move and
have their roots. The conditional components of this sphere indirectly
determine the actual performance and with that also the speech situation
inherent in the text, that is, they are intuitively taken into consideration by
the author during textual composition in the same way as the performance
situation. The literary and sociological conditional components for the rise

and spread of the street ballad, set out in chapter 1, must be taken as vital socio-cultural presuppositions (in the context of speech-act theory), directly affecting the construction of the street-ballad texts.[12]

The relationship between the street-ballad speaker and his listener is to some extent socially, economically, and culturally fixed. Class-specific common ground forms the basis for communication, although the ballad-monger – like the author – as someone only slightly integrated socially and having little financial security would be socially inferior to his audience, who as a rule belonged to the lower and middle classes. He would try to compensate by giving himself higher status in his self-presentation, a strategy which accords with the métier of the showman. As a purveyor of broadsides he is dependent on the sale of his literary merchandise and has therefore to contend with a buyer's market. The ballad producers' early capitalist readiness to take risks, and their business efficiency, must have rubbed off to a certain extent on the distributor. His communicative actions were nevertheless likely to succeed, as he could count on his poten-tial listener's interest due to the latter's foreknowledge of the widespread practice of balladmongering. The cultural milieu in which street-ballad distribution took place was of the people and therefore familiar to them. Literature of instruction and amusement had an immensely formative influence on literary taste. These general socio-cultural preconditions for street-ballad speech acts left their mark on the performance, and were realized in an intensive speaker–listener relationship in a finite time and place. Personal, temporal, and local indications of this relationship are found in the texts, which take account of the special conditions of the per-formance situation. Contact must first be established by attracting an audience and securing its attention. To this end, the balladmonger had to compete with other acoustic and optical distractions in the street, market-place, at the fair, or in the public house. We can only guess, from the texts, at the paralinguistic and extra-linguistic realization and form of the street-ballad speech situation. We do have the melody to go on, as far as acoustic reproduction is concerned. Gesture and mime are certainly indicated in the textual wording; how these were incorporated into the performance depended of course on the acting ability of the balladmonger. Although we must limit ourselves to an interpretation of existing written texts, it is precisely an analysis according to speech-act theory which affords us an approximate insight into the performance situation.

2.3 Communication levels in the street ballad

On the basis of the communicative levels of the literary text, we have estab-lished an analogous system of levels in speech acts and speech situations. The communication level of the street-ballad presenter (balladmonger) and of his correlative, the listener, who is already preformed in the text, is defined both by the fact that it can be pinned down comparatively precisely to a real-life situation and by the special nature of the illocutionary acts involved. In contrast to the narrator, dramatic character, discursive speaker and also the 'message of the text as a whole', they have clear, pragmatic functions. The instructional function of the street ballad is quite apparent in the speech acts of the presenter, which will be described in more detail in the next chapter on the basis of textual analysis. This function cannot, however, be separated from more comprehensive literary and aesthetic intentions. Amusement and instruction are embedded in the respective narrative, dramatic role-play, or discussion of a topic; the attention has to be directed towards the subject of the text; and it is precisely the action-orientated selling process which makes use of literary camouflage techniques. Pragmatic intention as a direct invitation to act and overall literary intention frequently merge into one another. To sum up and clarify the theoretical conditions described in this chapter, the textual and non-textual communication levels of the street ballad have been set out in diagram form; from now on this will be used as a basis for our study. Figure 2 is a further adaptation of the communication model for the production and reception of the street ballad in its socio-cultural context (p. 37). Only the components 'speaker and listener' in their textual and non-textual positions have been taken into account, however.

A thick line marks the divide between textual reality and socio-cultural environment. The deictic and illocutive interference which takes place, in spite of the actual dividing-line, between the performance level (BM – L/RSB) and the presenter level (P – SB/Ad is represented by the use of hatching and cross-hatching in this section of the non-textual area and in the corresponding section of the textual area. At the same time, the hatching marks those communication levels which should be seen as specific features of the street ballad: the performance and sale situation, which has already been described in detail (see above, chapter 1), and the 'presenter' level of communication, which will be examined in the next chapter.

The other textual and non-textual positions of the communication partners apply principally to literary texts, where some of the positions would be omitted and others partially taken over.[13] The graphic placing of the level of textual meaning (M – iAd) right on the textual border signals its higher rank in relation to the other textual levels but no particular closeness to socio-cultural reality. Direct, that is, pragmatic correspondence is only found, as we have said, between the two hatched communication levels. The term 'addressee' was chosen as opposed to 'listener/reader' in order to indicate the different textual levels of these listening positions.[14] At the same time, the degree of explicitness in being addressed has to be taken into account.

On the whole we can say that the levels of communication which have been segmented here for reasons of a clearer analysis are functionally related to each other. Interferences of function are of course possible in individual cases, that is, the presenter can assume at will certain functions of the explicit narrator, dramatic character or discursive speaker. I shall be examining this aspect more closely in my classification of street-ballad sub-genres in chapter 4. My description of the procedures of the presenter in the next chapter ignores to a large extent the correlation with the other communication levels, since in the first place it is essential to document the presenter's communication level with its functions of reference to self,

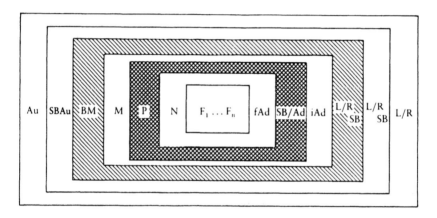

Fig. 2.

Au   empirical author as a member of society (with various social roles)

L/R   empirical listener/reader as a member of society (with various social roles)

SBAu   street-ballad author (author in the role of text-producer with street-ballad competence)

L/RSB   empirical listener/reader in the role of street-ballad recipient (with street-ballad competence)

BM   balladmonger

L/RSB   in concrete transmission situation (direct communication with the balladmonger)

M   message of the text as a whole

iAd   implicit addressee

P   presenter

SB/Ad   ballad public as addressee of the presenter

N   narrator

fAd   fictional addressee

F   fictional character

appeals to the listener, and reference to the outside world, and also its specific speech acts. In chapters 1, 3 and 4, therefore, my study of the street ballad follows the model of the communication levels 'from outside inwards'.

3 Procedures of the presenter and his relationship to his audience

3.1 Definition

The term 'presenter' is the one best suited to the speech situation concerned with performance and sale, as far as this can be ascertained in the text and established as empirical historical reality,[1] although 'showman' includes the fairground aspect and will therefore also be used to designate this function. Balladmonger and presenter share many similarities which have to do with both entertainment and selling. In the case of the street ballad as the object and at the same time final form of the presenter's message, the indications in the text of the appropriate actions and behaviour are particularly marked. The similarity to the speech activities of a juggler, 'one who entertains or amuses people by stories, songs, buffoonery, tricks, etc.',[2] is illustrated by a contemporary document. In the fifth dream apparition of his *Kind-Harts Dreame* (1592) Henry Chettle imitates the speech of one such fairground entertainer and conjurer of his time. A certain William Cuckoe, who has been forced out of business by the competition, is speaking to his colleagues from beyond the grave. Although he condemns their activities he continues to use the methods of their craft:

William Cuckoe To All Close Juglers Wisheth The Dis-Couery Of Their Crafts, And Punishment For Their Knaueries.
    Roome for a craftie knaue, cries William Cuckoe, nay, it will neare hand beare an action. Bones a mee, my trickes are stale, and all my old companions turnd into ciuill sutes. I perceiue the worlde is all honestie, if it be no other than it lookes. Let me see, if I can see; beleeue mee theres nothing but iugling in euery corner; for euery man hath learned the mysterie of casting mysts, and though they vse not our olde tearms of hey-passe, re-passe, and come aloft, yet they can bypasse, compasse, and bring vnder one another as cunningly and commonly as euer poore Cockoe coulde command his Jacke in a boxe.
    Yet, my maisters, though you robde me of my trade, to giue recompence, after death I haue borrowed a tongue a little to touch their tricks.[3]

It is first of all interesting to note here the cultural and historical information on the widespread nature of this kind of entertainment. Its milieu was shared by the street ballad, which gained from the fact that the public was already familiar with it. The practices of the craft, ranging from playfulness to downright roguery, and the cut-throat competition amongst the jugglers, are equally clearly indicated. The set phrase 'Room for' derived from popular drama and was in common use. It condensed self-presentation, attracting an audience and a request for attention – also characteristics of the street-ballad text – into one speech gesture. Its dramatic use further aided the self-advertisement and self-praise which was a necessity of the profession, and of course was meant to gain its user a pitch for his presentation. References to himself and his own point of vantage and activity place the figure of the presenter/showman in the usual exposed position for his presentation and indicate a common communication area for speaker and listener. Even though here the recipients of the address are former colleagues who are still alive, William Cuckoe is, from habit, treating the situation as though it were a performance. The spoken references to the practising of conjuring tricks through his punning use of the technical jargon[4] establish a relationship to concrete objects and actions, just as the street-ballad text does with its references to the broadside itself and its content. Amplification of the appeal dimension through colloquial fraternization – here contact is established through the abuse of fellow professionals – is also a street-ballad procedure. Further showman-type speech acts will be demonstrated when we come to analyse actual street-ballad texts.

In the following sections, the presenter/speaker's behaviour relative to his speech situation, in its various textual manifestations, will be described according to whether the respective function is predominantly orientated towards reference to self, appeals to the listener or reference to the outside world. This distinction regarding self-presentation, relationship to the public, and subject of communication corresponds to the basic components of the speech situation (speaker, listener, message). Any further differentiation into speech-act categories, that is, consideration of purposes of actions, time, and place as concrete conditional components of communicative action, or of certain conditions surrounding the relationship between speaker and listener, will also become clear when the 'presenter' level of communication is investigated. This communication level overlies narrative, semi-dramatic and discursive street ballads[5] in equal measure, and functions as a principle of textual cohesion, though it is present in varying degrees in individual texts. The following comprises indicators to be found in the text which refer to the procedure of the presenter. They also signify, some more clearly than others, an abandonment of the narrative, semi-dramatic, or discursive speech situation:

personal pronouns for clarification of speaker–listener relationship;

forms of address;

constative utterances regarding thought, feeling, opinion and belief which contribute to a clearer outline of the person of the speaker;

performative utterances, which indicate the nature of what is being said. These can function as appeals to the listener (entreating, requesting, advising, warning, etc.), as references to the outside world (informing, asserting, promising, evaluating, exaggerating, etc.) or as references to self (speaker);

references to time and place, which can be transferred to the actual performance situation: tenses, adverbs of time; adverbs of place, demonstrative adjectives, verbs indicating movement.

3.2 The presenter's reference to self

It is one of the presenter's functions to attract the attention of the audience by his marketplace behaviour and projection of himself. What he can illustrate in a variety of ways during his appearance can of necessity only be fixed in a limited way in the street-ballad text, so that in a sense the text is the score for the balladmonger's activity as showman. While to a large extent the juggler can back up his appearance with his manipulation of objects and performance of tricks as extra-linguistic acts, the presenter of the street ballad is limited by the text and by the fact that he has to transmit a message. He can introduce himself by giving speaker-related information, and help to create, through language, a reception area for his performance. In the absence of any concrete actions to perform, he makes his mark through the personalization of his message.

3.2.1 Speaker-related information

A very precise fixing of the presenter/speaker in the street ballad would tend to be a hindrance in the transmission of the text. His personality markers, then, usually relate to textual content. Sentimentally exaggerated expressions of feeling and attempts to create sensation and horror are inserted where the text allows and demands these.

> In sorrow and compassion great,
> I of a story sad will treate
> A story full of wonderous woe,
> As by the sequell you may know.[6]

> My heart doth bleed to tell the wo
>   or chance of grief that late befel
> At *Biglesworth* in *Bedfordshire*
>   as I to you for truth will tell,
> There was . . . [7]

The speech act which dominates here is not the explicit 'I will treate a story', 'I will tell . . . ' but the expression of a mournful attitude which gives the presenter a certain aura. As a function of an appeal to the listener, sympathetic involvement in his story is at the same time asked of the audience:

> Mee thinkes I heare a grone,
>   of death and deadly dole,
> Assending from the graue
>   of a poore silly soule:
> Of a poore silly soule,
>   vntimely made away
> Come then and sing with me,
>   sobbs of sad welladay.[8]

As the communicator of a piece of information, the presenter is indirectly also defined by the subject of his message. Thus, for instance, amusing and entertaining topics mark him out to be a comedian. This can even happen through the title, which we must assume was read out and displayed:

> *An Excellent Medley*
> *Which you may admire at (without offence)*
> *For euery line speaks contrary sense*[9]
>
> *The praise of Nothing:*
> *Though some doe wonder why I write in praise*
> *Of Nothing, in these lamentable daies,*
> *When they have read, and will my counsell take,*
> *I hope of Nothing Something they may make.*[10]
>
> *Faire fall all good Tokens!*
>   *Or,*
> *A pleasant new Song, not common to be had,*
> *Which will teach you to know good tokens from bad.*[11]

The joke in the following ballad is that the word 'tokens' in its meaning: signs for characteristics, patterns of behaviour and processes, is taken over-literally. The signalling function of the word serves as a peg on which to hang all kinds of statements – sometimes commonplace, sometimes vicious:

> Yet by all signes and tokens,
>   as I may judge or thinke,
> The man that hath lost both his eyes,
>   he cannot chuse but winke.
> But some will winke when they may see –
>   but that is nothing unto me:
> Some shut their eyes to have a fee,
>   which are in love with chinke.   (ibid., v. 3, lines 17–24, p. 343)
>
> But this is a true token, –
>   then marke my word aright! –

When Sol is setting in the West
the world will lose her light.
So when an old man's head growes gray,
    he may thinke on his dying day,
For to the grave he must away,
    and bid the world good night.   (ibid., v. 11, lines 81–8, p. 345)

The argument in this ballad is based on the connection between a sign and the conventional meaning it has acquired through common experience. The fact that this experience is shared by both speaker and listener consolidates their relationship through the medium of the textual content. The street-ballad presenter is furthermore confirmed in his role of purveyor of entertaining platitudes, which is reinforced by complacent references back to himself. The first two verses are devoted to the presenter's introduction of himself and the presentation, with examples, of the subject of his message:

To you that have bad tokens
    this matter I indight,
Yet nothing shall be spoken
    that shall your minds afright:
Be silent, therefore, and stand still!
    marke what proceedeth from my quill;
I speake of tokens good and ill,
    and such as are not right.

But first Ile have you understand,
    before that I doe passe,
That there are many tokens
    which are not made of brasse;
It is a token of my love
    that I to you this matter move;
For many tokens bad doe proove,
    we see in every place.   (ibid., vv. 1–2, pp. 342–3)

It is already clear at this point that to a large extent the presenter's character is determined by the subject of his message, and that he is defined as its communicator. Speech acts implying sympathy, amazement, criticism, thought and judgement, which are sometimes of a serious and sometimes of a humorous and joking nature, contribute to a contouring of his personality. They are also communicable through gesture and mime, but their purpose is always to convey the message in hand. The limiting of speech-related information in the text to cognitive and emotional attitudes guarantees their transferability on to the concrete performance situation which is linked to the direct addressing of the audience.

3.2.2 Establishment of a reception area for performance which is also relevant to the listeners

Indications of a common reception area for performance, where communication takes place and the perlocutive dimension of the speech act becomes possible, are important specifications for the concrete realization of a speech situation. In the street ballad, the presenter achieves this through a procedure which is already inherent in the text, usually in a combination of reference to self and appeals to the listener which are concerned with the link between text and performance. The request to come up and listen, and possibly to examine the 'wares', indicates the idea of a concrete spatial area which is capable of being transposed by means of the performer's technique. The ballad author had fixed formulas at his disposal such as 'listen to . . . lend me an ear, come . . . draw near, here is', etc.

> List to my dity Country men[12]

> Come grant me, come lend me
> your listning eares:[13]

> Come hither, good fellowes, come hither,
>   Good counsell, if you will learne it,
> I heere in a song will shew it,[14]
>
>   . . .
>
> Give eare, my loving countrey-men,
>   that still desire newes,
> Nor passe not while you heare it sung,
>   or else the song peruse;[15]

> And if you please to stay a while,
> You shall heare how . . . [16]

> Faire Maydens come and see,
>   if heere be ought will please you:
> And if we can agree,
>   Ile giue you iust your due,
>   or nere trust me.[17]

> Here's that will challenge all the Fair:
> Come buy my nuts and damsons, my Burgamy pear.[18]

The last two examples are taken from texts which actually describe presenter/showman situations. One is a dramatic poem recited by an itinerant pedlar, the other by an advertiser of fairground amusements. Fiction and street-ballad reality merge into one another here, a strategy not infrequently used by the street ballad.[19] A characteristic example is the discursive ballad *A Fooles Bolt is soone shot* (1629) (*PG*, No. 55, pp. 316–22). The text contains speech acts which are easily transposed by the presenter according to their gesture and mime potential, and depending on his relationship with his audience:

> Stand wide my Masters, and take heed,
>   for feare the Foole doth hit yee,
> If that you thinke you shall be shot,
>   I'de wish you hence to get yee;
> My Bowe you see stands ready bent,
>   to giue each one their lot,
> Then haue amongst you with my Bolts,
> *for now I make a shot.*   (ibid., v. 1)

The title of this ballad is a modification of the saying 'A foole's bolt may sometimes hit the mark' (F. P. Wilson [1970], p. 276). It concerns a wise fool who turns the weapon of criticism of himself on to his listeners and can hit the target. The reversal of the proverb – the unerring aim of the fool – corresponds to the exchange of roles between marksmen and targets, where the latter now appear as the actual fools. It is possible that during the process of aiming and evading there was an extra-linguistic inter-action between the balladmonger and individual listeners. This is pro-grammatically formulated as illocutive act and perlocutive effect in the opening verse. Each verse deals with a stock figure of contemporary society, and the closing refrain of each reminds the listener that the under-lying speech situation is one of mocking criticism aimed directly at the audience.

> The Miser that gets wealth great store,
>   and wretchedly doth liue,
> In 's life is like to starue himselfe,
>   at 's death he all doth giue
> Unto some Prodigall, or Foole,
>   that spends all he hath got,
> With griping vsury and paine,
>   *at him I make a shot.*   (v. 7, *PG*, p. 319)

More concise indications of the presenter's position are found at the end of the ballad, often in conjunction with a request for money. Diectic infor-mation of space is particularly obvious in the following example:

> And thus you now have heard the praise
>   of Nothing, worth a penny,
> Which, as I stand to sing here now,
>   I hope will yeeld me many:[20]

3.2.3 Personalization of the message

The clarification of the speech act in the street ballad through reference to self provides the presenter/speaker with a profile which is appropriate to the performance situation. He is projected as one who acts through speech, in an area for the presenter's action which is at least intimated in the text itself and is then particularized by the individual performance. The main task of this speaker is to convey a message. Recent research in communication, especially on strategies of influence and advertising, has shown empirically that the personalization of a message through the figure of the speaker is particularly effective. The mere presence of the speaker suggests authority; and the credibility, prestige, and attractiveness attached, together with the obvious membership of a certain class, are value categories which are more or less consciously projected by the receiver of the message on to the message itself.[21] Because of its particular mode of communication and distribution the street ballad as a literary form is both suited to, and compelled to adopt, a personalization of its message. The presenter with his speech acts specific to the street ballad, realized in the balladmonger, is a familiar figure in the social context of fairground amusements. His attraction lies in his claim to offer amusement and instruction, and he is very concerned to build up in words his prestige as a conveyor of sensational news items and true stories, so that at least a conventional claim to credibility is established. Whatever the balladmonger's prestige was, the assignment of the various communications and stories to one centre of orientation, manifested in the balladmonger and his speech acts, meant a substantial ease of reception for a public unaccustomed to literary texts. This in turn served as a basis for the exertion of influence of various kinds.

The simplest form of message personalization is the explicit reference to the speaker's communicative function. The speech act is described as a communication, whereby a closer definition of the subject of the communication (the narration of a story, report of an incident, etc.) is possible. There is frequent evidence in the street ballad of the speaker's thus coming to the fore in the text, often in conjunction with an introductory announcement of the textual content which follows. The procedure covers, therefore, reference both to self and to the outside world.[22]

> I'le tell you a Iest which you'l hardly beleeue –
> No matter for that, you shall hear't, right or wrong –[23]

> For, ere you heare it, I must tell,
>   my newes it is not common;[24]

> You who would be inform'd of forraine newes,
> Attend to this which presently insues,[25]

> Now I must here declare my Ditty,
> To all, both Countrey, Towne, and Citie,[26]

> Young maids, and young men,
>   I pray you give eare,

And with hand and pen
  Ile plainly declare
Of a maid's resolution,[27]

I heere in a song will shew it,[28]

Ile write of an age that for euer shall last,[29]

Whose storie I doe meane to write,
  and tytle it, True Loues delight, . . . [30]

Examples are practically endless. Probably the most frequent illocutive formula is 'I will tell', as a denotative reference to the communicative intention. Other expressions such as 'narrate', 'enumerate', 'make known', 'report', 'state', are found according to whether the context is narrative, a list of examples pertaining to a topic, a report of an event, or an expression of opinion. Such a connotative specification of the communication method which derives from the actual subject of the message also marks the transition from the presenter's general to his particular role, that is, as narrator, dramatic figure, or discursive speaker (see below, chapter 4.1). The formula 'I will declare' has various nuances of meaning, according to context: 'to make clear' (until 1691, see *OED*), 'to make known' and 'to relate' (until 1703, see *OED*). Finally, the reference to the writing process in 'I'll write' relates to the ballad author in his speech function, and is in its literal sense inappropriate for translation on to the performance situation. Since, however, the writing process is frequently mentioned in the text together with the communicative function of the performer and singer,[31] the meaning of 'write', seen pragmatically, can also be understood as a signal of communicative intention.

In forms of literature which were intended for oral transmission, and also otherwise as introductory formulas, it is quite usual to find explicit references to the communicative function of a speaker who is implied in the text. This is evident, for instance, in verse romance. Taken by themselves, these formulas do not constitute a characteristic of the street ballad. In conjunction, however, with other procedures which are specific to the showman/presenter and which relate to street-ballad performance and the sale of broadsides, the frequent articulating of the communicative intention does help in the construction of the presenter's persona.

The speaker's and storyteller's act of maintaining that he is speaking the truth is also a traditional topos (see E. R. Curtius [1965], pp. 95–9) which was adopted by the street ballad, but at the same time modified in a characteristic and situation-specific way. As I see it, the claim to be reporting the truth, and a corresponding sense of expectancy on the part of the audience, are even more prominent than is the case in medieval literature. 'True' is virtually the motto of ballad literature, and the entrance of Autolycus in Shakespeare's *The Winter's Tale* is an illustration of this:

CLOWN: What hast here? Ballads?
MOPSA: Pray now, buy some, I love a ballad in print a'life, for then we are sure they
    are true.[32]

At the same time an ambivalence regarding the street-ballad's claim to
truth set in. The 'intellectuals' of the time were not convinced, and we can
assume that the producers and the relayers of the street ballad inserted
such claims for manipulative purposes. As early as 1589, Thomas Nashe
was sneering at the supposed credibility of ballads and other products of
hack writers (see appendix B 16), and Ben Jonson attacks the conveying of
news in broadsides where the motivation is not a duty to report facts
reliably but rather the printer's desire for profit.

PRINTER: Indeed I am all for sale, gentlemen; you say true, I am a printer, and a
    printer of news; and I do hearken after them, wherever they be, at any rates;
    I'll give anything for a good copy now, be it true or false, so it be news.
FACTOR: And I have hope to erect a Staple for News erelong, whither all shall be
    brought, . . . news that when a man sends them down to the shires where they
    are said to be done, were never there to be found!
    . . .
PRINTER: Sir that's all one, they were made for the common people; and why should
    not they have their pleasure in believing of lies are made for them, as you have
    in Paul's, that make them for yourselves?
    . . .
PRINTER: . . . a great many who will indeed believe nothing but what's in print.[33]

It can clearly be seen here how the new topic area of news transmission, taken up also by the street ballad, in combination with a desire to
lend an air of topicality to other subjects of communication extends the
function of the claim to authenticity as well as calling it into question for
a critical minority. The catchword 'news' – 'latest news', 'strange news',
'wonderful news' – in numerous ballad titles[34] signals the announcement
of sensational information and implies an assertion of the truth of the
subject-matter communicated. At the same time, however, the author is
counting on a belief in marvels, familiarity with the practices of magic, and
a lack of logical and sophisticated thought on the part of the audience.[35]
He would also expect from them a readiness to accept sensational and
horrific events on the basis of their entertainment value. The speech act of
truth assertion presupposes a close interaction between the claims of the
speaker and the attitude of the listeners.

Forms of an explicit claim to authenticity, together with the necessary
fictions proving such authenticity, are found predominantly in reports of
miraculous happenings, such as blood rain, freaks of birth, etc. They are
also found in accounts of sensational murders, that is, in narrative street
ballads whose subject-matter seems to require a declaration of credibility.
Claims to authenticity are not necessary in first-person narrative or ballads

with dramatic role-play, as the (fictional) authenticity is provided in the person of the narrator/actor himself. The most obvious way of asserting the truth of what is being communicated is to say that it is true. But the claim to authenticity is also made in the form of fictions such as eye-witness reports of references to an oral or written source, supported by realistic detail including actual place, time, and names. A clear separation cannot be made between claims to authenticity referring to the speaker, and those referring to the outside world, as they always relate to the subject of the communication and at the same time to the speaker himself as a source. There is, underlying the speech act, a declaration which is not always formulated in the first person but refers predominantly to what is about to be reported.

> It is for certain true,
>   and is approved plain;
> From earth, I say, it came[36]

> Thus have you heard the doleful end,
>   of *Gibbs*, which is too true,[37]

The true reporte of the forme and shape of a monstrous Childe borne at Muche Yorkesleye, a village three myles from Colchester, in the Countye of Essex, the XXI daye of Apryll in this yeare 1562   (*AB*, no. 8, pp. 38–42)

The true description of two monsterous children, lawfully begotten betwene George Steuens and Margerie his wyfe, and borne in the parish of Swanburne in Buckynghamshyre the iiij of Aprill, Anno Domini 1566[38]

The tvvo inseparable brothers. Or A true and strange description of a Gentleman (an Italian by birth) about seventeene yeeres of age, who hath an imperfect (yet living) Brother, growing out of his side (1639)
    (*POA*, no. 2, pp. 7–14; by Martin Parker)

Two unfortunate Lovers; Or A true Relation of the lamentable end of John True and Susan Mease (between 1601 and 1640)   (*RB*, II, pp. 643–50)

Strange Newes from Brotherton in Yorke-shire, being a true Relation of the raining of Wheat on Easter *day last*, . . . (*c.* 1648)   (*POA*, no. 7, pp. 36–43)

There is particularly frequent occurrence of titles in which the formula 'true relation', and similar combinations with the epithet 'true', appear. In the mouth of the balladmonger this declaration of the truth of what is being related takes on the specific function of the market-crier's prot-estations, giving him the appearance of guarantor of the truth. The claim to authenticity becomes more convincing through the fiction that the speaker is supposed to have witnessed the events he is reporting, and his reference to his role as eyewitness is an indirect illocutive act of delaring his narrative to be true.

Not infrequently the street ballad makes use of the late medieval intro-

UNIV.

ductory topos 'as I was walking', which usually sets the scene for the eye-
or earwitness of a quarrel between a man and a woman or a woman's
solitary lamentations (see E. Sandison [1913]; R. Dähne [1933]).

> In the gallant month of June,
>   When sweet roses are in prime,
> And each bird, with a severall tune,
>   Harmoniously salutes the time,
>   then, to delight
>   my appetite,
>   I walkt into a meddow faire,
>   and, in a shade,
>   I spyed a maide,
> Whose love had brought her to dispaire.[39]

> As 't was my chance to walke abroad
>   One time, to take the ayre,

> I heard a faire maide make a great moane,
>   And she was in great care:[40]

This introductory topos occurs in the street ballad most frequently
within the theme of *mal mariée*. An example of this is found in the
dramatic ballad about a bachelor musing on the disadvantages of married
life,[41] as the frame for a conversation between a courting lover and a girl
who scornfully rejects him.[42] At the same time it provides a platform for a
socially critical dialogue where the way of life and outlook of a well-to-do
peasant and a town servant are contrasted.[43] The idea of the eyewitness,
inherent in the topos 'as I was walking' as a claim to truth, is clearly
restricted to the reporting of speech as the subject of communication and
occurs therefore only, though by no means always, in ballads with
dramatic role-play and dialogue. This type of claim to authenticity would
presumably seem too idyllic and long-drawn-out for the narrative ballad
of sensation and wonders, although the latter does tend to refer to an infor-
mant as the source rather than to the presenter/speaker as eyewitness. In
one of Martin Parker's ballads he has as an eyewitness the 'reporter' of a
freak. This reporter makes use of his extensive experience in the field to
produce a 'one better' topos:

> I many Prodigies haue seene,
> Creatures that haue preposterous beene,
>   to nature in their birth,
> But such a thing as this my theame,
> Makes all the rest seeme but a dreame,
>   the like was nere on earth.[44]

References to informants, that is, shifting the role of eyewitness on to a
third person, can take various forms. The narrator of *A feareful and*

*terrible Example of Gods iuste iudgement executed vpon a lewde Fellow,
who vsually accustomed to sweare by Gods Blood* (between 1591 and
1603)[45] can name as his source the master of the servant who is punished
with a repellent mortal illness for his blasphemous cursing. The report of
a young man from the country who is relieved of his money by a prostitute
in London is said to stem from a member of that profession, if not from the
girl herself:

> For I will here vnfold
> A iest that was done lately,
> As I for truth was told
> By a City Lasse most stately,
> of Cupids mould.[46]

*A Lamentable List, of certaine Hidious, Frightfull, and Prodigious
Signes* (1638) refers back to 'good testimonies hither brought' (*POA*,
no. 4, pp. 21–5; 2, 3, p. 22), *A Maruellous Murther, Committed vpon the
Body of one* George Drawnefield of Brempton (1638?) similarly refers to a
documentary report.[47] A number of different informants gives added
weight to the claim to authenticity.[48] The event may through this attain
such a degree of fame that the audience is called upon as witness: *The
father hath beguil'd the sonne. Or, a wonderfull Tragedy, which lately
befell in Wiltshire, as many men know full well* (1629).[49] *The Tragedy of
Doctor* Lambe, *The great suposed Coniurer, . . .* (1628) (*PG*, no. 48,
pp. 276–82) reports the lynch-mob justice carried out on a feared magician
and can similarly call on the audience's experience:

> Neighbours sease to mone,
> And leaue your lamentation:
> For Doctor *Lambe* is gone,
> The Deuill of our Nation,
> as 'tis knowne.   (ibid., v. 1, p. 278)

A claim to authenticity of this kind, orientated towards an appeal to the
listeners, operates on an emotional basis, a persuasion strategy with which
we are familiar from our experience of modern advertising.[50] A similar
claim is made in the classical topos of *adtestatio rei visae*.[51] Even those who
had only heard tell of Doctor Lambe, and were not present at his death,
were supposed to feel relief. Excitement and sympathy reinforce the subjective impression of authenticity.[52] The author of *Youth's Warning-peice*
(1636) (*RB*, III, 1–4) makes express use of this strategy, basing his proof
of authenticity solely on the shattering effect of his narrative:

> If it was feigned, or not true indeed,
> It should not in men such dolour breed;
> Or had it beene some fable, or old thing,
> It might have past without much sorrowing.   (ibid. v. 2, p. 2)

The contrast with events which take place in the distant past links the claim to authenticity, based as it is on affective and aesthetic aspects of reception, to the criterion of topicality. This last is for the most part a fundamental component of the street ballad's claim to authenticity, as can be seen in the profusion of ballads containing the word 'newes'. Details of place and time are usually implicit. In contrast, reference to written sources of the type:

> In searching ancient chronicles
> It was my chance to finde . . . [53]

which are typical of medieval literature,[54] are found comparatively seldom in the street ballad.[55]

Claims to, and fictions proving, authenticity recur constantly in the street ballad. As I see it, claims to authenticity are of more central concern in the street ballad than in medieval literature. Although the street ballad adopts elements from the traditional topos, it expands it through its claim to topicality and through direct conversion into didactic literature.[56] The public is to be offered not so much truths propagated by scholarly tradition, but instruction in the ways of the world, to be gleaned from events which are contemporary, either because of their actual core of reality or because of the fiction adopted. The presenter has to grip his listeners directly with events which happened next door, so to speak, and which could also happen to them. The truth assertion is therefore related to the subject of the ballad, stresses its news value, and refers back to informants. The reference to older sources is consequently less appropriate, and an eyewitness report in lyrical form is ill suited to the news ballad. The arousing of emotion and fear, however, which is also part and parcel of the presenter's projection of his persona (see above, p. 41) reinforces the topicality of what is reported in the same way as the fictions proving authenticity. In all the forms of the claim to authenticity the presenter sets himself up as guarantor of the truth and therefore of the importance of his message. The realization through the balladmonger of the illocutive act of truth assertion in the speech situation of the street ballad increases the effectiveness of the act.

Proof of the quality of his message is also inherent in the presenter's claim to authenticity, and the intention to instruct and amuse, specific to the street ballad, is reinforced by it. Warnings and advice involving appeals to the listener, and comments in the title and opening lines,[57] referring to the outside world, on the entertainment value of a ballad serve to emphasize further the particular worth of the literary product. It is always the presenter who conveys this idea, especially as in referring to his communicative function and to his persona as speaker he clearly reveals himself as guarantor of value. With this the street-ballad text appears at the same time to have an inbuilt sales-orientated procedure. Such a procedure is used in modern advertising, as when an advertisement is personalized by competent-looking manufacturers of a product, or by customers' recommendations or typical (fictionalized) consumer situations (see I. Hantsch [1972], esp. pp. 95–7). A speaker figure vouches for the quality of the goods, so to speak, offering thereby an opportunity to identify with him.

In the street ballad the speaker figure of the presenter, as implied in the text, is realized during the performance in the balladmonger, who puts the sales intention into effect immediately after the performance at the very latest. The presenter's demonstrative, market-crier's projection of himself makes him a particularly suitable figure for advertising purposes. He can also indicate or formulate the 'consumer situation' by an anticipatory description of the subject of his communication as 'merry', 'pleasant', 'lamentable', 'wonderful', 'fearful' – and whatever other emotive words may appear in the title – or by giving warnings and advice. The balladmonger arouses or reinforces the public's 'consumer needs' as soon as he appears and starts making announcements. He achieves this not least by inducing emotional responses in the listeners when he exposes his own deep emotion regarding his subject, at the same time commenting on its pathos:

> Come, mournful Muse, assist my quill, whilst I with grief relate,
> A story of two Lovers true, cut off by cruel fate:
> Death onely parts united hearts, and brings them to their graves,
> Whilst others sleep within the deep, or perish in the waves.[58]

It is reference to the subject of communication as an advertising technique – here applied to literary texts – which gives this process its special character. The presenter, as a major component of the textual and performance procedures of the street ballad, functions as both cohering principle of the textual structure and mere fairground entertainer, and as both personalization of his wares and as salesman. The illocutions involving reference to the speaker's self which have so far been described also serve indirectly the purpose of selling, disguised though they are, by marking the presenter out, with his various functions, as a competent and reliable sales representative. Literature and advertising thus work in close liaison. The special structural characteristics of the street ballad, the identity of the balladmonger, and the coupling of performance and sale, make possible a particularly intensive form of self-advertising. This last is catered for in the text itself, and would take place in an atmosphere of naïveté and unconcern regarding functional literature, whereas other printed literary products had to rely on title announcement and preface alone.

3.3 The presenter's appeals to the listener

On the presenter/showman communication level it is not only the speaker who is clearly profiled, but also his correlative, the listener, who is also in various ways taken account of in the text. Explicit appeal functions are frequently made use of in the street ballad in order to attract the public's attention, and in the presenter's speech act they are directly translated on to the performance situation. An explicit appeal function of this kind must be distinguished from the implicit addressee, who is assigned to the text as a whole with its global intention which is on a communication level of its own.[59] Textually explicit information involving appeals to the listener which in performance address a recipient can elucidate and clarify textual intention, but they may also, through the use of irony, run counter to it.[60] The presenter's relation with the audience involves various textual procedures: forms of address, exhortations to act in a certain way or to change one's attitude, colloquialism, and refrain.

3.3.1 Forms of address: of a general kind; specific address relevant to topic; early forms of address

The most frequent form of address is of course the unspecific 'you', with which the speaker can establish a relationship with the listener even when his function is predominantly one of self-reference, for example if he is referring to his communicative function or setting up a reception area for his performance. The frequency and self-evidence of the occurrence of this form of address clearly show the dominant communicative intention of both author and balladmonger. Forms such as 'young and old',[61] 'good folks',[62] 'good fellowes' (see above p. 45 and n. 14) and similar, are almost as common. Where forms of address are more precise in content this usually relates to the relevant topic, which is directed at a specific target group. This would be a group of potential listeners of whom it can be assumed some were present at the relevant performance. The differentiation in street-ballad address, as an appeal-orientated pragmatic element in textual construction, can thus be realized in the performance situation. In *The wiuing age* (between 1621 and 1625) (*PG*, no. 41, pp. 234–8) the presenter/speaker sides unequivocally with the young girls who are elbowed out of the marriage market by rich old widows, emphasizing his view with an explicit address at the end of the ballad:

> My song vnto Virgins is chiefly directed,
> Who now in this age are little respected,
> Though widowes be chosen and maids be reiected,
> They will be esteemed, though now they'r neglected,

Yet not in this wiuing age,
Yet not in this wiuing age.   (ibid., v. 18, p. 238)

Here begins a pleasant song of a Mayden faire (*c.* 1630?) (*PB*, no. 72, II,
pp. 157–61) warns young girls against money-grabbing young men,
reinforcing the message with an appeal to potential victims:

All you young Maydes, by me be warned,
Lest you by false youngmen be harmed:
Be careful in the choosing of your honey,
Vnlesse you lose your mayden-heads and mony.   (ibid., v. 24, p. 161)

The Pedler opening of his Packe (*c.* 1620) (*PG*, no. 19, pp. 116–20)
wisely directs his advertising of cosmetics and toiletries chiefly at young
girls, in the manner of a presenter:

Faire Maydens come and see,
    if heere be ought will please you:
And if we can agree,
    Ile giue you iust your due,
        or nere trust me.   (ibid., v. 2, p. 116)

A Ditty delightfull of mother Watkins ale (*c.* 1590) (*AB*, no. 76,
pp. 370–5) warns young girls against the dangers of being easily seduced
when under the influence of alcohol:

I wish all maydens coy,
That heare this prety toy,
Wherein most women ioy,
    How they doe sport;
For surely Watkins ale,
And if it be not stale,
Will turne them to some bale,
    As hath report.   (ibid., 6, 5–12, p. 373)

In the following textual examples the thematic basis for the respective
form of address, which refers explicitly to the text itself, is immediately
obvious from the title and is reinforced in the text through direct address:

Nobody his Counsaile to chuse a Wife: Or, The difference betweene Widdowes
and Maydes (*c.* 1626):

Let Young men giue eare
    vnto that I reherse,
And thinke good the subiect
    though set downe in verse: (*PG*, no. 46, pp. 263–9, 1, 1–4, p. 263)

The Cruell Shrow: Or, The Patient Man's Woe (between 1601 and 1640):

Come, Batchelers and Married men,
    and listen to my song,

And I will shew you plainely, then,
   the iniury and wrong
That constantly I doe sustaine   (*RB*, I, pp. 93–8; 1, 1–5, p. 94)

A Penny-worth of Good Counsell

To Widdowes, and to Maides,
   This Counsell I send free;
And let them looke before they leape,
   Or that they married be (between 1624 and 1660)   (*RB*, II, pp. 294–9)

The Essex *man coozened by a* VVhore (1631):

You Countrey-men that are
   And trauell vnto *London*,
And there doe sell fat ware,
   Take heede you be not vndon
      by Cupids snare.   (*PB*, no. 78, II, pp. 191–5; v. 1, p. 192)

John Spenser a Chesshire Gallant, his life and repentance, who for killing of one Randall Gam: was lately executed at Burford *a mile from* Nantwich (*c.* 1626):

Kind Youngmen all to mee giue eare,
   obserue these lessons well;

For vndeserued my death I tooke,
   and sad is the tale I tell.[63]

There are many further examples of the addressing of a specified section of the public. It is usually one section at a time that is addressed; only seldom are different social groups called upon to consider a ballad's moral implications and didactic appeal. It is particularly clear in the next example that the ballad author reflected on the thematic relevance to his audience of his text and that he was bent on achieving an effective communication of it:

Parents come bend your eares,
   listen what followed on,
Masters come shed your teares,
   mothers come make your moane,
Seruants with sad laments,
   rue the calamity,
Those gentle children had;
   liuing in missery.[64]

The frequency of what we might call personal forms of address, which are bound up with the thematic content of the text in question, increases with the expansion and differentiation of the subjects of communication in the street-ballad corpus at the beginning and during the course of the seventeenth century.[65] There seems to be here a close connection with the secularization of textual content which took place at the same time. In early street ballads, namely those which were predominantly religious, moral, and theological in content, collective forms of address such as 'Christians', and 'man', or apostrophizations of God and the saints were the norm. These texts convey inviolable religious truths and address their audiences *sub specie aeternitatis* in corresponding forms of appeal which are of general application, when they address them at all. Reference to self and appeals to the listener are often fused in the collective first-person plural, so that no difference in conviction between speaker and listener can begin to emerge, even from the point of view of the speech act.[66]

In this context we will first give examples of typical forms of address used by the early street ballad:

> O Christian hartes, relent;
>   prepare your soules to saue –
> When fethered foules shall help
>   for vs to make a graue![67]

> True Christian hartes, cease to lament,
>   for greefe it is in vaine;
> For *Christ*, you know, was well content
>   to suffer bitter payne,[68]

> Wherefore, good Christian people, now
>   Take warning by my fall, –[69]

> Triumph good Christians and reioyce,
>   This wondrous newes to heare:
> Wherein the power of mightie Ioue,
>   So greatly doth appeare.[70]

> Remember well, o mortall man, to whom god geueth reason,
> How he truly, most ryghtfully, doth alwayes punyshe treason.[71]

> Ye Adams broode and earthly wightes, which breath now on the earth,
> Come . . . [72]

> *Remember man both night and daye,*
> *Thou must nedes die, there is no nay.* (1566)   (BB, no. 59, pp. 177–9)

As a general rule forms of address have reference to the topic of the text: the martyr's exemplary conduct, warnings against the sinful behaviour described, and victory over unbelievers, affect Christians directly. It appears that human beings who are not specifically Christians are addressed only when the generally applicable topic of death is treated. As far as the audience is concerned the forms of address are of an exhortatory nature, though without the phatic component which occurred so frequently in later street ballads. They do not add in any way to an explicit self-reference function whose standpoint or dramatic role-play are geared towards a specific audience. The speaker withdraws behind his 'object of concern'.

The link between the topic, and that section of the public which it is meant to affect, can lead to a specification of the public addressed, as was common in the seventeenth-century street ballad. There are already signs of this in the early street ballads. *A Triumph for true Subiects, and a Terrour vnto al Traitours* (1581) (OEB, no. 10, pp. 62–9) addresses at the beginning the large community of Protestants and patriots under Queen Elizabeth:

> Good Subiectes of ENGLANDE, reioyce and be glad;
> Gyue glorie to God . . .   (ibid., 1, 1–2)

Also in *It is not god but we our selves seke the euersion of our own countrey*[73] it is, in line with the thematic content, the Queen's subjects who are addressed as responsible citizens of a country:

> Ye *Britaines*, borne of *Brutus'* bloud,
>   leave of[f], therfore, to walcke at will,
> That all your woordes and deedes may be
>   to reason's lore attentive still.   (8, 5–8, OEB, p. 283)

A differentiation in address is seen in *A pretie dittie and a pithie intituled O mortall man* (1563?) (OEB, no. 47, pp. 265–9), where there is an arrangement according to position and age and the warnings are hierarchically ordered in the individual verses. However, it is here less a question of public than of apostrophic address which is implied in the text, since presumably neither king nor judge would have been present in the audience.[74]

It is often the case that the speaker does not address an audience at all, but rather invokes God, Christ, or the saints with prayer-like requests for support or lamentations on the sinfulness of the world. If an exalted person or transcendental sphere is addressed, a possible perlocutive effect is shifted in that direction and communication with the listeners reduced; however, the latter are urged in the text to participate in the hymn-like invocations:

> Our liuyng God, to thee we cry,[75]
>
> Correct vs, Lord, by thine own hand,   (ibid., 2, 2, p. 177)
>
> Soyled in sinnes (O Lorde,) a wretched sinfull Ghoste,
> To thee I call, to thee I sue, that shewest of mercie moste,[76]
>
> O happie marterèd saintes,
>   to you I call and crye,
> To helpe vs in our wantes
>   and begge for vs mercie![77]

The frequency of religious invocations[78] and also of poems in praise of religious figures[79] in the early street ballad shows that forms of address were certainly known and used within the text corpus. It is also apparent, however, that a relationship with a real-life audience was hardly envisaged: it is possible that such a relationship was either taken for granted or simply not taken into account. A change can be seen here clearly at the beginning and during the course of the seventeenth century: as religious thematic content waned, so the dimensions of self-reference and appeals to the listener of the communication level of the showman/presenter expanded.

3.3.2 Encouragement of the audience to immediate action during the performance: requests to come closer, listen, join in the singing and buy

The presenter's speech act is particularly clearly shown where it contains explicit requests. These establish a speaker–listener relationship, whereby influence can be exerted so that the performance will have practical consequences for the audience. The illocutionary act can here be so structured that its perlocutionary dimension remains directly involved in the temporal and local schema of the speech act or is, on the other hand, shifted to an indefinite future date, as with warnings and advice.[80] The course of the performance is directly influenced by the presenter's request for attention combined with an invitation to come closer. In consideration of probable acoustic disturbances, and of audience fluctuation, a reception area for performance is established,[81] which is characteristic of the presenter's procedure. The short, formalistic request to listen, *herken*, *lysten*, part of the introductory convention of the Middle English verse romance,[82] does not, however, involve references to place and time, nor does it resort to market-crier repetition and intrusiveness. The minstrel appeared before an assembled audience for whom a request to listen closely was seen more as an opening statement, whereas the balladmonger had the job of attracting his audience, persuading them to stay, and keeping their attention. Thus the communication situation was taken into account in the ballad text.

> Come hither yongmen and giue eare,
>   and good example take,[83]

> Attend, my Masters, and listen well
> Vnto this my Ditty, which briefly doth tell[84]

> Give ear you lusty Gallants,
>   my purpose is to tell[85]

Listen a while dear frinds I do you pray,
And mark the words that I to you shall say[86]

Good People all pray lend an eare
   to this my Song, that's strange and true,
Wherein I breifly shall Declare,
   the full Relation here to you.[87]

List to my dity Country men,

     . . .

giue eare to that which will insue[88]

Give eare unto my story true,
   you gracelesse men on earth,
Which any way, in secret, seeke
   your neighbour's timelesse death![89]

Kind hearted men, a while geue eare
   and plainely Ile vnfold
The saddest tale that euer yet,
   by mortall man was told.[90]

The examples given above are representative of many others, although by no means every street ballad from the first half of the seventeenth century contains an initial request for attention and an invitation to 'come and listen'.[91] Conventionalized in the neat formulas 'come listen' and 'give ear', this request was probably a stimulus for the habitual ballad-listener, which could be interpreted behaviouristically as it may well have triggered off an automatic reaction of standing still and listening. The repetition of the illocution in different words even in the same line reinforces the urgency of the presenter's object of concern, whereby the request to give him attention just for a short while (see also the example above, p. 44), as a singer's modesty topos, indicates at the same time some of the difficulties involved in ballad performance. Alongside its predominantly phatic function, the request for attention has the further function of to some extent manipulating reception, since it implicitly stresses the importance of the subject of communication and usually involves a transition to the topic.

Invitations to join in the singing, which in fact do not often occur, also serve to attract attention and have the additional purpose of stimulating the audience to participate in the performance. The fact that such a procedure was fairly common is also shown by the numerous refrains constituting further, though less explicit, encouragement to participate. This kind of request is linked to the topic in hand, in so far as a corresponding arousal of emotion in the audience is thereby ensured. In *The cryes of the Dead* (c. 1625) (*PG*, no. 39, pp. 222–5) the request to join in the singing also involves an invitation to feel moral outrage at a horrendous deed. In *A most delicate, pleasant, amorous, new Song* (c. 1638) (*PB*, no. 98, 11, pp. 249–52) the audience is asked to share in the euphoria of the lover:

Come then and sing with me,
   sobbs of sad welladay.   (*The cryes* . . . , 1, 7–1, 8, *PG*, p. 223)

Sing, O sing, the day is cleare.
   sad misfortunes are estranged,
       . . .

Come, O come and sing with me,
   at my Feasts and Banquetings
Louers all, that speeders be,
   come reioyce like petty kings:
All our songs shall still approue,
All content doth liue with loue.
     (*A most delicate* . . . , 1, 1–1, 2, *PB*, II, p. 250 and v, 14, p. 252)

The invitation to buy the broadside is an unambiguous illocutionary act and a very direct example of the advertising process used. It is usually at the end of the text, and concludes the performance by ensuring some income for the performer. Other, less obvious, selling techniques are used during the course of the text, such as personalization of the advertising process, appropriate opening lines, and answer-ballads (see above, chapter 3.2.3, and below, chapter 3.4.1 and 3.4.3). These will have prepared the audience for a request to buy, and will already have persuaded a few listeners to do so. Now, before the audience disperses, the final, supreme, effort is made to sell as many broadsides as possible:

And thus to conclude,
   an end for to make,
Colen doth grumble,
   my stomacke doth ake:
A packing penny,
   if you will bestow,
I will goe to Dinner,
   I tell you but so.[92]

The request to buy is often linked associatively with the topic of the ballad: the value of the goods on offer is based on the textual message, in order that it should seem desirable to buy copies. A ballad on the topic of 'money': *The World's Sweetheart: . . . Mistris Money* (between 1633 and 1643) closes with the logical *salto mortale*:

Because their love on it they doe settle:
Yet I would not have you to set your heart
   On worldly treasure, to make it your hony,
But to buy this ditty before you depart,
   If that you doe love sweet Mistris Money.
     (*RB*, III, pp. 81–5, v. 13.5–13.9, lines 110–14, p. 85)

The contradiction between the invective against the power of money as apparent in the text recited, and the closing request to buy, makes especially clear that the intention was to put the audience under obligation to buy. The same process can be seen in *The praise of Nothing* (between 1601 and 1640), where the singer first outlines in forthright fashion the reprehensible and vain nature of this world, and of worldly goods in particular, and then at the end demands in no uncertain terms the price of a penny for his good advice.

> And thus you now have heard the praise
>   Of Nothing, worth a penny,
> Which, as I stand to sing here now,
>   I hope will yeeld me many:
> But if that price be held to[o] deare,
> Or any dislike this counsell here,
> He may depart with a flea in's eare;
>   For I will give him Nothing.
>   (*RB*, II, pp. 339–44; v. 14, lines 105–12, p. 344)

A more sophisticated advertising technique for promoting sales is to exploit the possible identification of the audience with the thematic content or standard characters of the text. This is a procedure which is also used in modern advertising (see J. Hantsch [1972], p. 101 and *passim*).

> *Round boyes indeed.*
>   *Or*
> *The Shoomakers Holy-day,*
> *Being a very pleasant new Ditty,*
> *To fit both Country, Towne and Citie,*
> *Delightfull to peruse in every degree,*
> *Come gallant Gentlemen, hansell from you let me see.* (1637)

Laurence Price's opening announcement uses the title of Dekker's comedy *The Shoemaker's Holiday* (1600) as an advertisement. The request to buy is founded on the interest in this ballad which it is anticipated will come from all classes. At first, the request is directed only towards the better-off members of the audience, which may have been a hint that 'gentlemen' were also to be found among ballad-listeners. The final verse, however, is addressed in the first instance to those who will identify with the praise of shoemaking and indeed of every honest craft, as expressed in the ballad. Such members of the audience are also expected to have some fellow-feeling for the shoemaker's, and the balladmonger's, partiality to a drink:

> I trust none of this company,
> *round boyes, round,*
> Will with this song offended bee,
> *round boyes, indeed,*

therefore let some kind Creature heare
  giue hansell for to buy me beere,
To make my throat more shrill & cleere
  you see I haue great need.   (PG, no. 78, pp. 443–8; v. 16, p. 448)

Similarly, in another ballad, Laurence Price combines the request to buy with an appeal to the audience's sympathy for the singer's fondness for drink, thus integrating a description of his wares thematically into the ballad context. His *Good Ale for my money* (between *c.* 1628 and 1680) justifies its praise of beer-drinking by the fact that you actually get something for your money, implying also that the text is worth buying because the author and balladmonger are only asking for payment so that they can spend it on beer. This request for money is at the same time situationally reinforced, since we can assume that such drinking-songs were often performed in taverns and inns, and often served as wall decorations there (W. Chappell, *RB*, I, p. 412).

Thus to conclude my verses rude,
  would some good fellowes here
Would joyne together pence a peece,
  to buy the singer beere:
I trust none of this company
  will be herewith offended;
Therefore, call for your Jugs a peece,
  and drink to him that pen'd it.
                    (*RB*, I, pp. 411–17) v. 14, lines 127–34, p. 417)

One of the techniques of modern advertising is to target the product at a certain consumer group and imply that it is a status symbol. This ploy is found in the balladmonger's address, in which those members of the audience are appealed to who feel that they represent the positive norm in the context of the ballad they have just heard. In *Man's Felicity and Misery* (1632) there is a dialogue between two married men where one has the best and most dependable of wives, while the other is cursed with the proverbial slattern. In the last verse the presenter declares:

You wives who have heard this discourse,
Now shew who's better and who's worse;
The best will freely buy this song,
The worst will shew she hath a tongue.
The head's soone broken that is scald,
And jades will kick if they be gall'd.
                    (*RB*, II, pp. 182–8; v. 21, lines 121–6, p. 188)

A Pleasant new Ballad (1630) tells of a scold who was even capable of taking on the Devil. Using the strategically ingenious advertising technique of inviting identification, the presenter/speaker concludes thus:

Then, honest wives and maides,
    and widdowes of each sort
Might live in peace and rest,
    and Silence keep her court:
Nor would I have a scold
    one penny here bestow;
But, honest men and wives,
    buy these before you goe.
                    (RB, II, pp. 366–71, v. 19, lines 145–52, p. 371;
                                    for dating, see bibliography)

This manoeuvre inviting the audience to identify can also replace altogether the explicit request to buy. In *The Honest Age* (1632) the presenter flatters his listeners by identifying all of them with the shining examples of honest craftsmen which he has just been describing:

All this honest company which I haue nam'd,
I trust will like of it I shall not be blam'd,
For this rare new Ditty in loue I haue fram'd,
I know no plaine dealing man will be asham'd,
    To heare of this honest age,
    This is a plaine dealing age.   (PG, no. 71, pp. 406–9; v. 16, p. 409)

The selling intention as illocutionary act is concealed here behind the presentation, as a proposition, of an identification between the opinion of the presenter/speaker and the intended audience. Such veiled advertising techniques offering identification models or presenting the 'value of the product' by means of sensational announcements can be found more frequently in the street ballad than the direct request to buy. Furthermore, we can assume that additional requests of the type 'come and buy . . . ' were made, which were not integrated in the text. In addition, every instance of a balladmonger beginning his performance with a sheaf of broadsides over his arm would have constituted a common extra-linguistic sales appeal.

3.3.3 Exhortation to the audience to change their attitude and behave differently in future: warning and advice

Warnings and advice constitute a substantial proportion of the activities of the presenter/showman. He is not urging his listeners to act immediately; the aim is to achieve a long-term didactic effect. It is usually at the end of a story or in connection with an event or a topic that the speaker formulates a moral or practical instruction which is supposed to act as a warning deterrent or be taken as positive advice. The affective and cognitive effects of the street-ballad message should be initiated and fixed, through the influence of the presenter, even during the performance. This would be achieved through the visual and acoustic impression made by the presenter's speech act. Warning and advice are usually given in conjunction with other elements of the showman's speech act, for example in the address to the audience – often relevant to the specific topic – or, together with his phatic functions, announcements of subject-matter, or summaries.

The special nature of the presenter's speech act consists in the fact that the speaker is here in a position of superiority *vis-à-vis* his listeners. The illocutionary dimension of his address is based on a greater experience of life, more comprehensive information, and on his didactic evaluation of the same. His power to convince is also increased because he is referring to common social values and morals and to typical everyday behaviour. He thus makes it clear that he is acting in the interest of the audience. The thematic spectrum of his didactic influence is in fact fairly wide. Serious and even dramatic warnings against morally reprehensible and criminal acts follow deterrent examples of, for example, the ease with which the young are led astray, betrayal, greed, murder, and suicide. The extreme nature of the examples, and their graphic description, probably involved the same ambivalence of sensationalism and didactic intention as present-day reports of motor accidents in their function as pedagogical deterrents. Equally important in the street-ballad text corpus are the minor, worldly-wise warnings against trivial, everyday vices, and advice regarding personal relations, which would be relevant to the listeners' own experience. From the standpoint of advertising technique, the examples depicted can be seen as typical consumer situations devised in order to encourage the audience to purchase (see J. Hantsch [1972], p. 97 and *passim*) within the literary and fictional sphere. One is always willing to hear advice in matters of courtship, choice of partner, marriage and married life, jealousy, and judgement of people. For those who do not feel directly concerned by them, warnings against abuse of alcohol, extravagance and associating with prostitutes have at least a morally reinforcing effect. The entertainment element is always there too, though the proportion of *delectare* and *prodesse* is difficult to determine. At any rate the audience is given, directly and explicitly, a didactic evaluation of the detailed narrative of an individual's fateful life story.

The recurrence of warnings and advice in the street ballad should on no account be understood as merely 'genre-typical'. At the same time, however, the presenter's use of them, including such terms in the titles as 'warning' and 'advice', and insistent stock appeals, such as 'take heed', 'be warned', 'beware', 'take example', 'learn from this', 'bear in mind', must in my view be seen as a specifically street-ballad characteristic.[93] It was the didactic observations involved, especially the moral guidance, which served to justify the existence of an entertainment literature that was as popular and widespread among the people as it was despised by contemporary men of letters.[94] The didactic aim follows from the respective content, and from the claim to authenticity, which enabled the listener to make the connection more easily between the example depicted and the actuality of his or her own life. The difference between the claims to didactic justification of medieval literature and those of the street ballad lies in the fact that the former uses historical and traditional events and narrative, whereas the warning and advice given in street ballads are related more to topical incidents, or at least to 'real life' individual experiences. The genre-typical tendency towards topicality is effective here also from the commercial aspect, the appeals to the audience being not without an eye to prospective sales.[95]

The predominantly religious thematic content of the earlier street ballad allowed the speaker to base his observations on scriptural truths and standards rather than on the illustrative individual destinies described in seventeenth-century ballads. He was thus not obliged to allude constantly to the example of the subject of his communication,[96] nor to justify his own role as presenter. Since the early street ballads were not restricted to the individual case as illustration, there is seldom a reference in them to contemporary topical events.[97] They are concerned rather with generally applicable ideas and events within the sphere of Christian ethics, especially those dealing with the saving of souls. Their solemn, dignified linguistic style thus also owes much to that of homiletic literature, whereas later 'warnings' emphasize the didactic intention in the language of the market-crier, achieving their heavily insistent note through extreme hyperbole, colloquial style, and personal address.

> Let euery good father
> A warning here gather,
>   by this old mans punishment:
> And let euery young Lasse,
> (As in a glasse,)
>   looke on this disastrous euent;
>
> For both were to blame,
> And both suffer'd shame,
>   the old man yet liuing doth run
> In mad franticke wise
> And alwayes he cryes
>   *for casting away his owne sonne.*[98]
>
> Let all good wiues a warning take,
>   in Country and in City,
> And thinke how they shall at a stake
>   be burned without pitty.
> If they can haue such barbarous hearts,
> What man or woman will take their parts,
>   *Oh women,*

> *Murderous women,*
> *whereon are your minds?*[99]

> Great store of abuses,
>   vnto you Ile shew,
> Good counsell refuse not
>   *I tell you but so.*[100]

By contrast, religious, edifying street ballads remain within the sphere of abstract ideas such as sin and punishment, reform and promises of everlasting life, Christian charity, and the God-fearing life. The warning appeal is addressed to all Christians, acquiring a hymn-like character in the absence of any concrete realization.

> Aryse and wak, for Cristis sake,
>   Aryse, I say agayn;
> Awake, all ye that synfull be,
>   Awak, for fear of payn;
> Amend your lyff, both man and wyff,
> Whils youe have tym and sppace,
> For God hath sent his punisshment,
>   Which shortly wyll tayk place.[101]

> Take hede in tyme, whylste youthe dothe reane,
> Lest that in age thoue soore complayne;
> Thys world yt ys so unsertayne;
>   Therfor take hede.[102]

> Awak, rych men, for shame, and here
> The powars owtcry and playnte,
> Let mercy ons in youe apear,
>   So eays them of ther streante.[103]

A rich tradition of Christian exhortation in song form[104] preceded the sensational warnings of the street ballad. Attempts at concrete realization seldom occur,[105] and the practical advice on worldly matters, characteristic of the seventeenth-century street ballad, is not found in this early period of public address.

The extreme deterrent effect intended by ballads of crimes and marvels is related to the religious songs of exhortation in so far as it makes similar appeals to ethical norms whose validity is reinforced by the principle of poetic justice during the course of the narrative. Such reinforcing is 'based on real life', however, while the early street ballad resorts at best to biblical examples, preferring to deal for the most part in abstract concepts. The concrete realization of the didactic intention through reference to a topical example corresponds to the general tendency towards secularization observable in the diachronic development of the street ballad. A typical ballad of the transition period is *A new Ballad against Unthrifts* (between c. 1560 and 1582; *AB*, no. 44, pp. 226–9). It describes certain forms of extravagance and waste – regular drinking in the alehouse, expensive clothes, games of dice, work-shy loitering, and pawning one's possessions – warning of what they can lead to: loss of honour, poverty, minor thefts, robbery with murder, and finally to Newgate prison and Tyburn gallows. While later ballads illustrated this theme using the example of an individual's life, it was still customary at this period to present typical episodes and types of behaviour as examples. Although no personal deictic information was given, the examples were quite concrete, however. It is already apparent here that through the use of concrete examples it is possible to conclude with the relevant warning. The presenter's didactic intent, both as individual intellectual offering and separate speech act, is thus set apart from the subject of communication:

> Wherfore al ye that vse this trade,
>   Leaue of betimes, yf ye be wise,
> Lest that perchaunce this way ye wade
>   Ful sore against your owne deuise;
> For heer ye see the end of suche,
> As little haue and wil spend muche.   (ibid., v. 13, p. 229)

A later ballad, which mentions its didactic intent and target group in the title, takes the fateful life story of an individual as an example: *Youth's Warning-peice. In a true Relation of the woefull Death of William Rogers of Cranbroke, in Kent, an Apothecary, who, refusing all good counsell, and following lewd company, dyed miserably since Christmas last, 1635.* (1636, RB, III, pp. 1–5). In the final verses the presenter–adviser reveals himself as the narrator and sets out to establish a consensus of opinion with the audience regarding this life story:

> So you have heard his end: I wish you all
> To take a warning by his fearefull fall
> Of all leud company, and drinking too,
> Which alwayes are the harbengers of woe.
>
> Reject not councell, nor God's ordinance scorne,
> Nor yet church discipline, as men forlorne;
> Follow your callings diligently still,
> So God shall keep you in your wayes from ill.
>   (ibid., vv. 27–8, lines 105–12, p. 5)

In passages containing warnings and advice the address to the audience is, almost without exception, topic-related (see also above, pp. 54–6). The link thus established between message and addressee reinforces the illocutionary act, although this must to a large extent remain fictional in the case of criminal accounts, since the audience was not entirely made up of potential murderers and swindlers. The warning in the final verse of *The Norfolke Gentleman, his last Will and Testament* (between 1610 and

1675, *RB*, II, pp. 214–21; see v. 20, lines 153–60, p. 221) is addressed to all guardians and advises them to fulfil their obligations conscientiously and selflessly. *A most notable example of an ungracious Son, who in the pride of his heart denyed his owne Father, and how God for his offence turned his meat into loathsome toades* (between 1601 and 1640, *RB*, II, pp. 73–9; see v. 21, lines 161–8, p. 79) is addressed to 'All vertuous children . . .' And *A Warning to all Lewd Livers. By the Example of a disobedient Child, who riotously wasted and consumed his Father's and Mother's goods, and also his own, among strumpets and other lewd Livers, and after died most miserably on a Dung-hill* (between 1623 and 1661, *RB*, III, pp. 22–8) appeals to several groups:

> You disobedient children all,
> Draw neer, and listen to my fall;
> Example take, repent in time,
> Lest that your woes be like to mine.　　(ibid., v. 14, lines 53–6, p. 25)

> You fathers dear, and mothers kinde,
> Bear you this lesson in your minde:
> Trust not too much a wicked child,
> For oft times men are so beguil'd.　　(ibid., v. 15, lines 57–60, p. 26)

> Take warning, young men, by this vice,
> Learn to avoid both cards and dice;
> Lewd women's company forbear;
> They are the high-way unto care.　　(ibid., v. 30, lines 117–20, p. 28)

Whether the recurrence of urgent warnings and exhortations with their almost unvarying topoi increased their didactic effectiveness is debatable.[106] It can, however, be assumed that the practical advice which followed accounts of less sensational events and experiences presented at least a wider scope for identification purposes. L. B. Wright sees street ballads as the 'conduct-books' of the lower classes:

In addition to formal treatises on manners, there were other even cheaper sources of instruction for the citizen or apprentice who did not wish to lay out more than a penny on good conduct, for the broadside ballad did not neglect to give advice as to both the details of behavior and the general rules of life. Most of these ballads of good counsel mix admonition to godliness with practical suggestions.

(L. B. Wright [1964], p. 130)

Warnings and advice on everyday practical matters differ radically from the dramatic, urgent exhortations of the criminal ballad. In the former, the presenter's illocutionary act is not concerned with ethical norms; it takes as its yardstick a pleasant life free of conflict, whereby human egoism and malice are fully taken into account. A realistic view of life is expressed, and offered by the presenter at bargain price. Constant jealousy is proved to be detrimental to married life.[107] Excessive drinking leads to financial ruin, as is immediately clear in the presenter's introduction to his story of a young man:

> All you good fellowes who loue strong beere,
> In time be warned the same to flee
> For I can make it plaine appeare
> How tis strong beare that has vndon me.[108]

For young girls there is the danger of being more susceptible to seduction if under the influence of strong beer. This is expressed as a humorous warning in *A Ditty delightfull of mother Watkins ale / A warning wel wayed, though counted a tale* (*c.* 1590, AB, no. 76, pp. 370–5). At the same time the consumption of beer is used as a metaphor for erotic enjoyment. By means of jokes, lewd remarks, and clichés the presenter establishes a lighthearted and familiar relationship with his audience:

> Good maydes and wiues, I pardon craue,
> And lack not that which you would haue;
> To blush it is a womans grace,
> And well becometh a maidens face,
>   For women will refuse
>   The thing that they would chuse,
>   Cause men should them excuse
>   Of thinking ill;
> Cat will after kind,
> All winkers are not blind, –
> Faire maydes, you know my mind,
>   Say what you will.
> When you drinke ale beware the toast,
> For therein lay the danger most.
> If any heere offended be,
> Then blame the author, blame not me.   (ibid., v. 8, pp. 374–5)

A favourite theme of the street ballad is that of association with prostitutes. The topic is often accompanied by the relevant warnings regarding the latters' arts of seduction, their thieving, and the substantial cost involved for the victim: *A warning for all good fellowes to take heede of Punckes inticements* (*c.* 1625, PB, no. 44, I, pp. 262–8); *A Caueat or VVarning. For all sortes of Men both young and olde, to auoid the Company of lewd and wicked Woemen* (*c.* 1620, PB, no. 20, I, pp. 128–32, esp. vv. 11 and 12, pp. 131–2); *The Essex man coozened by a VVhore* (1631, PB, no. 78, II, pp. 191–5):

> You Countrey-men that are
> And trauell vnto *London*,
> And there doe sell fat ware,
> Take heede you be not vndon
>   by Cupids snare.   (ibid., v. 1, p. 192)

Detailed advice on how to distinguish between good and false friends is also given. After a sensational announcement in the title, a series of positive and negative characteristics is then contrasted: reliability versus flattery, generosity versus meanness, loyalty versus malicious gossip, sympathy versus underhandedness, etc.

> *Friendly Counsaile.*
> *Or,*
> *Here's an answer to all demanders,*
> *The which I'le declare to all by-standers,*
> *Thereby to teach them how to know*
> *A perfect Friend from a flattering Foe.*   (1633; *RB*, I, pp. 65–9)

The theme of marriage provides wide scope for devising practical, psychologically useful rules of behaviour, though it is here that the plurality of views apparent within the street ballad is especially predominant. Various points of view are found regarding the same problem, from which differing aspects emerge. Thus one ballad warns against being too hesitant and choosy when deciding to wed: *A pleasant Ditty of a mayden's vow / That faine would marry, and yet knew not how* (between 1601 and 1640, *RB*, II, pp. 197–202, esp. v. 16, lines 120–8, p. 202), while others advise against rushing into marriage:

> *A Penny-worth of Good Counsell.*
> *To Widdowes, and to Maides,*
> *This Counsell I send free;*
> *And let them looke before they leape,*
> *Or that they married be.*
>   (between 1625 and 1660; by Martin Parker; *RB*, II, pp. 294–9)

The stating of the price has a double function: it not only arouses interest in buying the broadside but also brings home the generosity of the presenter in offering his important advice so cheaply. Another ballad warns young girls by reeling off, as a deterrent, negative examples of men's bad characteristics and unpleasant behaviour: *The Married-womans Case: OR Good Counsell to Mayds, to be carefull of hastie Marriage, by the example of other Married-women* (*c.* 1630, *PB*, no. 74, II, pp. 169–73, by Martin Parker):

> You Maidens all, that are willing to wed,
>   before you are well aduised,
> Make not too much haste to the mariage bed,
>   lest the sheetes be too dearly prized: (ibid., 1,1–1,4, p. 170)

But men, too, are advised against succumbing to the yoke of marriage, in urgent, vociferous tones. The speaker makes continual use here of the adviser's role in contriving his presentation of himself as showman:

> Come, Batchelers and Married men,
>   and listen to my song,
> And I will shew you plainely, then,
>   the iniury and wrong
> That constantly I doe sustaine
>   by the vnhappy life,
> The which does put me to great paine,
>   by my vnquiet wife.[109]

Marriage remains nonetheless a socially institutionalized and therefore desirable goal which others seek to attain through the arts of persuasion and manifold psychological ploys. That is why there is:

> *Good Counsell for young Wooers:*
>   *Shewing the Way, the Meanes, and the Skill,*
>   *To wooe any Woman, be she what she will:*
>   *Then all young men that are minded to wooe,*
>   *Come, heare this new Ballad, and buy't ere you goe.*
>   (between 1620 and 1655; *RB*, I, pp. 422–7)

The speaker in this discursive ballad recommends the suitor to flatter his girl constantly, indulge her in her moods, adapt in all situations, find out about her dowry, be in her company as much as possible, go to weddings with her to encourage that idea in her head, seek eye-to-eye contact with her in the company of others, and pounce as soon as she shows willing. The presenter–adviser's claim to superior wisdom is particularly evident in the closing verse:

> Yet be thy sweet-heart either blacke, browne, or ruddy,
> These Lessons, kind Wooer, are fit for thy study:
> Be she fayre, be she foule, be she Widdow or Maid,
> In wooing, a man must doe as I have said.
>   (ibid., 12,3–12,7, lines 93–6, p. 426)

Other ballad authors warn girls against such practices and against false promises of marriage.[110] A familiar theme encountered in the street ballad is one of rich widows, desirable catches for young men on the lookout for advantageous marriages. Martin Parker gives the balladmonger a virtuoso presenter's role where rich widows are actually recommended as 'wares':

> All you Young-men who would Marry,
>   and enioy your hearts content,
> In your mindes this Counsell carry,
>   then you shall no whitt repent:
>   now is the time
>   that Men may clime
> Unto promotion by good lot,
>   this Prouerbe old

> hath oft bene told,
> Tis good to strike while the Iron's hott.
>
> Wealthy Widowes now are plenty,
>   where you come in any place,
> For one Man thers Women twenty,
>   this time lasts but for a space:
>   She will be wrought,
>   though it be for nought,
> But wealth which their first Husband got,
>   let Young-men poore
>   make hast therefore,
> Tis good to strike while the Irons hott.
>
> Doe not dote on Maydens features,
>   Widowes are the only ware,
> It is many Young-mens natures
>   to loue Maydens young and fayre,
>   tis *Cupids* wile
>   thus to beguile
> Young Louers, therefore trust him not,
>   get one with Gold,
>   though nere so old,
> Tis good to strike while the Irons hott.[111]

The semantic level of the marketplace with the presentation of widows as 'wares', references to the lasciviousness of old women and the greed of young men, specious arguments discrediting marriage between young people together with gross exaggeration make it clear that this ballad, with its urgent exhortation to do the profitable thing, is intended to be satirical. *Nobody his Counsaile to chuse a Wife: Or, The difference betweene Widdowes and Maydes* (c. 1626, *PG*, no. 46, pp. 263–9) also compares the two groups, recommending marriage for the first. The attitude is similarly that of the superior adviser, but the satirical intention is less clearly and effectively expressed. Another 'advice ballad' explicitly warns 'Widdowes' against the exploitative practices of young men:

> Old women take good heede,
>   and trust your selues with no man:
> For as you doe heare,
> She hath paid full deare.[112]

Along with thematically fixed 'advice ballads', there are those in which a discursive speaker strings together various pieces of advice.[113] He can also function as adviser while playing a specific dramatic role. Thus a schoolmaster hands out warnings by virtue of his office,[114] and in *The merry Old Woman; ... Her Counsell is good* (1633, *RB*, II, pp. 163–9) the speaker's competence is enhanced by the experience which age bestows.

The advice given is characterised by a realistic and in part ironical world view whose basic idea is that one must be able to adapt to circumstances. The extent to which the 'advice ballad' was accepted as a set type within street-ballad literature is shown not only by the frequency of such texts but also by the fact that it was possible to parody the genre with 'mock advice'. In *Doctor Dogood's Directions. To cure many diseases in body and minde, lately written and set forth for the good of infected persons* (between 1633 and 1652, RB, I, pp. 234–8) the knife is prescribed for uncomfortably long hair, work for overweight layabouts, and abstinence from drink for those with red noses. Garrulousness is cured by pruning the mouth, pains in the limbs through reluctance to work are cured with elderberry oil, fainting fits in lovesick girls by marriage, etc. The respective therapy prescribed is either obvious, or related to human weaknesses which are described as illnesses.

It is questionable whether the presenter's act of warning and giving advice in its various thematic guises, although impressive as a speech act, was in actual fact effective. As far as practical performance is concerned, it makes possible a close appellate and phatic contact with the audience which at the same time helps to convey the respective message on which the spoken exhortation is based. Warning and advice frequently appear as the formulaic close of a narrative or of a ballad with dramatic role-play. Sometimes, but less often, they appear as the motivating lead-in to a ballad. They can also be elevated to the level of a constant and general principle in a discursive ballad. It is above all in the presentation of extreme deterrent examples of wrong behaviour that the didactic effect has to be questioned. Instead of being given opportunities to identify, the listener/reader is placed in the role of self-righteous judge, and the effectiveness of deterrent appeals is in any case uncertain.[115] Where a gradual slide into criminal activity or difficult circumstances is depicted it is more likely that the ballad would carry conviction. Down-to-earth everyday advice relating to the limited experience of the average person would have met with a general appreciation comprising amusement, glee at the downfall of others, and possibly even new insights. The entertainment value of warning and advice, contained in both the presenter's communication of his subject and in the thematic content itself, should not be underestimated in comparison with the didactic effect.

3.3.4 Use of the colloquial element as a form of audience approach

Even with his importunate manner, in the speech act of warning and advice the balladmonger as presenter is able to impute to himself superior wisdom. Use of colloquial speech style and idiom as a means of establishing a friendly relationship with the audience works against this, however. Familiarity with the style register, especially with certain turns of phrase, indirectly helps to boost the recipient's ego and steer his attention positively in the direction of the presenter. Colloquial language can be used explicitly as an appeal in order to create an understanding with the audience, as for instance in the presenter's approach: 'take this from me',[116] reinforcing 'Ile tell you ...' (ibid., 1,8, line 8, p. 423). It is also made use of in affirmations of the truth with hidden *captatio benevolentiae*: 'to tell you the troth',[117] or 'speaking my mind' (ibid., 15, 12, p. 159). But even where the colloquial element is not obviously an address to the audience, it has an implicit appeal function which determines the relationship between speaker and listener on the presenter level of communication. The common area of linguistic experience was especially emphasized by the use of proverbs, which implicitly reinforced, from the point of view of the speaker, the good understanding with his listeners. 'Strike while the iron is hot' is a popular formula which described tactically correct behaviour in courtship and proposals of marriage in 'advice ballads'.[118] John Tomson, a dramatic figure who is complaining about his wife's constant jealousy, makes his position clear to all through his allusion to the well-known saying, 'to wear yellow stockings',[119] in the refrain:

> Give me my yellow hose againe,
>   give me my yellow hose;
> For now my wife she watcheth me,
>   see, yonder! where she goes.

Similarly, a disappointed lover makes his theme clear right at the beginning of the ballad: 'But now I see all is not gold, / that makes a glistring show'.[120] The speaker in a socially critical ballad ensures the confidence of his listeners from the start with his idiomatic refrain: 'I smell a Rat',[121] which assigns to him the critical perspective. Another speaker, who appears as a market-crier and is thereby particularly marked out as a presenter, illustrates his playful or satirical questions to the audience with phrases reminiscent of old sayings. When a person has been engaged in a long lawsuit, his situation is referred to with the words: ' ... to regaine the saddle / is glad to lose the horse'.[122] And one becomes wise after the event: 'But now the steed is stolne be sure / to shut the stable doore'.[123]

Since proverbs usually have the function of referring through metaphor to some aspect of general human experience, they are particularly suitable for taboo subjects. Because the proverb was in such common usage, a tacit understanding, with a nudge and a wink, would be established between speaker and listener. If it is a question of the tendency of young girls to be easily seduced, the proverb 'cat will after kind' (see F. P. Wilson [1970], p. 107) can be used to denote frequency of copulation and thus also erotic responsiveness.[124] In the context of this ballad the dangers of an erotic relationship to a girl's reputation and health are humorously played down. By referring with the words 'It is no iesting with edge tooles' (ibid., 6,16, p. 374) to the saying 'Children and fools must not play with edged tools' (see F. P. Wilson [1970], p. 120) the speaker communicates to the audience not only the dangerous consequences in figurative language, but implies also that the sensible use of dangerous instruments is perfectly possible. For tactical reasons relating to his listeners, the presenter changes the wording of a saying in order to reprove those who do not agree with the ballad's content and price, in a *captatio benevolentiae ex negativo*:

> But if that price be held to[o] deare,
> Or any dislike this counsell here,
> He may depart with a flea in's eare;[125]

Colloquial speech and idiom as typically popular means of emphasis reinforce the intended effect of the presenter in combining expressions of self and appeals to the listener. Whereas John Donne, for example, used colloquial elements stylistically to bring about a distancing shock effect within an otherwise highly sophisticated linguistic context, the colloquialism of the street ballad was intended to create an atmosphere of confidence and familiarity. The colloquial element, embedded as it was in a language that was in any case simple or at most given to sentimental exaggeration, helped in large measure to effect ease of reception.[126]

3.3.5 The refrain: an appeal for creating a sense of community

The implicit function of appeal to the listener, as a tactical approach to the partner, which is performed by the colloquial element on the level of style, is fulfilled by the refrain on the level of song. It is true that explicit requests to join in the singing are relatively seldom found in the street ballad, but implicit invitations to do so are frequent.[127] They are backed up by the audience's familiarity with the ballad melodies, together with the regular settings of different ballads to the same tunes. This is in principle a formal function of the appeal to the listener which is directed towards the audience's readiness to participate in the performance by singing one or more lines. The particular form of the refrain tended to reinforce this effect. As far as content is concerned, the refrain summarizes and explains the text,[128] either commenting or encouraging an emotional response. The colloquial nature of the refrain and its easily assimilable rhythm practically demand spoken or sung repetition, and the semantic vagueness of the idiomatic content can with its emotional undertones create an atmosphere of communal feeling.

The refrain in the discursive ballad *Knauery in all Trades* (1632) both comments and, through the speaker's colloquial function of expression, has the effect of heightening emotion:

> All honesty is decay'd,
>> here's an age would make a man mad.
>>>> (PG, no. 72, pp. 410–14; by Martin Parker)

The first-person narrator of a murder comments from verse to verse in an exaggeratedly sentimental way:

> oh murther,
>> most inhumane
> To spill my Husbands blood.[129]

The public punishment of a scold[130] as the central theme of a report is hammered home in the refrain which also encourages passers-by to stop and listen:

> The cucking of a Scold,
>> The cucking of a Scold,
> Which if you will but stay to heare
>> The cucking of a Scold.

The evocative description of the punishment for the intolerable behaviour of a woman can certainly be understood as an identification opportunity for those men in the audience who perhaps have wives at home who are constantly scolding them.

In *The cunning Northerne Begger* (between 1626 and 1681),[131] a ballad with dramatic role-play, the refrain has the function of both commenting and clarifying. At the end of every verse it reminds the listener of the basic situation of the beggar, finally revealing his fraudulent practices, his play-acting as the impoverished father, robbed sailor etc., with the allusion to the way he spends his ill-gotten gains:

> For still will I cry 'Good your worship, good sir,
> Bestow one poore denier, sir,
>> Which, when I've got,
>> At the Pipe and Pot
> I soone will it casheere, sir.

The appeal factor creating a sense of community is seen here on the level of communicating to the audience together with a corresponding understanding on the part of the listeners. In *A Fooles Bolt is soone shot* (1629)[132] members of the audience are supposed to adopt a satirical attitude themselves when they join in the refrain 'for now I take a shot' which is especially conceived with audience reaction in mind. The allusion to a well-known saying supports this reaction. The refrai.1-like reinforcement, 'Tis good to strike while the Iron's hott', in *A Prouerbe old* . . . (between 1625 and 1650)[133] ensures a consensus with the audience based on elements of both style and song. Attempts to win over the audience through the use of colloquial idiom, implicit invitations to join in the singing, and explicit claims on listeners' agreement are all present in the refrain: 'Which nobody can deny'.[134] Having similar functional aspects, the refrain 'that shall be tryde', with its incitement to common action, goes even further. Its somewhat vague content is specified through the context. The ballad *A Mad Crue: Or, That shall be tryde.* (*c.* 1620, *PB*, no. 31, I, pp. 190–4) tells of a pleasurable, besotted stroll through the streets of London, with its amusements, temptations, dangers and some typical inhabitants:

> Walking of late through London streets,
> A crue of good-followes together meets,
> Not one of them sober, if not belyde,
>   Well, quoth the *Maultman*, that shall be tryde.
>
> From thence I traueld, to see a new Play,
> Whereas an old Widdow in gallant array,
> Sate pleasantly smirking, like a yong Bride,
>   Well, quoth the *Fiddler*, that shall be tryde.
>
> Then to a Tobacco house, smoking hote
> Went I, and call'd for my Pipe and my Pot,
> The Weed was strong, but hardly well dryde,
>   Well, quoth the *Horse courser*, that shal be tryde.
>
> (ibid., vv. 1–3, p. 191)

The refrain, 'Well, quoth the . . . now that shall be tryde', a character's utterance integrated into the action and adapted to the particular situation, encapsulates the bold and enterprising basic mood of the ballad in a turn of phrase which is both familiar to the audience and capable of being used in a variety of ways according to circumstance. The audience is furthermore involved in that mood, precisely through the refrain. The refrain also implies the risky nature of the various enterprises, drawing the listeners' attention to the possible dangers:

> Moore Fields being pleasant, the same I would see,
> Where Maids of our City, stil whiting cloathes be,
> For forty weekes after, my loue I there tyde.
>   Well, quoth the *Midwife*, now that shall be tryde. (ibid., v. 8, p. 192)

The intention of the street-ballad refrain to effect a sense of community, a way of relating to the audience which is not commonly found until the beginning of the seventeenth century, differs from the intention behind the forms of collective address as seen in the early street ballad. The aim of the refrain in the street ballad was to unite the audience through communal singing, thereby backing up the message. By contrast, forms of audience address such as 'good Christians' and 'good men' assume common audience attitudes and beliefs which are already ideologically fixed. It is clear here, too, how much more the seventeenth-century street ballad was dependent on its own resources, relying on explicit communicative procedures to back up the respective message.

The function in the street ballad of appeals to the listener on the communication level of the presenter is particularly rich and varied in form, and shows the extent to which the street ballad sets out to relate to the audience. The appeal dimension of the street ballad is thereby so integrated into the text as a whole that it correlates with other components of the speech situation. Forms of address directed at target groups reflect back on the respective subject of communication. Requests to come up, listen, join in the singing, and buy the broadside, that is, to take immediate action, also relate to the reception area where the street-ballad speech act takes place, without the details of the performance being fixed in the text. Warning and advice develop out of the chosen topic, marking out the speaker as an educator. Through his use of the colloquial element he is also felt by his listeners to be equal with themselves. Finally, the refrain both summarizes the textual content and activates the audience's attention and readiness to participate.

It is possible, on considering the variety and widespread occurrence of textual constituents in the street-ballad corpus which have the function of appeals to the listener, and bearing in mind the wide distribution of broadsides and the frequency of performance,[135] to reconstruct something of the ballad audience's receptive impression. The audience was subject to intensive, almost importunate approaches by the balladmonger. Direct and specific forms of address singled out certain groups of the public, establishing, so to speak, personal contact with them. Requests to the audience relating to the course of the performance, as also to the refrain, were intended to persuade the audience to act themselves. Audience action such as listening, heeding a warning, participating in the refrain and generally enjoying the performance would in each case create a common area of activity in a way which was uncharacteristic of most other forms of literature. The sense of community would also be reinforced by the presenter's use of the colloquial element in his approach. Finally, moral and didactic appeals would place, despite their entertainment value, certain demands on the audience. Even though it remains open how far individual members of the audience responded to the recurrent and multifarious appeals of the street ballad, the dominant communicative intention is unmistakable. Since these procedures persisted with particular variety of form in the first half of the seventeenth century and were also well in evidence during the rest of the century, it is not unreasonable to suppose that they were highly successful.

3.4 The presenter's reference to the outside world

Starting out once more from the analogy between the street-ballad presenter/showman as a procedure of textual interpretation and the contemporary juggler, one can see a further common functional element, namely that both are concerned with performing or presenting. With the fairground or street-trade showman it is tricks, objects, and spoken or sung items which are on offer. The presenter's 'object' in the street ballad is the subject of communication. What for the juggler is a display and performance of something concrete, has in the case of the street ballad to be converted into language, that is, pre-programmed in the text. The subject of communication is introduced through announcement in the title and opening verses, and it is conveyed with accompanying comments and allusions. Other ballads from his repertoire can become display objects if they are alluded to by the balladmonger. The manipulation of a subject of entertainment by an entertainer presenting it to an audience, whatever form it takes, will have the effect of easing reception – through reference to self, appeals to the listener, and reference to the outside world, the latter in particular. With the juggler as with the street-ballad presenter, the display of 'wares' is very much connected with purposes of advertising.

3.4.1 The street-ballad 'trailer': metatextual advance information and advertising technique

One way the ballad content is 'displayed' is in the detailed title and opening verses, where the content is briefly summarized; at least the topic is presented or partial information given which is likely to whet the public's curiosity. The actual textual message is announced and its character defined, so that it is possible to speak of metatextual advance information. This information is given by the presenter. The illocutionary dimension of his speech act can in its performative aspect be divided into giving information, stating, asserting (the truth of what he is saying), promising (with regard to the rest of the text), evaluating and exaggerating. These illocutionary acts are based on the brief advance information given, although they are rarely explicit. It is the presenter's functions of reference to self and appeals to the listener which, as explicit illocutionary acts within the framework of the ballad opening, reinforce his implicit, specifically introductory speech acts.

The intention of giving advance information is at the same time combined with that of stimulating the public's interest, thereby also advertising both the performance and the broadsides on sale. These street-ballad procedures and intentions are present in what is termed in modern film, television and radio the 'trailer': a brief summary of and information about a programme, including excerpts – previews shown for advertising purposes. Participants are named, introductory music played, and the content of the programme possibly anticipated in a short publicity spot immediately prior to the showing. It therefore seems appropriate to apply the term 'trailer' to the title and opening verse(s) of the street ballad, since these are intended to give advance information in a similar way. What the street-ballad trailer and the modern trailer have in common – with all their historical difference in detail – is their function, their public nature due to their wide distribution, the need to attract a fluctuating audience, and finally the way they are structured. If the street-ballad trailer is compared with the announcement of the theme in the verse romance, which was similarly dependent on performance,[136] it can be seen that the latter confines itself to the naming of the main figures, sometimes expanding into a characterization, whereas the former usually gives quite precise circumstances and important details of the action or states the central idea of the ballad. Not infrequently the intention of the text as a whole is formulated at the same time. The street-ballad trailer is more comprehensive and more precise than the rhetorical topos of the announcement of a theme, as it has to satisfy the special demands of the street-ballad speech situation.

However showy, exaggerated and recurrent to the point of cliché the street-ballad trailer may appear at first sight, it is certainly differentiated in intention and often well suited to the demands of the context. The ballad-monger gives details of content, evokes the prevailing mood of the ballad, indicates the street-ballad sub-genre to be expected, and casts a bait for the recipient or perhaps consciously misleads him. His role as presenter is already evident in the trailer; sometimes the latter is confined to very brief indications.

The story of Hero and Leander is introduced in the first verse of a ballad on the subject and made out to be exactly what it is: a paradigm of true love between two ideal figures, without revealing the outcome of the story. The intention to evoke compensatory pleasure in such ideals is likewise intimated:

> Two famous Louers once there was,
>   whom Fame hath quite forgott.
> Who loued long most constantly,
>   without all enuious blott;
> Shee was most faire, and hee as true:
>   which caused that which did ensue; fa la,
> Whose storie I doe meane to write,
>   and tytle it, True Loues delight, fa la.[137]

The announcement of a report of the activities of three witches sounds quite different. Here it is not only a description of their wicked deeds that is promised, but an atmosphere of horror is also evoked and the presenter's moral outrage conveyed at the same time:

> Of damned deeds, and deadly dole,
>   I make my mournfull song,
> By Witches done in *Lincolne-shire*,
>   where they haue liued long:
> And practisd many a wicked deed,
>   within that Country there,
> Which fills my brest and bosome full,
>   of sobs, and trembling feare.[138]

Turners dish of Lentten stuffe, or a Galymaufery (1612, PG, no. 5, pp. 30–8) announces in the trailer pleasurable entertainment, giving as the main subject of the text: street-cries in London:

> My Maisters all attend you,
>   if mirth you loue to heare:
> And I will tell you what they cry,
>   in London all the yeare.   (ibid., I, 1–4, p. 31)

The fateful life story of a criminal places value on the didactic content of the narrative, with the promise of impressive exemplification to follow:

> That all young men from him may learne
>   to liue in better awe,
> Foule vice from vertue to discerne,
>   according to the law:
> A wicked life this caitiffe led,
>   reiecting vertues lore,
> The grace of God from him was fled,
>   all good he did abhorre.[139]

A most notable example of an ungracious Son, who in the pride of his heart denyed his owne Father, and how God for his offence turned his meat into loathsome toades (between 1601 and 1640, RB, II, pp. 73–9):

> In searching famous chronicles,
>   it was my chance to reade,
> A worthy story, strange and true,
>   whereto I tooke good heed –
> Betwixt a farmer and his son
>   this rare example stands,
> Which well may move the hardest hearts,
>   to weepe and wring their hands.   (ibid., v. 1, p. 74)

The title follows the same lines as, say, a television trailer, in introducing the two main figures, mentioning the conflict and a climactic scene, and indicating an interpretation. The first verse amplifies the title by giving sources, directing reception in advance with claims to authenticity and appeals to the emotions, and mentioning the main figures again.

The trailer in the title announcement differs from that in an introductory verse through the graphic layout of the former in larger characters which stand out clearly from the rest of the text: the title also tends to summarize more briefly. Both these characteristics are shared with the modern newspaper headline and lead. Thus the title was clearly visible, often to be seen on placards or displayed separately from the rest of the text, and probably recited or called out. Repetition in the first verse of elements in the title took account of the fact that newly arrived listeners had to be brought up to date. Similarly, for domestic consumption and private recital the title would also have the function of giving advance information and stimulating interest:[140]

A most excellent new Ballad of an Olde man and his Wife, in their olde age and misery, which sought to their owne Children for succour, by whom they were disdained, and scornfully sent away succourless; and how the vengeance of God was justly shewed upon them for the same
(end of sixteenth century and seventeenth century; *RB*, II, pp. 347–52; p. 348)

Ballads which recount sensational, horrific, or marvellous events have particularly long and involved titles. The advance information given is in fact sometimes so detailed that it reduces the trailer's function of stimulating interest, although it gains in apparent authenticity. The intention here is possibly to direct audience expectation not only towards the material but also towards the method of communication, namely a realism of detail employed as proof of factuality:

A Warning-peice for Ingroosers of Corne: BEING *A true Relation how the* Divell *met with one Goodman* Inglebred *of* Bowton, *within six miles of* Holgay *in* Norfolk; *as he was comming from* Linn Market, *and Bargain'd for a great quantity of Barly for eight shillings a Bushell and gave earnest; and when he came to fetch it, brought Carts and Horses (to their thinking) and while 'twas measuring the Divell vanished, and tore the Barne in pieces, and scattered all the Corne with such Windes and Tempest, which hath done such great harme both by Sea and Land, the like was never heard of before; the Farmer now lyeing destracted.*
(1643; *POA*, no. 6, pp. 31–5, p. 32)

It is also evident here that the trailer can be varied according to the street-ballad sub-genre, indicating a genre-specific procedure which would signify to the contemporary ballad-listener a directing of reception. In *The praise of Nothing* (between 1601 and 1640, *RB*, II, pp. 339–44), the title of the first verse announces the parodistic inversion of a song of praise, the pessimistic and satirical attitude of the speaker, and the use of anticlimax.[141]

The first-person narrative requires as trailer the main figure's introduction of himself. This is often an exposition of the action in the form of
a succinct retrospective résumé together with an anticipatory view of the
years yet to be described, interpreted by the figure himself, which is
guaranteed to arouse suspense in the audience. Thus the life story of the
first-person narrator becomes the subject of communication and object of
display, and the narrator becomes the presenter. At the same time the
formal principle of the first-person narrative becomes clear: an
interpretive retrospective survey according to a (fictional) autobiographical pattern:

> From *Cornwal* mount to London faire,
>   to trie all fashions did I repaire,
> Soone came I to a Cornish Chuffe,
> Left by my father rich enough,
> Yet riches could not me content,
>   Vntill at London all was spent.
>   *The causes why I am so poore,*
>   *Are Dice, Strong-waters, and a whore.*[142]

> When I was a Batchelour
>   I liv'd a merry life;
> But now I am a married man,
>   and troubled with a wife,
> I cannot doe as I have done,
>   because I live in feare;
> If I goe but to Islington,
>   my wife is watching there.[143]

> My Mother to Heauen is gone,
>   ten Pounds she gaue mee;
> Now neuer a Penny's left,
>   as God shall haue mee:
> Yet still my heart is free,
> I liue at liberty,
> And keepe good company,
>   taking Tobacco.[144]

The trailer of the ballad with dramatic role-play, which is not necessarily assigned to the main figure's introduction of himself, emphasizes the
situational facts, in accordance with the structure of this genre of street
ballad:

> *The Wooing Maid;*
>   *Or,*
> *A faire maid neglected,*
> *Forlorne and rejected,*
> *That would be respected:*
> *Which to have effected,*

This generall summon
She sendeth in common;
Come tinker, come broomman:
She will refuse no man.   (*RB*, III, pp. 52–6, p. 52)

A Batchelour I haue beene long,
    and had no minde to marry,
But now I finde it did me wrong
    that I so long did tarry,
Therefore I will a wooing ride,
    there's many married younger,
Where shall I goe to seeke a Bride?
Ile lye alone no longer.[145]

The girl in the role-play ballad *The Countrey Lasse* (1620 or 1621, *RB*,
I, pp. 165–70) formulates in the opening lines the evaluation underlying
her presentation of herself as a representative of country life:

Although I am a Countrey Lasse,
    a lofty mind I beare a;
I thinke my selfe as good as those
    that gay apparrell weare a: (ibid., 1,1–4, p. 165)

Drinking songs are easily recognizable as such by their toasts,
expressions of welcome, and references to the merry atmosphere of the alehouse (see below, pp. 177–9).

In discursive ballads the advance information is often confined to the
title, since a theme can be more easily encapsulated than a narrative in one
or two abstract terms:

A Ballad against Slander and Detraction (between 1560 and 1582, *AB*, no. 3,
pp. 12–18)

The Poore Man Payes for All (1630, *RB*, II, pp. 334–8; *CM*, no. 37, pp. 102–5)

A godly ballad declaring by the Scriptures the plagues that haue insued whordome
(1566, *AB*, no. 26, pp. 149–53)

*Nobody his Counsaile to chuse a Wife: Or, The difference betweene Widdowes
and Maydes* (c. 1626, *PG*, no. 46, pp. 263–9)

The stimulatory function of the trailer is increased when partial information only is given which at the same time arouses suspense in the
recipient as to details of the topic or the course or outcome of the action.
In *A pleasant history of a Gentleman* (1633, *RB*, II, pp. 262–7) the happy
ending of the story is indeed revealed, but the audience is thrown a bait by
the suggestion that the task of identifying the true heir could only be
accomplished with great difficulty in a miraculous way; the solution, of
course, is not disclosed:

A pleasant history of a Gentleman in Thracia, which had foure Sonnes, and three of them none of his own; shewing how miraculously the true heire came to enjoy his inheritance.

Come, buy this new Ballad, before you doe goe: / If you raile at the Author, I know what I know (1620, RB, I, pp. 115–21) is an announcement of the speaker's advance information *vis-à-vis* the audience which is bound to excite curiosity. At the same time there is an indication of the provocative content of what follows, by means of an anticipation of possible audience reactions together with the discretion formula (for further analysis of this ballad, see below, p. 203. A similar procedure is evident in *I smell a Rat* (c. 1630, PB, no. 69, II, pp. 139–44; see below, pp. 204–5).

Setting a bait in the trailer can be taken to the lengths of actually misleading the audience, for instance in the following where a catalogue of ugly features is heralded as:

A peerelesse Paragon;

Or,

Few so chast, so beautious or so faire,
For with my love I think none can compare.   (1633, RB, II, pp. 299–304)

Martin Parker's nonsense song, *A Bill of Fare: For a Saturday night's Supper, A Sunday morning Breakfast, and A Munday Dinner, Described in a pleasant new merry Ditie* (1637, RB, I, pp. 70–4, see below, pp. 210–11) does not reveal in the opening verse that the repasts will consist of fantasy food. Only the reference to the unbelievable nature of the following 'jest' indicates this:

> I'le tell you a Iest which you'l hardly beleeue –
> No matter for that, you shall hear't, right or wrong –
> A hungry appetite may perhaps grieue
> To hear such a Banquet set forth in a Song:
> He rather would haue it then heare on't, hee'l say,
> But I cannot promise him such a faire sight;
> All that I can doe, is with words to display
> What we had to Supper on Saturday night.   (ibid., v. 1, lines 1–8, p. 70)

Other titles and introductory lines confine themselves to very brief indications:

> Stay a while with pacience, my freends, I you pray,
> Of the orders of fooles somewhat I wyll say:[146]

> *A merry new Song how a Bruer meant to make a Cooper*
> *cuckold, and how deere the Bruer paid for the bargaine.*
>   (c. end of the sixteenth century, AB, no. 17, pp. 88–93)

The trailer as a detailed, differentiated and multifunctional modification of the rhetorical topos of theme announcement is a recurrent feature of the street ballad. In its function of presenter's reference to the outside world it relates to the message of the ballad, not only by giving information regarding content but often also by indicating the procedure of the particular street-ballad sub-genre. In addition, it signals the lighthearted or serious tenor of the message and manipulates the recipient's expectations. The trailer is especially suited to announcements relating to performance, and to arousing audience interest. Its literary-aesthetic and journalistic function is thus closely bound up with an implicit concern to attract an audience to hear the message.

It eases the reception of what follows for both listener and reader, first exciting his curiosity about it and persuading him to stop, listen, or even buy the broadside. The more separate the claims to satisfy customers are from the actual theme of the ballad and the more clearly the intention is that of amusing and instructing, the closer the trailer is to explicit advertising. The request for attention which often accompanies the trailer also contains both the street-ballad reference to the subject of communication and the implication that something important is on offer which is worth listening to and buying.

In the text itself, statements about the content are closely related to sales promotion. The tendency to conventionalize in the title and trailer is similarly ambivalent: certain formulations and types of trailer would give the ballad-listener an almost definitive indication of particular street-ballad sub-genres. Genre terms such as 'Medley', 'Song', 'Ditty', 'Story', 'Relation', 'Warning', 'Advice', 'Lament', and 'Strange News', although by no means reliable, do have the character of poetological headlines and thereby also to a certain extent the signalling value of a literary brand article which only has to be mentioned for the recipient and buying customer to react as of habit (see I. Hantsch [1972], p. 93). The advertising is more obvious where the conventionalizing is combined with superlative announcements and certain epithets used which are well known for their consumer effectiveness – a procedure also used in modern advertising:

A most excellent new Ballad (end of sixteenth century and seventeenth century; *RB*, II, p. 348)

An Excellent Medley (between 1601 and 1640; *BBLB*, p. 118)

A famous dittie of . . . (1584; *AB*, no. 52, p. 270)

A Ditty delightfull (*c.* 1590; *AB*, no. 76, p. 370)

Here begins a pleasant song of . . . (approx. 1630?; *PB*, II, no. 72, p. 158)

A most delicate, pleasant, amorous new Song (1638; *PB*, II, no. 89, p. 250)

A most wonderful and sad judgement (1660; *POA*, no. 11, p. 63)

A most notable example of an ungracious Son (between 1601 and 1640; *RB*, II, p. 74)

A peerelesse Paragon (1633; *RB*, II, p. 300)

A Warning for all Murderers. A most rare, strange, and wonderfull accident (1638; *RB*, III, p. 137)

A Lamentable List, of certaine Hidious, Frightfull, and Prodigious Signes (1638; *POA*, no. 4, p. 22)

Here is a true and perfect Relation (1661; *POA*, no. 15, p. 87)

The true description of . . . (1566; *AB*, no. 65, p. 321)

A prettie newe Ballad (1591/2; *AB*, no. 77, p. 377)

Strange Newes from . . . (*c.* 1648; *POA*, no. 7, p. 36)

The implicit advertising appeal in the title involved the use of unspecific emotive words such as 'most . . . ', 'excellent', 'famous': general references to the textual content, its underlying mood and emotional, didactic and suspense effects, and also to its authenticity and novelty value. 'Merry', 'true' and 'new' are particularly popular epithets.[147] Adaptation to audience expectation is obvious here: as far as factuality and topicality are concerned, its fulfilment usually remains confined to the promise initially intended to attract an audience. That the eye-catching titles of short printed works of entertainment were there to draw the public was already recognized in 1628 by John Earle in his character sketch of a 'Pot-Poet':

His works would scarce sell for three half-pence, though they are given oft for three shillings, but for the pretty title that allures the country Gentleman.

(see appendix B 61)

The street-ballad trailer follows so precisely the pattern of the traditional proem of ancient classical literature that we can be almost certain that it was orientated towards this model. Practically all the elements of the exordial topos (see E. R. Curtius [1965], pp. 95–9) are used in the street ballad: information regarding theme, justification of intention and choice of material, comment on a particular predecessor, claims to authenticity, and invocation of the muses. The modifications which are evident are due on the one hand to the demands of the context and on the other very often to the new-found need to attract an audience. Changes of such a kind in a topos are indications of the type of effect non-literary factors can have on a text.

We have already touched on the advertising aspect involved in announcing the theme of a ballad. In comparison with the preliminary announcements of the classical proem, the information regarding content given in the street ballad is often more precise, deals more with the basic points of the 'story', states a problem, and gives the subject of the text certain emphases – moralistic, sensational, socially critical – thereby narrowing down the particular audience expectation. The proem, on the other hand, counts on the broad horizon of an educated public so that only hints are necessary. This is seen in the opening of Spenser's *Faerie Queene*, for instance, which refers to the literary world of knightly deeds, pastoral poetry and classical epic. The street ballad, similarly, counts on a certain type of audience, its needs, and its familiarity with this genre. But it is precisely here that the trailer has to present more exactly what is on offer in order to hold a particular audience for a particular performance.

For the 'justification of theme' and for choice of material, the decisive grounds and motivational factors in the street ballad are literary, didactic, socially critical, informative, and to do with advertising. The appeal to traditional authorities is missing, however, since the ballad author would neither feel dependent on them nor count on a corresponding audience expectation. In the claim to novelty and topicality there is an implicit comment on what has gone before, which corresponds to the audience's need for entertainment and information and also to the pressures of competition within the ballad business. Claims to authenticity are also influenced by this; it is a question in the first instance of an apparent factuality, while there is no claim to an ideal system of values for explicit proof of authenticity in the street ballad. The invocation of the muses has no relevance for audience attraction and is only occasionally used, partly in jest and partly in earnest.[148] The author's introduction of himself, as envisaged by the proem pattern, is transformed into the presenter's function of reference to self, as has already been described. All the elements of the exordial topos used in the street ballad differ from those of the classical proem in their more marked tendency towards appeals to the listener.

One thing that is definitely missing in comparison with the exordial topos of the proem model is the dedication to the patron. In its stead appear requests to buy and other, less explicit, advertising techniques. The poetological demands of the structural elements of the proem, fixed in a topos after long use, were penetrated and transformed by one factor: the pressure of the new need to sell. It is in such a drastic change that the original effect of the non-literary factor can be measured most easily. The changes which the proem model underwent in the street-ballad trailer show particularly clearly that the street ballad, in contrast to the book of the time, and even more in comparison with urban theatre, sought to reach a paying public directly. Alongside the 'respectable' sphere of literary activity which was dependent on patronage, there developed on the popular level, as was also the case with strolling players for instance,[149] a system of direct financial reward which quickly established itself. The patron, representing a prospective audience, usually occupied a high social position and extended his patronage 'downwards' to the author. The street-ballad author, on the other hand, was on the same social level as his audience and could therefore ask for financial patronage more directly. In addition he was in closer contact with his audience, a fact which had an effect on textual structure.

The street-ballad trailer as part of the presenter's speech act whose aim was to give advance information, arouse interest, and advertise the broadside, illustrates particularly clearly the situational presuppositions of ballad performance which were mentioned earlier (see above, pp. 34–5). Its particular features were very much conditioned by the socioeconomic status of the author and balladmonger, the social class of the audience, and the special circumstances of communication and sale. Within the limitations of the street ballad, there emerged an unquestionably artistic form of street-ballad exordial topos, capable of modification according to the demands of the context. Through the procedure of the trailer, 'conveying situations using the most general of statements at the beginning, moving on to more concrete statements later', textual understanding is increased in a way that is also recommended today, in a text dealing with advertising (see P. T. Teigeler [1968], pp. 41–2). The needs of the audience for street-ballad entertainment, information, and instruction are taken into account from the start, and author and balladmonger make every attempt to satisfy them.

3.4.2 The presenter's use of linguistic markers for the display of his subject

The presenter's display of his subject of communication in the trailer, which is accompanied by the offering of the broadsides for sale, is not infrequently continued in the rest of the text by means of linguistic markers, which can be converted during the performance into corresponding non-linguistic gestures. Included in these are indications of the beginning and end of the ballad, explicit references to an essential point or notable detail of the message, and playing on words.

The clear announcement as such of the beginning and end of a text is a very common procedure in functional texts as in literary works.[150] For the street ballad it has the performance-specific function of directing reception and of implicitly giving instructions to the audience. The indication that the recital is about to begin is meant to persuade the audience to be silent, and the announcement, usually at the beginning of the last verse, that the ballad is coming to a close, dismisses the audience while at the same time giving them an opportunity to come up to the balladmonger and buy a broadside. The beginning and end of a ballad text are implicitly signalled by a series of conventionalized procedures which include, at the start, reference to the presenter's communicatory function, requests to come up, listen, and buy, and the trailer, and end with warning or advice. There are in addition explicit markers such as:

Here begins a pleasant song of a Mayden faire[151]

My merry medley here I end,[152]

Thus to conclude and end my song,[153]

And thus I doe conclude,[154]

Introductory and concluding formulas of this kind which lack any connection with the text appear somewhat clumsy. Less obvious, and semantically more integrated markers such as trailer, summary and some forms of audience address usually fulfil the function of marking textual beginning and end more adequately, and are more frequently used. There were more possibilities available for the opening of the ballad than for the ending, especially as the (usually very comprehensive) title was obligatory. This could be one reason why the explicit marking of the begining appears with less frequency than the corresponding conclusion formula. Obviously the demarcation of the text is clearly shown in the graphic layout, where the ballad appears as broadside and commodity. The title is printed in larger characters, and the name of the tune forms the dividing line between title and running text. The end is quite often marked by the word *Finis*, and gives the name of the printer and sometimes also the author.

The subject of communication of a street ballad is understood as a 'display object' mainly where it features sensational or marvellous events; the showman points to it as a moral or didactic example. This speech act differs from other explicit comments which can be assigned to the communication level of the narrator in its visually realizable, performative character. Requests to the audience to observe more closely, together with demonstratives, characterize this speech act.

> Loe here you see a fearfull end,
>   of Sir *George Sands* his sonne,[155]
>
> But now, behold and see
>   God's vengeance on them all![156]
>
> All you that fathers be,
>   look on my misery![157]
>
> Let me a warning be to Wiues,[158]
>
> Come take a view good People all,
>   observe it well with heed,
> A stranger Wonder Nature did
>   ne're frame of Humane Seed;
> A Monster of mishapen Forme
>   I here to you present,

By this Example you may learn
   to feare Gods Punishment.

Strange Wonders hath been lately shown
   within our *English* Nation;
But none so strainge as this was known,
   you'l find by this Relation;
Then give attention to the same,
   I'le show you how it was,

To tell the truth it is no shame,
   for thus it came to passe.[159]

Here the presenter implies the actual presence of the display object, hinting at a pictorial reproduction of the freak whilst at the same time promising to give a verbal description. The presenter's own reference to himself in his function of communicator (see above, pp. 46–7) also contains, of necessity, a reference to the subject of communication, whereby the formula 'I will show you . . . ' in its double meaning of 'exhibit' and 'explain/report' acquires a particularly demonstrative character.[160] In the act of communication the street-ballad message is to a certain extent at the disposal of the presenter, a factor which is reinforced in a general sense by his references to self and appeals to the listener.

A favourite stylistic feature of Elizabethan and Jacobean literature was the play on words. This involved unusual combinations of speech elements or rapid alternation of original literal meanings and the figurative meanings which had since become established. The street ballad also makes use of this, sometimes throughout a whole text. By analogy with the showman's act, one could perhaps refer to it as 'juggling with words'. There is a linguistic display here which may not be realizable in any concrete way during the performance, but certainly requires attention and powers of imagination on the part of the listeners, in accordance with the presenter's intentions.

An example of this is *The Praise of Brotherhood: Or, a description of Hoodes, writ in Verse* (1634; *RB*, II, pp. 361–6). With a folk-etymological naïveté in keeping with the presenter's social and linguistic level, the speaker uses the homonyms 'hood' (headgear) and '-hood' (abstract suffix) to link certain social phenomena with changes in fashion. He arranges them alongside each other, describing them as he goes: 'brother-hood' is the simplest, most durable, and weatherproof headgear; 'priest-hood' is suitable for those unable to pay for their own schooling; 'knight-hood' is the appropriate reward for the brave; 'man-hood' is the fashionable hallmark of masculinity, while 'woman-hood' indicates a woman's increase in value; 'neighbour-hood'[161] he says has unfortunately gone out of fashion and 'French-hood' should be rejected as too foreign a style; 'child-hood'

can only be worn at a certain age, and 'false-hood' helps those with two
faces:

> In dayes of old, when I was but a boy,
> Then brother-hood went for a fashion each day;
> But brother-hood now is out of request,
> And other hoodes are accounted best.
> For now strange tricks and trifles they use,
> Which makes the poore man to stand in a muse;
> I doe say no more th[a]n all the world knowes,
> *For brother-hood best becomes the nose.*
>
> (v. 5, lines 33–40, *RB*, II, p. 363)

The ballad *Faire fall all good Tokens!*, already quoted as an example of
the presenter's introduction of himself in the role of joker (see above,
p. 43, for more detail), similarly uses linguistic games to illustrate its
theme. The underlying idea that tokens can be deprived of their situational
and contextual connotations serves to produce nothing more than a con-
fused mixture of truisms and sayings, but it no doubt answered the ballad
audience's expectations as regards entertainment. Proverbs and sayings
are not only a favourite stylistic device of the street ballad (see above, chapter 3.3.4): their usage, origins and meaning are also treated in their own
right. In *A merry new Ballad, both pleasant and sweete, / In praise of the
Black-smith, which is very meete* (1661; *RB*, II, pp. 126–31) the praise of
this craft is justified by the fact that a large number of proverbs originate
in the activities and products of the blacksmith: 'Strike while the iron is
hot';[162] 'to come to buckle and bare thong' (to be stripped of everything);[163] what he pulls out of the fire is indeed saved for good: 'out of the
fire';[164] if someone is in unfortunate circumstances, 'off the hooks',[165] it is
only the blacksmith who can help him. Comical similes are traced back to
him: 'as dead as a door-nail',[166] 'as plain as a pike-staff'.[167] Many of the
verses illustrate his contribution to the enriching of the language:

> The common proverb, as it is read,
> That a man must *hit the nayle on the head,*
> Without the Black-smith cannot be said,
>   *Which no body can deny.*   (ibid., v. 11, lines 41–4, p. 128)
>
> And if a schollar be in doubt,
> And cannot well bring his matter about,
> The Black-smith he can *hammer it out*
>   *Which no body can deny.*   (ibid., v. 26, lines 97–100, p. 130)

The blacksmith's job is also rich ground for puns using homonyms: he
exerts himself 'at the bar' more than any lawyer (v. 18, lines 69–72,
p. 129); he can also do more for the success of a racehorse than the jockey,
'to give him a heat', that is, in forging the horseshoe and in running a cer-

tain part of the race.[168] He can also 'forge what he will' without becoming a forger,[169] and 'file' is not only one of the blacksmith's tools, but also a swindler, not least to be found among soldiers, who of course march in 'rank and file'.[170] The inclusion of this text in a well-known anthology of the time, *An Antidote against Melancholy* (1661) leads us to conclude that the ballad was widely known for a considerable period.[171]

The praise of Nothing (between 1601 and 1640: *RB*, II, pp. 339–44), a parody of a song of praise, uses these key words in an ironic play on reflections of a critical and pessimistic nature: the use of the word 'Nothing' as an anticlimax makes all the assertions seem relative. Within the framework of such an analysis, the speaker describes his task as a manipulation of the term 'Nothing' which will further wisdom and perception:

> The praise of wisdome some doe write,
>   And some the praise of money;
> And every one, like bees to th'hive,
>   From something gather hony:
> But if my genius doe not faile
> To promp[t] me, ere I end my tale
> You'l finde that Nothing will prevaile;
>   For all must turne to Nothing.   (ibid., v. 1, lines 1–8, p. 340)

Owing to his profoundly negatory function, the key word 'Nothing' is ideal for a hyperbolic, emphatic criticism whose object is for its part characterized by obvious triviality.

> Nothing in all the world we finde
>   With sorrow more perplexed
> Th[a]n he that with a scolding wife
>   Eternally is vexed;
> Whose tongue by nothing can be quel'd,
> Although with red-hot pincers held;
> For shee will to no reason yeeld,
>   But scold and brawle for Nothing.
>
> Nothing is swifter th[a]n the winde,
>   Or lighter th[a]n a feather;
> Yet I another thing have found,
>   Which quite excelleth either:
> A harlot's love, that every day
> Is chang'd and swiftly blowne away;
> But what's more light th[a]n her, I pray?
>   The wise man answers, Nothing.   (ibid., vv. 3–4, lines 17–32, p. 341)

The treatment of the subject ranges from worldly-wise and banal reflections, on the one hand, to moralizing recommendations based on eschatological considerations on the other. Language games in the street ballad are ideally suited to show up the presenter as a skilful juggler with words. Since the audience is thereby made aware of elements of meaning, the message content of the ballad becomes a concretized display object at the disposal of the presenter. The presenter's function of reference to the outside world, as written into the text, can be accompanied during the performance by gesture and mime. This is made clear in these contexts by expressions which have the function of reference to self, such as 'I doe say no more',[172] 'if my genius does not faile',[173] and 'Yet I another thing have found' (ibid.).

3.4.3 Reference to other street ballads (the 'answer ballad'): plurality of opinion and advertising techniques

On the presenter–audience communication level, the so-called 'answer ballads' represent a further procedure concerned with reference to the outside world. A ballad which has perhaps already proved a hit is given an 'answer' by the same or a different author. The second text may be an imitation, reply, continuation, or attack on the first. Similarities in content and methods of presentation, and often the same tune, link the answer-ballad with its predecessor. The presenter becomes the vehicle for reference and allusion to the previous text, to which he wishes to draw the audience's attention. If he has before him an audience of experienced ballad-listeners he can establish a common agreement on textual correlations. For the subject of communication itself there is a contrasting and variation of theme involved, which again makes possible a plurality of opinion within the street ballad. At the same time a form of serial advertising can be discerned here. The extent to which the original ballad is well known or popular with the public – an implicit precondition for the success of an answer-ballad – or at least close proximity of times of publication, would have a substantial effect on answer-ballad sales. The idea that publications bolster each other up, as put into practice in modern publishing programmes and book series, is already apparent here in the beginning stages. The answer-ballad was a common literary procedure and advertising technique within the seventeenth-century street ballad.[174] As a presenter's speech act it again implies, through reference to an outside object, a concretizing of the message and creates an incentive to buy.

Both the following are particularly suitable as answer-ballads: the role-play ballad, where a standpoint is dramatically personalized which can then be opposed in another; and the discursive ballad, as far as it consistently treats a theme from the same angle which can then be picked up by an answer-ballad. The two dramatic monologues *A good Wife, or none* (before 1629) and *A Batchelers Resolution*[175] present two bachelor figures who are both concerned with the marriage question. The first ballad shows a man who, on the basis of his previous unhappy experience of women, is determined only to marry if he can find a suitable partner. The second involves a passionate decision to finish with bachelorhood, a state seen as causing inner conflict and pessimistic insecurity. The bachelor puts the blame on women for all his disappointments. Their refrains, corresponding to each other, show the wavering emotions of the one – 'Ile choose to lie alone' and the determination of the other – 'Ile lie alone no longer'. This topic was bound to interest many in the audience; as well as the various ways of looking at marriage, listeners were also shown just how subjective and personal these views were. Success with the audience would be reinforced by the already popular tune which was common to both ballads.[176]

The two ballads by Martin Parker, *Keep a good tongue in your head* and *Hold your hands, honest Men!* (both between 1633 and 1643),[177] similarly present contrasting aspects of marriage. The dramatic figures, a man and a woman, each have an ideal marriage partner whose merits they describe eloquently: 'But she cannot rule her tong'; 'He cannot rule his hands'. Nagging and violence weigh heavily in comparison with the other, good qualities which are listed after the manner of a catalogue of beauties. The exact correspondence in thematic content, structure, and verse form of the two texts, together with the duplication of incidents, serves to underline the everyday, practical character and worldly wisdom of the street-ballad message.

The Merry Cuckold (c. 1689) and *The Scolding Wives Vindication: Or, An Answer to the Cuckold's complaint* (c. 1698)[178] are a pair of ballads with very closely related contents. The first is the dramatic monologue of a husband who does not seem to mind that his wife is unfaithful to him, while he enjoys himself eating and drinking at her expense. The psychology and behaviour of this figure only become fully understandable through the wife's answer-ballad, in which the husband's failure in his work and in his marital duties supply both the motives for his unconcerned attitude and the justification for her adultery.

In *The Honest Age, Or There is honesty in all Trades* (1632) and *Knauery in all Trades,* OR, *Here's an age would make a man mad* (1632)[179] two extreme viewpoints are expressed. At the same time the two discursive ballads illustrate a minor literary feud between the doyens of ballad poetry, Laurence Price and Martin Parker. 'M.P.' counters the utopian ideal of an economic balance in the world of middle-class trade, as outlined by his competitor, with sharp social criticism, pessimistically lamenting the contemporary decline. Laurence Price's lines of equal length and almost regular triple-accented dactyls, which in combination with the content evoke a measure of cheerful self-confidence, are answered by Parker with irregular dactyls in lines of unequal length. With this textual content the dactyls produce the effect of an ironically alienated echo and accentuate particularly sharply the pessimistic statements in each short line.[180]

In the answer-ballads, commercial motives combine with the intention to use literary means of presentation in diverse, complementary and contrastive ways, achieving an effectiveness which goes beyond the individual text. In some cases the street ballad can turn into a kind of discussion forum. The repeated and varied use of common themes such as love, marriage, sexuality, criminality, moral behaviour, and the like within the whole ballad corpus has still to be investigated from the point of view of such genre- and reception-related coherences. Musical counter-structures and those relating to content would also have to be investigated.[181] The answer ballad shows a particularly high degree of awareness on the part of the ballad author with which he referred to a common repertoire of themes and certain texts.

Such awareness with regard to the possibilities of the street ballad as a genre can also be seen generally in the treatment of the street-ballad message. The presenter, in his function of reference to the outside world, announces it in the trailer and accompanies it with linguistic indications marking the beginning and end of the text, requesting the audience to observe closely the subject of communication and taking linguistic functions as a theme. Finally he refers back to well-known ballads for amplification and reinforcement of his text. The subject of communication appears in the performance to a certain extent as a linguistic display object.

3.5 Summary

3.5.1 The presenter's procedures as specific to the street ballad

We started out from the assumption that literary and sociological conditions, especially the specific communication situation in which the street ballad was communicated and distributed, could have an influence on textual construction (see above, chapter 1). To investigate this assumption on the basis of the extant texts, a communication model was set up which takes into account all known deducible or possible conditional components for the rise and spread of the street ballad. At the same time the model takes into consideration the procedures for directing communication which are inherent in the text (see above, chapter 2.1). For a more precise classification of the links between literary–sociological conditions and the communicative conditions and instructions apparent in the text, speech act theory proved a suitable starting-point. Certain modifications to the purely linguistic definition of this theory were of course necessary before it could be applied to literary texts (see above, chapter 2.2). Within the framework of the special conditions of literary communication the street ballad has its own level of communication, on which there is a correlation between the textual and non-textual components of a speech situation. It serves the specific communication needs of the street ballad, without the latter's forfeiting any of its literary character. The description of the various individual procedures on the presenter's level of communication shows that the street-ballad text, more than most other literary forms, takes account of a specific concrete speech situation in the text itself, namely the context of performance and sale. The street ballad incorporates components of this situational context in such a way that they can indeed be transposed on to various conceivable street-ballad performances.

The individual textual procedures with which reference is made to the speech situation show varying degrees of explicitness. The request for attention is more straightforward in comparison with the attempt to attract an audience by referring to the subject of the ballad in the trailer or in a topic-related address to a certain section of the public; similarly with the request to join in the singing as opposed to the importance of the refrain as an appeal to the listener with the purpose of reinforcing the sense of community, and the request to buy compared with the more subtle advertising techniques of the trailer, answer-ballad, and personalization of the wares on offer. The request to 'come closer' fulfils in practical terms what the colloquial element as an approach to the audience sets out to achieve on the psychological level. The showman's presentation of himself involves relevant expressions of attitude and indications of his function as speaker, but is also indirectly implied in the nature of his subject of communication, his claims to authenticity, and his understanding of his role as dispenser of warnings and advice. The less clearly and precisely the concrete speech and communication situation is articulated in a textual procedure, the more the speaker's functions can be integrated into the intention of the respective text as a whole. With its diversification of presenter's procedures the street ballad satisfies both literary demands and those of functional language which are found to the same degree in a street-ballad performance. Similarly, the illocutionary dimension of the presenter's speech act varies in the explicitness of its instructions to act, from direct imperative to literary and aesthetically based influence of reception.

The nature of the performance and of the textual procedures for controlling communication, in their mutual correspondence, mark out the street ballad as a functional and popular form of literature. The performance belongs in the socio-cultural sphere of alehouse and fairground amusements, street trade, and occasional poetry. The speaker inherent in the text with his highly developed audience relationship has the features that go with it – of the poseur, market-crier, and salesman – and is characterized by the intensity of his actions. He poses as joker, reporter of sensational events and narrator of sentimental stories, and can take on fictional roles. With this the figure of the presenter enters the literature – not as material,[182] but as a form of linguistic structure.

Considered as a whole or in its variety of individual forms, the presenter's procedure can be seen as specific to the street ballad. Certain elements of this procedure are of course indebted to medieval literary traditions: claims to authenticity and fictions with prove authenticity, some forms of audience address, didactic intentions and the trailer. These were, however, modified and adapted for the street-ballad context and performance situation. Other individual procedures, such as establishing a reception area for performance, invitations to the public to perform a direct action supplementary to the speech situation, forms of address targeted at specific groups, personalization of the literary wares on offer, forms of ingratiation with the audience, and street-ballad markers of various kinds are largely or indeed exclusively features of the presenter's communication level in the street ballad. The analogy with the juggler and the fairground showman is obvious; in the street ballad, however, the presenter's activities are translated into textual strategies which correspond both to the literary subject of communication and to the needs of performance and sale of broadsides. His level of communication should be understood as a genre-specific speech act in a speech situation which is conditioned by literary and sociological factors.

The interpretation of the presenter's procedures in the individual text leads beyond these functions of speech structure to certain essential characteristics of the street ballad, which will be examined in detail later. The secularization of content goes hand in hand with the development of a speaker inherent in the text who, as the messenger, has to justify and vouch for a message whose authenticity and conformity to fixed norms can no longer be taken for granted. The authority of the speaker provides a system of order for the rising pluralism of opinion and the relatively large variety of subjects of communication. It is also primarily on the presenter's level of communication that the message is given an air of topicality, whether through claims to present-day relevance and newness, or reference to what are obviously day-to-day practical matters. Literary advertising techniques are essential to the street ballad and fall similarly within the structural province of the presenter.

3.5.2 Literary integration of advertising techniques in the street ballad

These advertising techniques can be only loosely compared to the methods of modern advertising, however. They obviously have the common purpose of selling, but this is obviously much more subtly handled in today's advertising texts (and pictures). Disguising the intention to influence and mythologizing the product are genre-typical devices of present-day advertising (see I. Hantsch [1972], pp. 93–114) which are largely absent from the street ballad, as are fluctuations of sense and transfers of meaning, that is, a wealth of connotation for selling purposes hidden beneath seemingly common, everyday denotations. Street-ballad disguise tactics are confined to the use of implicit illocutions for the presenter's selling purposes. The combination of street-ballad advertising of broadsides with the literary textual intention shows a use of artistic elements and procedures which can be compared to the modern advertisement. Different elements predominate here, however, since street-ballad wares are themselves literary products which, in the context of the advertising process, are not only presented to the public but also simultaneously offered for sale.

It is only the request to buy, found at the end of the ballad in appeal formulas to the listener, intended to catch the possibly rapidly dispersing audience and persuade them to open their purses, which is clear and unmistakable in function. The trailer, on the other hand, combines its advertising intent in the description of 'wares' with the literary and communicative function of preparing the ground for the ballad message itself. By arousing interest in the actual message, however, and facilitating the audience's understanding of it as it appears in the text to follow, the trailer indirectly also creates an incentive to buy. This intention is reinforced by sensational formulations in praise of the ballad content. At the same time the trailer in its respective form is, as we have seen, fairly differentiated as regards mood and atmosphere, and adapted to the context according to the particular street-ballad sub-genre. Advertising function and literary intention cannot be clearly separated here. This is also apparent in the broad spectrum of the trailer's illocutionary acts of giving information, stating facts, asserting, promising and evaluating. It can be said at this point that the street-ballad trailer is somewhat more informative than the bulk of modern advertising. In addition, the concretization of the message as a linguistic display object by means of textual and non-textual markers exhibits the literary product immediately, and may at the same time help to explain the subject of communication.

The specific audience address relating to the topic, frequently used in the seventeenth century, has in the first instance the function of attracting attention and creating an effect favourable to the communication of the ballad message. At the same time it offers the target group addressed an opportunity to identify, a technique also used in modern advertising (see I. Hantsch [1972], p. 101 and *passim*). The advertising intent behind this becomes clear when the topic-related address is combined with a request to buy. The opportunity to identify is only one of the possibilities of turning ballad content to personal use. From the advertising point of view the didactic influence of street-ballad warning and advice presupposes a need which the balladmonger meets with his range of products. Such needs are admittedly to do with morals and 'lifemanship', and are satisfied in literary form in the text with the help of entertainment components. The 'personalization of the goods on offer', as realized in the person and manner of the balladmonger with the aid of his textual score, it also no mere advertising technique but at the same time a vehicle for literary intentions. The street-ballad presenter is not only a guarantor of the 'quality of his goods' but is also perceived, acoustically and visually, as both transmitter of the ballad message in its totality and visible entertainer. The specific proof of quality implied in a claim to authenticity is certainly a description of one of the presenter's functions, but in addition it relates to the topical value of the textual content itself and its use for didactic purposes. Finally, answer-ballads combine the advertising of a 'production programme' with the literary procedures of allusion, contrast, and the representation of diverse opinions.

Advertising purposes and intentions of literary presentation in the street ballad are closely connected in multifarious ways, showing mutual influence in their structural realization. This often involves a combination of the literary intention of the text as a whole with specific activities of the presenter; the latter participates in the functions of the 'message of the text as a whole', thereby personalizing them. Much as the presenter is the textual manifestation of the ballad-seller, he is as much if not more the transmitter of the respective textual message, being also defined by it. It is precisely in this functional multiplicity that the presenter is shown to be a popular cultural phenomenon and not just a hawker of wares. Behind the whole process, accessible to us only through the end result – the structure of the text – there are both the demands of the concrete situation of performance and sale, and literary–aesthetic regulatory factors which also determine genre. The advertising effect in the street ballad is achieved by means of linguistic and literary devices. We note again here the extent to which this genre was determined by literary and sociological conditions without, however, losing its character as literature. The street ballad cannot belong to the esoteric system of references and values of a world of lofty ideas or aesthetic freedom, but takes part in concrete, practical processes. This applies not only to its particular economic position within the contemporary sphere of literary activity but also to its intention to entertain and its functional, down-to-earth, and sometimes trivial content, all of which presupposes a relationship with an audience of a specific class.

3.5.3 Virtual absence of the presenter in the early street ballad: transition forms

We have been investigating the procedures of the presenter with their effects on textual construction and performance, together with their advertising aspects, as a particular characteristic of the street ballad. This does not however apply until the period when this literary phenomenon was both quantitatively and qualitatively fully developed, which was approximately between 1600 and 1650. It is largely absent from the early texts. If we assume some structural intention fulfilling demands related to the text, it is reasonable to suppose that there is a connection between obvious changes in thematic content and the development of a clearly defined speaker. We have described this as part of a process of secularization (see above, pp. 56–7). In the communication of moral and religious truths, the showman's presentation of himself and vociferous appeals to the listener are out of place; serious, religious content rules out his jesting and sensationalism.

A few examples will show how the specific content of the text and the speech structure of the early forms of street ballad largely prevented the emergence of the presenter element, even where there was ample opportunity provided for it in a particular speech situation. *A declaration of the death of* Iohn Lewes, *a most detestable and obstinate hereticke, burned at* Norwich (1583: OEB, no. 9, pp. 54–61) describes this man's ordeal from the perspective of his judges. The moral indignation at the obstinacy of the 'heretic' could be given vent to in relevant comments and audience address. The speaker goes no further, however, than ask rhetorical questions and talk as if to himself:

> Shall silence shrowde such sinne,
>   as Sathan seemes to showe
> Euen in his impes, in these our dayes,
>   that all men might it knowe?
>
> No, no, it cannot be;
>   but such as loue the Lorde,
> With heart and voyce, will him confesse,
>   and to his word accord.[183]

The secularized form of the 'exhortatory ballad', the warning, was the first to take advantage of a strong accentuation of the message by the presenter.

A counterpart to the repressed and sublimated emotions of *A declaration . . .* is *A Triumph for true Subiects, and a Terrour vnto all Traitours: By the example of the late death of . . .* (1581; OEB, no. 10, pp. 62–9). The triumphant joy at the execution of three adherents of a different faith, at the same time viewed as a political victory over Roman Catholicism, is certainly expressed in an audience address but immediately merges into a general feeling of community among all patriotic Englishmen, addressing a prayer to God:

> Good Subiectes of ENGLANDE, reioyce and be glad;
>   Gyue glorie to God – with humble knees downe! –
> That *Campion* the Traytour his hyre hath now had,

Who sought for to spoyle our queene and her Crowne;
And all vnder colour of *Iesuits'* profession,
To perswade the Queenes Subiects to their own destruction.
    Therfore vnto God for our Queene let vs pray,
That the Lorde may preserue her lyfe many a day.   (ibid., v. 1, p. 64)

This call to rejoice and pray remains in the notional world of general political activity and is in no way related to the situation of performance and sale, a link frequently established by the presenter. The reciter also fails to exploit the victory news to enhance the status of his own person.

In the depiction of a fateful life story it was similarly almost impossible in this early period for a showman-like self-presentation to emerge. The self-knowledge of the character depicted, with regard to the purely exemplary value of his own fate as an instance of God's justice on earth, did allow for express reference to the protagonist in a first-person narrative; such references would, however, have an air of humility rather than reflect the self-satisfaction characteristic of the presenter of the later period:

Let all men viewe my woefull fall,
    And rue my woefull case,
And learne hereby in speedy sort
    Repentaunce to embrace.[184]

That this is true the world may plainly see,
And view a fearfull spectacle in mee;[185]

In 'A Ballad without title, having a large cut representing five figures' (second half of the sixteenth century; *AB*, no. 25, pp. 143–8) there are initial signs of presenter activities which are typical of the early period of the street ballad. This ballad text explains and interprets several woodcuts which accompany it: 'Marke well the effect purtreyed here in all';' (ibid., 1,1, p. 143). There are five figures, portrayed separately and – in a further woodcut – sitting together eating in an arbour. Their status and attitudes are explained in the text. There is a bishop who represents the church's function of intercession with God and has spiritual power in his hands; there is the king who keeps order in the land and defends it against its enemies; the loose woman as ruler over all men; a lawyer as the arbiter in all disputes; and a farmer, on whose produce all are dependent. Death steals in from the side and puts an end to the power contest. In the text the figures are treated in the following way:

The contry clowne, full loth to lose his right,
Puts in his foot and pleads to be the chiefe;
What can they do, saith he, by power or might,
If that by me they haue not their reliefe?

> For want of food they should all perish than;
> What say you now to me, the countrey man?   (ibid., v. 6, p. 146)

The text relates here to the figure of the farmer in the woodcut who is taking a determined step forward with left foot first, to which the proverbial metaphor 'puts in his foot': 'raises an objection' is a direct reference. In the iconographic portrayal he also has his mouth open in speech. The ballad thematicizes the performer's function of comment and allusion, but only through description and interpretation and as a didactic task relating to the subject of the ballad; he has a subservient function, behind which he himself withdraws completely. The relationship with the audience is also limited to a call to put a religious interpretation on the textual amplification of the pictorial material:

> Here you may see what as the world might be,
> The rich, the poore, Earle, Cesar, Duke and King,
> Death spareth not the chiefest high degree. –   (ibid., 10,1–10,3, p. 148)

The principle of a textual structure which takes the presenter into account cannot really make any headway in these ballads. It exists as a possibility for any text that is to be performed, as with the early street ballad, but blossomed only at the turn of the sixteenth century. There is an undoubted correlation here with the secularization process and considerable broadening of topic areas. There is insufficient material available for an investigation into changes in the concrete speech situation which took place at the same time.

4   Sub-genres of the street ballad

4.1 Definition according to mode of communication; demarcation of presenter level of communication from the other textual speech situations

The street ballad as a genre is characterized by the additional communication level of the presenter. The text corpus comprises various literary forms which can be termed 'street-ballad *sub*-genres'. These can be classified according to the criteria of recent genre theory, where Aristotle's rhetorical criterion for the definition of literary genres or 'primary styles'[1] has been adapted for communication theory purposes. A distinction is made between a 'reporting' and a 'performative' speech situation, that is, in a narrative text the narrator reports on characters – their spoken and other acts – while in a dramatic text the figures as speakers act and speak independently, without further mediation. In the narrative the figures are projected by means of the overriding narrative communication level, thereby becoming the subject of communication; this communication level is absent in the dramatic genre (see above, chapter 2.3). In this division into two, determining all further sub-categorization, Aristotle's original third category of 'lyric' does not feature.[2]

According to this scheme the street ballad can be divided into the following sub-genres:

1 Speech situation of reporting:
Narrative street ballad: the speaker inherent in the text is the explicit narrator with his (occasionally explicitly addressed) fictional addressees on a more or less clearly defined communication level (deictic information of a personal though seldom temporal or local nature). The subject of communication is the narrative with its own deictic orientation according to figures, space, and time.
2 Performative speech situation:
2.1 *semi-dramatic* and *dramatic street ballad:* I shall term 'semi-dramatic' the role-play ballad, in which the dramatic figure's performative situation is relatively precisely fixed through the (fictional) content. This dramatic figure's addresses to the audience can contain partial transitions to the actual speech situation of the performance (*ad spectatores*). The term 'dramatic' will be applied to the *dialogue ballad*, in which there are usually

two (fictional) speakers, who are defined as to personal information, engaged in dialogue without any audience address. Such texts are as a rule performed by only *one* actual speaker – the balladmonger. Temporal deictic information concerning the figures is usually indeterminate, and local information largely confined to (textually implied) gesture and mime. *2.2 Discursive street ballad:* an explicit speaker who, in contrast to the dramatic figure, is not further defined deictically, has as his subject of communication a set of circumstances or state of affairs, or equally minimal deictic structure, with cognitive and emotive content. The term 'discursive' indicates that a topic is discussed. The coherence principles of the subject of communication are not deictic in nature, but semantic and argumentative.[3]

The speech situation of the presenter differs from those which characterize the street-ballad sub-genres, in its potential and realizable partial congruence with the general situation of performance and sale. The textual deictic references to his person, place, and time can be transposed on to the concrete functional situation, and the street-ballad illocutions of vociferous self-presentation, attracting attention, sales promotion, and the communication of an entertaining and instructional textual message in literary form, have an immediate audience-related function. The role of presenter is assumed and put into practice by the balladmonger. It is not always easy to draw a clear line between this and the speech acts of the narrator, the dramatic figure or the discursive speaker, however. The balladmonger can take on elements of what are clearly fictional roles.

The narrator can be distinguished from the presenter as speaker by his deictic indeterminacy, although it is possible for the presenter to take over in part the fictional role of narrator. This is the case, for instance, where the narrator functions in a vague and general way as communicator of the story ('I'll tell you . . .' and the like) or sets himself up as the guarantor of authenticity. On the other hand, where the narrator refers to his story with explanatory and evaluative comments he is clearly remaining within the bounds of his own function. Comments orientated towards appeals to the listener during the course of the narrative, similar in form to the presenter attracting attention, are borderline cases in which a change of role is conceivable. Where such utterances are semantically integrated into the narrative, they differ from the presenter's general requests for attention at the beginning of the text. On the whole, in assigning utterances to the narrator, their specifically narrative function and the degree of integration into the message narrated are the deciding factors.

For the semi-dramatic form of the street ballad, the problem of the presenter partially taking on fictional roles is different; here a basic distinction must be made between two of the balladmonger's textually defined functions: he can, as an actor, 'take on a role', that is, embody, however well or badly, a fictional and self-contained first-person situation; and he must be aware of his task as presenter. In the monologue utterance and in the *ad spectatores* (role-play ballad), as in the dramatic dialogue (dialogue ballad), the introduction of metatextual advance information, and requests to the audience to listen, join in the singing, and buy, signify a break in the fiction on the part of the presenter within the illusion which has been established. The deictic fixing of the fictional dramatic figure distinguishes it from the actual deictic characterizing of the presenter himself. There is, however, some convergence of the reality-orientated role of the presenter with the fictional dramatic figure, which is structurally intrinsic in the latter's often demonstrative behaviour and market-crier tones, making the balladmonger's task of both acting and presenting somewhat easier. Presentation of self, personal appeals to the listener from within the fictional situation, and the dramatic figure's presentation of his or her own problems remain integrated in the fictional role, however. Exceptions to this tendency to maintain the fictional illusion, in the dramatic figure's *ad spectatores*, only prove the rule.

There is a particular convergence of the speaker in a discursive ballad with the presenter as speaker, due to the former's deictic indeterminacy and the absence of fictional speech situations as subjects of communication. From the deictic and illocutionary aspect his functions can, again, he divided into the situationally determined speech acts of the ballad-seller, the organizer of a performance, and the metatextual announcer. A doubling of the reality-based and the fictional role in a quasi-role-playing identification with the tenor of the respective topic is always possible; it merges with presenter characteristics particularly where demonstrative commitment or satirical comedy are called for. The discursive speaker's instructional intentions can be easily and effectively taken over as a fictional role by the presenter. This proves to be a determining factor in the structure of numerous warning and advice ballads whose discursive procedure is accompanied by relevant appeals to the listener.

The possible correlations between the presenter's speech situation and those of the narrator, dramatic figure, and discursive speaker, which can be understood as a doubling of the presenter's role functions, often allow a certain leeway in analysis and in the determining of classification. The naive ballad-reader/listener was able more or less to make the distinction intuitively. Altogether, analysis and interpretation reveal the communicative complexity of the street ballad in a performance situation which is not apparent on the linguistic and aesthetic levels. The effect and effectiveness of this complexity lie not in any stylistic pretensions, but rather in a relationship with the audience where ease of reception had to be taken into consideration. The presenter here had the task of taking over as much as possible of the narration, self-presentation of a particular role, and the point of view of the discursive speaker into his own reality-based speech acts.

4.2 'Reporting' speech situation in the street ballad: the narrative street ballad

By far the largest proportion of the street-ballad text corpus is made up of narrative texts: criminal biographies, often with some historical and factual substance, or other life stories which can be didactically exploited, reports of sensational and marvellous events, comic tales and love stories and, in the early street ballad, biblical material and the stories of martyrs. The tenor of the narrative is determined by the explicit and implicit attitude of the narrator and can where necessary be taken over by the presenter. It can be serious and instructional, sentimental, entertaining or humorous. The shortness of the narrative, determined by the broadside format allowing no more than between about 80 and 120 lines, limits the number of characters to (usually) one or two main figures with few, or more often no, minor characters at all. There is similarly no scope for complicated narrative techniques giving information, connecting events, and introducing characters. Simple structural principles can however be established which have a complementary and indeed transparent function in the subject of the narrative. Explicit authorial communication and comment on the events narrated assume particular importance. The development of an explicit narrator, almost unknown in the narrative prose of the time,[4] can be seen in conjunction with the evolution of the presenter as speaker, especially as both these elements were still largely absent in the early street ballads at the close of the sixteenth century and only became textual constituents when the genre had been fully developed in both quantity and quality.

4.2.1 The explicit narrator and his subject of narration: types of comment, subjective emphasis in the first-person narrative

The explicit narrator in his function of communicator of the story is most clearly recognizable when a comment on the events reported is combined with a reference to the activity of authorship:

> Which straunge event whilst that I do
>   perpend and to minde call,
> My penne, in troth, is readie prest
>   out of my hand to fall:
>   . . .

> But yet, good pen, hold on thy course,
>   to write do thou not linne,
> For I the truth to prosecute
>   hereof will now beginne.[5]

The process of communication is much more frequently articulated in explicit comments which emphasize, with reference to the outside world, particularly important events and decisive turning-points in the course of the action. This type of comment can be termed 'action-syntagmatic' and distinguished from the 'action-semantic' type, which evaluates the content narrated and exploits it didactically. Action-syntagmatic comments are almost always part of the narrator's fictional role, although they frequently occur within the context of the presenter's speech acts, with possible transitions between the two.

In *The Constant VVife of Sussex* (1632) such an action-syntagmatic commentary accompanies the narrative, working towards the main point of the story, the birth of the longed-for heir on the same day as an illegitimate daughter, with an explicit reference:

> But time that tempereth euery thing,
>   did to this house contentment bring,
> Ere fortie weekes were gone and past
>   the man had his desire at last
> Then marke the sequell while I tell
>   how euery thing in order fell.   (PB, no. 85, II, pp. 229–33, v. 7, p. 231)

Again, at a decisive point in the action when the wife agrees to help cover up her husband's act of infidelity, the narrator points out the advantages of such a course: since the two children are born on the same day they can be passed off as twins:

> *Lucina* lent a helping hand,
>   as you may plainly vnderstand.   (ibid., 14, 1–2, p. 232)

The concluding words of praise for the loyal wife, together with a blessing, lead into an audience address. The topic-related street-ballad topos of a blessing directed at a particular section of the audience allows the presenter to take on the fictional role of narration, transposing it on to the performance reality as an audience address:

> But for the woman which did saue,
>   her husbands credit, I do craue,
> Good fortune on her may attend
>   and guide her to her later end:
> And vnto euery constant wife
> I wish long dayes and happie life.   (ibid., v. 22, p. 233)

The narrator's commentary is of obvious functional character in *A merie newe Ballad intituled, the Pinnyng of the Basket* (between 1570 and 1593),[6] a comic tale describing the domestic power struggle between three couples in all, involving repetition with imitative correlation. The woman's basket-weaving has the function here of both leitmotiv and symbol. A carpenter sends his journeyman to the chandler with an order, where he is witness to a violent marital quarrel. The husband is the victor, as the wife is forced finally into basket-weaving. On his return the journeyman reports to his master what he has seen, thereby setting off a test of strength which ends in the same way. At the same time he has to prove his own success over the housemaid. The first chance encounter, which sets in motion a whole chain of events, is highlighted by the narrator with the words: 'But see the chaunce, the chandler drie / Was gone to drinke' (v. 3, 1–2, p. 154), and the first marital quarrel marked out as a motif which will later recur: 'Now doeth the sporte beginne' (v. 6, 6, p. 156). The second is also labelled as such, with an indication of the result: 'And here you see a second iarre, / The basket bredde' (v. 16, 3–4, p. 159), and the recurrence factor of the third is pointed up: 'The thirde doeth now beginne' (v. 16, 6, p. 159). At certain points in the narrative further explicit narrator's remarks summarize, with anticipatory overtones, the action so far and indicate new turns of events:

> The basket pinde, the page departes,   (ibid., v. 10, 1, p. 157)

> For now the joigners wife to pinne
>   The basket must prepare.   (ibid., v. 20, 7–8, p. 160)

> This combate beyng doen, . . .   (ibid., v. 22, 6, p. 161)

Although the narrator is only implicit during the rapid conveying of the action, the humoristic distance is still perceptible, by which also more explicit action-syntagmatic references underline the comic element in the mechanical autonomy of the chain of events in this ballad. Thus the concluding warning cannot be seen as having any kind of importance either; the presenter can without difficulty assume the distance of the narrator's role as textually coherent, offering it to the audience as a satisfactory attitude for reception:

> Now all good wiues, beware by this
>   Your names to blot;
> The basket pinne with quietnesse,
>   Denie it not, –
> Tantara, tara, tantara, –
>   Be counsailed by your frende;
> And of this baskettes pinnyng now
>   Enough, and so an ende.   (ibid., v. 26, p. 162)

Humorous and mocking distance also characterizes the narrator's attitude in *The Cucking of a Scould* (*c.* 1615). This ballad illustrates in a series of episodes the typical behaviour of the forever scolding and nagging wife who becomes a general public nuisance. Her punishment – the usual public exposure and mockery whilst being tied to a chair – is already anticipated by the narrator's stance in the first part: he shows experience in such matters, with the pseudo-serious air of a conscientious reporter which exposes the woman all the more to ridicule:

> A Wedded wife there was,
> I wis of yeeres but yong,
> But if you thinke she wanted wit,
> Ile sweare she lackt no tongue.   (*PG*, no. 12, pp. 72–7; v. 1, 1–4, p. 72)

> Each man might quickly know,
> When as the game begun,   (ibid., v. 3, 1–2, p. 73)

> But once, the truth to tell,
> Worse scolding did she keepe,   (ibid., v. 5, 5–6, p. 74)

> And first of all behold,
> He clapt her in the Cage,
> Thinking thereby her deuillish tongue,
> He would full well asswage.
> But now worse then before,
> She did to brawling fall.   (ibid., v. 9, 1–6, p. 75)

Sarcastic and derisory comments are scattered throughout the narrative:

> A neighbours maid had taken halfe
> Her dish-clout from the hedge:
> For which great trespasse done,
> This wrong for to requite,
> She scolded very hansomely,
> Two daies and one whole night.   (ibid., v. 4, 3–8, p. 73)

> As nimble as an Eele,
> This womans tongue did wag,
> And faster you shall haue it runne,
> Then any ambling Nag.   (ibid., v. 2, 1–4, p. 73)

The proud and ill-considered departure of the 'prodigal son' in *A New Ballad; Declaring the Excellent Parable of the Prodigal Child*[7] is commented on by the narrator in a way that enables the balladmonger to refer to the relevant woodcut. This portrays the protagonist as a jaunty, elegantly dressed rider with drawn sword:

> Thus, in his jollity he rides along,
>   And, in his apparel most sumptuous and brave,
> To view this brave gallant much people did throng,
>   (ibid., v. 5, 1-3, lines 30–2, p. 394)

The ballad 'The Children in the Wood', current until well into the nine-teenth century, was known in the seventeenth century under the title *The Norfolke Gentleman, his last Will and Testament: And how hee committed the keeping of his children to his owne brother, who dealt most wickedly with them: and how God plagued him for it* (between *c.* 1610 and 1675). It is particularly touching and sentimental in character; this comes out especially clearly when the narrator/presenter comments on the point in the action where the children unsuspectingly follow the more kindly disposed murderer after he has killed the other in front of their eyes:

> And looke they did not cry!
> And two long miles hee led them thus.
>   (*RB*, II, pp. 214–21; v. 14, 4–5, lines 108–9, 220)

Owing to the preponderance of sad, horrific, and stirring narrative subjects it is sentimental, scandalized comments together with those of a serious moralizing nature which on the whole predominate in the narrative street ballad. Humoristic and ironic distance is comparatively seldom found, while the dramatic and discursive ballads more frequently show a cheerful serenity combined with reference to self, and a sense of the comic. Compared to the action-syntagmatic commentary, the action-semantic commentary with its explicit moral evaluation and concomitant legitimizing of the narrative is still more effective. A typical example is the criminal story *The life and death of M. Geo. Sands, who after many enormous crimes by him committed, with Iones and Gent his confederates, was executed at Tyburne on Wednesday the 6 of September, 1626*. The moralizing role of the narrator, through his integration of references to the outside world into the course of the action, can be distinguished from the presenter's role of attracting an audience and introductory praise of the didactic value of the ballad in the first verse (first textual example):

> Come hither yongmen and giue eare,
>   and good example take,
> By this which is related here
>   for admonitions sake.   (*PG*, no. 44, pp. 248–55, v. 1,1–1,4, p. 250)

> A wicked life this caitiffe led,
>   reiecting vertues lore,   (ibid., v. 2, 5–6, p. 251)

> His wicked heart so bent to sin,
>   in villany tooke pride,   (ibid., v. 4, 5–6, p. 251)

But no such crimes can be conceal'd,
old time will find them out,   (ibid., v. 9, 1–2, p. 252)

But *Sands* hath run so vild a race,
that few bewaile his death,   (ibid., v. 14, 5–6, p. 253)

A less explicit but certainly even clearer vehicle of expression for the narrator's comment is the popular generalization found in proverbs and sayings. These are frequently made use of by the street-ballad narrator:

But now I see all is not gold,
that makes a glistring show.[8]

Dice, Wine, and Women (c. 1625) describes the dangers of a life of pleasure in London to which the first-person narrator had fallen victim as a young man. The refrain draws its retrospective conclusion from the present point of view:

The causes why I am so poore,
Are Dice, Strong-waters, and a whore.   (PB, no. 39, I, pp. 237–41)

During the narrative there is a good sprinkling of comments of the type: 'I poore asse' (ibid., v. 7,5, p. 239), 'poore man' (v. 11,1, p. 240), 'lucklesse day' (v. 12,1, p. 240), evaluating his actions in retrospect.

Explicit comments and judgements at the conclusion of a story are indeed closely related to the action, but are also by virtue of their position designed to implement the change of role from narrator to presenter, thus easing the balladmonger's transition to the concrete activities of distributing and selling the broadsides. If such a concluding remark contains an explicit audience address or marking of the end of the text, the role-change is textually preformed:

Let no marry'd couple, that heare this tale told
Be of the opinion this couple did hold,
(To sell reputation for siluer or gold)
For credit and honesty should not be sold.
  Thus ended the song of the Cooper,
  That cry'd, Ha' ye any worke for a Cooper?
                         (RB, I, pp. 98–104; v. 26, lines 151–6, p. 104)

The point of this comic tale, *The Cooper of Norfolke* (between 1625 and 1660) is that the deceived husband is compensated by a substantial sum of money; the speaker of the commentary obviously feels bound to make a somewhat flimsy concession to public morals.

A Pleasant new Ballad you here may behold,
  How the Devill, though subtle, was gul'd by a Scold

(1630) tells of a scolding wife's trouncing even of the devil himself. Husband and narrator, both resigning, fall, so to speak, by the wayside:

> The man halfe dead did stand;
>   away the Devill hyde.
> Then, since the world, nor hell,
>   can well a scold abide,
> To make a saile of ships
>   let husbands fall to worke,
> And give their free consents
>   to send them to the Turke.
>
> (RB, II, pp. 366–71, v. 18, lines 137–44, p. 371)

The connotative correlation between figure and explicit narrator, by which the point of this comic tale is emphasized, effects here an integration of the commentary. In contrast to the previous textual example, the commentary can be ascribed to the role of the narrator.

In a general overall picture of narrative comments in the street ballad, examples of particularly naive comments and those having hardly any function at all must be included.

An Admirable New Northern Story, Of two Constant Lovers (first half of seventeenth century), a particularly simple ballad with regard to narrative method, syntax, and verse form, has a correspondingly naive narrator. He announces his story:

> Two Lovers in the North,
>   Constance and Anthony,
> Of them I will set forth
>   a gallant history: (RB, I, pp. 23–9; v. 1,1–4, p. 24)

During the course of their adventures at sea, which test Constance's loyalty and steadfastness, the narrator himself encourages her:

> 'What shall become of me,
>   why do I strive for shore,
> Sith my sweet Anthony,
>   I never shall see more?'
> Fair Constance, do not grieve,
>   the same good providence
> Hath sav'd thy lover sweet,
>   but he is far from hence.   (ibid., v. 9, lines 82–9, p. 27)

The well-deserved happy reunion of the lovers as the climax and finale is prepared by the narrator with the words:

> Now mark what came to pass,
>   see how the fates did work.   (ibid., v. 13,1–2, lines 121–2, p. 28)

Narrative anticipation is seldom employed within the course of the action in the street ballad. As action-syntagmatic comment it is distinguishable from the metatextual advance information given in the trailer by its integration into the fictional speech situation of the narrator.

While in the third-person narrative, sections of the explicit narrator's role can be taken over by the presenter and integrated into a concrete speech situation, the personal deictic congruence of narrator and protagonist prevents this happening in the first-person narrative. This congruence is emphasized and given textual coherence by the information given regarding the first-person narrator through the use of the first-person pronoun. Such information is deictically structured as to time and place and constitutes a fictional world. The only metatextual advance information which clearly remains the province of the presenter is the title; warning and advice and other audience appeals can be seen as breaks in the fiction of the first-person narrator; an explicit claim to authenticity would be superfluous here, since this is already satisfied by the fiction that the story is the narrator's own experience.

For the first-person narrative as distinct from the third-person narrative, the narrative perspective in the constructing of the subject of communication is of cognitive and emotive relevance. The first-person narrator's level of information is confined to his experience as participator in the action. The limitation of perspective in the first-person narrative street ballad is hardly noticeable to the reader/listener, however, owing to the shortness of the texts and the absence of explicit references to it. The first-person perspective does become relevant from the emotive point of view: here the street ballad makes use of the possibility of the narrator/protagonist's being himself affected as a personal mode of conveying a story.

The ballad *John Spenser a Chesshire Gallant, his life and repentance, who for killing of one Randall Gam: was lately executed at* Burford *a mile from* Nantwich. (c. 1626; *PG*, no. 45, pp. 256–62) tells of a well-to-do, popular man whose business and social successes make him thoughtless, arrogant, and hard-hearted. He gives himself over to all sorts of foolish fashions, neglects his wife and finally commits murder when drunk, 'by mischance' (10,1, p. 259) according to the narrator. At the instigation of the dead man's friends he is condemned and executed. Two white doves and two white butterflies on his corpse testify, however, that he has been granted God's mercy for his repentance. This material is presented twice, as a third-person narrative in Part I of the ballad and again in Part II where the repentant sinner himself speaks. Neither text is particularly sophisticated, but variations in procedure can be detected.

They both have an audience address and request for attention and both give advance information, matching even in individual formulations. The third-person narrator, however, using a superlative, indicates that his account is just one narrative subject amongst many in a repertoire of stories known to him, while the first-person narrator places the same narrative subject – as his personal fate – in a moral and metaphysical light. The third-person narrator sees the quintessential point of the story, in his version, as being John Spenser's betrayal of the trust vested in him and his failure as a member of society. John Spenser himself experiences this process as a change in his fortunes – and well deserved, as he later avers. His lament: 'and sad is the tale I tell' is – even to the sounds of the words – more expressive of personal involvement than the objective statement of the third-person narrator: 'The saddest tale that euer yet, / by mortall man was told', which is designed to raise his prestige as communicator of the story:

> Kind hearted men, a while geue eare
>   and plainly Ile vnfold
> The saddest tale that euer yet,
>   by mortall man was told.
> One *Spenser* braue, of *Cheshire* chiefe,
>   for men of braue regarde:
> Yet hee vnto his Countries griefe,
>   did good with ill reward.   (ibid., v. 1, p. 257)

compared with:

> *Kind Youngmen all to mee giue eare,*
>   *obserue these lessons well;*
> *For vndeserued my death I tooke,*
>   *and sad is the tale I tell.*
> *In prisond pent, I lie full fast,*
>   *sure Heauen hath decreed:*
> *That though I thriued, yet at last,*
>   *bad fortunes should proceed.*   (ibid., v. 13, p. 260)

The third-person narrator's opening verses can easily be taken over by the presenter as a trailer within his performance-related activities. The first-person narrator's emotional and subjective audience address, however, with its allusion to the performance situation, must be seen as a break in the illusion, especially as the speaker is at the same time deictically establishing his communication situation as that of imprisonment. From this fictional situation of present suffering, the emotive connotations of which help to determine the narrative point of view, he tells his tale in retrospect. We have already had in the third-person narrative a chronological account of external events, whereby the 'informed reporter' places the course of earthly justice in the foreground, mentioning only briefly the 'true repentance' (12,5, p. 259) which then gives rise to the confessions of the condemned man. In contrast to the merely chronological linking of events in Part I, the protagonist of the first-person narrative in Part II establishes clear mental connections between his earlier neglect of his wife and the sentence just pronounced on him, which he sees as a fit punishment

(vv. 14–15, p. 260). John Spenser sums up the account already given in Part I in a remorseful contrasting of God's goodness with his own abuse of His gifts (15,5–8, p. 260), commenting on his life under the aspect of regret and remorse: 'my hopes I did counfound' (18,2, p. 261), 'falce she did me find' (15,4, p. 260), 'For onely by bad company, / poor Spenser is vndone.' (22,8, p. 262) and other similar expressions. Whereas Part I is predominantly factual in content, though containing implicit judgements, in Part II John Spenser as narrator is more clearly profiled in his lamentations:

> When as (God knowes) his wife at home
>   should pine with hungry griefe,
> And none would pitty her hard case,
>   or lend her some reliefe.   (ibid., v. 5,5–8, p. 258)

as against:

> *I haue a wife, a louing wife,*
>   *a constant, and a kind;*
> *Yet proud of gifts, I turned my life,*
>   *and falce she did me find:*   (ibid., v. 15,1–4, p. 260)

What in Part I is offered as an example of the adage 'pride goes before a fall', from the perspective of a communicator who is not directly involved, is presented in Part II as personal experience, understandable from the human point of view. Few ballads exploit the structural possibilities of narrative perspective so effectively. Any implementation of literary techniques within the street-ballad text corpus depends on the talent of the individual author, and there is a very wide range in quality here.

Because of its strict complementary correlation there is a successful perspective change in *The Woful Lamentation of Mrs. Jane Shore, A Gold-smith's Wife of London, some-time King Edward the Fourth's Concubine, who for her Wanton Life came to a Miserable End. Set forth for the Example of all wicked Livers* (between 1603 and 1675).[9] Here two first-person perspectives are set against each other through the exploitation of the emotional and subjective possibilities inherent in the technique. In Part I Jane Shore herself tells of and laments her fate, and in Part II the listener is again told of the behaviour of the goldsmith's wife and royal mistress, this time from the point of view of her unfortunate husband. Jane Shore's account of her life, expressed in simple street-ballad chronology, monotonous paratactic structure and unvarying line pattern and inter-spersed with moralizing self-criticism, is given a new dimension by the lament of the honest goldsmith, forlorn, unhappy and mocked by his neighbours. A comparison of verses with the same content through differ-ing perspectives makes clear the development of misunderstanding and mental and emotional separateness, achieved here not so much through linguistic style as through the speech situation.

> My Parents they, for thirst of gain,
> A husband for me did obtain;
> And I, their pleasure to fulfil,
> Was forc'd to wed against my will.   (ibid., v. 3, lines 11–14, p. 484)

compared with:

> I married thee whilst thou wert young,
> Before thou knewst what did belong
> To husband's love, or marriage state,
> Which now my soul repents too late:
>   Thus wanton pride made thee unjust,
>   And so deceived was my trust.   (ibid., v. 42, lines 177–82, p. 489)

> In heart and mind I did rejoyce
> That I had made so sweet a choice;
> And therefore did my state resign,
> To be King Edward's Concubine.   (ibid., v. 10, lines 39–42, p. 485)

compared with:

> Ah! gentle Jane, if thou didst know
> The uncouth paths I daily go,
> And woful tears for thee I shed,
> For wronging thus my marriage bed,
>   Then sure I am thou wouldst confess
>   My love was sure, though in distress.
>   (ibid., v. 49, lines 219–24, p. 490)

Jane Shore presents herself retrospectively as a vain and lustful sinner — even though in the period of her good fortune she showed charity to the poor — who got her just deserts. Matthew Shore not only laments his own fate but also maintains a perspective of pity and understanding for his wife. He sees himself as having partly contributed to her guilt by encouraging her youthful irresponsibility by spoiling her and making concessions to her freedom. What the narrative could not provide in one go, by way of double perspective and objective judgement, is presented in two stories which articulate the respective personal involvement. This procedure is rare, however.[10] Critical and repentant confrontation with the past in the repentance ballad is usually restricted to one explicit narrative perspective, that of the protagonist.[11]

The preference for first-person narrative as opposed to third-person narrative, for a subjective and emotional presentation of events, can be seen particularly clearly where there is an unexpected change of perspective within the same text. *The Sailor's onely Delight* (between 1626 and

1681; *RB*, IV, pp. 408–10) tells of a battle between an English merchant vessel and a French pirate ship. The beginning of the English crew's voyage is told in the third-person plural, but on the outbreak of fighting the text changes to the first-person plural, signalling increased involvement in the action. At the same time the implicit claim to authenticity of a consistent narrative communication is thereby interrupted. The same revealing artistic fault occurs in a later ballad by Laurence Price, *The Honour of Bristol* (*c.* 1635; *RB*, VI, pp. 428–30), which deals with the historic victory over the Spanish Armada. At the point where the crew and armory of an English ship are described and the captain gives the first orders to attack (vv. 7ff), the author uses the plural pronoun suited to a collective perspective of experience and a sense of pride at having been present at the victory.[12]

The subjective emotionalizing of and commenting on one's own learning process, characteristic of *John Spenser* and *Jane Shore*, can be replaced by an aphoristic objectivity. Linguistic indicators for this are the deictic deviations from the individualized narrative action through the change of personal pronoun (from first-person to third-person singular) and the use of the present in place of the fictionalizing past tense. Such an objective distance with regard to his own experiences is maintained by the first-person narrator, a harassed husband, in:

A merry Jest of John Tomson and Jakaman his wife,
  Whose jealousie was justly the cause of all their strife.

>   When I was a Batchelour
>   I liv'd a merry life;
>   But now I am a married man,
>   and troubled with a wife,
>   I cannot doe as I have done,
>   because I live in feare;
>   If I goe but to Islington,
>   my wife is watching there.   (1586; *RB*, II, pp. 136–42, v. 1, p. 137)

In the comparison of 'then' and 'now' the typical time structure and narrative perspective of the first-person narration is thematicized as well as the personal problem, constituting a feature of the rest of the text. On the level of the narrative speech situation, aphoristic generalization is then also possible, offering an implicit appeal to the listener to identify without interrupting the fiction of the explicit audience appeal:[13]

>   Thus marriage is an enterprise
>   experience doth show;
>   But scolding is an exercise
>   that married men doe know;
>   For all this while there were no blowes,
>   yet still their tongues were talking:

> And very faine would yellow hose
>   have had her fists a walking.[14]
>
> This maketh batchelers to wooe
>   so long before they wed,
> Because they heare that women now
>   will be their husband's head:
> And seven years long I tarried
>   for Jakaman my wife,
> But now that I am married,
>   I am weary of my life.   (ibid., v. 12, lines 115–22, p. 141)

The plausibility of the pithy aphoristic commentary can be attributed to the syntactic clarity and lexic aptness, in combination with the regular metric alternation of three- and four-stressed lines with the corresponding alternate rhyme scheme. The worldly wisdom which derives deictically from the life story is thematically integrated as a lesson to be drawn from it.

The actively productive communicative role of the explicit narrator in the action-syntagmatic and -semantic commentary, with its possibilities for explanation and perspective, is a vital and recurrent textual constituent of the narrative street ballad in the quantitative and qualitative heyday of the genre. In the early forms of the street ballad a personalized centre of orientation, either as presenter or narrator, is largely absent. One reason for this lies in the nature of the narrative subject. A series of events which, due to its biblical origins or religious/theological exemplifications, is largely pre-structured hardly requires communication by a productive narrator; comments are limited to sermon-like references and admonitions.

A proper New balad of the Bryber Gehesie (1566/7; AB, no. 13, pp. 61–5) follows in essentials the action of the biblical original (2 Kings, ch. 4), with the omission of certain details.[15] The function of the 'narrator' consists here in the sermon-like commentary on the action, which seems more important to him than does his audience. He is to a certain extent himself immersed in the instructive course of events. This is shown in the use of rhetorical questions instead of audience address:

> Was not the bryber Gehezie
>   Rewarded iustly of the Lord,
> Which for example verelie,
>   The Holie Scripture doth recorde?
> If this be true, as true it was,
>   Of his rewarde,
> Why should not Christan men, alas,
>   Than haue regarde?   (ibid., v. 1, p. 61)

The narrator's scant regard for the structure and communication of the story as a narrative production is shown by the outraged speech to the sinful protagonist with which he simply interrupts the course of the action:

> Alas, how was thou, Gehezie,
>   Rauished in worldly gaine!
> How was thou brought to mizerie,
>   Of God appointed for thy paine,
> And all thy ofspringe after thee,
>   For thy rewarde!   (ibid., 5, vv. 1–6, p. 62)

The exploitation of this cautionary tale for the instruction of others is limited to a résumé of events and the vague ejaculation: 'O haue regarde!' (see v. 10 and 9,8, p. 64), whereas in later writings certain sections of the audience, to whom these would specifically apply, are very explicitly addressed. The conclusion of the ballad is a prayer for God's help and support in a world full of temptations. This ballad can be seen as a typical form of transition from a hymn-like text to the moral and didactic street ballad. Explicit comments remain solely within the sphere of reference to the outside world, humbly dedicated to the subject of narration and his God. There is neither an explicit function of appeal to the listener nor any sign of a presenter level of communication.

The historie of the Prophet Ionas (*c.* 1615(?); *PG*, no. 11, pp. 66–71) follows the biblical original far more faithfully than *The Bryber Gehesie*, often lifting the text word for word.[16] There is a corresponding reduction of explanatory comments of the type: 'And thus the Lords word he did disobey' (v. 2,7, p. 67). The most important lesson to be derived from this story appears in the comment of the refrain: 'But God through repentance his vengeance doth spare.'

A sermon-like instructional commentary on and exploitation of the action was also appropriate for the martyr ballads of the time. For their fellow believers the martyrs were a shining example of steadfastness, while politically they were condemned as traitors and executed. The narrator of martyr stories gives corresponding emphasis to the aspect of shedding blood for one's faith. In *A ballad concernynge the death of mr.* Robart glover (1555; *OEB*, no. 7, pp. 33–46) Robert Glover's personal fate fades largely into the background behind religious panegyric. The listing of his qualities, especially his courage and steadfast faith, from which others, above all those remaining behind, should draw their hope and strength, is more important than the action itself. The explicit narrator assumes an appropriately admiring attitude, while playing no part in the structure of the action narrated:

> What stedfastnes, what manfull[ness],
>   he showèd at his deathe
> (A numbre ther cann witnes bay[r]),
>   in all his moste distrese.   (ibid., v. 6, p. 35)

General exhortations to piety and the fear of God, steadfast faith and trust in God, humility and repentance accompany and virtually swamp the actual story. Only thirteen out of altogether seventy verses are devoted to the description of the judgement and execution (vv. 48–61). The ballad is more in the nature of a devotional song than a narrative text:

> Prepare your hart to bear your chrose
>   for *chryste* and his gosple,
> The which, trullye, will folowe you,
>   as scripture dothe vs tell.   (ibid., v. 24, p. 38)

The songe of the death of mr. Thewlis (1616; *OEB*, no. 13, pp. 87–100) is closer to the third-person narrative form. Hymn-like invocations of God are placed only at the beginning and end:

> O god aboue, relent,
>   and lissten t[o] our cry;
> O *Christ*, our wooes prevent,
>   let not thy Children die!   (ibid., v. 1, p. 88)

The remaining sixty-three verses are devoted to an account of Mr Thewlis's temptation (to renounce his faith), torture, and execution. Explicit reference to his cheerful steadfastness of faith, of the type which appears in *A ballad concernynge the death of mr.* Robart glover as apostrophizing comment on the protagonist, is here included in the past-tense account:

> When they could not preueile
>   to wrest his constantie,
> They did him treator call,
>   and said that he should die.[17]

Explicit action-semantic comment remains within the sphere of reference to the outside world; allusion to the degree of the audience's knowledge or to the significance of a detail of information is directly and logically linked to the action:

> And, as all people knowe,
>   he took it patientlie.   (ibid., v. 19,3–4, p. 91)

> His gesture little shranke –
>   such was his constantsie.   (ibid., v. 32,3–4, p. 94)

The explication of the 'message' is increasingly integrated into the subject of narration, also through implicit evaluation in epithets; the explicit narrator appears as the creative communicator of the narrative, no longer merely as a preacher making use of an example.

Just as the third-person narrator in the early street ballads is largely without narrative function, assigning his subject of communication to the biblical and religious thematic area, so the first-person narrator, in contrast to later texts, shows little of the subjective perspective of narrative communication. *Franklins Farewell to the World. With his Christian Contrition in Prison, before his Death* (1615 or 1616; AB, no. 22, pp. 124–7) is the retrospective account of the fate of a criminal who is condemned to death. In contrast to later criminal ballads, we are given very few details of his past life. The brief autobiographical résumé as subject of narration takes up only thirteen lines (lines 19–32, p. 125) out of a total of eighty-six. Full of remorse, Franklin cites his fate as an example in the context of general expressions of an understanding of the world based on religion and the Bible: renunciation of vain worldly goods which he had valued too highly. The discovery of his crime is also communicated, not as a personal experience, but exclusively as a sign of God's wisdom and as a warning and piece of advice of such moment that the whole of Christendom is addressed:

> Then let a dying friend good counsell giue
> To all estates and sexes how they liue:
> Oh, let my ending of my loathed breath
> Make all men care to shun eternall death!   (ibid., lines 41–4, p. 126)

The plea for mercy in the next world, repentance and the certainty of being saved take on again here the character of an example; the subjective effects of this individual fate merge into the idea of redemption:

> My Sauiour Christ hath tooke me to his folde;
> Hee true repentance vnto me hath giu'n,
> And for me (through his merits) purchas'd Heau'n.
>   (ibid., lines 62–4, p. 126)

4.2.2 Structure and functional transparency of the subject of narration: chronology, logic of events, motivational and thematic links, comic emphasis, presentation of figures

From the turn of the sixteenth century the explicit narrator in the English street ballad, as a narrative authority conveying information, played an essential part in the total structure of the narrative and in the constitution of its intended message. The narrator interprets and judges the action, moralizes or underlines the comic aspect of human weaknesses and faults, and in some instances takes on the subjective perspective of the figures. He draws the audience's attention to decisive moments in the narrative and to the thematic unity of episodes and scenes. On this level of narrative communication the explicit narrator is an essential structural factor.

At the same time the subject of narration contains within itself a number of procedures affecting structure. The time structure is as a rule chronological, whereby an alternation between simultaneous scenic narrative and summarizing report is possible. We can distinguish the logical connection of events from the chronological as a further structural principle. The logical consistency with which events succeed each other is frequently determined by social norms (transgression is followed by punishment), the practical consequences of actions (arrival follows departure) or by the laws of nature (after illness comes either recovery or death). A further important structural principle of the subject of narration is the motivational correlation between figure and action. The figure functions first of all in its capacity of furthering the plot. In addition the figure can be presented to varying degrees as a psychological entity on whose motivation his or her actions, and therefore also the plot, are founded. This affects the presentation of the figures, which in turn is linked to the question of characterization. The thematic correlation between isolated events can similarly be described as a structural principle. If 'event' is defined as a significant change in the circumstances of one or more persons, the significance of a particular event can be understood in the abstract (see W.-D. Stempel [1973]). The investigation of the significance of events enables us to recognize semantic isotopes within a series of events. Finally, the course of the action can be affected by concentration on one central event, a procedure which applies mainly to the comic tale. All these structural procedures, in varying combinations, are brought into play in the individual street-ballad text in such a way as to aid clarity and understanding of the story and the textual message. A structural description of the street ballad can elucidate this 'reader's impression' analytically as functional clarity.

A typical structural procedure of the street-ballad subject of narration is the strict observance of the congruence between chronology and logic of action. This serves syntagmatically to suggest a teleology whose content frequently conveys a connection between guilt and expiation/punishment. Motivational grounds, as far as they are made explicit, are subordinated to this textual message. The alternation of scenic narrative and summarizing report can in different ways underline the intended message, through description or increase of pace. The explicit narrator's comments do the rest.

Life stories, especially criminal ballads, are predominantly structured according to this pattern. *A new Ballad, intituled, A Warning to Youth, shewing the lewd life of a Marchant's Sonne of London, and the misiere that at the last he sustained by his riiotousnesse* (beginning of seventeenth century?; *RB*, III, pp. 35–41) tells the story of a profligate. The young merchant's son, a substantial inheritance at his disposal, spends his time breaking hearts and visiting prostitutes, at first in his native London. His carnal way of life features a rapid change of sexual partner:

> A night he could not quietly
>   without strange women sleep;   (ibid., v. 4,3–4, lines 31–2, p. 37)

But in his heart desir'd a change
   of wanton pleasures so,
That day by day he wishes still
   strange women for to know.

And so, discharging of his traine,
   and selling of his land,
To travell into countries strange
   he quickly took in hand;
And into Antwerpe speedily
   thus all aflaunt he goes,
To see the dainty Flemish girles
   and gallant Dutchland froes.   (ibid., v. 7,5–8, lines 57–68, pp. 37–8)

The restlessness of the protagonist, as a motive of obvious relevance to the course of action, takes him to a fresh hunting-ground where the repetition of his behaviour leads on to a new phase. The erotic adventures already described at the outset by the explicit narrator as a sinful and indisputably criminal are now crowned by the merchant's son: he rapes a virgin of good family, who becomes pregnant. His victim's suicide is set at his door. His punishment follows both logically from the action and chronologically, here in a supernatural way according to the curse of the girl's mother: the guilty man decomposes while still alive.

A most notable example of an ungracious Son, who in the pride of his heart denyed his owne Father, and how God for his offence turned his meat into loathsome toades (between 1601 and 1640; RB, II, pp. 73–9) combines two motifs common to the ballad to produce an intensification of the guilt syndrome: dissipation in a large city (here for once not London but Paris) and ingratitude towards parents, represented here by the father. The first motif is given less prominence as a phase in the action than the second, which is presented in more detail. The former consists of a brief account of the protagonist's business success, wealth, carefree life and ensuing impoverishment. By selling all he possesses the father secures his son's release from debtors' prison and gives him a new start in business so that he may again accumulate wealth. The son's hard-hearted, dismissive attitude towards his old and impoverished father is in sharp contrast to the preceding sentimental begging-letter sent from the debtors' prison, which stretches over several verses. Through a miracle involving toads the son is moved to remorse and a change of heart just in time for salvation. Motivational considerations – such as the occasional remorseful lament under pressure of incarceration and the father's tearful compassion as sentimental accentuation – are subordinated to the stringency of the plot which makes clear the moral warning in the textual message, as formulated also by the presenter as speaker in the final verse.

There is a structural principle within the stringency of plot which further underlines the message, and that is the intensification from phase to phase of the action. The son's first feelings of remorse over his life of dissipation have no effect on his behaviour after his father has stepped in and he is back in his old happy circumstances. Only God's intervention with a visible signal leads to a lasting change The criminal career of one George Sands (see above, pp. 112–13) also begins with minor thieving and leads via robbery with murder and rape to the worst deed of all – encouraging other young men to become his accomplices in a life of crime. The intensification of the criminal acts in accordance with a hierarchy of values which have been violated, described in chronological order, underlines the inevitability and justness of the punishment as a turning-point and finale having action-syntagmatic and action-semantic relevance. The trials which the steadfast lovers in *The Marchant's Daughter of Bristow* undergo begin with parental opposition and continue via parting, adventures at sea for both, reunion at the moment of one partner's mortal danger, readiness of the other to die likewise, until the happy ending which though not logically predictable is in accordance with poetic justice. The trivial effect of this procedure, so frequently used in the street ballad, derives not from the aesthetic principle of intensification itself but from the action-semantic messages thereby conveyed.

A distinction can be made between the type of narrative street ballad containing a number of events in chronological order and the type whose action is concentrated on one central event. The latter either presents the turning-point in a briefly described set of previous actions, or has representative function for a number of the figures' similar experiences. The contraction of the dimension of time and logic of action results in a pointing up of the one central event. This emphasis then becomes the structural bearer of the textual message. Apart from its concern with moral themes this narrative type often portrays the comic showing-up of fools.

A fearefull and terrible Example of Gods iuste judgement executed vpon a lewde Fellow, who vsually accustomed to sweare by Gods Blood (between 1591 and 1603; *BBLB*, pp. 42–7) presents the guilt–punishment pattern only in its final phase when the punishment has begun and the incorrigible offender is continuing to sin even while suffering divine retribution. A young servant who would not desist from the blasphemous profanities he had early acquired, and who even while dying curses the death-knell with blasphemies about Christ's sacrificial blood, himself perishes miserably by bleeding from the fingers, toes, nose and heart. The concentration of wrongdoing and its penalty in one event makes clear their logical correlation through emphasis and not consecutively, as is the case where a chronological chain of events determines this correlation.

The basic principle of logic of action in the comic tale, the outwitting of a fool by his superior with or without the help of circumstance, is simplified and exaggerated through episodic reduction. Causality of action and its motivational grounds run congruently here. The didactic value is not of a moral nature but is concerned with worldly wisdom, and is overlaid with the element of amusement. In *A merry new Song how a Bruer meant to make a Cooper cuckold, and how deere the Bruer paid for the bargaine* (c. end of sixteenth century)[18] an attempt at deception (adultery) is discovered and punished by the prospective victim (husband) through a combination of chance and cunning. The cooper returns home unexpectedly in order to fetch a tool he has forgotten. Through his wife's clumsiness he discovers the concealed brewer, whom she was hoping to pass off as a pig she had hidden. The exposure of the deception provides an opportunity for double meanings in the married couple's dialogue, whereby the connotations common to the subject of conversation – 'pig/ brewer' – give expression in passint to the pleasurableness of both eating and sexual activity:

> It is hard if a woman cannot haue a bit,
> But straightway her husband must know of it.
> A bore-pig, said the Cooper, so me thinks;
> He is so ramish, – fie, how he stinkes!
>
> Well, sayd the Cooper, so I might thriue,
> I would he were in thy belly aliue. (ibid., vv. 14,1–15,2, p. 91)

The discovery is followed by a punishment whose potential ethical function is superseded by one which confirms the success of the victor: the cooper does not allow himself to be fobbed off by his rival's offers of minor favours, but helps himself to a substantial sum from the brewer's moneybox.

That this comic tale was widely known is shown by the fact that Martin Parker published a version of the story twenty or thirty years later: *The Cooper of Norfolke* (between 1625 and 1660; *RB*, I, pp. 98–104). This ballad-author's expertise is seen both in his linguistic dexterity and effective descriptive detail, and in the clear syntagmatization of action. It is now not chance but methodical planning which takes the brewer to the house of the cooper, whom he keeps out of the way by asking for some work to be done elsewhere (see v. 5, lines 25–30, p. 100). It is not the wife's clumsiness that leads to the discovery of the lover but the canny suspicion of the cooper on his unexpected return home. Concern with motivational links in the interest of a cohesive plot can also be seen in the introductory characterization of the figures as a precondition of the interaction:

> This Cooper he had a faire creature to's wife,
> Which a Brewer i'th Towne lou'd as deare as his life;
> And she had a tricke which in some wiues is rife,
> She still kept a sheath for another man's knife,[19]

The narrator participates functionally in the perspectives of the figures. Apart from frequent direct speech, Parker also uses this procedure for purposes of psychological and action-syntagmatic clarification:

> Now when the good wife and the Brewer did heare
> The Cooper at doore, affrighted they were:
> The Brewer was in such bodily feare,
> That for to hide himselfe he knew not where,
>   To shun the fierce rage of the Cooper:
>   He thought he should die by the Cooper.
>
> (ibid., v. 9, lines 49–54, p. 101)

Since the figures are largely types and subordinated to action and plot, this kind of concern for the psychological dimension is relatively seldom encountered.

An important figure in the arsenal of the comic tale and the street ballad is the scold. In *The Cobler of Colchester* the triviality of the matter of dispute, an 'Apple Pye', indicates the recurrence of a behaviour pattern with a different context each time. The pointing up of the theme through a symbolic object is brought to a final climax in the woman's demand for the return of the pie, which is taken to absurd extremes:

> And though, quoth she, indifferent well,
>   Thy carcas I did bumme,
> Yet from thy carion greedy guts
>   I'le fetch out euery crumme.
> With that she did a feather take,
>   And in his throate it thrust,
> Till vp he cast the apple pye,
>   The fruits as well as crust.   (*BBLB*, v. 7, p. 34)

A Pleasant new Ballad you here may behold, / How the Devill, though subtle, was gul'd by a Scold (1630)[20] accentuates the hopeless inferiority of the husband with a different emphasis: longing for domestic peace, he tries to deliver her into the clutches of the Devil. The latter, however, is illtreated by the vigorous wife during the ride to hell, and after seeing the place of punishment especially set up for scolds she forces him to take her back:

> 'Here, take her!' quoth the Devill,
>   'to keep her here be bold;
> For hell will not be troubled
>   with such an earthly scold.
> When I come home, I may
>   to all my fellowes tell,
> I lost my labour, and my bloud,
>   to bring a scold to hell.'   (ibid., v. 17, lines 129–36, p. 371)

The parallelism of the scold's double victory over her husband and over the Devil, an otherwise invincible partner, has the rhetorical quality of the topos: 'outdoing', through which the textual message is effectively conveyed. Parallelism of episodes, with different characters each time, is a feature of *The Pinnyng of the Basket* (see above, p. 110). The recurrence of marital power struggles, here with a victorious outcome for each of the husbands, indicates the general validity of the significance of the events. The narrator does not formulate this but merely comments on the action with humorous and mocking objectivity.

Comic highlighting of the action through restriction to one episode with an unexpected outcome, usually with reduced motivational and sometimes also causal links, effects a reception which tends to be rapid and orientated towards the present moment, without doubts being raised regarding the lack of motivations and links. The clarity, entertaining nature, and comic suspense of the action offers ease of reception and compensatory distractions. This is why comic material is so suitable for street-ballad treatment.[21] The interrelation of motifs in the street ballad and in the corresponding prose texts of the time certainly deserves investigation. In our context we are primarily concerned to show that the street ballad is orientated here towards a literary form whose structure conforms to the street-ballad principle of functional clarity within a given limited length. The mediation of the presenter, together with the additional possibilities of accentuation within verse texts, effect fundamental modifications as compared with comic tales in prose.

Parallelism of episodes, as seen in the last three ballad examples, is based on a correspondence between the significance of each event (the scold's two victories; three marital quarrels in succession between different couples ending in victory for the respective husbands). There is here a semantic structure based on isotopes[22] which exist between complete events (various quarrels between married couples) and which combine these into one theme (marital power struggle). In episodic parallels of this kind the semantic correspondence is particularly evident and consequently the theme isotopically conveyed is particularly obvious. But even if the events have only partial semantic correspondence, a common denominator can be found and with that also thematic correlation. Thus, for instance, theft, robbery with violence, rape and murder are variations on the theme of criminality in the fictional life history of a protagonist, and cards, alcohol, and whoring are variations on the theme of dissipation. The isotopic conveying of a theme is still clear enough to be relatively easily recognized. Looking back on the examples already discussed, we can see that in those life histories where the main theme emerges less clearly from the significance of events, other structural procedures, such as chronology and logic of events, dominate. These correlations are completely absent, however, if the strong similarity in the significance of events allows a direct thematic build-up on the isotopic level. The episodes are chronologically and logically almost interchangeable, though all the more closely linked thematically. The structural procedures available to the street-ballad author are, then, selected and applied with a varying predominance of one or the other.

Thematic structuring comes into its own primarily where separate events are meant to illustrate a certain recurrent and therefore typical behaviour pattern of a figure. The theme can at the same time be encapsulated in generalizations, and further clarified by the narrator's comments. In *The Cucking of a Scould*,[23] single episodes illustrate the recurrent behaviour of the wife, which are amply commented on by the narrator reporting them. The following intrusions into her domestic sphere of control bring on bouts of nagging and scolding which last for days: an item of washing on the hedge is moved to one side; someone accidentally wakes her lapdog; a 'Constable' 'did but pisse against her wall' (v.7,7–8, p. 74). The description of her public punishment (vv. 11–17, pp. 75–7) takes the aspect of 'dangerousness' in the scold theme further, as she is led away under close guard. The description ends with a sense of earthly and poetic justice having been done, so that the theme can be summarized in a concluding warning on the level of the explicit narrator. In *John Tomson and Jakaman* (see above, p. 111) much space is devoted to the self-commentary of the first-person narrator, where his suffering under his wife's jealousy is thematicized. This is illustrated in separate episodes having no chronological coordination: the harmless greeting of another woman in an inn leads to a violent quarrel;[24] a well-meaning neighbour, sometime instigator of the marriage, tries in vain to persuade the jealous wife to behave in a more sensible way;[25] the visit of a female neighbour is a welcome excuse for a jealous scene.[26]

In the following ballad, also, the thematic correlation of events is flanked by explanation and clarification on the level of the explicit narrator: *The cryes of the Dead. Or the late Murther in South-warke, committed by one Richard Price Weauer, who most vnhumaynly tormented to death a boy of thirteene yeares old, with two others before, which he brought to vntimely ends, for which he lyeth now imprissoned in the White-Lyon, till the time of his triall* (*c.* 1625). The theme of the ballad can be described as 'brutal cruelty to children', whereby the didactic deterrent effect obviously lies in the reprehensible nature of the action itself, so that the punishment of the wicked perpetrator is only briefly referred to. On the level of the narrator the theme is personalized and evaluatively accentuated through explicit outrage which merges into a summarizing report. Individual cases, deictically distinct as to person, illustrate the weaver's cruelty to his apprentices:

Many poore Prentisses
   to himselfe did he bind,
Sweete gentle children all
   of a most willing mind:
Seruing him carefully
   in this his weauing Art,
Whome he requited still,
   with a most cruel heart.   (*PG*, no. 39, pp. 222–8, v. 3, p. 224)

The first a pretty boy,
   had with a suddaine spurne,
One of his eares strooke off,
   woefully rent and torne:
Where vnder surgeons hands,
   he liued long in woe,
By this same grieuous wound,
   this vilaine gaue him so.   (ibid., v. 7, p. 225)

In the following series of examples, where a chronology is at least implied, what could here still be seen as a violent outburst turns into systematic cruelty with fatal consequences: one apprentice is slowly beaten to death (v. 12, p. 226); another is tortured with a closely described whip for showing clumsiness and incompetence when working in the cold (vv. 13–15, pp. 226–7) – a realistic difficulty for a weaver's apprentice. The mutilated corpse of the third victim is discovered, and in the last verse the narrator hands over the criminal to justice, with a role-change to the presenter giving a warning:

(Oh *Price*,) deare is the price
   for this blood thou must pay,
Life for life, bloud for bloud,
   on thy domes dying day,
Pray thou for mercy there,
   to saue thy sinfull soule,
For me thinks I doe heare,
   thy passing Bell doth toule.   (ibid., v. 19, p. 228)

The structural procedures in the narrative street ballad which have so far been described apply largely to the action where the figure has the function of furthering the plot. An integration of the figure into the context of the action in a wider sense, as a psychological entity, is usually limited to brief information on the figure's characteristics merely as preconditions for the action to follow, or a description of direct reactions to new circumstances. A more complex presentation of character or even of individual psychological processes is largely absent, and would in any case not correspond to the possibilities and intentions of the street-ballad short narrative. Where there is no explicit information given on the figure relevant to the action, he or she is at any rate indirectly characterized by his or her deeds – as a murderer, blasphemer, wastrel, hen-pecked husband, nagging or jealous wife, prostitute, etc. On the whole a congruence can be discerned between motivational elements, whether implicit or explicit, and chronological and thematic syntagmatic elements including those relating to the logic of the action.

The first-person narrative is particularly suited to motivational structuring because of the subjectivity inherent in the first-person perspective. In it, there is a tendency to break the chronological pattern in favour of a mental and emotional working out of moral and psychological links such as guilt and atonement, as was shown in the examples *John Spenser* and *Jane Shore* (see above, pp. 115–19). When commenting on the careless, pleasure-loving phase of his life, John Spenser draws a causal link between his good looks, success with girls, his arrogant behaviour towards his wife, and finally his committing murder under the influence of drink:

> Heauen shewed his part in making me,
>   proper in limbes and face,
> Yet of it I no true vse made,
>   but reapt thereby disgrace.

> For being proud in dancings art,
>   most womens loues I gaynd:
> By them a long time was my life
>   in gallant sort maintaynd:
> No Mayden young, about the towne,
>   but ioyfull was to see
> The face of *Spenser*, and would spend,
>   all for to daunce with mee.

> I spent my time in Ryoting,
>   and proudly led my life,
> I had my choyce of damsels fayre,
>   what card I for my wife,
> If once she came to intreat me home,
>   I'd kick her out of doors,
> Indeed I would be ruld by none,
>   but by intising whores.

> At length being pledging of a Glasse,
>   my hopes I did confound:
> And in my rag[e] I feld my friend,
>   with one blow to the ground.   (vv. 15,5–18,4, *PG*, pp. 260–1)

The protagonist's self-knowledge is developed, through his narrative perspective, to include an appreciation and value of his wife, the only person to visit her now friendless husband in prison (see vv. 19–20, p. 261), and an acceptance of a just punishment.

Jane Shore's account of her life follows the chronological course of the rise and fall of the king's mistress which, at the same time, shows a logic of guilt and punishment in the course of events as seen from the perspective of the repentant narrator. A fairly detailed and explicit psychological rationale for her actions is given alongside these links: marriage to the goldsmith against her will at the instigation of greedy parents (see v. 2, lines 7–10, RB, I, p. 484); her job as saleswoman in her husband's shop, which is frequented by fine gentlemen of the town, increases her vanity (vv. 4–5, lines 15–26, p. 484); it still needs the influence of a woman friend to persuade her to agree to the king's wishes; her new status then fills her with joy and triumph:

> Yet mistress Blague, a neighbour near,
> Whose friendship I esteemèd dear,
> Did say it was a gallant thing
> To be belovèd of a King.

> By her perswasions I was led
> For to defile my marriage-bed,
> And wrong my wedded husband, Shore,
> Whom I had lov'd ten years before.

> In heart and mind I did rejoyce
> That I had made so sweet a choice;
> And therefore did my state resign,
> To be King Edward's Concubine.

> From City then to Court I went,
> To reap the pleasures of content;
> And had the Joys that love could bring,
> And knew the secrets of a King.   (ibid., vv. 8–11, lines 31–46, pp. 484–5)

The account of her sudden fall after the king's death also articulates the feelings of humiliation and remorse connected with it, which establish the link with the fictional present of the events narrated. The complementary account of her husband's life in Part II of the ballad has a similar psychological dimension concerned with motivational links. He regrets the mistake of his rash marriage to a young and inexperienced girl (v. 42, lines 177–82, p. 489), and gives the reason for his decision to leave the country as a feeling of shame and outrage:

> But when the King possest my room,
> And cropt my rosie, gallant bloom –
> Fair London's blossom, and my joy –
> My heart was drown'd in deep annoy
>   To think how unto publick shame
>   Thy wicked life brought my good name.

> And then I thought each man and wife,
> In jesting sort, accus'd my life;
> And every one to the other said,

> That Shore's fair wife the wanton plaid.
>   Thereby in mind I grew to change
>   My dwelling in some Country strange.
>
> (ibid., vv. 43–4, lines 183–94, p. 489)

The psychological motivation for his action becomes more complex owing to the contradiction in his feelings: alongside shame and outrage is the sadness of departing (v. 47, lines 207–12, p. 490), and his eager interest in her fortunes, which he follows from afar with the help of a magician (v. 53, lines 243–8, p. 491), is accompanied by a reluctance to return until he believes his shame to be forgotten (v. 56, lines 261–6, p. 491).

A goodfellowes complaint against strong beere (c. 1630; PG, no. 63, pp. 361–4) is by contrast extremely simple, hammering home the message with redundant repetition. In the continual contrasting of past and present, with the use of clear adverbial markers ('once – but now'; 'when I had . . . – but now' and the like), the structure of the first-person narrative is used to prove that alcohol addiction was the cause of a change in fortune leading to poverty and the loss of all friends. The protagonist's ruling passion is the direct logical cause of his past behaviour and its present consequences. The quantitative intensification and emphasis of the motivational link serves to further the textual warning intent which is at the same time made explicit by the speaker.

> I once enioyed both house and land,
> But now 'tis otherwise you see,
> My moneys spent my cloathes are pawnd:
> And tis strong beere that has vndone mee.   (ibid., v. 3, p. 361)

> My little hostes at the crowne,
> Would often sit vpon my knee,
> But now sheele cry away thou clowne,
> Because strong beere has vndone me.   (ibid., v. 15, p. 363)

> All you good fellowes that heare my case,
> Take heede least it your owne case be,
> I might haue liu'd void of disgrace,
> Had not strong beere thus vndone me.   (ibid., v. 25, p. 364)

It is a characteristic of the first-person perspective that it takes into account the psychology of the figures, a feature which does not only apply to the narrative street ballad. The role-play ballad also contains motivational links far more frequently than the third-person narrative. A rare example of motivation consistently determining action in a third-person narrative is *Any thing for a quiet life; Or the Married mans bondage to a curst Wife* (c. 1625; PB, no. 49, II, pp. 16–21). The need for domestic peace and a modicum of personal freedom is the reason for the husband's compliance which is shown in a series of episodes. This basic idea behind the events described, as also the psychological motivation formulated in the refrain, overlays the loose chronological order, to a certain extent levelling it out. The nature of this marriage is determined by the husband's accommodation to the changing moods and extravagant wishes of the wife.

> His wife (yong Lasse) grew wāton sick,
>   within a day or two:
> And long'd, she knew not well for what,
>   as many women doe.
> The daintiest things that could be got,
>   he gaue vnto his wife,
> And for her sake, did vndertake
>   any thing for a quiet life.   (ibid., v. 3, p. 18)

> At last her Child-bed time drew on,
>   where money must be spent:
> In dainty Lawnes & Cambricks fine,
>   or else no way content.
> Her house must be as well set out,
>   as any Citie wife:
> Thus fill'd with care, he must not spare,
>   any thing for a quiet life.   (ibid., v. 7, p. 19)

The most frequent motivational force in literary fictions is love. Additional motivation is found to be unnecessary, and an explication of this psychological condition is optional. Romantic and sentimental love stories in the street ballad, whose action is determined by this motivation, presume similarly that it is well known to all. Rarely is it presented in more detail, as for example in *The Marchant's Daughter of Bristow* (see above, p. 126), where the emotions of the protagonist are described through both the explicit narrator and the figure's own speech:

> 'Now will I walke, with joyfull heart,
>   To viewe the town whereas my darling doth remaine,
> And seek him out in every part,
>   Until I doe his sight attaine.' (ibid., v. 35, lines 137–40, RB, II, p. 91)

The motivational link between love and the overcoming of obstacles and dangers in order to realize this love is only at this point made explicit, although it is of course the basis for the sequence of events with the accompanying expressions of suffering uttered by the figures. The core of the plot, the motif of the faithful maiden who follows her lover with great difficulty (often disguised as a male), goes back via the dramatic ballad *The Nutbrown Maid* (see below, chapter 4.3.1) to the folk-ballad tradition (see 'Child Waters', Child no. 63). The girl's conduct is proof of her faithful love which, as the impetus for the plot, determines the sequence of events. In the Grizel material, this motivation underlies events which as hyperbolical test situations lose their credibility and should rather be understood symbolically. It is perhaps for this reason that the street-ballad version *A most pleasant Ballade of Patient Grissell* (seventeenth century; *RB*, II, pp. 268–74) shows the psychological motivation explicitly to be obedience and the topos of Grizel's patience, both in the speech of the figures and in narrative comment.

Apart from isolated instances, in the text corpus as a whole there is relatively little concern for motivational links, although again these are not expected of the short narrative. What is noticeable is that they are usually completely subordinated to the demands of the logic of the action. This characterizes the street ballad as predominantly orientated towards action, which indeed applies to all the contemporary narrative literature and corresponds to requirements for its entertainment value. A detailed presentation of motivational grounds for the course of the action is therefore the exception. One rare example is Martin Parker's ballad:

> *The father hath beguil'd the sonne,*
> *Or, a wonderfull Tragedy, which lately befell in*
> *Wiltshire, as many men knovv full well.*
>
> (1629; *PG*, no. 54, pp. 309–15)

The deception announced in the title and repeatedly emphasized in the refrain is that of the father stealing the son's girl. This leads to suicide first of the son and then of the girl, which leaves the father insane. In each of the phases of the sensational plot, motivation is treated with a detail most unusual in the street ballad. The opening description of the son's falling in love prepares the motivational ground for his later act of despair. As a motivational link for the ensuing rivalry, the father's falling in love is also described, with the narrator's attitude shown in the epithets.

> A pretty young maid,
> In the place aforesaid:
>   in a Gentlemans house did dwell
> And this youthfull lad
> So much view of her had,
>   that with her in loue he soone fell:
> By day and by night
> He wisht for her sight,
>   and she at the last was wonne.   (ibid., v. 3,1–3,9, p. 310)

> So to haue a view
> Of his Louer true,
>   the sonne with his father went:
> And when they came there
> The Lasse did appeare,
>   so faire and so louely a one,
> That the old doting churle,
> Fell in loue with the girle
>   *and sought to beguile his own sonne.*   (ibid., v. 5,4–5,12, p. 311)

In keeping with the stock types of contemporary figure, the father is described as a lecherous old man. During his persuasion of the young girl to marry him, her motive for agreeing is conveyed in the dialogue: she is unable to resist the lure of riches. The incident of suicide, an unusual subject even for the street ballad, as an act of despair is given comparatively differentiated motivation: for the son it is dismay and shame at the disgrace, for the girl the sudden insight into the stupidity and irresponsibility of her actions in the light of the consequences (see vv. 8–13, pp. 312–14). The father's remorse is manifested in his madness:

> The young-man with griefe,
> Heard of this mischiefe
>   and blaming this monstrous part,
> Before both their faces,
> Unto their disgraces,
>   he stab'd himselfe to the heart:
> The vnnaturall dad,
> Ran presently mad:
>   repenting of what he had done,
> He runs vp and downe,
> From towne vnto towne,
>   *and hourely calles on his sonne.*
>
> The faithlesse young wife,
> Weary of her life,
>   (to thinke what folly befell)
> Ran straight in all hast,
> And headlong shee cast
>   herselfe in a deepe draw-well.
> And there shee was found,
> Next morning quite drown'd
>   these things for certaine were done,
> Some sixe weekes agoe,
> As many men know,
>   *that knew both father and sonne.*   (ibid., vv. 14–15, p. 314)

In this ballad emotional reactions play an essential part in determining the sequence of events; they are also important quantitatively, taking up a large proportion of the text. One reason for this unusual procedure could be the literary skill of this author, who tends to pay particular attention to the psychological dimension of his plots.

The establishing of motivational links between the figure and its actions is part of a process of figure presentation which will now be investigated more closely. The fictional figure as both determiner of the action and psychological entity is an essential component of the subject of communication in the narrative speech situation. As conveyed in the text the figure can be understood as an information paradigm correlating functionally with other figures through semantic composition while at the same time distinct from them.[27] The presentation of figures in the narrative text can thus be described from the following viewpoints: information on a figure's spectrum of characteristics and psychological processes can be given both by the narrator and on the level of communication of the figures, whereby the latter characterize either themselves or others. The information can be graded according to the level of explicitness or implicitness involved; within the textual content, implicit presentation of figures means that a particular textual element or pattern of elements (e.g. a type of behaviour) is a connotative indication of a characteristic or immediate state of mind of a figure. On the level of the figures there is seldom explicit characterization, either of themselves or others. Implicit information about figures is primarily conveyed through the all-important action and its various structural procedures: the significance of the events points connotatively to a characteristic of a figure (losing a marital quarrel indicates an inability to stand up for oneself, murder indicates brutality and lack of conscience, card-playing and drinking indicate a frivolous nature, etc.). The semantically isotopic ordering of events thematicizes a characteristic even more clearly, and logical links in the action imply possible corresponding changes in character (from immorality to insight, from culpability to remorse, etc.) which have to be in chronological order. It will not be necessary to give further examples of the implicit characterization function of the street-ballad plot. The extent of information on a figure in the street ballad is necessarily small, so that the result is the presentation in most cases of a stock type.

As far as the position in the text is concerned, it is a feature of the street ballad that a brief characterization of the main figure or constellation of opposing figures precedes the account of events. An explicitly conveyed introduction of the figures before the action commences gives information exclusively about the characteristics which influence the course of events. The motivational link has a function which is quite clear and strictly geared to the action. In this it also has an expositional and anticipatory function which contributes to the textual coherence of the individual ballad. Its value to the recipient is proved by the recurrence of this procedure in the text corpus.

> A Wedded wife there was,
> I wis of yeeres but yong,
> But if you thinke she wanted wit,
> Ile sweare she lackt no tongue.
> Iust seventeene yeeres of age,
> This woman was no more,
> Yet she would scold with any one,
> From twenty to threescore.   (PG, no. 12, pp. 72–7, v. 1, p. 72)

The first verse of *The Cucking of a Scould* (*c.* 1615?)[28] gives information about the ruling passion of the scold which is shown in some of its excesses in the rest of the ballad and taken as far as public punishment. Garrulous-ness ('tongue' as a metonymical reference) acquires a pejorative conno-tation through the comparison with 'wit', a connotation which is reinforced by the reducing of this garrulousness to scolding and nagging. This characteristic, now well established as a negative quality, assumes particular importance through the ironic reference to the special achieve-ment of the woman in successfully mastering the art of scolding at so early an age, as the following episodes show.

In *The cryes of the Dead* (*c.* 1625)[29] the weaver's cruelty to his apprentice is based on his disposition. This is explained by means of a hierarchy according to the respective level of commonness of his trans-gressions. Starting with the establishing of his moral and theological state of sinfulness the narrative goes on, via the reference to his continual wickedness, to describe his specific bloodthirsty cruelty:

> One *Price*, in South-warke dwelt
>   a Weauer by his trayde,
> But a more graceles man
>   I thinke was neuer made:
> All his life wicked was,
>   and his minde bent to blood,
> Nothing but cruelty
>   did his heart any good.   (ibid., v. 2, p. 224)

The introduction of the protagonist in Part I of *John Spenser* is particu-larly detailed. This is a ballad in which the motivational grounds for the crime and for the repentance of the perpetrator are taken into consider-ation far more than usual.[30] It is indicative that only this third-person part of the narrative gives a total character summary, while the first-person narrative of Part II consistently reflects the relationship of personality structure, circumstances and action. The information in Part I concerning the figure, which precedes the actual account of events, is a necessary complement to Part II. It presents a detailed picture of John Spenser as a popular and successful citizen, whose lapses and decline appear at first astonishing but can later be explained psychologically. In this – from a motivational point of view – relatively complex ballad, the introductory characterization of the figure can have an expository function, but no longer one which is strictly in anticipation of the action.

> At *Acton*, neere *Nantwich* was borne
>   this man, so famde of all;
> Whose skill at each braue exercise,
>   was not accounted small:

> For beating of the war-like Drumme,
>   no man could him surpasse:
> For dauncing, leaping, and such like,
>   in *Cheshire* neuer was.
>
> For shooting none durst him oppose,
>   hee would ayme so faire and right;
> Yet long he shot in crooked Bowes,
>   and could not hit the white:
> For striuing still more things to learne,
>   the more he grew beloued;
> No Shomaker but *Spenser* braue,
>   by women was so prooued.[31]

These examples represent a substantial number of narrative ballads showing similar procedures, where the account of events is prefaced by information concerning the characteristics of figures which explains the actions following on directly from them. The motivation for the protagonist's actions is not necessarily restricted to one figure, however, but can also derive from an opposing or complementary constellation of figures as the basis for interactions which determine the course of the action. In the following textual examples pairs of figures are introduced: a peace-loving husband and his scolding wife whose superiority is proved during the course of the action even over the devil (. . . *How the Devill . . . was gul'd by a Scold*);[32] a pair of lovers whose faithfulness overcomes all obstacles (*The Marchant's Daughter of Bristow*);[33] and another pair, Leander and Hero, who through their noble origins and beauty are introduced as the ideal couple they then prove to be during the course of the romance-like action (*Leanders loue to loyall Hero*, 1614; PG, no. 8, pp. 49–53).

> A woman well in yeares
>   liv'd with a husband kinde,
> Who had a great desire
>   to live content in minde:
> But 'twas a thing unpossible
>   to compasse his desire;
> For night and day with scolding
>   she did her husband tire.   (RB, II, p 368, v. 4, lines 25–32)
>
> Behold the touchstone of true love,
>   Maudlin the Marchant's daughter of Bristow towne,
> Whose firme affection nothing could move,
>   Such favour beares the lovely browne.
> A gallant youth was dwelling by,
>   Which many yeeres had borne this mayden great good will,
> She lovèd him as faithfully,
>   But all her friendes withstood it still.   (RB, II, p. 87, vv. 1–2, lines 1–8)

> Two famous Louers once there was,
>   whom Fame hath quite forgott.
> Who loued long most constantly,
>   without all enuious blott;
> Shee was most faire, and hee as true:
>   which caused that which did ensue; fa la,
>
>   . . .
>
> Leander was this young-mans name,
>   right Noble by dessent:
> And Hero, she whose beautie rare,
> might giue great Ioue content,
> He at Abidos kept his Court,
>   and she at Sestos liued in sport, fa la,
>
> (PG, pp. 49–50, v. 1,1–1,6 and v. 2,1–2,6)

The introduction of figures before the start of the action can be seen as
constituting an element of functional clarification. The figure and the
action are first presented separately in the text, making for ease of comprehension, but at the same time attention is implicitly drawn to the
functional motivational link. Explicit information on figures' characteristics accompanying the course of the action can also be segmented and
therefore easily and clearly recognized. It provides the psychological
motivational link directly at the precise and relevant point in the text. A
clarifying procedure of this kind, where motivational links are given in the
presentation of figures directly by the narrator, can be seen for instance in
A most notable example of an ungracious Son:[34]

> For, having now the world at will,
>   his mind was wholly bent
> To gaming, wine and wantonnesse,
>   till all his goods were spent.
> Yea, such excessive riotousnesse
>   by him was shewèd forth,
> That he was three times more in debt
>   then all his wealth was worth.   (ibid., p. 3, lines 17–24, RB, II, p. 75)

The young man's wealth and business success – described in the preceding verse – lead to a recurrent behaviour pattern which can be summed
up in the characteristic 'excessive riotousnesse'. The motivational link is
already made explicit by the conjunction 'for' at the beginning of the verse.
A further consequence of the action ('that') is debt and an ensuing change
of fortune. When, after the father's intervention, his former way of life can
be resumed,[35] the hard-heartedness appears which although a consequence of wealth ('so') is presented at the same time as a contradiction
('but') of the opportunities for generosity provided by that wealth:

few men were found so rich.

But as his goods did still increase,
   and riches in did slide:
So more and more his hardened heart
   did swell in hatefull pride. (ibid., vv. 13,8–14,4, lines 104–8, p. 77f.)

A happy-go-lucky nature and a tendency to dissipation are the characteristics and behaviour which frequently constitute the basis for a life history or phase of life ending at the very least in financial ruin if not in a harsher punishment.[36] The relevance to the action of these motivational grounds has already been pointed out in the example *A Warning to Youth* (see above, pp. 124–5). In so far as they suggest the individual's responsibility for himself, the motivational grounds of immoral behaviour have a clarifying function for the moral and didactic intension of such ballads. Where, on the other hand, character weaknesses derive from external circumstances (*Dice, Wine and Women*),[37] the didactic effect is reduced. Significantly, the tenor of this ballad is humorous and the fulfilment of poetic justice limited to loss of money and the protagonist's return to his home in the country. The refrain refers explicitly to the motivation as being primarily linked to the situation:

> *The causes why I am so poore,*
> *Are Dice, Strong-waters, and a whore.*

Only a gradual distinction can be made between figures' characteristics which are fixed or effective over a long period, rapid changes of attitude, and immediate psychological processes which determine behaviour and the ensuing course of action. Distinctions can be recognized not only in the information content but also in the nature of the narrative communication; a fixed characteristic can be attributed to the figure as something relatively common through an explicit statement of the narrator, as is the case in most of the examples given so far. In contrast, immediate psychological processes are characterized as transient; they are therefore expressed in verbs whose subject is the figure him or herself. Where patterns of behaviour are presented as repetitive and therefore typical, a fixed characteristic emerges: the habitual nagging of the 'Scold',[38] the habitual swearing of the blasphemer (see above, pp. 114–15), the socially integrating activities of John Spenser (see above, pp. 115–17) and an ideal pattern of behaviour of a pair of lovers (see above, pp. 117–18).

A presentation of figures accompanying the course of the action and explaining every phase of it, correlating the affective processes with the corresponding individual reactions, is relatively seldom found in the street ballad. Alongside the first-person narratives already discussed, Martin Parker's version of the comic tale of the cooper and the brewer[39] is an example of a complex procedure of this kind:

> Now when the good wife and the Brewer did heare
> The Cooper at doore, affrighted they were:
> The Brewer was in such a bodily feare,
> That for to hide himselfe he knew not where,
>   To shun the fierce rage of the Cooper:
>   He thought he should die by the Cooper.
>   (ibid., v. 9, lines 49–54, p. 101)

> The Cooper mistrusted some knauerie to be
> Hid vnder the brewing Fat, and therefore hee
> Was fully resolu'd for his mind-sake to see.
>   (ibid., v. 15, 1–3, lines 85–90, p. 102)

> He feared the rage of the Cooper,
> Yet still he intreated the Cooper. (ibid., v. 19, 5–6, lines 113–14, p. 102)

> Iohn was so farre in affection with that,
> That he tooke up handfuls and filled his Hat.
>   (ibid., v. 23, 1–3, lines 133–5, p. 103)

> Thus money can pacifie the greatest strife;
> For Iohn neuer after found fault with his wife.
>   (ibid., v. 24, 1–2, lines 139–40)

The two last quotations refer to the cooper's successful blackmailing of the brewer, now revealed as a rival. The former helps himself generously from the cooper's moneybox, providing a basis for a reconciliation with his wife through his new-found prosperity. However simplistic and directly related to the action this character psychology may be – fear of discovery, canny suspicion, and avarice – it adds a further dimension to the action, providing, within the aesthetics of reception, an opportunity for identification. This also applies to the first-person comic narrative of the husband plagued with a jealous wife.[40] He reflects on his situation not only on the explicit narrative level, but also describes his reactions in events given as examples. This iterative–durative method points up the static nature of the correlative characteristics of the figures: the wife's jealousy and the husband's inability to stand up for himself:

> Thus when I come in company,
>   I passe my mirth in feare,
> For one or other, merrily,
>   will say my wife is there;
> And then my look doth make them laugh
>   to see my woful case;
> How I stand like John Hold-my-staffe,
>   and dare not shew my face. (ibid., v. 3, lines 22–9, RB, II, p. 138)

The most important and didactically effective change of attitude in the narrative street ballad is repentance as a reaction to preceding phases of the action. The effect of repentance on the following action is usually only slight. It is mainly in serious cases, where a crime has been committed, that repentance ensures the protagonist at least the prospect of forgiveness in the next world, though no happy end in this one. This psychological state therefore frequently characterizes the narrative perspective in street ballads with first-person narrator where, usually shortly before execution, a criminal past is reappraised with insight and contrition. The account of the past in such 'good-nights' or 'hanging-ballads', a sub-category of the 'repentance ballad', is essentially determined by the protagonist's perspective of remorse with its concomitant reflection and evaluation (see also the examples above, pp. 115–18). The woman who murdered her husband (*The vnnaturall Wife*, 1628; *PG*, no. 49, pp. 283–7) realizes: 'But now too late I doe repent . . .' (v. 2,5, p. 284) and during the course of the description condemns her deed as 'murther most inhumane' (v. 1,7–1,8, p. 284), 'bloody crime' (v. 5,4, p. 285), 'foule and bloody fact' (v. 10,3, p. 286) and the like. The child murderess (*No naturall Mother, but a Monster*)[41] formulates her remorse primarily as a lament: 'woe is me, woe is me',[42] with which she accompanies her account of the unwanted pregnancy, birth, and the final rash act of desperation. There are also other elements of repetition in the account (in the second line of each verse) which underline the consistent emotive tenor of the ballad. It can be seen here also that the first-person perspective is particularly suited to a detailed presentation of motivational links – usually recurring grounds for the plot consisting of one characteristic only – indeed this perspective practically cries out for such a method of presentation.

Remorse taking place as an immediate change of attitude during the course of the action is also a common motivational link, although this occurs predominantly in third-person narratives. A representative example of this is *A most notable example of an ungracious Son* . . . (see above, pp. 141–2, where the son's first severe setback in life, accompanied by insight and remorse, is cancelled out by his father's aid and support:

> And living in this wofull case,
>   his eyes with teares he spent;
> The lewdnesse of his former life
>   too late he did repent:
> And being void of all reliefe,
>   of helpe and comfort quite;
> Unto his father, at the last,
>   he thus began to write: (ibid., v. 5, lines 33–40, *RB*, II, p. 75)

In this ballad the rare instance occurs where, in spite of his serious misdeeds, the repentant protagonist is granted a second chance to change his ways and reform:

For when the fayrest pye was cut,
    a strange and dreadfull case,
Most ugly toades came crawling out,
    and leapèd at his face.
Then did this wretch his fault confesse,
    and for his father sent;
And for his great ingratitude
    full sore he did repent.   (ibid., v. 20, lines 153–60, p. 79)

The procedures of figure presentation dealt with so far are characterized by explicitness, whether this involves naming characteristics outright or describing psychological states and inner processes. Implicit presentation of figures is achieved by means of the action itself, which connotatively points up the figure's role in furthering the plot. The speech of the figures also contributes to implicit presentation, in so far as it contains intentions to act or actions themselves. In the lover's words of farewell, the sorrow of parting and the extent of his love are expressed,[43] and in the promise of support, the helper's loyalty (v. 36, lines 141–4, p. 91); the refusal to commit a certain action shows strength of character;[44] the appeal for help reveals the figure's dire straits and inability to cope, the content of which, since this is a characteristic dependent on situation, is always specified;[45] the assurance of loyalty gives a direct indication of the corresponding characteristic and attitude;[46] the intention of persuading another to commit a wicked deed shows the speaker to be morally degenerate;[47] a command shows him to be superior and mindful of retaining and confirming his (e.g. domestic) authority;[48] abuse reveals a malicious and aggressive nature.[49]

The presentation of figures in the street-ballad narrative is mainly orientated towards the action. A figure's characteristics and changes of attitude both cause and directly explain his or her actions. Information about the figure is given primarily by the explicit narrator, whether it is at the beginning of the text or accompanies the action as it happens. The figures are outlined in simple, clear terms. The explicit, unambiguous, and reliable nature of the information about the figure is in keeping with a tendency to clarify which can be observed elsewhere in the street ballad.

The analytical segmentation of the structural procedures in the narrative street ballad's subject of narration shows that there is clarification on several levels which, in combination, are intended to elucidate the textual message. The number, predominance, and complementary association of the structural levels are determined by this intention. If the textual message is expressed through the structural principle of logic of action, reinforced by chronological congruence, the semantic structuring plays only a minor role. If the subject of narration is limited to one episode, the clarification of the total message is effected by a pointing up of the links in the action. Where several episodes are neither linked chronologically nor connected through logic of action, the thematic correlation predominates. In all these cases motivational links remain subordinate. That is, information about the figures' characteristics is given functionally as a reason for their actions, in keeping with the other structural procedures. Only rarely does the figure as a psychological entity acquire an overriding complexity and autonomy compared with the course of the action. Within this procedure, explicit information is primarily given by the narrator. The frequent position of the information at the beginning of the text, with its expositional and anticipatory function, similarly aids the understanding of the motivational link. Where this remains implicit, it is indicated by action which is reported or communicated through dialogue.

The coordination of structural procedures is on the whole characterized by the predominance of one level, with the complementary support of others. The resulting structural clarity is matched by redundant reference to the theme within a text. Both of these have the object of clarifying the textual message as fully as possible. Thus 'functional transparency', as a basic structural principle of the subject of narration, means that a simplifying clarity, from the syntagmatic and semantic points of view, serves above all to help in understanding the text. It will be shown that this structural principle predominates not only in the narrative street ballad. It is augmented by the personalization of the communication process on the level of the presenter, the narrator, the dramatic figure, and the discursive speaker, all of which effect a communication-orientated ease of reception.

4.2.3 Overriding importance of the event and reduction of the figure in the 'news ballad'

The English broadside ballad has frequently been referred to by literary historians as an early form of journalism, whether in the wider sense, embracing all 'light' material,[50] or in the narrower sense of news reporting as a separate area of the text corpus labelled 'journalistic ballad' as opposed to the section labelled 'literary ballad'.[51] 'Literary' means here that a ballad is based on contemporary literary tradition as regards both form and content, implying at the same time a higher evaluation. The 'journalistic' ballad, on the other hand, with its close connection with topicality and pseudo-topicality, is held to be far more inferior in quality, especially as its tendency to lies and sensation exposed it to ridicule and contempt.[52] From the point of view of the history of newspapers the matter has been presented more precisely: within the whole spectrum of the forerunners and early forms of English journalism the street ballad has its fairly fixed position and is characterized by set functions. Before the emergence of periodicals with news content and commentaries in the third decade of the seventeenth century,[53] the street ballad, together with other broadsides with prose texts, chapbooks, pamphlets, and the more extensive books,[54] was a form of journalistic communication of political and moral–theological panegyric. It was also a vehicle of expression for pressure groups (especially for political and religious propaganda), and above all a means of communicating didactically orientated news of an entertaining nature.[55] During the course of the seventeenth century there is an increasing functional division between the street ballad as 'yellow journalism' on the one hand, and on the other the journalism of the *corantos* (circulating newsletters), periodical newsbooks, periodicals and newspapers which were gradually taking on a more serious character.[56] The distribution method of the broadside ballad by performance and street sales very probably constituted a distinct advantage as regards reaching potential receivers of news, especially in the early period of journalism, as long as most other printed matter was sold on permanent stalls and without the energy and effort of the presenter which was peculiar to the street ballad.

The concept of 'news', however, with its factual content, topicality value, and relationship to 'comment' in the modern understanding of the term, cannot simply be transposed on to the sixteenth- and seventeenth-century environment. It is well known that the 'news transmission' of the time was in no way constrained by an obligation to provide factual authenticity, even when this was claimed and often believed in. Claims to and fictions proving authenticity combined with a new need for topicality, a need which not only involved a short time lapse between events and report but also relevance for the recipient (see K. Koszyk and K. H. Pruys [1969], p. 27). Within the street-ballad genre this can be observed in the titles, where the term 'true relation', ('reporte, description' and the like) is combined with exact details of place and time and the epithet 'new' in conjunction with 'ballad, ditty, song', etc., signals uniqueness and topicality.[57] As far as I can ascertain, the formula 'news from . . . ', widely used synonymously with 'true relation', is not in common use until the middle of the seventeenth century.[58] The lapse of time after the actual event, or what was claimed as such, tended to vary. In the case of the street ballad it was in fact rather greater than with other forms of 'reporting', since the former was often based on a previously published prose text.[59] The relevance for the recipient was greatly stressed, and made explicit through a moral/didactic reflection which is possibly comparable to the 'comment' of today. Comment in the street ballad is, however, less clearly separated from the 'news' than is at least normally expected of modern journalism. It predominates above all in early ballads, where events are used merely as 'pegs' on which to hang sermons, exhortations, and attempts to persuade and influence (see R. Köster [1969], p. 77). In this they form part of a long tradition of religious and political song (see T. Wright [1895–61]; 1839). M. A. Shaaber summarizes the journalistic importance and function of the street ballad amongst the forerunners of the newspaper in England as follows:

Normally a news-ballad is not so much a record of events as a commentary upon them; it is not a harbinger of news but a follower in its wake, expressing the opinion of the mass of the people about it. That it served to some extent, nevertheless, to give currency to the news is not to be doubted, but its own substance is chiefly emotional rather than literal. A ballad on the queen's opening of Parliament is likely to be not so much a description of what took place as an enthusiastic huzza for the most famous, gracious, wise, and splendid of sovereigns and a sincere testimonial of loyalty; a ballad on the French king's defeat of the league will probably have little to say about military operations, but it will be sure to emit a crow of triumph over the discomfiture of the pope and to warn England against Catholic machinations; a ballad on a flood in the north may very well omit all but the meagrest particulars, but it will not fail to expatiate plentifully on this evidence of God's mercy in chastening the sinful or to exhort his people to repentance. The ballad, then, tends to distil the essence of a recent event rather than to disperse itself among the details; unlike a true report of news, it is derived not from the circumstances of outward occurrences, but from the impression they make on the popular mind. As contemporary historical documents these ballads are highly unsatisfactory, but as revelations of the majority opinion on passing events they are perfect.[60]

In attempting to place the news ballad systematically within the text corpus, thereby facilitating its more precise description, it is necessary to see its journalistic features from the standpoint of literary analysis. The question of reliability and factualness can then be understood in terms of frames of reference and the problem of fictional inventions. The relation between news and commentary concerns the nature and extent of the subject of communication in relation to the speaker. That is, where the commentary predominates we have a discursive ballad with the news as a 'peg', and where there is an event, however conveyed, we have a narrative ballad with commentary from a sharply defined explicit narrator. The reduction of the figures to mere agents furthering the plot is relevant as a criterion for classifying the news ballad as a sub-category of the narrative street ballad. Such agents would then also include as 'figures' natural phenomena, demons, animals, the dead, and objects of all kinds which can similarly constitute the subject of the street-ballad news broadcast (e.g. storm, fire, appearance of the devil, taking of cities, monsters etc.). Human beings may participate in the action but are not presented as psychological entities. The level of motivational correlation, the presence of which is a criterion of fictionality, is omitted in favour of an emphasis on events. Seen from the standpoint of journalistic analysis, serious news items and commentaries refrain from giving information on people's emotional life unless it is expressly specified as background knowledge or interview.

Thus if the street-ballad narrator gives information on a figure's emotional life he does not describe this as something which has been researched but suggests it – in the modern sense at least – as a fiction. The personal statement of the first-person narrative (and in the role-play ballad) is certainly similar to the interview in form, but reference to factual investigation in the person of an interviewer is absent.

The structural distinction between absolute predominance of the event in the news ballad and motivational links in the other narrative ballads enables us to delimit the two types according to our observation of the texts. The assessment of fictionality on the basis of fictional centres of awareness in the text, and also with regard to reference and allusion, is, of course, dependent on the attitude of the recipient and therefore historically variable. Since this is in the end the decisive pragmatic criterion of fictionality[61] it is necessary to differentiate between the modern reader of the street ballad and the majority of ballad recipients of the time. While the modern reader will recognize a report of a fire disaster as news, verifiable by reference to sources, and criminal biographies of psychological interest and ballads retailing marvels as fictional, most ballad recipients of the time would accept all these indiscriminately as true accounts. The true, possible, or impossible references of the journalistic message are thus from the pragmatic standpoint historically variable and therefore of only limited use as a criterion of classification. The textual distinction according to structural criteria is by comparison more objective; we must, however, expect to find smooth transitions between fictional narrative and pure reporting, since many street ballads show a definite predominance of events. There is obviously a difference, however, between, for example, a criminal ballad with motivational links which are subordinated to the logic of the action, and a report of a church tower collapsing after being struck by lightning. As to aesthetic effect this difference can be described – leaving out the question of fiction – as that between the quasi-factual and unambiguous event on the one hand, and on the other the more subtle appeal of the motivational dimension of the action to the recipient's psychological sensitivity towards the fortunes of a fictional individual.

The narrative contents of the news ballad can be grouped thematically as follows: political events of far-reaching importance (coronation or death of a sovereign, rebellion and high treason, civil war); important events of the day of an official, military, or catastrophic nature (processions, sieges, fire disasters, and the like); and miraculous happenings, which include both a description of human and animal freaks and what are clearly marvellous events, since both of these are interpreted as miracles. Political events of far-reaching importance are almost always used as a peg for a discussion involving appeals to the listener and will therefore be dealt with in more detail in conjunction with the discursive ballad (see below, chapter 4.3.3). It is interesting to note here that in the diachronic sequence this type of street ballad appears in the first half of the sixteenth century, and only reappears with any regularity after 1640. During the Cromwell period party-political debate predominated in the street ballad, and at the same time there was an increase in crude and sensational reporting. The reasons for this may have been both the turbulent political events of the Civil War and stricter censorship measures, which the ballad trade was particularly skilful in evading.[62] For the moment we must assume that political debate was largely absent from the street ballad between 1600 and 1640.[63] Similarly during this period, events of the day such as the appearance of monsters and miracles are fairly rare in the street ballad. For the first half of the seventeenth century it can be said that the street ballad's purpose was seen by its producers to consist in entertainment and instruction, which although of immediate relevance to the listeners did not in the main include reference to topical events. The street ballad certainly reflected the social life of the time, with its norms and concepts,[64] but in the narrower sense it remained non-political. Life histories and crimes are billed as news but reproduced as narratives; in the same way, sensational accounts of miracles having entertainment and instructional value can be described as 'entertaining news with a didactic message'. Everyday problems are frequently presented in role-play form, and socially critical topics in discursive form. If the street ballad is described as 'journalistic' in the global sense, then it certainly does apply on the basis of its method of distribution, ease of comprehension, and greater topicality compared with 'orthodox' literature. But it is a contemporary 'news' medium only to a very limited extent.

These general journalistic concerns of the street ballad, as distinct from the more narrowly defined news ballad's concentration on sensational events, are expressed in a piece of street-ballad self-examination: *The Post of Ware: With a Packet full of strange Newes out of diuers Countries* (1620 or 1621; PG, no. 22, pp. 139–43) deals with the bringing of news by courier[65] and the content of the news. The plurality of the news brought is closely allied to the form of the *coranto*, which was at that time becoming popular, where several items of news from various places and points in time were strung together.[66] In contrast to the *coranto*, however, this ballad contains mainly satirical comments on trading and dealing in England, whose inhabitants are praised, with hyperbolic inversion, for their honesty, virtue, and unselfishness. As far as actual news is concerned, the ballad contains merely a reference to the possible threat of war between Spain and the Netherlands, criticizing in this context the neglect of home news compared with continental news. Rollins rightly describes the text as a parody of the *coranto*. As such, the ballad may be interpreted as a self-examination of the purpose of the street ballad – a purpose other than the transmission of news which is represented as being the function of the *coranto*. The ballad refers to themes which actually do become common in the street ballad after 1600: the fraudulent behaviour of craftsmen,[67] the immorality of courtiers and arrogance of the ladies of town society, exploitation by landowners and increasing poverty, prison life, the threat of bankruptcy in a risk-filled business life, moneylending, bachelors' reluctance to marry, and the fraudulence of prostitutes. What is announced and sold as 'strange Newes out of diuers Countries' turns out to be aspects of social reality at home. Within the street ballad of this period such aspects are usually treated in detail individually, either in discursive mode or in fictions where they are presented as examples. By contrast, such material as is treated in the news ballad proper – fires, monsters, miracles, prodigies – is not mentioned at all in *A Packet full of strange Newes*.

In the classification as narrative street ballads of the small group of those ballads which communicate news, we see that in their narrative presentation of monstrous phenomena, miraculous happenings, and current events they have procedures in common which at the same time show slight differences in emphasis in comparison with other street-ballad narratives. They concern the narrator in his role of reporter, his commentary, and the particular importance assigned to detailed description.

An obvious feature of the news ballad is that it should require the speaker to be specified quite clearly as a 'reporter', that is, he must be identified as an eyewitness or at least a reliable transmitter of news. This function of 'guarantor of authenticity' is performed by the balladmonger in his own person, reinforcing a direct relationship with the audience, with the result that the structurally fixed role of the narrator merges into that of the presenter.[68] This congruence of roles is aided by the nature of the subject of communication: the absence of fictional centres of awareness marks out the transmitter of the 'news' (external events, description of objects) as an observed as opposed to a narrator. The difference in aesthetic effect is clearly illustrated in the following ballad:

The deserued downfall of a corrupted conscience, degraded from all Authority and titles of Knighthood, censured in the high Court of Parliament, and executed at the Kings Bench barre vpon the 20. day of June last, 1621, in the presence of foure great Peeres of this Kingdome. (PG, no. 23, pp. 144–9)

While street-ballad narratives of crime and punishment usually present the dimension of the protagonist's personal experience together with the external circumstances, the 'report' of the public degradation of Sir Francis Mitchell, the Middlesex Justice of the Peace found guilty of corruption,[69] confines itself to a purely objective description. The speaker establishes himself immediately as an eyewitness, making further references later to his standpoint of observer:

It was my chance of late
  in Westminster to be,
Whereas in gallant state
  great numbers I did see,
  attending all
  in that great Hall,
Where Iustice is decreed,
  and people store
  came more and more,
Which did amazement breed.[70]

At last, my longing eyes
  (expecting some strange thing)
Knight Marshals men espies.   (ibid., v. 2,1–2,3, p. 145)

It seem'd he was a Knight,
  and Iustice by degree.   (ibid., v. 3,1–2, p. 145)

The information he gives is concentrated on the detailed description of a ritual procedure: the accused is divested one by one of the attributes of his power and esteem; not a word is said about what this man might have been feeling.

Official events such as Queen Elizabeth's entry into London, 12 November 1584,[71] the ceremonial procession in honour of the High Court of Justice,[72] the conferring of the Order of the Garter on Aulgernon Percie, Earle of Northumberland, 13 May 1635,[73] and the Opening of Parliament by Charles I, 13 April 1640, are particularly suited to being recounted by a narrator in the capacity of observer. In the first two this is only suggested by the nature of the presentation – the minute detail of the description of the proceedings. Martin Parker'a account of the conferring of the Order mentions the standpoint of the observer during the course of the text (see v. 7, lines 47–53, RB, III, p. 223), and his ballad on the reopening of Parliament in 1640, which gave rise to such political hopes, explicitly introduce a reporter:

The order how they rode that day
To you I will in briefe display,
In the best manner that I may,
    For now my minde is bent
To publish what my selfe did see,
That absent (Loyall) hearts may be
Participants as well as wee
    Ith' joy oth' Parliament.   (v. 3, CP, pp. 78–9)

The actual presence of the author at such events, as distinct from the textual role of the reporter, is very much open to doubt, as can be shown in precisely this example. The printing licence for this ballad had already been granted on 9 April, four days before the event reported, and the title entered in the Stationers' Register (see Rollins, *CP*, commentary, p. 77). We must therefore assume that Martin Parker now only wished, as a staunch royalist, to secure the reporting of the event but also wrote the account in advance on the basis of what he had gleaned through his experience as a 'reporter'. The use of the invocation of the Muses at the beginning of this ballad, as also at the beginning of another report of his,[74] points in the same direction. Rollins mentions elsewhere further examples of ballad entries in the Register before the event reported had taken place (Rollins [1919], pp. 269–70). Thus the terms 'exact description' and 'true reporte', which occur with particular frequency in the news ballad, should be understood in the first instance as alluding to the method of presentation and as claims to authenticity, justified by the detail of description, and not as proof of authenticity. The role of the reporter is usually a fictional one in correlation with the principles of presentation of his subject of communication. There are, however, also cases where historical sources show a description to be true to fact, as with the street-ballad accounts of the ceremonial procession or the conferring of the Order, both also by Martin Parker (see Rollins [1919c], p. 118).

Claims to authenticity as mere statements by a speaker who is not further defined, in the form of epithets, the term 'news', and through illocutions, are not specific to the news ballad, although this topos is very often employed when sensational and marvellous happenings are related (see above, pp. 48–9). In such 'news' communications the declaration in the title is often considered inadequate and is further supported by corresponding assertions in the text itself together with reference to informants.[75] In accounts of public processions, conflagrations, sieges, and other particularly credible happenings, which can often be historically proved, it is the precise details of time and place which furnish proof of authenticity. This procedure can however also be employed as a fiction proving authenticity in ballads concerned with miraculous events.

The main justification for the street-ballad message lies however not in its truth content – whether claimed or actual – but in the commentary. The predominance and propagandistic importance of the commentary, established also from the journalistic viewpoint, can now be defined more closely both as to content and in the wider context of the didactic intention of the street ballad. The fictional narrative street ballad can orientate its moral and didactic evaluation towards a particular case of wrongdoing which is fixed in the textual content. The corresponding didactic potential of the subject of communication in the narrative news ballad is, however, usually less clearly definable, so that its conclusions are likely to be somewhat vague moral and political generalizations and warnings. Symptomatic here is the preference for a general call to repentance and change, the key words being 'sinne' and 'repent' as opposed to the 'warning' and 'advice' in both serious and humorous fictional ballads. The latter are concepts which in street-ballad usage imply the deliberate purpose of helping the listener in everyday life, assuming concrete form in the context of the narrative. In this explicitly intentional aspect of the commentary it can again be seen how the news ballad occupies a separate position within the text corpus as a whole with its bias towards advice on the practical problems of day-to-day living.

In both subject and mode of interpretation, mircale and monster ballads owe much to a strong tradition of prodigy literature[76] in the narrower sense and to the sixteenth- and seventeenth-century specialist literature of magic, philosophy and science.[77] The dividing-line between the miraculous and abnormal on the one hand and the normal and scientifically explicable on the other was still fluid even at the end of the seventeenth century. The interest in miracles and monsters continued,[78] even for serious scholars such as Bernard Connor, Fellow of the Royal Society and the Royal College of Physicians (see Thorndyke [1958], VIII, pp. 627–8) or Robert Plott, Oxford's first professor of chemistry and curator of the Ashmolean Museum.[79]

To many the fantastic world of demons and witches was more real and actual than the pretensions of physical or chemical experimentation. Others would not be surprised at any freak of nature, startling phenomenon of the sky, or apparent miracle, but would confidently account for it by the influence of the stars or by occult virtue in inferior objects. Others were ever on the search for 'secrets' of nature rather than for laws of nature.[80]

The definition of the prodigy as a phenomenon which transcends the laws of nature[81] and may therefore be divine, demonic, or occult in origin[82] forms the basis for theological and moral–theological interpretation. The decision as to what counts as a miracle in an individual case, and in what numinous powers it originated, remains open, however (Thorndyke, *passim*). Prodigies have the function of stimulating human belief in the divine, of directing attention towards the heavenly sphere,[83] and, more specifically, serving as a warning or punishment of wickedness.[84] That which has so to speak its systematic place in scholarly writings is confirmed in the area of popular ideas where it is revealed in widespread superstition and a prevailing awareness of magical relationships.[85] The predominantly moral–theological interpretation of prodigies in popular literature is clearly reinforced by the homiletic tradition and the effectiveness of its functional literature.[86] The correlate of prodigy literature with regard to aesthetic effect is an audience that lives for the most part in a world of miraculous signs, only rarely taking the sceptical viewpoint, as is expressed for example by Thomas Nashe:

Yea, the Country Plowman feareth a *Calabrian* flodde in the midst of a furrowe, and the sillie Sheephearde committing his wandering sheepe to the custodie of his wappe, in his field naps dreaming of flying Dragons, which for feare least he should see to the losse of his sight, he falleth a sleepe; no star he seeth in the night but seemeth a Comet; hee lighteth no sooner in a Quagmyre, but he thinketh this is the foretold Earthquake, wereof his boy hath the Ballet.[87]

The consistency of the message of prodigy ballads, as of their recurrence – though with less frequency in the first half of the seventeenth century – can be explained by their adherence to certain literary and historical ideas. Although in the second half of the sixteenth century they conform to the Christian and religious orientation of the street ballad, they remain outside the secularization and other literary diversity of the text corpus in the ensuing period, fitting more easily into the general picture of political propaganda and 'yellow press' of the second half of the seventeenth century,[88] when their number was once more on the increase.

Adherence to tradition and the typical mode of interpretation can be seen particularly clearly in the following ballad:

A Lamentable List, of certaine Hidious, Frightfull, and Prodigious Signes, which have bin seene in the Aire, Earth, and Waters, at severall times for these 18. yeares last past, to this present: that is to say, Anno. 1618. untill this instant. Anno 1638. In Germany, and other Kingdomes and Provinces adjacent; which ought to be so many severall warnings to our Kingdome, as to the said Empire.
(1638; *POA*, no. 4, pp. 21–5)

The list of miraculous events is, as with most miracle ballads, based on a prose source of the same year, and in turn provides a model for a number of subsequent ballads using similar material (see Rollins, *POA*, p. 21). What is criticized or ignored in the street-ballad parody of the *coranto* of 1620 (see above, pp. 150–1) is presented here twenty years later towards the end of that phase of the street ballad concerned mainly with entertainment, thus pointing to the future trend: a collection of 'forraine newes' – items referred to as 'marvels' and 'strange sights' from a period of eighteen years and attested to by witnesses (see vv. 1–2, p. 22): terrifying heavenly signs, the bleeding of bread, water or leaves, blood rain, freak births, bird battles, and the like. The final commentary bases the call to repentance and penance on a reference to analogous numinous warnings of the fall of Jerusalem,[89] thereby demonstrating the historical basis for this mode of argument which in other miracle ballads is simply taken for granted:

> Such wonderous signes, & tokens Heaven sent,
> That faire *Ierusalem* might in time repent:
> Prodigious sights, and fearefull blazing starres,
> As learn'd *Iosephus* speakes in's Iewish warres.

> But all these tokens served to no end,
> For the rebellious Iewes did still offend;
> And slighted these Celestiall warnings still:
> The Viols of Gods wrath their sins did fill.   (ibid., vv. 19–20, p. 25)

A battle between birds,[90] similarly part of the repertoire of prodigy literature, is the main subject of the following ballad and occasions a call to repentance:

A battell of Birds Most strangly fought in Ireland, vpon the eight day of September last, 1621. where neere vnto the Citty of Corke, by the riuer Lee, weare gathered together such a multytude of Stares, or Starlings, as the like for number, was neuer seene in any age.   (1622)

> Marke well, Gods wonderous workes, and see,
>   what things therein declared be,
> Such things as may with trembling feare,
>   fright all the world, the same to heare:
> for like to these, which heere I tell,
> no man aliue remembreth well.   (*PG*, no. 24, pp. 150–4; v. 1, p. 151)

The astonishment at the battle between two flocks of birds, described in detail, again leads to a concluding call to repentance, 'for sure it is that God it sent, / that of our sinnes we should repent' (v. 18,5, p. 154). The moral-theological mileage that can be derived from miraculous phenomena – the opportunity to call people to penance and implicitly threaten punishment – can also be gained from the exploitation of historically documented fire disasters having natural causes, since the interpretive potential of events is so generally applicable. The analogy of the destruction of Jerusalem may also have influenced such a commentary on the news where this is not mentioned as such. The report of the great fire at Corke refers to the battle of the birds as an omen and comments with a comprehensive *memento mori* containing reference to eternal fire and repetition of the words 'repent' and 'sinne'.[91] The collapse of a church tower after being struck by lightning, with an ensuing fire in a neighbouring monastery, is also exploited as a miraculous event, with a corresponding moral interpretation:

A newe Ballad of the most wonderfull and strange fall of Christ's Church *pinnacle in* Norwich, *the which was shaken downe by a thunder-clap on the 29 of* Aprill *1601, about 4 or 5 a'clocke in the after-noone: with a discription of a miraculous fire, which the verye next morninge consumed and burnt downe a great part of the cloyster.*   (1601?)[92]

Two early ballads on a fire disaster, the destruction in 1586 of Beckles (*sic*) a small town in Suffolk,[93] certainly give a detailed description of the conflagration, together with its cause (inadequately controlled fire during a gale), and also of the damage wrought. The report has however at the same time the structure of a lamentation on the sins of the personified city. The call to repentance and penance in *Miraculous Newes from the cittie of Holdt in* Germany (1616?; *SHB*, no. 16, pp. 75–80) is, from the point of view of the subject reported, more stringently related to the content. The call to repentance is put into the mouths of three men temporarily risen from the dead, and reinforced by the commentary. The connotative allusion to the Last Judgement is implied in the event whose fearful effect is included in the description, as a strategy of deterrence. It is accompanied in the commentary with references to the immanent possibility of death, especially through plague. The significance of events together with the commentary show a similarly moral–theological interpretation in:

A dolefull dittye of five vnfortunat persons that were drowned in their drunknes in crossing over the Thames *neare* Iuy Bridge, *vpon sundaye night the 15 of* October *last, 1616: set forth for an example for all such prophaners of the Lord's Sabaoth daye.*   (1616?)

> What hart so hard, but will relent
>   of Strangers' suddaine deathe to heare;
> And, of God's dreadful punishment,
>   he cannot choose but stande in feare.
>   (*SHB*, no. 14, pp. 67–71; v. 1, p. 68)

In contrast to such events the usual 'prodigies' have for the most part an even less fixed range of significance which, although usually exploited morally and theologically, allows of a political interpretation. *Strange Newes from Brotherton in Yorke-shire* (*c.* 1648)[94] reports on wheat-and-blood rain, hail, the appearance of two suns, and the well-known fast miracle of the German virgin (Eva Fliegen from Moers) who lived for six-teen days on the fragrance of a rose. The commentary contains the obliga-tory call to penance (v. 2,1–2,4, p. 40), but extends the omnipotence of God, which becomes apparent in the prodigies – 'The wonders of the Lord' as it says in the refrain – to include political events: the victory over the Spanish Armada, the discovery of the Gunpowder Plot, King Charles's successful public relations journey to Spain in 1623 and his preservation from death in battle (see vv. 10 and 11, p. 43). This interpretation of God's intervention in historical events, by no means unusual for this period, gives a list of examples which have the preservation of the state in common. The divine right of kings thereby implied reinforced the vigorous royalist standpoint of the time, which culminated in this miracle ballad:

> And since there's none hath power,
>   to do him any harme,
> God him defend against his foes,
>   with his out-streaching hand: (ibid., v. 12,1–12,4, p. 43)

Just as historical events *per se* are certainly not miraculous in character, the occurrence of human or animal abnormalities should not necessarily be classified as transcending the laws of nature. In scientific writings they are both given a natural explanation and accounted for on theological and cosmological grounds; or they are traced back to a general disharmony with the cosmos.[95] The commentary in the relatively numerous monster ballads of the early period[96] interprets the phenomenon as a sign of divine punishment, while in the few examples of the subsequent period[97] a general link with the supernatural is established, from the connotations of the extraordinary with regard to deviation from the norm, and expression is given to the admiration of God's works:

The true reporte of the forme and shape of a monstrous Childe borne at Muche Horkelleye, a village three myles from Colchester, in the Countye of Essex, the XXI daye of Apryll in this yeare 1562.

> This monstrous world that monsters bredes as rife,
>   As men tofore it bred by native kinde,
> By birthes that shewe corrupted natures strife,
>   Declares what sinnes beset the secrete minde.
> (AB, no. 8, pp. 38–42 and lines 1–4, p. 38)

In the following report the orientation towards a scientific source can be discerned in the combination of attempts at medical and theological explanation.[98] Another ballad from the same year treats the same event with a similar interpretation, at the same time ranging it alongside Old Testament prodigies.[99] Less horrific, if not less cliché-ridden, is the more 'modern' commentary on the monster as proof of divine intent, as is shown in two ballads by Martin Parker:

A description of a strange (and miraculous) Fish, cast upon the sands in the meads, in the Hundred of Worwell, in the County Palatine of Chester, (or Chesshiere). The certainty whereof is here related concerning the said most monstrous Fish.
(between 1632 and 1636)

> O mark what maruels to our sight
>   our Potent Lord can bring.
> These secrets *Neptune* closely keeps
> Whithin the bosome of the deeps.[100]

The tvvo inseparable brothers. Or A true and strange description of a Gentleman (an Italian by birth) about seventeene yeeres of age, who hath an imperfect (yet living) Brother, growing out of his side, having a head, two armes, and one leg, all perfectly to be seene. They were both baptized together: the imperfect is called Iohn Baptist, *and the other* Lazarus. *Admire the Creator in his Creatures.*

> In seeing this or such strange things,
> Let vs admire the King of Kings,
>   and of his power conceaue.[101]

The stress on the extraordinariness of the phenomenon as a connotation of the miraculous makes possible that presenter-like behaviour of the speaker which had been increasingly evident since the turn of the century. His gestures of reference (see above, chapter 3.4.2) can be directed towards the verbal description and the woodcut illustration in equal measure:

> A Gentleman well qualifide,
> Doth beare his brother at his side,
>   inseparably knit,
> As in this figure you may see,
> And both together liuing be,
>   the world admires at it.[102]

> It is a fish, a monstrous fish,
>   a fish that many dreads,
> But now it is as we would wish,
>   cast vp o'th sands i'th meads,
> In *Chesshire*; and tis certaine true,
> Describ'd by those who did it view.

> O *rare*
> *beyond compare,*
> *in England nere the like.*[103]

A notable exception to the theological interpretation of monsters is seen in a ballad by Laurence Price about a girl with a pig's head, a figure which was the subject of several ballads and prose pieces around 1640 and later.[104] The humoristic form of the catalogue of ugliness has a corresponding commentary which does not assign the otherwise attractive and also rich eligible maiden to biblical or contemporary prodigies, with the appropriate interpretation, but ranges her alongside metamorphoses of the ancient world and native fairy-tale figures.[105]

Reports on subjects which can hardly be interpreted as miracles show a more precise concentration by the commentary on the actual event itself and its symbolic overtones. In the case of official processions it is not surprising that the demonstration of splendour, political power, and their possible topical significance should be formulated in the commentary. Thus the entry of Queen Elizabeth into London takes six verses to describe, and a further seven contain invective against earlier and future traitors, panegyric, cheers, and blessings on the monarch.[106] Glorification of state institutions (monarch, Court of Justice, aristocracy) is also of concern in other ballads of this type.[107] It is somewhat less easy to define precisely the significance potential of a siege; the taking of Rheinberg near Düsseldorf in 1601 serves to spread the fame of the victorious commander Prince Maurice,[108] while in the description of the fall of La Rochelle, a Protestant town on the island of Rhe, 28 October 1628,[109] the misery of the inhabitants is used as an occasion for a call to penance. Owing to the royalist perspective of the author Martin Parker, however, only veiled criticism is made of this use of force by the state (see v. 8, pp. 297–8).

An essential characteristic of the street-ballad news commentary is the topos of 'outdoing'; this also applies in the case of narratives which are made out to be 'newes'. The subject of communication is by this means characterized as sensational, and with the positioning of superlatives and hyperbolic comparisons in the title and trailer[110] the 'outdoing' topos serves at the same time to enhance the speaker's status as presenter. The commentary's emphasis on the exceptional features of an event is frequently accompanied in the news ballad by the narrator's communication of a reception perspective which is inherent in the event itself, a device which also reinforces the impression of an authentic report. In the case of public events the reaction of the onlookers serves to manipulate reception along emotional lines:[111]

> The people flocked there amain,
>   The multitude was great to see;
> Their joyful harts were glad, and fain
>   To view her princely maiesty.[112]

> His spurs of Knighthood then,
>   was from his heeles there hewen,
> And by the Marshals men
>   in high disgraces throwne
>   into the Hall,
>   amongst them all
> That stood with gazing eyes,
>   to marke and see
>   in what degree
> Degraded Knighthood lies.[113]

The victims of fire disasters and of starvation during a siege are of course directly involved in the events. The reference to their participation in the experience, although not as individuals, similarly lends support to the laments in the commentary exhorting listeners to pity and cathartic remorse.[114] Reception is deliberately manipulated in some miracle ballads through the astonishment and terror of the eyewitnesses.[115]

The primary function of the news ballad – processing with commentary a series of events which are often already known or fixed in a certain topos – is borne out by interpretation of the texts. According to analysis from the journalistic viewpoint,[116] such versions embrace popular opinion and ideas. The actual 'item of news' determines the commentary in so far as it offers a varying amount of interpretative leeway according to the political, scientific, magical, and theological ideas of the time. The content of the commentary is to a large extent conventionalized, while opinion in discursive ballads is clearly of a secular nature, as is also seen in the variation possible through the dramatic use of different perspectives with regard to certain problems in the role-play ballad.[117]

The manipulation of opinion through commentary is supported by the illustration of the news event. This is furthermore intended to produce a feeling of participation in far-off and extraordinary happenings on the basis of a real or imagined topicality. This is achieved in the presentation through as exact a description as possible, although it is only in the street ballad of the first half of the seventeenth century that this is effectively put into practice.[118] It is at the same time a strategy for rendering a report credible. The detailed information in Martin Parker's account of the Siamese twins in Italy is structured around the basic question of which bodily functions are shared by the two, and where they have individual control.[119] *A description of a strange (and miraculous) Fish* (PG, no. 77, pp. 437–42) conveys to the audience the monstrous dimensions of the stranded whale (?) through comparisons with familiar objects and through units of measurement: a rider together with his horse would fit into the fish's mouth (v. 11, p. 441) – also illustrated in the woodcut; 16 tons of oil have already been extracted from the fish (v. 13, p. 441); every tooth weighs 2 lb, and the weight of the whole fish is so great that twelve pairs of oxen could not move it (v. 7, p. 440 and v. 5, p. 439). The description of the tower of Norwich cathedral uses information about shape, material, and dimensions – exaggerated in comparison with the original – in order (with this account of the edifice's size and invulnerability) to prepare the ground for the climax of destruction by lightning.[120] The functional use of detail to convey through language the significance of an event with the formation of semantic isotopes, illustrating it at the same time, is effected in a simple and comprehensible way in the report sections of all news ballads. The description of the panic amongst the inhabitants of Beckles (*sic*) is particularly effective, with the anonymity it conveys through the use of verbal nouns connoting rapid movement and uncontrolled expressions of distress:

> To see such a burning, such flaming of fire,
> Such wayling, such crying, through scourge of Gods ire,
> Such running, such working, such taking of payne,
> Such whirling, such haling, such reauing in vaine,
> Such robbing, such stealing, from more to the lesse,
> Such dishonest dealing, in time of distresse,[121]

In the description of ceremonial processions the detail conveys splendour and show of power, and the public degradation of the Middlesex Justice of the Peace,[122] by being divested of his honours, is founded on the fixed symbolic function of dress, sword, spurs, and all the ceremonial of Westminster Hall. In another ballad the description with which this procedure is recounted (see vv. 4–11, pp. 146–8) suggests a slow pace, underlining the oppressive character of the ballad as a whole. Rollins's criticism that the news ballad is incapable of telling a story well (H. E. Rollins [1919a], p. 268) proves on the whole to be too sweeping. Effective narrative techniques of contrast of events, climax, and textual coherence through connotative correlation of details are certainly in evidence in these ballads. The journalistic device of giving the salient facts at the beginning to catch the attention is also to a certain extent already present in the very detailed titles.

In so far as it reports events and does not use them merely as pegs for discussion and warning, the so-called 'news ballad' should be seen structurally as a narrative street ballad where figures as experiencing centres of consciousness are replaced by predominantly non-human agents, and by freaks. The narrator is more frequently and explicitly endowed with the attributes of the role of reporter (observer's standpoint, repeated claims to authenticity, the importance of the event in the subject of communication) than is otherwise the case in the narrative street ballad. From the point of view of content, the narrator's normally extensive commentary constitutes in fact moral theology and pseudo-scientific theodicy. Analysis of the textual structure shows that the commentary's uniformity and vagueness can be explained by a lack of fictional life histories which would provide a precise point of orientation. It can also be explained from the historical angle by the fact that there was a traditional practice of interpreting prodigies in a certain way. The report section of the news ballad contains an even greater enthusiasm for detail than does the narrative ballad in general. The description of the respective happening or phenomenon is characterized, if it is not simply a list of several prodigies, by functionality and coherence. Up till now scholars have regarded the news ballad as especially typical and important – possibly on the grounds of its iconographic attractions and sensational content – and as proof of the trivial nature of the street ballad. It must however be stated that it in fact occupies a subordinate position in the area of contemporary news communication from the point of view of topicality, function, and quantity. Within the street-ballad text corpus it is quantitatively – and that includes the discursive news ballad which will be discussed later – of only slight importance, if one leaves out the narrative ballad with a system of motivational links (e.g. a criminal ballad billed as news). In intention the news ballad deviates from the purpose of entertaining and instructing where the main concern is with day-to-day problems of life. This is particularly true for the literary and historical heyday of the street ballad, where the news ballad is noticeably sparse on the ground, appearing rather to be an exercise based on a tradition extraneous to the street ballad.

4.3 Performative speech situation in the street ballad: semi-dramatic, dramatic and discursive street ballad

4.3.1 Role-play ballad: conflict situation and expression of opinion specific to the situation

The communicative structure of the role-play ballad is determined by the performative speech situation (see above, chapter 4.1, pp. 105–7) in which a speaker presents himself and which in this type of ballad must convey fairly precisely a sense of the immediate present. To this extent we are concerned with a dramatic figure. The drama, however, involves as a rule several figures in a fairly long confrontation in dialogue form. The figure in a role-play ballad is, on the other hand, as far as the conveying of information is concerned, dependent entirely on him- or herself, the dramatic action is reduced to one single situation, and the only possible communication partner is the audience. Thus, while in the drama direct and indirect characterization of self and others is conveyed through the figures' speech and the dramatic interaction, the characterization of the single street-ballad figure is to a very large extent limited to his or her own spoken self-presentation. Characteristics can be described explicitly, or implied through confrontation with the situation. To convey an immediate present situation often requires explanation and illustration out of the past. In contrast to the first-person narrative, however, this past is not reported in the preterite as a chronologically ordered period but rather made available to the audience through an iterative–durative presentation, with the use of the conditional, of typical experiences, possibilities, and wishes for the relevant situational present. Everything is related to the situation in which the figure finds him- or herself. The drama of the figure's spoken action derives on the one hand from confrontation with a situation perceived as a conflict, such as unfulfilled desires in love or for marriage, quarrels between husband and wife, life in a reformatory, and difficulties as a tenant. The dramatic figure is here confronted at the same time with other episodically described figures as representatives of contrasting values. On the other hand the decision following a conflict may be presented as already having taken place, whereby the dramatic figure represents a value which he or she feels obliged to defend against the listeners, or a section of them, as a representative of society. An example of this would be the point of view of the confirmed bachelor or drinker, the one-sidedness of the skinflint or the spendthrift, or the ideal of bucolic life.

The conflict perceived as immediately present or presented as already resolved can be described sociologically as a role-play conflict. The concept of the social role embraces a complex of behaviour patterns expected of an individual by virtue of his or her position in society (occupation, status, personal relationships) and which he or she exhibits in the 'role play' (see H. P. Dreitzel [1972]). Such behaviour expectations are understandable within the framework of contemporary social values, and there is a threat of sanctions if they are not fulfilled. If the individual is unable or unwilling to conform to a particular role, he or she either enters into a conflict or causes the interaction partner to be disappointed in his or her expectations, which leads to an interpersonal conflict. The figure in the role-play ballad articulates the problem as a wish (girl wanting to marry), as criticism of the partner (disillusioned wife) or of the respective circumstances (prostitute in a reformatory), or as a decision already taken (confirmed drinker). The concentration on one figure in a dramatic role in the role-play ballad can point up particularly clearly the respective socially conditioned conflict. The interaction with other members of society is shown here merely through the relationship with other figures.

The single figure at the centre of the miniature drama presents his or her own fictionally present problem and speech situation him- or herself. Since specifications of time and place are only minimal, transposition on to an actual performance situation is easily effected. To a limited extent this also applies to the drinking-song, where specific information about an alehouse situation fits in with the actual function of the street ballad as alehouse entertainment. In contrast to the role-play street ballad, the nineteenth-century dramatic monologue[123] contains detailed information regarding the speaker's scene of action and the temporal delineation of the speech situation, where other figures participate in the dialogue. Since these texts are meant for the reader only, the recipient's imaginative capacity will not conflict with the reality of his or her situation. In the case of the role-play street ballad this difficulty does arise for the speaker's relationship with his audience, and it is in fact twofold: fictional self-presentation of the figure *ad spectatores*, and communication on the showman/presenter level. Metatextual advance information and attracting of attention in the title and trailer are clearly the concern of the presenter. The explicit claim to authenticity is obviously considered superfluous in the role-play ballad, where the illusion of reality is conveyed by the dramatic presence of the figure itself; the request to buy is also absent, presumably since it was felt to be too drastic a break in the fiction. There is however an indirect invitation to buy contained in the dramatic figure's striking self-presentation and market-crier demeanour. The figure's attitude derives from a fictionally specified situation, such as the search for a husband, but in fact can be virtually transposed on to the presenter. In the combining here of practical objectives and literary intention in textually implicit advertising techniques (see above, chapter 3.4.3 and 3.5.2), the ballad-monger is assigned the dual function of actor and salesman. Where there

is predominance of expressions of opinion on an already resolved conflict
the textual speaker may similarly converge with the presenter. Audience
addresses, on the other hand, whose content is determined by the figure's
fictional world (for instance, proposal of marriage to members of the
audience), would to a certain extent be spoken by the balladmonger in the
manner of an actor's asides to his audience.

Martin Parker's *The Wooing Maid* (1636; *RB*, III, pp. 52–6 and *CM*,
no. CLIX, pp. 313–15) is an especially typical example of a literary version
of a role-play conflict. In its realization of genre-specific possibilities it is
also particularly successful. The basic situation of the girl left on the shelf
is communicated as the problem area in the metatextual advance information of the title, where reference is made to the figure in the third
person:

> *The Wooing Maid;*
>   *Or,*
> *A faire maid neglected,*
> *Forlorne and rejected,*
> *That would be respected:*
> *Which to have effected,*
> *This generall summon*
> *She sendeth in common;*
> *Come tinker, come broomman:*
> *She will refuse no man.*

Both the sanctions of isolation and of loss of respect are formulated here
as well as the wish of the figure in this role to conform to the norm of early
marriage. The first verse presents the concrete situation from the first-
person perspective of the protagonist who is experiencing it at first hand:

> I am a faire maid, if my glasse doe not flatter,
> Yet, by the effects, I can find no such matter;
> For every one else can have suters great plenty;
> Most marry at fourteene, but I am past twenty.
> *Come gentle, come simple, come foolish, come witty,*
> *Oh! if you lack a maid, take me for pitty.*   (ibid., v. 1, lines 1–6, p. 53)

The information given here forms the basis for the figure's self-
presentation in the rest of the text: the effort to bolster up her self-
confidence with praise of her own attributes,[124] the rhetorical question as
to the possible causes of failure,[125] the desperate attempts to find a
husband, and the comparison with other norm figures; sanctions are
mentioned explicitly only at one point (v. 2,4, line 10, p. 53). The girl tells
of her efforts in retrospect, illustrating in episodes related in iterative–
durative mode:

> When I goe to weddings, or such merry meetings,
> I see other maids how they toy with their sweetings,
> But I sit alone, like an abject forsaken;
> Woe's me! for a husband what course shall be taken?
> Come gentle, &c.   (ibid., v. 4, lines 18–22, p. 53)

The dramatic figure cites as representatives of the norm in contrast to herself: her mother who by the age of eighteen had had two sons and a daughter, her less pretty sister who rejected six or seven suitors yet was still married by the age of sixteen, and, in further intensification, a misshapen relative who managed to get a husband at the age of nineteen. The highlighting of the figure's own situation through the quotation of examples of the opposite shows at the same time women's competitive mentality with regard to the marriage-market.[126] It is less a question of psychological or erotic needs here than of achieving status. In face of such massive pressure, personified in those who conform to their social roles, the object of sanctions – 'the wooing maid' – takes positive steps. Although this constitutes a deviation from the woman's passive role as possession and status symbol, thereby producing a comic effect, it is meant to make up for a more serious deficit in the role assigned to females. She declares her assets and extols herself. The explicit self-characterization towards the end of the ballad mentions qualities which correspond to the expectations of the lower-middle classes of the time: money, thrift – while the husband is allowed to spend money in the alehouse and on similar pleasures – agreeable looks, no trace of the two most feared characteristics, 'to scold nor be jealous', and in addition a strong erotic side to her affections (see vv. 11–13, lines 54–68; RB, III, p. 55). This spectrum of the figure's qualities cannot be brought into line with the person of the balladmonger. It demands, together with the conveying of the whole situation of conflict, a dramatic realization which is supported by textually implicit gestures and mime: the searching look in the mirror (v. 1,1, p. 53), consternation and amazement at a fate peculiar to herself (v. 2,1–2, lines 7–8, p. 53), the outraged despair intensifying at the end of each verse, the disparaging scrutiny of her more fortunate rivals (vv. 8–10, lines 39–48, p. 55), and the defiant enhancing of her own value (v. 11, lines 54–8, p. 55). The role-play fiction of the girl seeking a husband, which has to be dramatically realized, has, in its quasi-deep structure, elements in common with the procedure of the presenter: exhibitionist behaviour, the self-praise of the market-crier and also the appeal to the audience by a subject which has been conveyed through the spoken word and which has to be got rid of – 'Ile goe without bidding' (v. 6,3, line 30, p. 54). (In this case the appeal is directed towards potential suitors, in a humorous break in the fiction.) Through this use of ambivalence the audience's attention and readiness to buy are thus manipulated by means of a role-play fiction.

Now judge, am not I a lasse well worth the having?
       . . .
Let none be offended, nor say I'm uncivill,
For I needs must have one, be he good or evill:
Nay, rather then faile, Ile have a tinker or broomman,
A pedler, an inkman, a matman, or some man.
Come gentle, come simple, come foolish, come witty,
O let me not die a maid, take me for pitty.[127]

The redundancy in the text, which manipulates and eases reception and
with which the topic of social status is communicated, is manifested in the
isotope levels: self-praise;[128] efforts to find a husband;[129] lack of success
with potential husbands;[130] success of other females perceived as rivals;[131]
lamentation and wishes;[132] plea for rescue.[133] The equal distribution of
isotopic information throughout the whole of the text, and its logical
correlation, effects a textual coherence where the conflict is presented in
the contrasting of isotopes. This redundancy, justified from the didactic
point of view and with practical regard to reception, is compensated by the
variation in the procedures used to convey the topic: self-characterization,
characterization of other figures, iterative–durative recounting of
episodes, summarizing observations, appeals to the audience. The
dramatic figure's conflict, communicated with functional textual transparency as the fictional portrayal of a social problem which the speaker of
the role presents to the audience as a wish and an appeal, remains
unresolved.

A role-play ballad with a similar theme is *This Maide would giue tenne
Shillings for a Kisse* (c. 1615; *PG*, no. 13, pp. 78–83). The way in which
the figure makes herself available, extolling her assets in the manner of the
market-crier praising his wares, is similar to the behaviour of the presenter
and can easily be adopted by the balladmonger. The large amount offered
for a kiss adds dramatic irony to the catalogue of beauty (vv. 3–6,
pp. 79–80):

My waste is small, and likewise long,
    my leg well calft, and boned strong,
My pretty foote you all may feele,
    is not in bredth an inch in th'heele.
From head to foote in euery part,
    I seeme a building fram'd by Art:
Yet since their hopefull loues I misse,
    come here's ten shillings for a kisse.   (ibid., v. 6, p. 80)

The role perspective complementary to the husband-seeking girl is that
of the wife or husband where the normative and therefore desirable status
of marriage usually turns out to have been a negative experience.[134] *A
Penny-worth of Good Counsell* (between c. 1624 and 1660; *RB*, II,

pp. 294–9) tells of a woman's experience of many years of marriage. The cliché of the 'penny-worth' as a reference to the monetary value of the advice, in combination with an epithet indicating its high quality, signals a cheap offer,[135] especially as the ballad costs only half that amount to buy. The presenter's offer of literary wares for sale is undercut in the sub-title which must be assigned to the speaker of the role. He specifies the content of the advice and the group at which it is targeted:

> To Widdowes, and to Maides,
>   This Counsell I send free;
> And let them looke before they leape,
>   Or that they married be.[136]

The marriage state is presented from the viewpoint of the wife as being full of disillusionment. It is not a question here of the role-player's desire to conform to the norm demanded; it is a description of the recurrent failure of the interaction partner to live up to a complex of behaviour expectations:

> 'Hee's not the man I tooke him for:
>   Alas! who would be so much tyed?
> I tell you, friends, now seriously,
>   my husband he doth nought but chide:
>   His lookes are sowre,
>   And he doth lowre;
> For nature no good parts hath gi'n him:
>   For which I grieve,
>   You may believe!
> My husband hath no fore-cast in him.   (ibid., v. 4, lines 31–40, p. 296)

> 'He doth not use me like a woman,
>   and doth not care what clothes I have;
> When other men's wives weare each fashion,
>   and are maintained rich and brave:
>   Thus to the wall
>   I may condole,
> Although that this same song I sing him –
>   Some counsell give,
>   Me to relieve!
> My husband hath no fore-cast in him.   (ibid., v. 8, lines 71–80, p. 298)

Since the conflict is not between the dramatic figure and an abstract norm still to be realized in the form of a person, as was the case in the ballads just discussed, but between two individuals, we are presented with two main figures: the speaker and the husband. The husband's failure to fulfil the role expected of him in any aspect of his behaviour determines the dramatic figure's disappointed state of mind. His carping and fault-finding cause her to lament (see v. 4, quoted above), the poor state of his finances[137] and his meanness prevent her from showing off her female charms with fine clothes in the company of others (see v. 10, lines 91–100, p. 298), and his patriarchal assertion of authority keeps her confined as a 'house-dove'.[138] Other men in general are cited as norm figures,[139] as also is her own husband at the time when he was courting her.[140] In the self-praise of the dramatic figure there is reference to both her youthful past with its concomitant opportunities (see v. 2,1–2,4, lines 11–14, p. 296) and to her present activities as a housewife (see v. 9, lines 81–90, p. 298). The plethora of detailed information precludes an episodic type of structure; everyday prosaic experience with a wide range of reference emerges as the overriding isotope level.

The complementary perspective of a similarly disillusioned husband is offered in *The Cruell Shrow: Or, The Patient Man's Woe* (between 1601 and 1640; *RB*, I, pp. 93–8), a role-play ballad based on the same type of interaction. Its literary presentation in the ballad differs from that of *A Penny-worth of Good Counsell* only in the clear development of the presenter level and the more frequent use of fairly tightly constructed episodes of an iterative–durative character:

> Sometime I goe i' the morning
>   about my dayly worke, –
> My wife she will be snorting,
>   and in her bed she'le lurke
> Vntill the chimes doe goe at eight,
>   then she'le beginne to wake;
> Her morning's draught, well spiced straight,
>   to cleare her eyes, she'le take.
>
> As soone as shee is out of bed
>   her looking-glasse shee takes,
> (So vainely is she dayly led);
>   her morning's worke shee makes
> In putting on her braue atyre,
>   that fine and costly be,
> Whilst I worke hard in durt and mire, –
>   alacke! what remedy?[141]

The division of sexual roles is seen here from the male perspective as stress involved in working for a living versus female inactivity and unproductive vanity. The conventional spectrum of characteristics denoting an unsatisfactory wife includes a predeliction for gossiping (see v. 5,1–5,4, lines 33–6, p. 95) and nagging,[142] moodiness (see v. 9, lines 65–72, p. 97), assertion of authority in not allowing the husband out, and surveillance.[143] The dimension in the text of appeals to the listener is integrated into the fictional role, where in the *ad spectatores* the dissatisfied husband begs the audience for sympathy, support, advice, and help.[144] A fusion of the roles of dramatic figure and presenter in a personal statement following the theme of the trailer, and in a warning marking the end of the ballad, effects a certain distance with regard to the role-play fiction, converting it into a subject of communication of didactic value:

> Come, Batchelers and Married men,
>   and listen to my song,
> And I will shew you plainely, then,
>   the iniury and wrong
> That constantly I doe sustaine
>   by the vnhappy life,
> The which does put me to great paine,
>   by my vnquiet wife.[145]

Whilst the situation where marriage has been experienced and practised demands a resigned and pessimistic perspective, the situation of a bachelor deciding to marry calls for a sceptical attitude to the future. In *A Batchelers Resolution* (1629; *PB*, no. 65, II, pp. 110–15) the weighing-up of possible interaction problems is bound to consist in a presentation in the conditional of potential marriage partners' characteristics and behaviour:

> A Slut would make me loath my meate
>   were I halfe dead with hunger,   (ibid., v. 4,5–6, p. 112)
>   . . .
> What if she should a Wanton be,
>   and make my forehead ake?   (v. 5,1–2, p. 112)
>   . . .
> If iealous she shall be of me,
>   that were as great a spight,   (v. 6,1–2, p. 112)
>   . . .
> Yet if she prooue a drunken sot,
>   'twill grieue me worst of all,   (v. 9,3–4, p. 113)
>   . . .
> I would not be a Widowes slaue,
>   Ide rather loose my life: (v. 12,3–4, p. 113)
>   . . .
> If she should haue a stinking breath
>   I neuer should abide her . . .   (v. 13,1f., p. 113)

The contents of this catalogue of the characteristics of an unsatisfactory wife are traditionally well known,[146] and they are presented here by means of imaginary personifications in relation to the speaker's reaction to them in the conditional mode. This constitutes a decision situation of a dramatic vividness which is intensified by the plurality of partner types and density of information contained in the pithy formulations. The formulation of the positive counterpart as an ideal (see v. 3, *PB*, II, p. 111; v. 8,5–8,8, p. 112) shows the difficulty of the decision which society's expectations are forcing him into (see vv. 15–16, p. 114) and which is not made any easier by his favourable position in the marriage market (see v. 10,3–10,7, p. 113). In the final verse the figure of the bachelor formulates his decision to marry, which he has managed to cling on to, in a kind of self-praise reminiscent of the presenter mode.

A somewhat different type of decision situation is presented dramatically in the role-play figure *The merry carelesse Lover* (1634; *RB*, II, pp. 105–10). The young lover, by no means sure of the girl he is courting, has the choice of two kinds of approach: as the 'foolish lover' (v. 2,1, line 13, p. 106) or 'man indifferent' (v. 5,1, line 43, p. 107). During the course of his own account of the situation he adopts both roles in imagination, whereby the choice of one or the other is related to the potential characteristics and reactions up to then of the girl, with whom he is still only slightly acquainted. The lover's sensible deliberation, his objective self-interpretation and the recognition of an interaction reference show the contrast between this role-play figure and both the suffering Petrarchan lover and the 'rebellious lover' type.[147] This is briefly formulated in the title and refrain:

> But let her chuse – if she refuse,
>   and goe to take another,
> I will not grieve, but still will be
>   the merry carelesse Lover.

As well as the frequent treatment of the problems of role in the spheres of love and marriage, the role-play ballad deals with other situations having similar relevance to contemporary reality. Prostitution as well as loss of fortune, due to a frivolous and irresponsible way of life, certainly belong to the standard themes of the street ballad in general, but with the role-play perpsective there is often less stress on moral and didactic appeals to the listener. Three prostitutes, compelled to exchange the practice of their profession for a term in Bridewell gaol, attempt to cope with their unpleasant situation with humour and gain the sympathy of the amused listener. *Whipping Cheare. Or the wofull lamentations of the three Sisters in the Spittle when they were in new Bride-well* (c. 1612; *PG*, no. 6, pp. 39–43) gives fairly precise details of the speech situation, in contrast to most role-play ballads. The three professional colleagues tell in chorus of their activities of hackling and spinning tow and hemp while being urged on and threatened by a strict female supervisor and an overseer brandishing a whip. The norm of a regular working life as represented by these figures is treated with irony by the 'three sisters' in the use of humorous and obscene double meanings and an imaginative preoccupation with their highly rated past experiences in their old pleasure haunts. The change in function of the invocation of the Muses, to a plea to the Fates for support in the difficult operation of spinning, through its exaggeration renders the activity slightly ridiculous (see v. 1, p. 40). The description of the overseer as a 'blinded whipper' associates Cupid's blindness as the previous ruler of their life with the present threats from the whip (see v. 2, p. 40). 'Hoglaine', their former base, as a street 'in which backs are arched', connotes a sexual position and recalls their previous occupation.[148] There the girls are missed, as the letter from their former clientèle shows with its evocation of underworld pleasures in the second part of the ballad. The compulsion of the situational present is expressed in the onomatopoeic refrain, which not only denotes the dreary occupation of the prisoners but at the same time connotes their erstwhile capturing of men in the 'tow to to to, tow to to to tero'. The refrain is furthermore a textual direction for the performer's non-linguistic actions, involving audience participation. Similarly, the contrast between the desires and the fictional situation of the role-play figures (see v. 3, p. 40; vv. 7 and 8, p. 41) may be converted into body-language signals of impatience and recalcitrance.

There is a similar conflict concerning adaptation to a new and undesirable situation in the case of loss of fortune. *No body loues mee* (c. 1625; *PB*, no. 51, II, pp. 29–35) personalizes and dramatizes such an experience, which has here the practical consequence of the loss of membership of a group. Each verse shows in a brief episode the change of attitude of certain people – drinking companions, landlady, moneylenders, girls, relations (see vv. 1–6, pp. 31–2) – in order to illustrate the figure's isolation and lack of pleasure opportunities. In predominantly iterative–durative presentation, the two time perspectives of past and present are in a short space given maximum priority with the incorporation of a fund of events:

> Faire Mayds would follow me fast for a Fayring,
> I was good company, Purse was not sparing:
> The finest Froe in this towne, I might haue kist her,
> And perhaps layd her downe, now I must misse her.
>   Now that my money is lost,
>   They bid me kisse the post,
>   Was euer man thus crost,
>   No body loues me.   (ibid., v. 5, p. 32)

The isotopic level of disappointment and dissatisfaction, as the psychological constant of the figure's account of his situation, is easily detected and is indeed explicit in the refrain and at various other points in the text (see v. 4,4–4,8, p. 31; v. 5,7, p. 32). The role-play presentation is all the more convincing in comparison with the second part of the ballad, which in a moral and didactic appeal exhorts the audience to thrift, a puritanical way of life, and to piety, drawing its thematic justification from the previous role-play section.

In its fictional role-play form, the problem of social roles can best be understood as a conflict situation, since the role-play figure presents the alternatives in his or her capacity as an experiencing and directly affected subject, with whom the audience can identify. It is characteristic of this type of role-play ballad that the conflict is not resolved, so that the recipient is required to appraise the textual message him- or herself to an extent which is otherwise unusual in the street ballad. In contrast to this, a different type of role-play ballad presents decisions already taken, whereby the alternative is shown to be undesirable and later explicitly rejected. On the other hand the negative alternative is also taken into account as a possible point of view of the listener, which can be deduced from the more or less clearly defensive attitude of such a role-play figure. This type of self-presentation of a figure corresponds socially and psychologically fairly closely to the model of the resolution of cognitive dissonance.[149] This describes the psychological dynamics which take place after an individual's decision, achieving a final harmonizing of alternative norms and values. The speaker of the role is primarily concerned to give information in support of his decision, putting forward negative examples and arguments for the rejected alternative. In this way the speaker intends to present a clear justification for his or her own decision. Such a ballad is characterized by situation-specific expressions of opinion, as opposed to the portrayal of a situation perceived as a conflict.

The differences between the two types of role-play ballad are seen particularly clearly in a comparison with thematically similar role-play ballads which deal with the same behaviour norms in a correspondingly different way. Whereas the husband-seeking girl of *The Wooing Maid* (1636) and the figure in *This Maide would giue tenne Shillings for a Kisse* (c. 1615) perceive the constraint of the marriage norm as a conflict and are prepared to take anyone, the role-play figure in *A pretty new Ditty: Or, A young Lasses Resolution* (between 1601 and 1640; RB, II, pp. 289–94) places herself so emphatically outside this social constraint that she is able to reserve her decision:

> No, I'm a lasse, sure,
>   That live unwedded can;
> And much will endure
> *For a handsome young man.*   (ibid., v. 5,5–5,8, lines 37–40, p. 291)

Her point of departure is of course all the more advantageous as she is not without means (see v. 6,5–6,8, lines 45–8, p. 291); and from her comparison of men she has been disparagingly critical of (see vv. 8–10, lines 57–80, pp. 292–3) with her ideal young man[150] it is not absolutely clear whether she has in mind a real person[151] and therefore intends to marry. Alongside the men who are out of the question as candidates for marriage to her, foolish females similarly serve as foils to her self-justification, which is underlined with the spoken gesture of mild contempt

– 'Some maidens . . .' 'And some . . .'.[152] The conviction 'I would have you know . . .' (v. 6,1, line 41, p. 291) is explicit, as also the anticipation of possible objections: 'Some happily [= haply, perhaps] will / Conjecture of mee . . .' (v. 5,1–2, lines 33–4, p. 291) and possible criticism in the final verse which moves over to the presenter level:

> And thus I conclude,
>   And here end my song;
> Let none thinke me rude,
>   Nor large of my tongue.
> For I am intended
>   As first I began;
> Then let me be friended
>   *With a handsome young man.*   (ibid., v. 16, lines 121–8, p. 294)

The difficult decision situation in *A Batchelers Resolution* (1629) is replaced by a definite standpoint in Laurence Price's complementary ballad, *The Batchelor's Feast,* or *The difference betwixt a single life and a double; being the Batchelor's pleasure, and the married Man's trouble* (between 1628 and 1667; *RB*, I, pp. 46–51).

> Wee Batchelors can flaunt
>   in Country and in Towne,
> And in good company
>   may meryly spend a crowne;
> Wee may doe as wee list,
>   our lives from cares are free,
> O 'tis a gallant thing
>   to live at liberty:
> *With hie dilldo dill,*
>   *hie ho dildurlie:*
> *It is a delightfull thing*
>   *to live at liberty.*   (ibid., v. 2, lines 13–21, p. 48)

The arguments justifying the present situation, which is characterized by cheerful self-satisfaction, are supported by an abundance of negative details concerning the duties of a husband and the expensive requirements of a wife. The role-play figure again seeks the approval of the listeners by anticipating possible objections (see v. 10,1–10,4, lines 88–91, p. 50), giving advice having the illocutionary potential of conviction (see v. 10, 5–10,8, lines 92–5, p. 50), conceding exceptions (see v. 11, 1–11,4, lines 97–100, p. 50) and by means of a *captatio benevolentiae* by the presenter at the end (see v. 12, lines 106–17, p. 51) together with the appeal dimension of the refrain (see above, chapter 3.3.5) with its swaggering gaiety:

The honest plaine dealing Porter:
VVho once was a rich man, but now tis his lot,
To proue that need will make the old wife trot.

(*c.* 1630; *PG*, no. 64, pp. 365–9)

The title informs us of the adaptation to a new situation brought on by impoverishment, as with the conflict seen in *No body loues mee* (*c.* 1625). In contrast to this role-play figure, the porter succeeds in compensating for the contempt of former friends (see v. 8, p. 367) by joining another group – 'We Porters are good fellowes' (see v. 11, p. 368) and orientating his self-esteem towards the positive norm of earning an honest living. The difficult resolution of the conflict which has gone before can be perceived by the recipient quite apart from the limited perspective of the figure, if the former is capable of interpreting psychologically the vehemence of the latter's contempt for idlers and parasites (see vv. 5–6, p. 366), recurrent self-praise,[153] obvious self-satisfaction,[154] and insistent presenter-type lectures to the audience[155] which are the result of the resolution of cognitive dissonances. If, however, the recipient identifies with the perspective of the figure, the textual message will be understood as moral instruction. In this dual possibility of reception Martin Parker shows his professional competence as a ballad-maker.

> At first to worke I was asham'd,
>   but pouerty hath me so tam'd,
> That now I thinke it no disgrace,
>   to get my liuing in any place,
> Tis more commendable to worke,
>   then idlely at home to lurke,
> Wishing for bread, and haue it not.
> *Thus need will make the old wife trot.*   (ibid., v. 4, p. 366)

Other role-play ballads, featuring representatives of certain professions and ranks, do not convey as clearly the resolution of cognitive dissonances. They offer an understanding of the role-play situation which is unproblematical as to perspective, affording no clue to evaluation in the psychodynamics of the speaker of the role.

The cunning Northerne Begger,
Who all the By-standers doth earnestly pray
To bestow a penny upon him to day.

(between 1626 and 1681; *RB*, I, pp. 136–41)

This figure invites an understanding of the role that is quite different from that of the 'honest plaine dealing Porter':

> I am a lusty begger,
>   and live by others giving;
>   I scorne to worke,

> But by the highway lurke,
>   And beg to get my living:
> I'le i'th wind and weather,
>   And weare all ragged garments;
>   Yet, though I'm bare,
>   I'm free from care, –
>   A fig for high preferments!
> *For still will I cry 'Good your worship, good sir,*
> *Bestow one poore denier, sir,*
>   *Which, when I've got,*
>   *At the Pipe and Pot*
> *I soone will it casheere, sir.'*   (ibid., v. 1, lines 1–15, p. 137)

The 'cunning begger' is a virtuoso at assuming the role of the war invalid, the robbed sailor, cripple, blind or infirm individual, and the impoverished father of a family, and he also knows how to present his plight convincingly with embroidered stories. The histrionic potential of the text, with its components of attention-seeking self-presentation, its fraudulent designs, and requests for money, is similar in nature to the activity of the presenter. Its type of reference and allusion places it within the tradition of *Conny-Catching Tracts* (1591 and 1592), whereby the realization of the roles and the public performance were probably more amusing and effective.

The figures of the country lass, usurer, and spendthrift were also of immediate social relevance. Various proclamations since the reign of James I had sought to stem the economically and socially disastrous development of an increasing flight from the country to the towns. This movement affected not only agricultural labourers but also several of the aristocracy who sold their land at the time of the enclosures (see L. C. Knights [1951], pp. 115–16). The two poles of town and country loomed large in the minds of the populace and developed into a topos of rhetorical and propagandist contrast. *The Countrey Lasse* (1620 or 1621; *RB*, I, pp. 165–70, probably by Martin Parker) embodies the idealized country life in traditional contrast to the artificiality of town life,[156] which is represented by the opposite type in the person of a lady of the town. The role-play figure contrasts herself polemically[157] with the latter at every point of her self-presentation.[158] While the country girl represents a normative ideal, the comparisons in *The usurer and the Spendthrift* (between 1625 and 1640)[159] are in both parts of the ballad satirical in intention. In each of the two figures a complex of characteristics is presented which in its onesidedness and exaggeration clearly leads to a negative judgement. The moneylender's avarice and meanness, his contempt for and cruelty towards those without means, are contrasted with an equally unacceptable norm – the senseless dissipation of a father's fortune in ephemeral pleasures. The satirical target of these two fictional roles – which are also figures common to the drama of the time[160] – has its correlative outside the text in the profession of the usurer and in the fate of numerous individuals. The economy was becoming increasingly based on large-scale capital investment, necessitating a system of credit which was to develop into a controversial topic of contemporary economic theory.[161] In addition, there was a general desire for a higher standard of living and the prestige that went with it, and the emulation of the well-to-do urban middle classes which this involved also led either to borrowing or to the wasting of already accumulated wealth (see H. V. Rowth [1909], pp. 316–18).

An important aspect of the costly life of pleasure, particularly frequently thematicized, is the consumption of alcohol. Criticized in the narrative street ballad as a component of a life ending in misfortune,[162] it is by contrast resoundingly defended in the drinking-song. Owing to its textually preformed speech situation, the drinking-song as a role-play ballad is most suited to performance in the alehouse, where it can be directly transposed on to the intended reality situation. This type of ballad does however contain components connoting procedures connected with the presenter: in the bragging self-presentation of the *plaine dealing drunkard*, in the marking of the end of the text with the call to pay (for the drinks or the broadside)[163] and leave, or in the formula 'Roome for a lusty liuely Lad'.[164] On the other hand the toast, an integral part of the drinking-song, is quite clearly specific to the situation.

> Come Hostesse fill the pot,
>> for a penny will neuer vndo mee.
> If thou hast no money to pay the shot,
>> my Guest thou art welcome to me.
> Come fill vs a dozen of Cannes,
>> though they be but a pint a peece,
> We sweare weele drinke 'em off euery man,
>> and then weele the Tapster fleece.
> *For after a while we are here,*
> *And after a while we are gone:*
> *And after a while we haue money,*
> *And after a while we haue none.*[165]

There are however drinking-songs which are formulated in such a way that they will fit various situations or which indicate that the drinking will be done later, thus offering the audience the prospect of further ballad entertainment in the alehouse:[166]

> Heeres a health to all good fellowes,
>> that intend with me to ioyne,
> At the Tauerne, or the Ale-house,
>> and will freely spend their quoyne.

> But for such as hate strong liquor,
>   are not for my company,
> O it makes my wits the quicker,
>   when I taste it thorowly.   (ibid., v. 1, p. 235)

To a large extent the main concern of the drinking-song is to evoke an atmosphere of conviviality advantageous to the performance of ballads. *Heres to thee kind Harry. Or The plaine dealing Drunkard* (1627; *PB*, no. 61, II, pp. 88–93 and v. 1, p. 89) also intends primarily to convey a cheerful and lighthearted atmosphere in the opening verse, through self-presentation and the internal refrain from the Robin Hood ballads. Such an atmosphere would enhance the aesthetic effect of the ballad perform-ance:

> Roome for a lusty liuely Lad,
>   *dery dery downe,*
> That will shew himselfe blyth be he ne're so sad,
>   *dery dery downe.*
> That cryes a fig
>   for pouerty
> And takes all troubles
>   patiently,
> Will spend what he gets,
> And drinke more than he eates,
>   That neuer meanes to vary
> From good fellowship free,
> If thou such a one be.
>   *Ile drinke to thee kinde Harry.*

The role-play figure's firm stand in his self-presentation, resolving cog-nitive dissonances, is revealed especially clearly in the drinking-song. The bibulous speaker of the role describes himself and those of like mind as honest, generous, merry, and good-natured. The norm with which he con-trasts himself is provided by representatives of various trades and classes who are noted for their fraudulent practices,[167] or figures whose inferior qualities[168] he attributes to a lack of enjoyment in life. Another type of argument stresses the merits of cheap, healthy beer in comparison with those of other alcoholic drinks: *Good Ale for my money* (between 1628 and 1680; *RB*, I, pp. 411–17), whereby this beverage connotes popularity with the common people and becomes a status symbol for the convivial gatherings of honest, upright men. The strengthening of the individual's position through group coherence in an alcoholic haze of togetherness is common to all drinking-songs. The acting of the part is determined by the text, where the role is one of swaggering self-esteem, with miming and gestures expressing distance between the figure and those not of like mind and his contempt for them:

I can fuddle, roare and swagger,
    sing and dance in seuerall sort,
And giue six pence to a begger,
    in all this there's little hurt.
Whilst some churle thats worth a million,
    will giue nought in charity,
But to himselfe he proues a villaine:
    iudge who's better he or I.[169]

The defence of the drinking of alcohol in the street-ballad drinking-song, together with the fact that the latter was situation-specific – often used and kept as wall decorations in alehouses – lead us to assume that it afforded not only the drinking customers an extra pleasure but also the landlords, who would welcome it as advertising and as encouragement to drink. The balladmonger as performer and purveyor of such songs belonged to this milieu in the same way as musicians and down-at-heel minstrels. The practical function of the street ballad is here particularized in a quite distinctive way.[170]

The procedures and topoi of the drinking-song acquire, so to speak, a feminist slant through female role-speakers: *Fowre wittie Gossips disposed to be merry / Refused muddy Ale, to drinke a cup of Sherrie* (c. 1630; *PB*, no. 75, II, pp. 174–9) follows the tradition of 'alewife poems',[171] in which a group of drinking women humorously or satirically criticize men and their activities. The four women's positive feeling of solidarity is particularized in their liking of the more refined sherry in preference to the ordinary, commonplace beer drunk by men.[172] The fictional situation of the drinking-song, here narratively conveyed at the beginning and the end of the text, connotes the realizing of a claim to equal rights in the consumption of alcohol and leisure activities outside the home; this is in fact clearly stated:

So let the health goe round about,
    this day weell take our pleasure:
Our husbands were last night all out,
    and weell goe home by leasure?
For sack and suger let vs ioyne,
    you see it is cold weather?
And blithly let vs spend our coine,
    wee seldome meet together,
Wee will not depart,
    weell drinke a quart
    of Sacke to make vs merry.
Your Barlie broth fild vp with froth,
    is nothing like old sherrie.   (v. 5, p. 176)

Analysis of the role-play ballad has shown that in its reference to reality it deals with contemporary social problems of immediate relevance to the audience. The figure of the girl searching desperately for a husband in order to conform to an obligatory role-pattern articulates the social problem of the substantial surplus of females in seventeenth-century England.[173] The man's greater sexual permissiveness and unwillingness to marry correlates to this, though it is not so much a conflict as – from the point of view of consumer needs in the marriage-market – a legitimate attitude. It is expressed in the roles of the confirmed bachelor and the rake. The girl left on the shelf and the unmarried mother would be their interaction partners. Although within the street ballad these figures are treated as autonomous and dealt with in separate texts, they belong to the same social context which provides stimulation and material for the production of ballads. The inferiority of women was based not only on their statistical surplus but also, more importantly, on a system of social norms which produced a sexually specific hierarchy (see R. Thompson [1974], *passim*). It finds expression in the devaluation of women to the types 'shrew' and 'scold',[174] in the comic figure of the lecherous old widow and the, in part, tolerant attitude towards prostitution. Occasional protests in the form of a refusal to conform to the normal social role also appear in the spectrum of eclectic opinion in the street ballad. Without exception the norm of the marriage state is presented critically and negatively, from the perspectives of both sexes. The puritanical disapproval of strong drink and the widespread tendency to alcohol addiction are processed by the role-play ballad in drinking-songs. These are either of the type where the norm conflict is removed and the figures defend themselves and their habits with a conviction borne of the situation, or they are laments where the financial ruin suffered is presented as a deterrent example. Economically determined roles and role-changes in the dynamic early capitalist system are embodied in the usurer, spendthrift, beggar, and a porter who has seen better days. The increased contrast between town and country is articulated by the figure of the country girl.

The role-play ballad portrays problems concerning social role either as conflicts or as resolutions of cognitive dissonances. Existing norms are thereby seen as causing conflict but are in the end accepted. The role-play ballad does not convey a harmonizing of opposites – even where through a subjectively limited perspective the norm conflict is (temporarily) resolved – and it also avoids idealization far removed from reality. The intention of didactic effect in the role-play ballad is integrated into the perspective of the role itself and the subjectivizing of opinion and events. The dramatic fiction predominates both quantitatively and structurally, so that we seldom find the explicit moralizing didacticism which is a feature of many narrative street ballads. Instruction is far more closely interrelated with entertainment in the role-play ballad and therefore less obtrusive.

This last is only true of ballads with secular content, however. Where self-presentation in a role-play ballad conveys spiritual concerns, it is particularly influenced by stock patterns of theological and redemption history. As a consequence of the unquestioning acknowledgement of these values of the spirit and the next world, the situation of the figure – for example, a martyr or a sinner – is presumed to be so well known that no detailed graphic description is deemed necessary. Similarly, audience reference remains very general, at most listeners are specified as 'Christendom'; appeals are addressed to God in the manner of prayers.[175] The main concern is not the realistic portrayal of an individual fate, but religious exhortation and edification. The sacrifice of one's life for the sake of one's faith in order to gain eternal life implies a conflict of norms which from the Christian point of view clearly involves a hierarchy. It is presented in the martyr ballad as already overcome – rarely as a conflict still to be resolved:

> True Christian hartes, cease to lament,
>   for greefe it is in vaine;
> For *Christ*, you know, was well content
>   to suffer bitter payne,
> That we may come to heaven blisse,
>   there joyfully to singe.
> Whoe doth beleeue, shall never misse
>   *to haue a joyfull rysinge.*
>
> And then why should I be afraid
>   to suffer constantlie?
> Sith in this cause soe manie saintes
>   did suffer patientlie;
> And left examples for vs all
>   that we with them may singe;
> God grant wee may for mercie call,
>   *and haue a happie ryseinge!*

In *The songe mr.* Thewlis *writ him selfe* (1616),[176] a late but typical example of a martyr ballad, famous martyrs are mentioned as positive norm representatives (see vv. 6–13, pp. 81–4). The brief description of their execution illustrates at the same time the dramatic figure's situation, which is not itself portrayed. Hints given by the speaker as to his own individual situation continually merge into an awareness of the universal validity of the certainty of salvation which he shares with his model predecessors. While the secular role-play ballad portrays the dramatic figure's situation as being that of a (fictional) individual, the dramatic figure of the martyr ballad is placed in a situation determined by a comprehensive history of redemption, where his death has exemplary character but very little value as subjective experience. This becomes even clearer where the martyrdom is conveyed as a collective experience, as in *A songe of foure Preistes that suffered death at* Lancaster (1601).[177]

> O god, of thy great might strengthen our frailtie soe,
> Stoutlie to stand in feight against our infernall foe!
> Thy Campe in Order standes, where many a Champion bould
> In their victorious handes eternall Tryumph hould.   (v. 1, p. 71)

The group feeling which causes them to range themselves with the host of those who follow Christ, sharing their lot with a further two hundred priests executed for their faith,[178] has an almost timeless universal validity, as the listing of famous martyrs from different centuries also shows (see vv. 4–14, pp. 72–4). The deictically fixed situation is replaced by the fundamental situation of the eschatological polarity of Satan and Christ,[179] in which the Christian must prevail. This is explicitly formulated in relevant appeals (see vv. 25–33, pp. 76–8). If we compare this collective experience with the specific situation and feeling of solidarity particularized in gesture and mime in the street-ballad drinking-song, the connection between secularization and individualization becomes clear.

The resolution of cognitive dissonances is never articulated in the role of the confessor as clearly as in the secular role-play ballad. A psychological stance of this kind is at most implied in an absolutely fearless determination and rebelliousness in face of religious oppression by a temporal power:

> Noe rope nor cruell tortour then
>   should cause my minde to faile;
> Nor lewde deuice of wicked men
>   should cause my corage quaile,
> On racke in *tower* let me be lead,
>   let Joynts at large be stretched;
> Let me abyde each cruell braid,
>   till blood frome vaines be fetched.
>
> And if they can devise worse waies
>   to vtter thinges vntrue,
> Let them proceede by all assaies
>   to frame Inventions newe;
> Let all distresse to me befale
>   to doe my Countrie good;
> And let the thirst of Tyrantes all
>   be quenchèd in my blood.

In this ballad: *Caluarie* mount is my delight (c. 1616; OEB, no. 22, pp. 147–51; vv. 9–10, pp. 149–50) there is no reference to other martyr figures, and at the same time the visualizing of the suffering to be endured in the conditional mode does tend towards an individualization of situation and protagonist. However, within a theological framework with a fixed hierarchy of values, a clear conflict can be thematicized only retrospectively as penitence and lamentations of sinfulness. The ballad *An*

Askew. Entituled, *I am a Woman Poor and Blind* (between 1546? and 1675)[180] dramatizes the martyr role by including the elements of guilt and penitence.[181]

> My spirit within me is vexed sore,
>   my spirit striveth against the same,
> My sorrows do encrease more and more,
>   my conscience suffereth most bitter pain.
>
>   (v. 3, lines 9–12, *RB*, I, p. 31)

Inner struggles and religious error are generalized during the course of the text in a garden allegory[182] and overcome by the dramatic figure. The minimal importance attached to the situation of the individual speaker in the religious role-play ballad is also shown in the version of the Job story: *A pleasant ballad of the iust man* Jobe, *shewing his patience in extremitie* (1564/65; *OEB*, no. 33, pp. 209–12), where the details of his suffering are presumed known, in order to emphasize the functional and exemplary value of the penitent as such. This Old Testament figure has through tradition and convention become a formalized example which only needs to be mentioned, so that presented in role-play form he is to a certain extent an icon figure for the instructional purpose of Christian ethics.

The dialectics of human guilt and God's grace can be presented as a personal conflict between fear and hope.

> I might haue liued merelie
>   If I had sinned never;
> But now, forsooth and verelie,
>   condemp'd I am for ever,
> Except I turne right towardlie
>   to god with hart and glee,
> And leaue my sinninge frowardlie,
>   and true repentant bee![183]

In lamentations of sin, however, the personal statement, indicated by frequent usage of personal pronouns, usually recedes behind the fundamentally religious and moral discussion which is characterized in fixed formulas from the homiletic sector – 'sin, condemn, repent, mercie, faith and hope in Christ'[184] etc. – and apodictic statements. The performative speaker does have the function of a textual centre of orientation, but apart from that he is only minimally specified, so that his theologically representative role covers a far greater reference area than his counterpart in the secular role-play ballad. It is not everyday problems which are presented here, but a fundamental religious attitude: *The sinner, dispisinge the world and all earthly vanities, reposeth his whole confidence in his beloved Saviour, Jesus Christ* (1569):

> Though the world tempt me sore,
>   though the flesh trouble me,
> Tho the devill would devoure,
>   my refuge is to thee;
> Though heaven and earth doe faile,
>   tho all perplexèd bee,
> Thou art and euer shall
>   *my cheefest comfort bee.*   (OEB, no. 30, pp. 198–202; v. 9, p. 201)

The awareness of sinfulness provides here, as in other ballads, the starting-point for general rejection of the world: *How happy and assured they are, in all stormes, that firmely depend vpon god* (before 1576),[185] or for the portrayal of the sufferings and sacrifice of Christ: *O blessed God, O Sauiour sweete* (c. 1616; OEB, no. 16, pp. 114–18). In theme and linguistic style these early street ballads follow a song tradition which was predominantly religious in content.[186] The personification of death in *Deth with houreglasse in the one hand and speare in the other threatneth all estates* (c. 1580)[187] can be distinguished, in self-description and reference to the figure itself and its attributes, only through its imperious content and lofty style from the type of linguistic behaviour of the presenter and fictional role-player, but it is just as effective in performance:

> Loe heare I vaunce, with speare and shield,
> To watche my pray, to spoyle, to kill;
> By day, by night, on sea, on land,
> Noe tyme I stay; but toyling still,
> My force I try, to worcke the will
> Of ruling *Ioue*: with deathfull dint,
> Eache hart I reave, though hard as flint.
>
> My shape is dread of wor[l]dly wightes;
> My piercing darte, abhorèd sore;
> Which them devides from vayne delightes, –
> From glaring pompe possest before,
> From scepter, croune, and earthly glore:
> With Pallas, throne, yea reign and power,
> I them bereave at 'pointed howre.
>
>   . . .
>
> Defer noe tyme, therfore, I say,
> Ye sonnes of men, your selves prepare;
> For hence, perforce, ye must away:
> No keyser, kyng, nor Quene, I spare;
> But when their times fulfillèd are,
> I strike them doune, whome none may save,
> But dust to dust I fling in grave.[188]

The figure of Death as precentor and leader of the dance of death comes particularly close to the role-play figure, fulfilling functions similar to

those of the presenter: *Remember Death, and thou shalt neuer sinne*
(1569; *BB*, no. 2, pp. 3–4).

> Ye Adams broode and earthly wightes, which breath now on the earth,
>   Come daunce thys trace, and marke the song of me most mighty Death.
> Ful wel my might is knowen & sene, in al the world about,
>   When I do strike, of force they yeld, both noble, wise & stout.
> Of liuing things which breath and bray, I raigne as puisant Prince,
>   No sooner take they lyfe, but I, pursue it to conuince.
> In Mothers wombe the Babe I slay, in birth sometime I strike,
>   No place nor state may exempt, to me all is a like.
> The Prince with Begger to graue I take, the yong eke wyth the old,
>   [The] wise graue men with fooles and dolts, I lodge them in one fold.
> Y[ea] courtly Dames, & town wyues fine, though neuer so trim they be,
>   W[i]th Malkins, Sluts, & sloyes they trudge, in graue I make the gree.
>
> The seming braue fine Courtiers, which square it out in gate,
>   With Hob and Lob I close in clay and bring them to one state.
> The tchuffe with tchinckes and ruddocks red, wherin is all hys trust,
>   In moment I wyth mysers poore, do hyde hym vp in dust.
> The Iudge seuere, and Counceller sage, with me they all must trudge,
>   I force not for their hye estate, nor feare their hate or grudge.
>   . . .
> No place so sure, no food so good, no exercise at all,
>   Me Death can barre, but at Gods becke to earth I make them fall.
> And yet behold how ech one thynckes, to scape me and my dart,
>   Though neuer so nere I come them to, and grype them to the hart.
> My Minstrell Sicknes pipes ech houre, by aches, stitches and cramps,
>   It soudes my daunce styll in their eares that they must to my damps.
>   . . .
> It makes me laffe oft times to see, their gate, their lookes, their walke,
>   How halting tryps, and fine wryde iestes they counterfet in talke.
> They would me blere, and make folkes think, they wer to yong for me
>   And yet forsooth if stript they were, faire Notamies might ye see.
>   (ibid., lines 1–18 and 23–8, p. 3; lines 43–6, p. 4)

The request for attention, and invitation to join in the dance of death
which no one can escape, create an area of action which can be incorporated ionto the actual performance. Gesture and mime expressing the
limitless power of the figure of Death and his contempt for the vain resistance of his victims accompany the evocation of his activities, which take
place beyond the sphere of the performative present. The inexorable certainty of his victory is illustrated by a large number of representative
examples of extreme conciseness and graphic vividness. In the portrayal of
the death figure's claim to power, his universal and all-embracing operations are translated into the individual performance situation.

As far as I can ascertain, the role-play quality of the self-presentation
and its particularization in situation and episode are features peculiar to

the street ballad. The genre may have taken as a point of orientation the tradition of carols[189] with texts which are regarded as being of a 'role-play' or 'dramatic' nature in the sense of a performative speech situation. This tradition continued into the mid-sixteenth century, overlapping with the emergence of the early street ballad. The social ranking of the carol as 'popular', as opposed to 'courtly' or 'folk',[190] and its functions of practical use and entertainment – though more broadly interpreted than those of the street ballad[191] – certainly indicate a possible connection. Occasional textual correspondences also point to this possibility,[192] as, for instance, the use of a narrative introduction of the type, 'As I was walking . . . ', which clearly derives from the *chanson dramatique* type of poem.[193] The following account by the figure of his or her situation, however, in contrast to that of the *chanson dramatique*, frequently reveals features of the role-play ballad. It is precisely the discrepancy between the traditional topos element and an unconventional treatment of further elements traditionally belonging to it that shows the independence of street-ballad texts.[194]

While in the *chanson dramatique* the figure's account of his or her situation usually shows minimal deictic structure (lament, reflection, religious instruction), among the carols which have no narrative introductory verse and are comparable thematically to role-play ballads, performative texts can be found where the first-person statement also contains iterative–durative episodes with illustrative function:

> Care away, away, away,
> care away for euermore.
>
> All that I may swynk or swet,
> My wyfe it wyll both drynk and ete;
> And I sey ovght, she wyl me bete;
>   Carfull ys my hart therfor.
>
> If I sey ovght of hyr but good,
> She loke on me as she war wod
> And wyll me clovght abovght the hod;
>   Carfull ys my hart therefor.[195]

The thematic similarity of this *chanson de mal marié* to the street-ballad role-play fiction of the discontented husband (or wife) merely indicates the conventionalizing of the theme. The type and treatment of episodes correspond in principle to that of the street ballad, but in this and similar texts[196] there is no particularizing of the immediate speech situation with its presenter components, into which the iterative–durative episodes are integrated and to which they are subordinated. The dimension created by the effect of direct contact with the audience through the medium of the role-play fiction is absent in the carols. Furthermore, the comparative shortness of the carol, which has verses of only four lines compared with the considerably longer role-play ballad with, for the most part, eight-line verses, does not permit full exploitation of a speech situation or of the episodes. The 'burden' is frequently emotive in content, and given emphasis by sound equivalences. Occurring after each short verse, it tends to dominate more than the street-ballad refrain at the end of a longer verse. From the point of view of deictic coherence, the burden also has a more segmenting effect.

Only a rudimentary shaping of the speech situation by the performative speaker in his own account of himself – not conveyed through a narrator or eyewitness – is found in the carols. This may be in the mention of an attribute, for example, a dagger, or in the description of a fashionable nobleman's attire:[197] in these contexts such elements have a characterizing and symbolic function rather than a deictic one. Somewhat more precise deictic information is found in some drinking-songs, where drinking companions are addressed (see ibid., no. 420, pp. 253–4) or the 'butler' is asked to pour out (no. 421, p. 254) or to bring various dishes listed like a catalogue (no. 422, pp. 254–5);. However, as with the street-ballad drinking-song, the speech situation here is fictionalized to such an extent that it can only be directly transposed on to a concrete situation if in a very restricted functional context. There is regular occurrence of audience address in carols, with obvious deictic reference to person. For example, this can be a warning to young men not to marry (nos. 404 and 405, p. 240), or to young girls to protect their innocence (no. 398, p. 235), or a request that the audience believe what the speaker has to say.[198] On the other hand there is only perfunctory signalling of a concrete performance situation and, except through an explicit speaker, there is little by way of deictic structuring. It can be seen from this brief survey that although isolated role-play elements do indeed occur in the carol and in the *chanson dramatique* – first-person statement of the figure's situation, explicit speaker, audience address, occasional references to the speech situation and iterative–durative episodes – their detailed and frequent application and, more importantly, their combination in a single text are features of only the later type of role-play ballad. Within the carol text corpus, predominantly performative texts are in the minority compared to those texts which are predominantly narrative.[199]

4.3.2 Dialogue ballad: dialogue action and perspectives of opinion

The fact that there are two speakers in the dialogue ballad, as distinct from the role-play ballad, affects the structure of the figures' fictional accounts of themselves. Apart from minor exceptions, the allocation of roles within the limited space of the broadside precludes the treatment of the figures' fictional past either as an expositional account, as frequently found in drama, or as a series of iterative–durative episodes, as found in the role-play ballad. Psychological subtleties and their illustration by means of realistic detail are thereby necessarily reduced in comparison with the role-play ballad. The fictional situation conveyed through role-play is replaced either by a rudimentary plot realized through dialogue or by a predominantly discursive argument, where the division into different speaking roles serves to demonstrate differing points of view.

The dialogue ballad has its origins in two literary traditions: the contemporary 'jig' and late-medieval dialogue poetry. As a brief version of a *singspiel* with dance[200] or as a group dance with song accompaniment combined with a certain amount of plot, the jig has a close affinity with the street ballad, from both the literary and the sociological point of view. It appeared in its various forms as an 'afterpiece'. The word 'jig' refers first of all to a particularly lively dance form which was presumably performed on the toes.[201] The term is also used to refer to *singspiel* farces, song-and-dance items, and dialogue ballads of the time. The extent to which dancing was involved is often unclear, and for most dialogue ballads remains open. Jig texts were also circulated on broadsides, often in shortened versions; on the other hand jig ballads found their way into the theatre or into the programme of annual festivals or country weddings.[202] They also occur as amusing interludes during plays (see C. R. Baskervill [1929], pp. 7–14). Alongside common features of bibliography, textual structure, and specific literary level between the street ballad and the jig as popular entertainment, there are also personal links which point to a traditional connection. Actors such as Tarlton and George Attowell are known to have been ballad-singers and authors.[203] Similarities of theme certainly indicate that the tradition of early dialogue poetry, the *débat*, exerted an influence on the dialogue ballad. Marriage problems expressed in dialogue form, 'gossips' song', the courtship situation of the pastoral, and discussion between faithful lovers of the *Nut-Brown Maid* type and her vacillating partner, all found their way into the dialogue ballad.

Dialogue ballads conveying dramatic action through the speech acts of rudimentarily characterized figures are in the minority compared with dialogue ballads using discursive procedures. It is possible that this is merely a bibliographic lack of extant texts due to excessive usage and consumption. *Frauncis new Jigge, betweene Frauncis a Gentleman, and Richard a Farmer* (PG, no. 1, pp. 1–10), written, significantly, by the actor George Attowell (see ibid., p. 1, n.), is thought to be the earliest and at the same time a very typical jig ballad (see ibid.). The social difference between the couple Besse and Richard on the one hand and the rival Francis on the other still contains an element of the figure constellation in the pastoral. Besse, however, only pretends to give in to the seduction attempt, which is

reinforced by gifts, in order to prove her faithfulness to Richard by means
of a trick involving disguise and to shame the city gentleman and seducer:
the latter's own wife is brought to him for the nocturnal rendezvous. This
motif, together with the brevity of the responses regardless of the verse
structure, indirect 'stage directions',[204] the communication of the plot
through the announcement of plans in the dialogue, the plotting of the two
women in the absence of the men, and the denouement after the night of
love, with all the characters 'on stage' – all reveal the influence of comedy
and farce. The text is not ideal for reproduction in the street ballad with
only one performer. This also applies to *A Country new Jigge betweene*
Simon *and* Susan, *to be sung in merr[y] pastime [by] Bachelors and
Maydens* (c. 1620; PG, no. 21, pp. 132–8). It is a ballad with less action,
and involves alternate singing between a young couple wishing to marry,
the mother, and the father whose agreement is procured in the second part.
The various speakers' utterances are segmented into verses and given song
character through the refrain and simplicity of language; they are of little
relevance to the plot, relating primarily to the couple's idealized future.

The courtship dialogue with only two speakers, where the responses are
divided into verses, is more suited to performance by the balladmonger.
The situation of courtship determines the course of the action which, conveyed in dialogue form, ends with the overcoming of the girl's resistance.
The arguments of the lover and the objections of the girl relate to differences in station, the property situation, the praise of beauty, and erotic
desires. In *The Louers Guift, Or a Fairing for Maides: Being a Dialogue
between* Edmund *and* Prisilly (c. 1620; PB , no. 25, I, pp. 162–7), a concrete offer of money turns the scales for the girl of slender means. *A Wench
for a VVeauer* (c. 1630; PB, no. 73, II, pp. 162–8) contains panegyric with
regard to station: the weaver's craft is defended with reference to 'lacke of
Nuberie' (see v. 11, p. 166) against the widespread view uttered by the girl,
'To be a Weauers wife / is to liue poore' (v. 4,3–4, p. 164). Colloquial
expressions and aggressive tirades show the affinity to popular tradition
despite occasional allusions of a highly literary nature.[205]

> *A most pleasant Dialogue:*
>   *Or*
> *A merry greeting betweene two louers,*
> *How* Will *and* Nan *did fall at strife,*
> *And at the last made man and wife.*   (1632; PB, no. 84, II, pp. 224–8)

The argument between Will and Nan is characterized by the stark aggress-
iveness with which the female character exposes the bragging of her lover.
Speech characteristics of the 'shrew' contrast with the well-turned phrases
of Will, who is attempting to appear elegant:

When I liued with my friends at home,
   I went in silke and rich arayment,
With Gallants I in Tauernes roard,
   ten pound at once in ready payment
I did disburse out of my purse,
   vnto the Vintner for good licker,
And so my Father allowd me to doe,
   to make my wits and spirits quicker.

Mvch like vnto a ruffian, rude,
   thou didst 'mongst Puncks & Panders wander,
And commpany keptst with Strumpets lude,
   as flockes of Geese keepe with the Gander.
To *Tom* of *Bedlam* wouldst thou skip,
   all this is truth which I doe tell yet,
And eate the meate out of his scrip,
   so glad wert thou to fill thy belly.   (ibid., vv. 6–7, p. 226)

The violence of the arguments in street-ballad courtship dialogues[206] gives them more potential for dramatic action than the pastoral, but at the same time deprives them of the latter's playful gaiety. This mood is still quite clearly retained in *A Ditty delightfull of mother Watkins ale, / A warning wel wayed, though counted a tale* (c. 1590; AB, no. 76, pp. 370–5), a ballad which also shows the link with tradition in its partial use of narrative. The enjoyment of a particular kind of beer is used throughout as an image for courtship and seduction, through which they not so much lose their taboo character as acquire a humorous slant. Alongside the component of beer consumption there are obscene connotations – the alcohol-induced mutual encouragement to prolong the pleasure, and the subsequent symptoms of illness (pregnancy).

Courtship and marriage problems are themes with immediate relevance for wedding celebrations, and we can assume that such dialogue ballads were used on these occasions as jigs. Whereas the situation in the courtship dialogue, where the lover is attempting to persuade the girl to marry him, admits of little dramatic action, the married status provides the conditions necessary to contrast or confirm various speakers' views whose situation can no longer be significantly changed. The treatment of marriage themes in the dialogue ballad is predominantly critical and negative, and in this respect as well as in its line of argument it does not differ from corresponding role-play ballads. However, whereas in the role-play ballad various points of view and norms are represented by the figures as reported by a single speaker, in the dialogue ballad each viewpoint is assigned to a certain speaker. In so far as the speaker's viewpoint is based on personal experience and possibly described iterative–duratively, he or she is also characterized as a fictional figure. In this way the speaker differs from the speaker of the discursive street ballad; the division of the limited textual space does mean, however, that the dialogue speakers cannot be portrayed as figures as consistently and precisely as can the individual speaker of the role-play ballad within his or her characteristic situation. This in fact corresponds to the main intention of the discursive dialogue ballad, namely to present and discuss a theme from different perspectives, whereby the function of detailed fictional information is to illustrate the theme rather than to help portray the figures.

The cunning Age. Or A re-married Woman repenting her Marriage, / Rehearsing her Husbands dishonest carriage. / Being a plesant Dialogue between a re-married Woman, / a Widdow, and a young Wife (between 1624 and 1626)[207] follows the pattern of the 'gossips' song'[208] which was possibly also the model for other dialogue ballads on the marriage theme which are not based on women's conversation:

> WIDDOW
>
> Good morrow, kind Gossip, why whither so fast?
> I pray stay a while, I know ther's no haste,
> And let's chat a while of some things that are past;
> I heare say y'are married since I saw you last;
>   *O this is a hasty Age,*
>   *O this is a hasty Age.*
>
> MAR. WOMAN
>
> 'Tis true. I am marry'd, which hath beene my bane,
> But if that I were now a Widdow againe,
> I so would continue; but griefe is in vaine,
> I must be contented to sing this sad straine,
>   *Oh fie on this coozening Age,*
>   *Oh fie on this* etc.
>
> WIDDOW
>
> Oh, doe you so quickly your bargaine repent,
> And yet you thought long e're about it you went?
> If marriage bring trouble, in time Ile preuent
> All future vnquietnesse, and be content
>   *To shun such a coozening Age,*
>   *To shun,* etc.
>
> MAR. WOMAN
>
> Oh, woe is me, Gossip, that e're I was borne,
> I marry'd a Boy, that now holds me in scorne,
> He comes among Whoores both euening and morne,
> While I sit at home, like a creature forlorne.
>   *Oh, this is a coozening Age,*
>   *Oh,* etc.   (PG, no. 42, vv. 1–4, pp. 239–40)

All three female participants can introduce their marital experience into the conversation, conveying it in iterative–durative descriptions of situations which all combine to produce a negative view of marriage. One of the women is converted to this view: the widow who has recently remarried succeeds in persuading the widow who has not yet done so to abandon her plans to remarry. The young wife who joins in later approves of this attitude on the basis of her own experience. The convergence of views of the three speakers renders the textual message particularly convincing.

The procedure of contrasting different opinions and experiences, on the other hand, gives the audience an apparent freedom of choice, although this is for the most part cancelled out by the unambiguous nature of the evaluation conveyed in the ballads. In *Man's Felicity and Misery: Which is, a good Wife and a bad; or, the best and the worst, discoursed in a Dialogue betweene Edmund and David* (1632; *RB*, II, pp. 182–8), positive and negative marital experiences are schematically contrasted: the two men compare notes as they go along, speaking in alternate verses. The emotional agitation of the two speakers is confined to the refrain. The dovetailing in the dialogue is effected by each speaker's seizing on what has just been said by the other and responding with the extreme opposite:

> EDMUND
> My wife for beautie beares the name
> From all i' th' towne from whence she came,
> For shape she might a lady be,
> And so all say that doe her see;
> Her middle I can easily span,
> O shee's the best wife that ever had man.

> DAVID
> My wife so lothsome is to view,
> She every morning makes me spew,
> For person she's scarce good enough
> To cry, 'Maids ha' ye any kitchen-stuffe?'
> She shineth like a dripping pan,
> O she's the worst wife that ever had man.[209]

The positive or negative assessment of marriage is presented here as depending on choice of partner. The schematic ordering of opposites is in line with the principle of functional transparency and reinforces the didactic intention. A similar procedure is followed in *A merry Dialogue betwixt a married man and his wife, concerning the affaires of this carefull life* (between 1619 and 1629; *RB*, II, pp. 158–63), by Martin Parker. It consists of an argument in which both husband and wife strive for the other's acknowledgement and appreciation of the male and female role respectively:

> (WOMAN)   I have for all good wives a song –
>   I doe lament the women's wrong,
>   And I doe pittie them with my heart,

To think upon the women's smart –
Their labour's great, and full of paine,
Yet for the same they have small gaine.

(MAN)   In that you say cannot be true
For men doe take more paines th[a]n you;
We toile, we moile, we grieve and care,
When you sit on a stoole or chaire;
Yet, let us do all what we can,
Your tongues will get the upper hand.

(w)   We women in the morning rise
As soone as day breaks in the skies;
And then to please you, with desire,
The first we doe is, make a fire.
Then other worke we straight begin,
To sweep the house, to card, or spin.

(M)   Why, men doe worke at plough and cart,
Which soone would break a woman's heart:
They sow, they mow, and reape the corne,
And, many times, doe wear the horne.
In praise of wives speake you no more;
For these were lies you told before.

(ibid., vv. 1–4, lines 1–24, pp. 159–60)

The areas of responsibility inside and outside the home are then further defined and contrasted – washing, cooking, and bearing and bringing up children, as opposed to earning money and maintaining prestige. Social contact is also contrasted: gossip with neighbours as opposed to the pleasures of the alehouse. The double perspective of two discontented individuals brings out these contrasts and reveals Martin Parker's remarkably critical awareness of the one-sidedness of each of the roles. This would have corresponded to contemporary reality (see R. Thompson [1974], p. 9 and *passim*), and is to a large extent still relevant today. The reconciliation at the conclusion of the ballad, where the two speakers end their striving for mutual acknowledgement, can be interpreted as a concession to prevailing public opinion. A counterpart to this ballad, similar in theme but differing in the kind of perspective used, is *A new Ballad, Containing a communication between the carefull Wife and the comfortable Hus*[band], *touching the common cares and charges of Household* (between *c.* 1620 and 1640).[210] As already indicated in the epithets used in the metatextual advance information on the two dialogue partners, the husband and wife describe their different roles in much the same way as in *A merry Dialogue* in their attempts to reach agreement on the extremely difficult task of earning a living.

Dialogue ballads in the early period of the street ballad were religious in theme. The allegorical figure of Death[211] proves his authority in the interaction with a youth who begs in vain for a delay: *A dialogue betwene death and youthe* (1563/64; OEB, no. 44, pp. 252–6). In contrast to the later dialogue ballads, the dialogue partners are here not representative types from everyday life but personifications of the traditional kind. In the figure of the youth there is no differentiation according to social status, individual fate, or situational factors. The confrontation does not take the form of schematic parallels but develops out of the discrepancy between the resistance and powerlessness of the victim and the omnipotence of death. The outcome of the dialogue, the youth's insight and submission, is determined by the theological frame of reference, whereas the secular dialogue ballad conveys different perspectives and opinions. The same applies to *A Dialogue betwene* Christe *and the pore oppressed synner* (1586; OEB, no. 48, pp. 270–1) and other ballads of this kind.[212] The sinner comes to Christ, in full awareness of his guilt, in the hope of grace and salvation. The dialogue turns on the discrepancy in the power positions and follows the traditional pattern of the doctrine of salvation in both argumentation and style of language.

The speech structure of the dialogue ballad is not conducive to the development of a presenter level of communication except in the metatextual advance information of the title. The fact that a number of dialogue ballads of the first half of the seventeenth century nevertheless have presenter-type verses, usually at the end, indicates a widespread awareness of the demands of the speech situation on the part of ballad authors. The final verse serves to summarize the didactic content and to clarify the close of the discussion with warnings or advice to the audience. This is specified as address by the 'Author',[213] or it is recognizable as a narrative ending[214] or it may be communicated by the speakers in chorus.[215] A breaking of the dialogue fiction by one of the speakers is also possible.[216] Invitations to buy,[217] marking the end of the text,[218] *captatio benevolentiae*[219] and audience address targeted at particular groups[220] are further features specific to the presenter.

4.3.3 Discursive street ballad: arrangement of examples according to theme; medley; advice ballad; religious exhortation ballads

The communication structure of the discursive ballad, like that of the role-play ballad and the dialogue ballad, is characterized by the performative speech situation. In contrast to the self-presentation and fictional situation of the role-play and dialogue figure, however, the performative speaker in the discursive ballad is only minimally defined. His function is to convey a theme, and any closer characterization is merely through the attitude expressed in his explicit and implicit comments. The coherence principles of his subject of communication are not, or only slightly, deictic in nature but of a semantic, syntactic, and argumentative kind (see above, chapter 4.1). With regard to the fundamentally thematic coherence principle, there is a similarity here to the type of narrative ballad in which the thematic linking of events predominates (see above, pp. 129–31). In the latter, however, the episodes are also correlated deictically through the respective figures, whereas the discursive ballad can mention a large number of figures, usually only once, using them merely as examples which are completely subordinated to the development of the theme. The criterion of difference involving the virtual absence of deictic structure in the discursive ballad compared with the narrative ballad also applies to the news ballad, which only becomes a discursive ballad when the report of events is merely a springboard for the discussion of a topic and moral instruction (see above, p. 148. The tendency for the thematic aspect to predominate was also noted in the 'discursive dialogue ballad' (see above, pp. 188–93), which can present a divergence of opinion by means of different perspectives, while in the purely discursive ballad there is only one speaker perspective.

The discursive street ballad can thus be distinguished through predominance of a theme from other sub-genres of the street ballad whose textual message is mainly conveyed via deictic structures – individuals and their actions in space and time. In order to explain more precisely the thematic structure of the subject of communication for purposes of interpretation and the investigation of textual manipulation of reception, it is convenient to use the textual–linguistic conception of the various interconnection possibilities of 'theme' and 'rheme'.[221] The distinction between theme and rheme serves on the one hand to assign semantic units to different hierarchical levels, and on the other to establish their respective information value; the theme is defined as the 'known information', and the rheme as the 'new information'.[222] The distribution of semantic units throughout the text can then be described according to their relationship to each other (repetition or derivation) and to their position (contact or distance; see F. Daneš [1976], p. 35). By this means it should be possible to describe more precisely thematic structure and the information given in a discursive ballad. In order to prevent complications unnecessary to this investigation, however, a modification is needed: while F. Daneš's procedure describes the 'thematic progression' sentence by sentence as an utterance consisting of theme and rheme, for an analysis of the far more comprehensive street-ballad texts (compared with his examples) it is more appropriate to start out from the larger semantic units (possibly a whole verse). The degree of intuitiveness which is usually attached to the formation of semantic units is doubtless thereby increased: for the understanding of the basic thematic structure of discursive ballads, however, it is adequate. Our primary aim must be to clarify and objectify, in a more differentiated way, the reader's impression of the fairly simple thematic structure and high degree of redundancy of these texts, using Daneš's types of thematic progression. It is possible to describe theme-orientated manipulation of reception in detail.

The status of the subject of communication as the development of a theme also determines the nature and function of the speaker. His lack of definition compared with the narrator and role-play figure is the result of the absence of any narrative communication function in respect of the fictional role-play situation conveyed as a characteristic of the speaker. It is all the easier to effect a change of function between the discursive speaker and the presenter as speaker. Expression of opinion and elucidation of the theme easily slot in with the illocutionary and deictic features of the presenter speech situation,[223] which is often quite clearly developed in the discursive street ballad. The presenter puts the theme before the audience, proclaims himself as an authority and source, makes didactic intentions explicit, and contributes to the entertainment element of the performance.

The discursive street ballad can be divided into various types according to the dominant role of the presenter, certain kinds of content and thematic structure, and different intentions:

1   Many texts convey social criticism by means of their clear thematic structure and numerous examples, interspersed with entertainment elements.
2   By contrast, the 'medley' takes lack of structure and coherence as a principle, in order to produce a predominantly entertaining effect by means of associative sequences taken to the point of nonsense.
3   The 'advice ballad' differs from the type of discursive ballad which presents a string of examples with predominantly socially critical intention, merely through the appeal dimension of advice, which provides an additional coherence principle.

The above three types, occurring in the first half of the seventeenth century, have in common the use of presenter procedures.

4   The early form of the discursive street ballad, however, to a large extent lacks the communication level of the presenter, as was already established with regard to other street-ballad texts of the second half of the sixteenth century. Such texts have a more or less clear thematic structure and are without exception didactic in intention and religious and edifying in content.

In an answer ballad[224] to Martin Parker's *Knauery in all Trades* (1632; *PG*, no. 72, pp. 410–14) Laurence Price, in competition with his rival, uses irony to turn the theme round and give an exaggeratedly utopian picture of society:

The Honest Age,
OR
There is honesty in all Trades;
As by this Ditty shall appeare,
Therefore attend and giue good eare.   (1632; *PG*, no. 71, pp. 406–9)

The development of the theme is typical of the discursive ballad and is
here particularly simple and transparent. The 'hypertheme' (T) is
announced in the title, then presented to the audience in two opening
presenter-type verses using the 'outdoing' topos, reference gestures, and
requests for attention, and there are constant reminders in the refrain.
Each of the following verses illustrates the theme with an example of
honest, altruistic behaviour of a tradesman or craftsman ('Broker,
Chandler, Taylor, Cooke, Tapster, Baker, Butcher, Miller, Brewer, Shoo-
maker, Weauer, Glouer, Mason, Painter', etc.). These representative
figures constitute the sub-themes (T_{n-n}), and each time we are given information regarding their typical behaviour patterns. According to Daneš's
classification of thematic structures, the thematic progression follows type
3: a number of sub-themes which derive from a hypertheme follow one
another in the course of the text, with the appropriate rheme each time (see
F. Daneš [1970], pp. 76ff.):

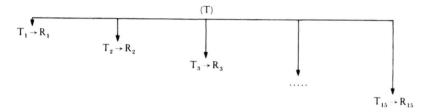

And first to goe forward as now I intend,
I heare that the Broker his money will lend
To any poore Neighbour his estate to amend,
How well is that man that hath got such a friend.
  O this is an honest age,
  This is a plaine dealing age.

The Chandler that keepes coles and fewel to sell,
Doth top heape his measure and soundly it fill,
For Sope, Starch, and Candle he wayeth so well,
That of his plaine dealing his neighbors can tell.
  O this is an honest age,
  This is a plaine dealing age.

That Taylor doth scorne to deceiue any friend,
But vnto plaine dealing his mind he doth bend,
If once he were false he hath sworne to amend,

> No more cloth, nor silke, lace, to hell he will send.
> *O this is an honest age,*
> *This is a plaine dealing age.*   (vv. 3–5, *PG*, p. 407)

The consistent principle of derivation, which may be described as the exemplification of a statement, and the regular sequence of sub-themes at practically identical intervals throughout the text determine the simple, transparent thematic structure. The large measure of redundancy in the information supplied similarly contributes to ease of reception. The audience is however expected to recognize the socially critical reference to a negative reality full of swindling and greed in the exaggerated portrayal of the positive ideal, as is thematicized often enough in other discursive ballads. The concrete detail in the series of examples has entertainment value.

The vast majority of discursive street ballads follow type 3 in their thematic macrostructure.[225] A basic theme is dealt with throughout the text, either split into partial statements or explained by means of examples which for their part provide detailed new information. Redundancy abounds, owing to the uniformity of the hypertheme which is apparent in all the sub-themes and to the latter's semantically isotopic interrelation, similarity of structure, and possible recurrence. This thematic macrostructure is not always as apparent as in the example just quoted. It may be, for example, that the derivation of the sub-themes from the hypertheme is not uniform, or that the sub-themes differ in their degree of abstraction (generalizing statement versus concrete example), or that repetition and change of position of sub-themes in the course of the text occur, or various rhemes are assigned to the same sub-theme in different parts of the text. Apart from such 'irregularities' or microstructural complications, the thematic macrostructure may also remain concealed owing to an abundance of detail within one semantic unit.

> *The wiuing age.*
> *Or*
> *A great Complaint of the Maidens of London,*
> *Who now for lacke of good Husbands are vndone,*
> *For now many Widowes though neuer so old,*
> *Are caught vp by young men for lucre of gold.*
>   (between 1621 and 1625; *PG*, no. 41, pp. 234–8)

In this ballad the thematic structure is complicated in so far as the hypertheme, 'competition between pretty young girls and rich old widows', can first be divided into three sub-themes which recur alternately during the course of the text and whose rhemes need further definition. The three sub-themes which can be clearly delineated are: the situation of girls at (T_1), of widows (T_2) and of eligible young bachelors (T_3). Each time new infor-

mation is given about the group (R'–n'), and these rhemes can be distinguished throughout in all the sub-themes according to positive (+R) or
negative (−R); assessment of the situation or characteristics of the respective group. The thematic progression can thus be represented diagrammatically as follows:[226]

Verse

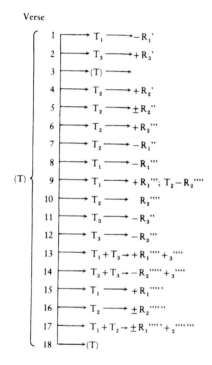

The wiuing age.
     Or
A great Complaint of the Maidens of London,
Who now for lacke of good Husbands are vndone,
For now many Widowes though neuer so old,
Are caught vp by young men for lucre of gold.

     To the tune of *the Golden age.*

1   The Maidens of *London* are now in despaire,
      How they shall get husbands, it is all their care,
      Though maidens be neuer so vertuous and faire,
      Yet old wealthy widowes, are yong mens chiefe ware.
          Oh this is a wiuing age.
          Oh this is a wiuing age.

2   A yong man need neuer take thought how to wiue,
   For widowes and maidens for husbands doe striue,
   Heres scant men enough for them all left aliue,
   They flocke to the Church, like Bees to the Hiue.
     Oh this is a wiuing age.
     Oh this is a wiuing age.

3   Twixt widowes and maids there is a great strife,
   And either of them would faine be a wife,
   They all doe cry out on this fond single life,
   And long to dance after a Taber and Fife.
     Oh this is a wiuing age.
     Oh this is a wiuing age.

4   The maidens I doubt will be put to the worst,
   And widowes though old, will be maried all first,
   To drinke the bride Posset good Lord how they thirst,
   Though they haue foule faces the're beautifull purst.
     Oh this is a wiuing age.
     Oh this is a wiuing age.

5   Most Widowes are impudent, they cannot blush,
   For speech of the people they care not a rush:
   They are very free and their money is flush,
   They will haue a young-man their aprons to brush.
     Oh this is a wiuing age.
     Oh this is a wiuing age.

6   Yong maidens are bashfull, but widowes are bold,
   They tempt poore yong men with their siluer and gold,
   For loue now a daies for money is sold,
   If she be worth treasure no matter how old.
     Oh this is a wiuing age.
     Oh this is a wiuing age.

7   For one maid now maried theres widowes a score,
   Their husbands scant dead a whole fortnight before,
   They cannot liue single they'le mary therefore,
   With any yong man though hees neuer so poore.
     Oh this is a wiuing age.
     Oh this is a wiuing age.

8   Oh is not this a pitifull case,
   That many a delicate beautifull lasse,
   Should thus by old widowes be put to disgrace,
   For euery yong lad has his widow in chase.
     Oh this is a wiuing age.
     Oh this is a wiuing age.

     The second part, to the same tune.

9   Let Maidens be patient, and neuer take thought,
    But stay vntill all the old widowes be caught,
    For now like to horses for coyne they are brought.
    They say that in *Smithfield* they'r cry'd twelue a groat.
        Oh this is a wiuing age.
        Oh this is a wiuing age.

10 Yet some of these widowes that marry so fast,
    I doubt will haue cause to repent of their haste:
    If they marry yong men their shoulders to bast,
    Oh then they will whine when the remedy is past,
        And curse such a wiuing age.
        And curse, &c.

11 Likewise many yongmen perhaps may repent,
        When all the old Angels are wasted and spent,
    Theyle wish the tongue out, that gaue first consent,
    Theyle say then I muse what a deuill I meant
        To match in that wiuing age.
        To match in that wiuing age.

12 A young man that marries a widow for wealth,
    Does euen much dammage vnto his soules health,
    For he will be toying and playing by stealth,
    Shee's iealous though neuer so iustly he dealth.
        Take heed of this wiuing age.
        Take heed, &c.

13 When young Lads and Lasses as them doth behoue,
    Doe lawfully marry together in loue,
    God poures downe his blessings on them from aboue,
    But youth and old dotage contrary doe proue,
        As tis in this wiuing age.
        As tis, &c.

14 It may be accounted a wonder to see
    An old crasse croane with a young man agree:
    Tis onely for wealth that they married be,
    Then take them who list, a young maid is for me.
        Oh this is a wiuing age.
        Oh this is a wiuing age.

15 Then let no yong maidens be displeased in minde,
    Though widowes are maried, and they left behinde:
    Those yong men who are thus contrary to kinde,
    You were better lose, then euer to finde,
        Leaue them to this wiuing age.
        Leaue them, &c.

16 Yet must I confesse many widowes there be
    Who from all libidinous thoughts are so free,
    They wed not for lust, but for loue as we see,
    Finde me such a one, and Ile quickly agree,
        To *match in this wiuing age.*
        To *match in this wiuing age.*

17 Of all sorts and sexes theres some good some bad,
    Theres choyce of both widowes and maids to be had
    He that happens well hath cause to be glad,
    And therefore let euery honest young Lad
        Make choyce in this wiuing age,
        Make choyce, &c.

18 My song vnto Virgins is chiefly directed,
    Who now in this age are little respected,
    Though widowes be chosen and maids be reiected,
    They will be esteemed, though now they'r neglected,
        Yet not in this wiuing age,
        Yet not in this wiuing age.

We can see from the diagram how the three themes are treated alternately, with a corresponding increase in the amount of information given. We have not taken into account the interdependence between T_1, T_2 and T_3: the marriage opportunities of young girls and widows are interrelated; the interests of the men can be directed towards one group just as much as the other. The dividing of the theme into multiple sub-themes makes possible not only a plurality of information about young girls, widows, young men, and their relationship to each other, but also differing assessments of their qualities and chances according to the respective additional information. If the financial advantage of widows is taken into account, their position has to be judged positively (vv. 2; 6) and that of girls negatively, despite their youth and beauty (vv. 1; 8). If one considers that girls are able to wait longer, however, until the venal men have all been weeded out and only wealthy bachelors are left for them, then the position of girls appears more favourable (vv. 9; 15). Men who marry for money certainly have an advantage at the start (v. 2), but they are likely to regret very quickly their rashness and greed (vv. 11; 12), and thus in the end they are far better off marrying young girls (v. 13) than old widows (v. 14). Taken as a whole this text provides, so to speak, a considered appraisal of the marriage-market, from which it emerges towards the end that there is more hope for girls than was thought at the outset. In the thematic structure of the subject of communication this is reflected in the feature of alternation of sub-themes with a new rheme each time, and in the implementation of the contrast principle in the arrangement of rhemes. Derivation from a constant hyper-theme, and semantic isotopic levels between sub-themes and rhemes, ensure transparency and redundancy here also. Because of the structure of his subject of communication, the attitude of the discursive speaker is characterized as one of weighing up and assessing; as presenter he identifies the hypertheme in the appeal dimension of the refrain ('Oh this is a wiuing age') and takes sides in his advice and encouragement to young girls, the group which is seen as being at a disadvantage (vv. 9; 18).

The majority of discursive ballads are not, like the ballads discussed above, restricted to one theme[227] but have social criticism of a very general nature as their subject. This criticism is however particularized more or less precisely in one hypertheme, from which a number of viewpoints are derived as sub-themes. If we follow Daneš's descriptive diagram, the social groups selected as examples have in this case the status of rheme within the hierarchy of semantic units, and the additional information given each time would have to be described as a series of 'sub-rhemes' (my term). An additional level of semantic units thus emerges. In fact the sub-themes here are simply a sub-set of the hypertheme, and their 'derivation' is more arbitrary than in the relation of 'statement – exemplification'. The next lowest levels of the hierarchy are more closely correlated, however.

A structure of this kind can be seen in the following ballad:

> *Come, buy this new Ballad, before you doe goe:*
> *If you raile at the Author, I know what I know.*
>
> (1620; *RB*, I, pp. 115–21)

From the hypertheme announced in the second verse, 'deviations from obligatory moral concepts of society' ('. . . many enormities I will display', v. 2,3–4, lines 11–12, *RB*, I, p. 117) four sub-themes are derived[228] which are exemplified in the text: these vary in frequency and extent of digression:

T_1 Pride and arrogance illustrated by Lucifer (v. 3) and all 'upstarts' (v. 8).

T_2 Hypocrisy illustrated by the fox (v. 4), religious and especially popish hypocrisy (vv. 5 and 7), women feigning innocence (v. 10), men who secretly drink and visit prostitutes (v. 11), bachelors' false declarations of love and promises of marriage (v. 12), the *miles gloriosus* (v. 15).

T_3 Material greed shown in the example of yeomen, gentry (v. 6), and moneylenders (v. 14).

T_4 Fraud shown in the bribery and corruption among holders of public office and their subordinates (v. 9) and in the dishonesty of traders (v. 17).

The thematic progression could be represented diagrammatically in the same way as *The wiuing age*, whereby the distinction between positive and negative assessment in the rheme would not apply, although each rheme would have to be further divided into sub-rhemes. The sub-rheme occurring most frequently in the text is hypocrisy (seven times) – the others only twice each. Their socially critical content and the individual examples are amongst the topoi commonly met with in the street ballad, especially the discursive type, and have therefore little novelty value for the audience. The special feature of this ballad lies in the nature and function of the speaker as he is presented in the title and opening verses:

It is an old saying,
    that few words are best,
And he that sayes little
    shall liue most at rest;
And I, by experience,
    doe finde it right so,
Therefore ile spare speech,
    but I know what I know.

Yet shall you perceiue well,
    though little I say,
That many enormities
    I will display.
You may gu[e]sse my meaning
    by that which I show;
I will not tell all,
    but I know, &c.   (vv. 1–2, lines 1–16, *RB*, I, pp. 116–17)

The attitude of one who knows but is withholding part of his information gives the speaker a special aura and air of authority. It can be expressed through gesture and mime, and is explicitly and deliberately fostered in the refrain, 'but I know what I know'. It determines the to some extent indirect treatment of the details of the theme, thereby manipulating reception by encouraging the audience to think for themselves along the lines indicated.

In other discursive ballads also it is the figure of the speaker who puts a new slant on the hackneyed, ever-recurring socially critical themes and their exemplification through representative figures within the text corpus, orientated as it is towards stimulating the audience. The principle of suggesting and hinting, intensified by the presenter's use of the colloquial element in his approach, is implemented by the following speaker who presents himself as being much-travelled and therefore well informed, though forced into caution owing to his low social station:

I Traueld farre to finde
    where honesty abides,
And found in England more
    then all the world besides;
But where true vertue growes,
    vice quickly ruines that:
A poore man must not speak,
    although he *Smell a Rat.*

When Iustice hath her sight,
  shee's beautifull in show:
But when she Masks her face,
  how vild she soone doth grow;
I doe perceiue the cause,
  but dare not speake of that:
Ile not offend the Lawes,
  but yet *I Smell a Rat*.[229]

The idiomatic expression of suspicion (see F. P. Wilson [1970]) regarding the external appearance of the world constitutes the hypertheme,
which in turn is differentiated into numerous sub-themes whose 'deriva-
tiveness' is constantly discernible in the refrain. The performance-
orientated personalization of the textual message is even more marked in
A Fooles Bolt is soone shot (1629; *PG*, no. 55, pp. 316–22). The speaker,
personalized as presenter, aims his mocking criticism like arrows at the
audience, marking out typical representatives of unacceptable social
behaviour which in his view always rebounds back on the perpetrator:

The Man that wedds for greedy wealth,
  he goes a fishing faire,
But often times he gets a Frog,
  or very little share;
And he that is both young and free,
  and marries an old Trot,
When he might liue at libertie,
  at him I make a shot   (v. 6, ibid., p. 318)

With a fixed repertoire of reprehensible behaviour and the discursive
ballad's predictable macrostructure of thematic progression, the possibilities for variation lie in the detail, in the speaker's communication of the
subject, or in the particular didactic pointing-up of the message, as here
through the fool's shot or in *Sure my Nurse was a witch* (c. 1626; *PB*,
no. 57, II, pp. 63–9) through a nursery-rhyme threat in the refrain:

The giddy headed Shopkeeper
  loues gadding here, and there,
And of his businesse at home
  hath no respect and care:
Still wasting, and consuming
  it quickly poore will make him
If once he counter tenor sing,
  come take him beggar, take him.
O take him beggar, take him,
  here take him beggar, take him,
Thus still she singes vnto her child,
  come take him beggar, take him.   (ibid., v. 7, p. 67)

Through a series of examples the world of adults is epitomized by anti-social, parasitic behaviour of inexcusable stupidity – the reckless, egoistic drinker, the work-shy layabout, the ostentatious debtor, the careless womanizer, the cursing gambler, the imprudent trader, the gullible shoe-maker and tailor, the arrogant academic. The inappropriateness of the proverbial threat of punishment (see n., ibid., p. 67) can be interpreted as signalling resignation or satirical intent. The simple listing of figures and their activities or behaviour patterns as rhemes makes quite clear their illustrative relation to the common theme. This is presented in a more humorous and complex way in:

> *The praise of Nothing:*
> *Though some doe wonder why I write in praise*
> *Of Nothing, in these lamentable daies,*
> *When they have read, and will my counsell take,*
> *I hope of Nothing Something they may make.*[230]
> (between 1601 and 1640)

The hypertheme announced in the title contains a contradiction within itself which refers connotatively to the nature of the world as it is presented in the text which follows. Owing to its universally negating function, the keyword 'Nothing' is ideal for both hyperbolically accentuating individual criticisms and pessimistically describing circumstances in general. It also gives rise to unexpected and absurd turns of phrase in the treatment of the sub-themes:

> Nothing in all the world we finde
>   With sorrow more perplexed
> Th[a]n he that with a scolding wife
>   Eternally is vexed;   (ibid., v. 3,1–3,4, lines 17–20, p. 341)
>   . . .
> In heat of war Nothing is safe;
>   In peace Nothing respected
> But ill-got wealth, which to procure,
>   No vice at all's neglected:
> The sonne doth wish his father's end,
> That he may have his wealth to spend;
> But let such lads their manners mend,
>   Or all will come to Nothing.   (ibid., v. 7, lines 49–56), p. 342)
>
> Nothing is swifter th[a]n the winde,
>   Or lighter th[a]n a feather;
> Yet I another thing have found,
>   Which quite excelleth either:
> A harlot's love, that every day
> Is chang'd and swiftly blowne away;
> But what's more light th[a]n her, I pray?
>   The wise man answers, Nothing.   (ibid., v. 4, lines 25–32, p. 341)

The manipulation of the word 'Nothing' within the framework of the parody of the song of praise[231] is the idea on which this ballad is based and through which it can combine both entertainment and instruction with a view to improving society.[232]

Other ballads tend simply to list examples, which are often quite disparate, of a hypertheme which can only be detected with difficulty. In *Euery Mans condition. Or euery Man has his seuerall opinion, Which they doe affect as the* Welchman *his Onion* (1627; PG, no. 47, pp. 270–5), it is: 'everyone follows his own wishes and goals' ('All men are inclinde, / To follow their minde / although their courses be bad'.[233]

> The Smith loues his Hammer,
> And the Captaine his Drummer,
>   the Souldier loues a good blade,
> The Pedler his packe,
> And the Collyer his Sacke,
>   and the Horse-courser he loues a Iade.   (ibid., v. 9,1–9,6, p. 274)
>
> The Usurer Gold,
> Idle Knaues endure cold,
>   because that they wil not labour,
> The Fiddler the fiddle,
> The Iester his riddle,   (ibid., v. 8,1–8,5, p. 273)
>   . . .
> The Thrasher his flaile,
> The Spanyel his taile,
>   the Carman his whip and his whistle:
> The Butcher his dogge,
>   the Swineherd his hogge,   (ibid., v. 5,1–5,5, p. 272)

In the accumulative stringing together of almost fifty examples the thematic progression becomes diffuse, and the abundance of sub-themes diverts the attention from the hypertheme. The direction of logical thought is levelled out so that there is only a selection of attention-seeking attractions on offer. This is also the case with *A merry nevv catch of all Trades* (c. 1624; PG, no. 34, pp. 196–9). On the hypertheme 'all trades', the ballad mentions a representative of a different trade in each line or half line, with largely redundant additional information. Similarities to the nursery rhyme are reinforced by onomatopoeic effects:

> The Taylor sowes, the Smith he blowes,
> The Tinker beates his pan:
> The Pewterer ranke, cries tinke a tanke tanke,
> The Apothecary ranta tan tan. The Apoth: etc.
>
> The Weauer thumps, his olde wife mumps,
> The Barber goes snip snap,

The Butcher prickes, the Tapster nickes,
The Farmer stops ap ap. The Farmer, etc.
(ibid., vv. 3 and 5, pp. 196 and 197)

Roome for Companie, heere comes Good Fellows (1614; *PB*, no. 8, I,
pp. 51–7) is a ballad which makes do with a simple list with no other
indication of the trade involved. The individual representative figures are
subsumed under the term 'good fellowes', and as a further coherence factor the speaker is brought in as market-crier and thus as presenter who is
specific to the particular situation. The speech situation which is consistently the basis of every verse can be concretely realized at every fair, but
in other performance situations it must remain fictional:

Roome for Company,
    here comes good fellowes.
Roome for company,
    in Bartholmew faire.
Pointers and Hosiers,
Salemen and Clothiers,
    Roome for company, etc.
Horse coursers, Carryers:
Blacksmithes and Farryers,
    Roome for company,
    well may they fare.   (ibid., v. 5, p. 53)

In 'list ballads' of this kind, with their undemanding evocation of everyday impressions within the audience's experience, the entertainment
element predominates over the didactic. This is further reinforced by the
sound and melody structures. The novelty value of such texts would tend
to be for children, although we do not know whether they were used as
nursery rhymes. In content and structure they are very similar to the
'medley', where the breakdown of thematic progression is raised to the
level of a principle and taken to the point of nonsense. The extreme
heterogeneity of the medley is purposely based on the evocation of other
ballad types and procedures, and of well-known material, motifs, hackneyed ideas, sayings, and set turns of phrase.[234] A mere mention was considered enough to set off the appropriate association processes in the mind
of the experienced ballad recipient who was part of the popular entertainment sector. Where the allusive character of an item of information is not
recognized or indeed not present, the text verges on nonsense, which in fact
has a further, sub-textual, range of associations. The structural autonomy
of this ballad type corresponds in large measure to the functions performed
by the jester and stage fool from the mid-sixteenth century onwards,
whose repertoire also included medleys. A representative example is
Richard Tarlton (d. 1588), who is also well known[235] as a writer of ballad
tunes and texts.[236] Functions characteristic of the presenter already obtain

in the activities of the jester and the theatre clown, together with an extremely varied and recipient-orientated range of entertainment. Such presenter functions are made use of in the street-ballad medley and constitute the only coherence factor on the level of the speaker.

In illustration of the allusive character of heterogeneous items of information I shall quote a few examples from Martin Parker's

> *An excellent new Medley*
> *Which you may admire at (without offence)*
> *For euery line speakes contrary sence*
>   (between 1624 and 1640; BBLB, pp. 118–24; RB, I, pp. 51–6)

and by the same author: *A New Medley, Or, A Messe of All-together* (between 1624 and 1660; RB, II, pp. 239–45):

> Strange news is come from Hounslo' heath,
> That all false theeues are put to death;
> Nell Collins has a stinking breath,
>   I heard Tom Phillips say:
> The cobler and the broome-man's wife
> Have made a match, Ile lay my life;
> Come drinke a cup and end all strife,
>   Sweet Kester.   (RB, II, p. 240, v. 1, lines 1–8)

The first verse contains allusions to two ballad types: the set formula 'Strange news' refers to the news ballad (sensational news or story of a criminal) and through the reference to the adultery motif, with the typical figures of the cobbler and the broom-man, the comic ballad is evoked. Audience expectations aroused by these promising beginnings are soon shattered by the abrupt change of subject. At the same time, the hyperbolic character of the second line already hints at the comical unreliability of the news, and the call to drink a conciliatory cup at the end of the verse can also be understood as an appeal to the audience to help create an atmosphere of conviviality. Sub-textually, an associative connection can be made between thieves and adulterers, via 'stinking breath' with its connotation of 'bad reputation'.[237]

Allusions to well-known ballad material such as *Jane Shore*,[238] the offer of money in exchange for a kiss,[239] or the popular ideal portrayal of a beautiful and faithful lover as 'the fair flower of . . .'[240] can also bring to mind individual ballads, to a certain extent testing the listener's 'ballad expertise'. The quoting in mid-text of the introductory formula, 'As I walkt . . .',[241] – normally used to authenticate the narrator's claim to being an eyewitness – has reference to a wider spectrum of ballad examples. Similarly, the evocation of more extensive subject areas such as 'rogery'[242] or the typical street-ballad nostalgia for the 'good old days'[243] is orientated towards the cultural horizons of the middle and lower classes which are conditioned by street ballads and other entertainment literature of the time. Those items of information which relate to an immediately accessible area of experience – even though this is conveyed through literature – also correspond to the social level of the audience. These include proverbs and sayings,[244] obscene allusions[245] and fictionalized gossip.[246] They certainly occur in other ballad types; here however, because they are concise and disparate – and consequently at the free disposal of the author – they are similarly allusive in character within their function of amusement. Reference is also made to well-known literary material:

> Dido was a Carthage Queene;
> As I walkt in a meddow greene;
> The fairest lasse that ere was seene;
>   that was the flower of Kent:
> Looke to your forehead, honest friend;
> The longest day must have an end;
> Good fortune unto thee, God send,
>   young bridegroome.[247]

The idea of waiting impatiently for the fulfilment of love links the figure of Dido with that of the bridegroom. The allusion to the typical ideal lover, 'fair flower', of folk-ballad provenance (see above, n. 240), forms a semantic isotopic link with a corresponding figure from the ancient world, and in the context of the themes of love and marriage the reference to a man's forehead can be interpreted as a warning against being horned. Here, too, the connections are intended to convey a wealth of experience.

Where the incoherence of the medley is neither justified by the allusive character of small semantic units nor compensated for by sub-textual coherence, we are left with lighthearted nonsense offering the recipient wide scope for associative connections. This is the overriding intention in a ballad by Martin Parker: *A Bill of Fare: For A Saturday night's Supper, A Sunday morning Breakfast, and A Munday Dinner, Described in a pleasand new merry Ditie* (c. 1637; RB, I, pp. 70–4). In the trailer in the first verse the speaker gives advance notice of actual culinary delights, only to present the listener with a menu of comic and satirical figments of the imagination.

> Imprimis, foure Fancies, two boyld, and two roast,
> A large dish of Endimions (good for one's drinke),
> Six Pelican Chickens, as hote as a toast,
> And six Birds of Paradise – braue meate I thinke.
> A couple of Phenix, a Cocke and a Hen,
> That late from Arabia had tane their flight;
> I thinke such a Banquet was ne're made for men,
> As we had to Supper on Saturday night.   (ibid., v. 2, lines 9–16, pp. 70–1)

The comic effect is produced by the incongruence between realistic references to the preparation and serving of the dishes on the one hand, and the fantastic nature of the food on the other. The latter includes fantasy images, moon-worshippers, and mythical animals, and later these are followed by inedible parts of animals such as 'A dish of Irish Harts' hornes boyld to a Ielly' (v. 4,3, line 27, p. 71) and 'Two paire of Elephants Pettitoes boyld' (v. 3,3, line 17, p. 71). In this Martin Parker goes beyond what we may presume was his model – a song in Ben Jonson's *The Gipsies Metamorphosed* (1621)[248] where there is satirical coherence in representative figures of society being served up to the Devil.[249] Satirical elements can be seen in Martin Parker's ballad where the sequence of dishes metaphorically brings in the bad mood of the wife at home.[250] On the whole, however, the comic fantasy element predominates, the fiction of the sequence of dishes providing a coherence principle.

The heterogeneity of the medley has on the whole a lighthearted, humorous intention which may simply be based on the items of information or may on the other hand be achieved through their isolation from the context and possible associative links. Martin Parker formulated this pragmatically within the function of the presenter:

> My merry medley here I end,
> Which to young men and maids I send;
> To make them mirth the same was pend,
>   although it seeme non-sense:
> Yet is there such variety
> Of sense for each capacity
> That old and young may pleasèd be
>   to learne it.[251]

The wide range on offer, in accordance with the motto, 'something for everyone', carries with it an obligation to the principle of variety, by means of which presenters of all types, from the court fool to the conjuror and market pedlar, sought to satisfy their customers. The free disposability of the textual elements used in the medley enables the speaker, to a certain extent, to manipulate them as if they were display objects.[252] The communication level of the presenter is correspondingly well developed in this ballad type. The speaker's function of linguistic communication is made self-consciously explicit – 'I'le tell you a Iest',[253] 'All that I can doe, is with words to display' (v. 1,7, line 7, p. 70), 'O that is a dainty'[254] – and numerous addresses are intended to secure the attention of the public. At the same time the performance situation, possible audience reactions, and individual sections of the audience (see above, chapter 3.3.1 and 3.3.2) are taken into account.

peace, peace, you bawling Curres.[255]

All people are not of one minde,
    hold Carmen.   (ibid., v. 3,7–8, lines 23–4, p. 53)

Moll is afraid that shee's with childe,
    peace Peter.   (ibid., v. 8,7, lines 63–4, p. 55)

Theres hardly one good friend in ten:
    turn there on the right hand.[256]

'Oh! neghbour Ralph, what doe you meane –
    to pawne your shirt for ale?[257]

The name 'Peter' is directed at all men in the audience with a bad conscience on that score. The truism of the rarity of a good friend is followed by the injunction to separate the good individuals from the bad after the manner of the Last Judgement. At the same time, this can be understood as a request to newly arrived listeners to come closer and take up a position to the right of the singer. The implicit warning of financial ruin through excess drinking, addressed to the common name Ralph, can only be understood if the appropriate ballad topos is familiar to the listener. It is precisely in the medley that ambivalent addresses to the audience abound, and in this they accord with the consistent intention of keeping unambiguous aids to reception to a minimum.

The special position of the medley within the sub-group of discursive street ballads becomes particularly clear when it is contrasted with the advice ballad, which is characterized by a distinct thematic progression and an abundance of explicit aids to reception. The hypertheme, to which the thematically coherent series of examples of type 3 of the thematic structure is assigned, is repeatedly formulated in the illocutionary function of advice (or warning). That is, in addition to the presenter/speaker's usual functions of manipulation of reception, we have the exhortation to the audience to change its attitude, with a possible consequent alteration of life style later. Advice and warning as a selective appeal function of the presenter during the course of the text are common procedure in all types of ballad (see above, chapter 3.3.3). Where they are directly and consistently combined with the theme, within the discursive ballad, we have the advice-ballad type, which is usually signalled by the words 'counsel, advice, lesson', etc., frequently in the title itself. The educational deterrent in the warning is quite often implicitly communicated in the examples; alternatively it can be made explicit in positive advice, although it is not raised to the level of a dominant illocutionary function.

Since the advice ballad corresponds to the socially critical discursive ballad in its thematic structure, remaining furthermore completely within the framework of the street-ballad text corpus in its thematic repertoire, only a cursory examination of a few textual examples, with particular reference to their advice function, is necessary. In *The Married-womans Case: OR Good Counsell to Mayds, to be carefull of hastie Marriage, by the example of other Married-women* (*c.* 1630; *PB*, no. 74, II, pp. 169–73) by Martin Parker, the exhortation to take great care when making a decision is again clearly formulated in the first and last verses, acquiring particular importance through its position at the beginning and end. The advice is supported by the deterrent examples of the 'quarrelling Coxcombe', the 'whore-monger', 'drunken sot', 'gamester', and 'iealous asse', whereby a detailed and vivid portrayal of their behaviour to their wives has particular didactic effect. The space devoted to the examples – two verses for each – and their relatively precise deictic structuring, with the retention of iterative–durative and typifying devices, exceeds the norm in the discursive ballad. However, the thematic progression with the hypertheme 'advice on being cautious when embarking on marriage' and the sub-themes 'illustration by means of representative figures' with an extensive rheme each time remains totally transparent.

A tendency towards narrative portrayal of the examples and a clear thematic progression also characterize *Nobody his Counsaile to chuse a Wife: Or, The difference betweene Widdowes and Maydes* (*c.* 1626).[258] While the discursive ballad *The wiuing age* (between 1621 and 1625; see above, pp. 198–203) gives a balanced consideration of the competition between widows and girls in the marriage-market, advice must of necessity be unequivocal and clearly stated. Here it is given from the point of view of the man and his own interests, which lead him to decide against girls and in favour of widows:

> For Maydens are wanton
>   and often times coy:
> But Widdowes be wilfull
>   and neuer say nay.

The explicit advice, reinforced by the presenter[259] at the beginning and end of the ballad, is kept fresh in the memory during the course of the text by the refrain. The two sub-themes 'widdowes' and 'maydes' are treated in alternate, contrasting verses. Their respective positive and negative rhemes of evaluation are so unequivocal that it is doubtful whether the advice is meant to be taken completely seriously, especially as the highly praised qualities of widows appeal primarily to the man's comfort, certainly not to his sensuality:

> He that's matcht with a widdow,
>   by that is a winner:
> Shee'le stay and heare Seruice,
>   and then prouide dinner:
> Shee is twise in a Saboath,

> at Church like a Woman:
> And not to learne fashions,
>   as some doe most common:
> Shee loues to goe plaine,
>   let who will disdaine:
> Shee needs must goe so,
>   that hath had Husbands twain:
> For Maydens, etc.   (v. 5, PG, p. 265)

The plurality of viewpoints and opinions, which has already been repeatedly noted, is also evident in the treatment of marriage, a theme recurrent within the text corpus. Alongside this ballad's advice on being cautious and choosing an absolutely safe and boring older wife there is a detailed catalogue of instructions for those prepared to take the risk of courting and marrying young girls in *Good Counsell for young Wooers* (1633):[260]

> Come, all you young Pupils, that yet have no skill
> In wooing to get a fine Lasses good will,
> If you will be rulèd, and take my advice,
> Ile teach you to wooe and [to] speed in a trice: (ibid., v. 1,1–1,4, p. 422)

There follows a series of various pieces of advice on how to achieve rapid success when courting (hypertheme), so that the illocutionary function of the presenter as speaker, who takes the role of a canny expert, remains constantly present throughout the text. This function is combined with a wealth of information regarding women's characteristics (sub-themes) and the appropriate behaviour recommended each time for the lover (rheme). Since the various tactics suggested – flattery, adapting to the girl's moods, promising financial support, being constantly in her company and providing a programme of amusements, and finally pouncing quickly – convey a somewhat negative image of women, the advice is mixed here too with humorous ambivalence.

The humoristic distance and the extreme, comic nature of the examples, together with the presenter elements inherent in the speaker's role of adviser, guarantee the entertainment value of most advice ballads which are secular in content, in contrast to the serious warnings contained in texts based on religious and moral precepts. The illocutionary function is predominantly humorous in intent in *A prettie newe Ballad, intytuled: / The Crowe sits vpon the wall, / Please one and please all* (1591/92),[261] a ballad attributed to the comic performer Richard Tarlton.[262] The speaker's recommendation that one should try to please all women is the hypertheme kept constantly before us in the refrain; it is rather called into question than supported, however, by the large number of contrasting examples of female appearance and behaviour. The principle of contrast and variation through which the sub-themes are linked serves to point up the range of alternatives, the diversity of possible experiences, and the wide scope of potential application. Running counter to this, the recurrent nature of experience is implied, both syntactically and phonologically, through parallelism, anaphora, refrain, and metrical uniformity of couplets, an implication correlating to the speaker's attitude of humorous resignation. It is also expressed in the ambiguity of the refrain: 'Please one and please all': either, 'try to please everybody' or 'if you manage to please one, you will have learnt so much that you will be able to please everybody':

> Be they wanton, be they wilde,
> Be they gentle, be they milde,
> Be shee white, be she browne,
> Dooth she skould or dooth she frowne,
> Let her doo what she shall, –
> Please one and please all,
> Please one and please all.
>
> Be she coy, be she proud,
> Speake she soft or speake she loud,
> Be she simple, be she flaunt,
> Dooth she trip or dooth she taunt, –
> The crowe sits vpon the wall, –
> Please one and please all,
> Please one and please all.
>
> Is she huswife, is she none,
> Dooth she drudge, dooth she grone,
> Is she nimble, is she quicke,
> Is she short, is she thicke,
> Let her be what she shall, –
> Please one and please all,
> Please one and please all.
>
> Be they ritch, be they poore,
> Is she honest, is she whore,
> Weare she cloth or veluet braue,
> Dooth she beg or dooth she craue,
> Weare she hat or silken call, –
> Please one and please all,
> Please one and please all.   (vv. 11–14, *AB*, pp. 380–1)

Distinctly serious, moralizing, and didactic elements are also to be found within the form of the advice ballad:

> *Friendly Counsaile.*
> *Or,*
> *Here's an answer to all demanders,*
> *The which I'le declare to all by-standers,*

> *Thereby to teach them how to know*
> *A perfect Friend from a flattering Foe.*   (1633; *RB*, I, pp. 65–9)

This theme is treated by the repeated contrast of the behaviour patterns of the good and the false friend, the appeal function being in evidence throughout. The underlying norms are unequivocally moral in character, as opposed to the advice concerning marriage which tends more towards opportunistic and materialistic expediency or down-to-earth worldly wisdom. A ballad which is distinctly moralizing in its series of warnings and was in circulation from *c.* 1640 until the end of the century is *An Hundred Godly Lessons, That a Mother on her Death-Bed gave to her Children, whereby they may know how to guide themselves towards God and Man, to the benefit of the Commonwealth, joy of their Parents, and good to themselves.*[263]

The discursive street ballad of the second half of the sixteenth century is akin to the advice ballad in so far as in the former the appeal to the listener is also predominantly advisory in function. Beyond the illocution of advice, however, the speaker shows no special features, and the audience is collectively addressed as Christians or included in the communal first-person plural, unless prayer-like invocations of God or eulogies addressed to those in power take their place (see above, pp. 56–9). As in the early forms of the narrative and semi-dramatic street ballad, the communication level of the presenter is absent here also. As regards the subject of communication, two thematic areas can be distinguished: religious and edifying exhortations based on biblical material, and political warnings and admonitions which are religious in motivation and invoke the divine right of kings. They usually take a factual event as their starting-point and could also be described as 'discursive news ballads' in which it could be said that the 'news' is totally subordinated to the 'comment' (see above, p. 148). I have used the term 'exhortation' to describe the recurrent illocutionary function of the discursive speaker in these ballads in order to point up the religious, moralizing, and transcendental aspects of their content as opposed to the everyday, worldly-wise, secular advice of the advice ballad. Humorous and entertainment elements are of necessity also absent in the early form of the discursive ballad, both as regards content and owing to a lack of presenter functions.

In contrast to the discursive ballad of the first half of the seventeenth century, the religious exhortation ballad often contains no examples at all, although the relevant thematic coherence is preserved. From this there emerges a different, simpler thematic structure. Whereas the series of examples provides a sequence of sub-themes of a hypertheme with the appropriate rhemes (Daneš's type 3), this level of sub-theme does not apply here. The thematic progression of the religious exhortation ballad can be described in terms of type 2: a continuous theme is constantly given new rhemes (see F. Daneš [1970], p. 77):

$$(T_1 \rightarrow R_1)$$
$$\downarrow$$
$$T_2 (= R_1) \rightarrow R_2$$
$$\downarrow$$
$$T_2 (= R_1) \rightarrow R_3$$
$$\downarrow$$
$$T_2 (= R_1) \rightarrow R_4$$

The theme of *To pass the place where pleasure is* (1561/62; OEB, no. 34, pp. 212–15) is the alternative that faces man of either heaven or hell ($R_1 = T_2$). It is presented in various abstract terms and norms (R_{2-n}), combined with collective exhortations in the first-person plural:

> Our perfett trust and confidence
>   must fixèd be on *Christ* onelie,
> Serueinge our lord with pure pretence,
>   and shunning all hipocrisie, –
>   which might vs draw, vs draw,
>   from godes true law,
>   marke well this saw:
>   all remedie gone
>   except in *Christ* alone, alone.   (ibid., v. 4, p. 214)

Through the absence of independent examples of at least a personal deictic nature, and the concomitant simplification of the thematic structure, the conceptual content is scaled down in favour of an increased appeal function. The recipient is not given scope for initiative in interpreting examples or making an independent choice. The theme of 'slandering others' is treated in just this way in *A Ballad against Slander and Detraction* (between 1560 and 1582; AB, no. 3, pp. 12–18), with varying exhortations which, in the alternation of formulations, at the same time provide a series of rhemes. The Christian/religious appeal to the listener can also be made *ex negativo*, where non-achievement of a required norm is formulated as a warning. This occurs in 'When I do cawll to mynd' (between c. 1550 and 1565; SB, no. 15, pp. 40–4). The theme is the sinfulness of man, manifested in the non-observance of Christian norms of behaviour (as rhemes) such as gratitude and obedience to God, love, charity, and forgiveness etc. (see vv. 2–6, pp. 40–2):

> We know what thankes we owe
>   To Gode for all hys gyftes,
> Yete contrarye we showe
>   To hym our selves unthryftes.
> The good frome yll we knowe,

> Yet in owr daylye dryftes
> The yll in us dothe growe,
> The good frome us yt shyftes.   (ibid., v. 2,1–2,8, p. 40)

The series of exhortations to lead a Christian life is characteristic of a considerable number of texts from the second half of the sixteenth century which are extant on broadsides.[264] Their possible use as hymns and their traditional links with homiletic literature have still to be investigated. Even where the theme is simply man's right and wrong conduct it is treated *sub specie aeternitatis*[265] and not, as in later warnings and advice, from the point of view of the consequences in this world.

Apart from texts whose appellant thematic progression can be assigned to Daneš's type 2 there are also those which illustrate their theme through examples, thereby introducing an additional thematic level; these texts follow type 3 in structure. *A godly ballad declaring by the Scriptures the plagues that haue insued whordome* (1566; AB, no. 26, pp. 149–53) begins with five verses of exhortation, going on to cite famous biblical instances of the punishment of fleshly desires: the Sodomites, Potiphar's wife and her designs on Joseph, Bathsheba washing, Samson, King Solomon, Herod, and others. Each story is for the most part presumed known and therefore only touched on. *A generall discourse vpon Covetousnesse* (1560)[266] chooses as a model for its depiction of greed and avarice the figure of 'the covetous carle', illustrating the corrupting effect of this vice on the person in question as well as on those around him, in the portrayal of typical behaviour patterns: anxiety at the prospect of loss, and compulsive acts. The warning appeal to the audience takes the form of rhetorical questions[267] which assume a consensus of opinion but also provide for the necessity of persuasion through direct exhortation.[268]

An interesting form constituting a transition to the socially critical discursive ballad of the seventeenth century is seen in *The XXV. orders of Fooles* (1569/70; AB, no. 23, pp. 128–36). The judging of man's foolishness, exemplified by various 'fooles'[269] and seen as both sinfulness and as a violation of social norms, already contains elements of secularization, and at the same time the speaker in this text shows definite presenter features. Here again we are confirmed in the supposition that there is a strong connection between the secularization of the message and the personalization of the way in which it is communicated. The speaker takes over responsibility for statements that are not unquestionably supported by a conception of the world orientated towards religious salvation.[270]

> Stay a while with pacience, my freends, I you pray,
> Of the orders of fooles somewhat I wyll say:
> Fiue and twentie iust a quarterne is, ye know, –
> Euery foole in his foolishness wyll I show.

And, as the prouerbe doth show very playne,
A hood for this foole, to kepe him from the rayne.[271]

Those ballads of the early period which take a topical event as the starting-point for political exhortations based on religious precepts, thereby sharing a common element with the news ballad, do not, however, implement any presenter procedures. The recurrent didactic appeal function of the speaker follows on directly from the development of the theme, usually vividly illustrated by means of examples. The combination of religious and political argumentation is again very much in evidence during the Cromwell period, though in a different form. In accordance with the debate between Royalists and revolutionary Puritans, party-political propaganda and polemics are founded on popular theology. During the period between 1600 and 1640, political and religious content is largely absent in the street ballad (see above, p. 150).

Panegyric on a ruler's accession to power combined with serious exhortations *sub specie aeternatis* and historical retrospect is a typical form of the 'discursive news ballad'. A ninuectyue agaynst Treason (1553)[272] celebrates the proclamation of Mary as Queen, 13 July in Norwich, and 19 July in London. The list of previous royal crimes and political struggles[273] is intended to emphasize the hope of political stability at home, whereby the history of England is finally made subject to divine justice:

> Remember well, o mortall man, to whom god geueth reason,
> How he truly, most ryghtfully, doth alwayes punyshe treason.
> Consyderyng oft the state of man, and of this mortall lyfe,
> which is but short and very full of mutabylyte,
> I callèd to remembraunce the hateful war and stryfe
> Which hath ben don within this realme thrugh gret iniquite, —[274]

The accession to the throne of Queen Elizabeth is presumably also placed in a historical context by A newe Ballade,[275] this time that of the struggle against the Pope and Roman Catholicism. The series of historical examples is combined with urgent rhetorical questions and warnings addressed to the Queen to the effect that she should learn from history, which might merge into an appeal to the audience for solidarity. The combination of political and religious exhortations becomes clearer in *Englands Lamentation For the late Treasons conspired against the Queenes Maiestie by Frances Throgmorton: who was executed at Tyborne, on the 10 day of July, Anno 1584* (BBLB, pp. 21–8):

> And where the Lord of Lords hath set,
> his handmaids pure and cleene,
> Annoynting her my rightfull Prince,
> to raigne a royall Queene:

> . . .
>
> Who to the sacred worde doth stande
>   with zeale and godly minde,
> Maintaining truth, embracing faith,
>   and to eche subject kinde.
> Alas! why then, my people deare,
>   what is the cause you swerue
> Against the Lords annoynted, so
>   your owne selfe willes to serue?
> Pray, pray, and praise the Lord, etc.   (ibid., v. 2,1–2,4 and v. 3, p. 22)

A considerable number of ballads, of which only some are extant, are
concerned with the Catholic rebellion under the leadership of the Dukes of
Northumberland and Westmorland in the autumn of 1569, which was
defeated after a few weeks but nevertheless aroused great excitement.[276]
The news value of the events, manifested in contradictory rumours,
prophecies, and widespread unrest among the people, is graphically presented in *A newe Ballade, intituled, Agaynst Rebellious and false rumours*
(1570; AB, no. 73, pp. 354–9) as a continuous theme and interspersed
with prayer-like invocations and warnings.[277] This ballad regards the
rebellion with its accompanying turmoil of war as God's punishment for
the sinfulness of the English people. William Elderton, on the other hand,
condemns it as a political rebellion in *A ballat intituled Northomberland
newes, / Wherin you maye see what Rebelles do vse* (1569/70).[278] The
abuse and mockery of the rebels can at the same time be seen as a warning
to all like-minded individuals, as is made clear in the refrain:

> Come tomblinge downe come tombling downe.
> That will not yet be trewe to the Crowne.

The vast majority of discursive street ballads of our period of investigation show a definite thematic coherence. Their thematic progression can
be described in terms of two similar types of thematic structure. Both types
of progression show quite clearly that the thematic structure of the discursive street ballad is as a rule simple and easily recognizable. In the one
case we have a clear hierarchical structure which allows the dominance of
a theme and its differentiation into individual statements and examples,
and on the other a continuous theme with the addition of supplementary
information. The thematic structure of the discursive street ballad can be
assigned to the general principle of 'functional transparency' (see above,
pp. 145–6) on the basis of the strict functionality of its semantic levels
and elements, simple relationships between dominant elements, and the
large measure of redundancy and explicitness. The strategy of audience
influence is thereby characterized by elucidation of the textual message,
without the complete scaling down of the conceptual content, and is thus

highly suitable for an audience of listeners with minimal cognitive demands. There is no question of an argument in the strict sense of logical inference. It is rather a case of moulding public opinion on a certain matter which is illustrated by examples from the world of the audience's experience, or, in the early form of the street ballad, of reminding the audience graphically of irrefutable moral–theological principles with reference to biblical authority.

An exception to the norm of functional transparency and intention to influence is seen in the medley and related forms. Here the principle of listing includes little if any thematic structuring, so that the heterogeneity of small semantic units determines the textual structure. The individual items of information may, as allusions, refer to other contexts, or they may be connected connotatively within the same ballad text. Where elements do not even acquire this degree of overall sense, we are dealing with nonsense verse.

The thematic repertoire of censurable behaviour, which is treated discursively with inclusion of examples, advice, and exhortation, is limited and therefore recurrent within the text corpus of the street ballad. This applies equally to the Christian canon of sins in the early street ballads and to the secular content of the ballads of the first half of the seventeenth century. In this period, however, possibilities of variation were sought in the differentiation of the thematic structure, in the detailed information, in the use of a particular 'peg' for the didactic intention,[279] or in the way in which the speaker communicated the message. The discursive speaker with simultaneous presenter function can have an additional manipulative effect on reception through his attitude to the subject of communication, which in the discursive street ballad is frequently conveyed in the refrain. Certain procedures and attitudes – for example, the careful selection of information and secrecy ('I know what I know'; see above, p. 204), the idiomatic intimation ('I Smell a Rat'; see above, pp. 204–5), the weighing up of different aspects and explicit appeals to the audience (see e.g. above, pp. 206–7) especially in the role of adviser – define the speaker further as the communicator of the textual message. The instructional and entertaining 'discussion of a problem' from the world of everyday experience is personalized in a way specific to the street ballad and brought into a presenter speech situation.

4.4 Classification and survey of street-ballad types: feature matrix

In this chapter a macrostructural analysis has been undertaken of a substantial selection of street-ballad texts from the period 1550 to 1650. Particular attention has been given to pragmatic aspects, and interpretations of individual ballads offered. The analysis reveals a considerable variety of textual strategies, of which a number predominate and combine in any one ballad type. 'Ballad type' refers here to a textual group which as a sub-category can be assigned to one of the 'street-ballad sub-genres' – narrative street ballad, role-play ballad, discursive street ballad. Before we consider the question of the unity of the street ballad as a literary genre we shall first present a survey of the ballad types which have been established in the form of a feature matrix.

We are dealing here with pragmatic features which can be clearly identified, that is the fictional or real speaker–listener relationships, and with macrostructural features. The presence of certain of these features in any one ballad determines the textual manipulation of reception. Difference in content is also taken as a criterion, since in its correlation to structure features it has proved consistently relevant; the distinction made here is between religious and secular content. The classification of a textual type is determined by the predominance of certain features. In some individual cases it is also possible to find a mixture of types. In order to distinguish the regular from the occasional occurrence of a feature, a distinction has been made in the relevant column between '+ +' and '+'. This does not indicate a mixed type of text, but rather the variation of feature distribution, together with the gradation of partial congruence of procedure, in the individual ballad types. The features are given equal ranking in the list, without reference to their position within the genre-theory system according to which we have dealt with them in this chapter. The importance of a feature's position in the system of street ballad types is indicated, however, by the frequency of its occurrence within the matrix, that is, if it is common to a whole group of ballad types. This can be seen for example in the case of the first three features.

The terms used to describe individual ballad types derive largely from the traditional terminology of literary forms and sub-genres, whereby aspects of both content and textual structure are given expression. The list of textual types eliminates the hierarchical order of the literary genre system in the wider sense. In accordance with the course of the investigation so far, however, it is appropriate also to include, despite conceptual overlaps, those generic terms which are relevant for our differentiation of features. This applies both to the first-person versus third-person narrative, both of which may occur as 'life story' and 'criminal ballad', and to the role-play ballad with its partial similarity to its earlier forms. The distinction between role-play ballads where the conflict situation predominates and those where opinions are predominant (within the resolution of cognitive dissonance) is not relevant to our feature catalogue, as these two characteristics are not found in any ballad type other than the role-play ballad; they are therefore combined under 'role-play ballad'. This classification of ballad types according to their predominant features is by no means complete, but it contributes to a further precise defining of textual types.

The feature matrix, relating to textual types extant as broadside ballads from 1550 to 1650, enables us first to gain an immediate overall picture of the feature distribution in the text corpus with particular reference to these ballad types. We are also able to restate more precisely the most important features of each type with regard to its description in previous chapters. It is furthermore possible, from the frequency of occurrence of features and the congruence of feature between individual textual types, to establish concise supplementary confirmation of our findings so far. A general feature of all ballad types of the first half of the seventeenth century is, as we have repeatedly emphasized, the presenter level of communication,[280] for the most part side by side with predominantly secular content. By contrast, the early forms of the street ballad are characterized by the virtual absence of the presenter level of communication, which clearly correlates with the almost constant use of religious content. There is of course a clear distinction between ballad types involving a reporting and those involving a performative speech situation. The former is realized in an explicit narrator who is for the most part present, although this is less well developed in early forms (biblical narrative, martyr narrative). The performative speech situation finds expression in various ways: in a simple personalized speaker (with no narrative or role-play function), a situational realization (speaker of a role) or two speakers correlated through dialogue. Over and above the genre-theory dividing line between 'reporting' and 'performative', based on the criterion of speech-structure difference, we have the 'speaker-centred subjective perspective', a feature of those texts whose subject of communication relates directly to the speaker. This applies to the first-person narrative and therefore, in certain cases, to the life history and the criminal ballad, to the role-play ballad and therefore, in certain cases, to the 'martyr figure', and on occasion also to the action-orientated dialogue ballad. Since this involves a psychological portrayal of the speaker as figure, this feature distribution correlates significantly with 'predominance of motivational links'.[281]

The following features concern the structure of the subject of communication. The most frequently occurring structural principle is the personal, temporal, and local deictic ('deictic structuring of subject of communication'), from which the categories 'predominance of events', 'congruence of chronology and logic of action' and 'iterative–durative portrayal of events' are also derived. In the decreasing frequency of the feature 'deictic structuring of the subject of communication' – from occasional to completely absent – there is a necessary correlation with the increase in occurrence of the thematic coherence principle. With regard to this prin-

FEATURES \ TEXTUAL TYPES	third-person narrative	first-person narrative	life-history (or extract)	comic tale	criminal ballad	biblical narrative	martyr narrative
presenter level of communication	+ +	+ +	+ +	+ +	+ +		
reporting speech situation	+ +	+ +	+ +	+ +	+ +	+ +	+ +
performative speech situation							
explicit narrator	+ +	+ +	+ +	+ +	+ +	+	+
simple personalized speaker							
situational realization of fictional speaker							
two speakers correlated through dialogue							
speaker-centred subjective perspective		+ +	+		+		
deictic structuring of subject of communication	+ +	+ +	+ +	+ +	+ +	+ +	+ +
predominance of events	+	+	+	+	+	+	+
congruence of chronology and logic of action	+	+	+ +		+ +		
iterative–durative portrayal of events	+	+	+		+		
predominance of thematic coherence principle				+			
predominance of motivational links	+	+ +	+	+	+		
concentration of action in one episode				+			
religious content	+	+				+ +	+ +
secular content	+	+	+ +	+ +	+ +		

Fig. 3. Matrix of features producing an open repertoire of textual types extant as broadside ballads from 1550 to 1650

news ballad	role-play ballad	martyr figures	allegorical figures	lamentation of sin	action-orientated dialogue ballad	discursive dialogue ballad	socially critical discursive ballad	medley	advice ballad	exhortation ballad
+ +	+ +						+ +	+ +	+ +	
+ +										
	+ +	+ +	+ +	+ +	+ +	+ +	+ +	+ +	+ +	+ +
+ +										
			+	+		+	+ +	+ +	+ +	+ +
	+ +	+			+					
					+ +	+ +				
	+ +	+		+						
+ +	+ +	+	+	+	+					
+ +					+					
+										
+	+ +									
+		+	+	+		+ +	+ +		+ +	+ +
	+ +	+			+					
+										
+		+ +	+	+ +				+		+ +
+	+ +				+ +	+ +	+	+ +	+ +	

ciple as a criterion of difference for certain ballad types it should be noted that we are concerned with its predominance over other structural procedures. Obviously the vast majority of street-ballad texts have a recognizable theme derived from the narrative or the role-play fiction, which is often also made explicit on the presenter level of communication. Thematic coherence is however a decisive structural factor only in the discursive ballad, with the exception of the medley and occasionally in narrative texts where there is a simultaneous abandoning of other correlation procedures. A tendency to thematic structuring can also be seen in performative ballads where the speech situation has only perfunctory realization and where content is predominantly religious: martyr figures, lamentation of sin. Here we see, in their common moral and didactic intention, transitions to the exhortation ballad. The correlation between 'predominance of motivational links' and the feature 'speaker-centred subjective perspective' has already been noted. Motivational links and a consequently more subtle portrayal of figures are for the most part only occasionally apparent or indeed completely absent. The oppositional features to these – namely, 'predominance of events', 'congruence of chronology and logic of action', and 'iterative–durative portrayal of events' – predominate, particularly in the case of the news ballad. This ballad type shows further a similarity with the comic tale on the one hand (concentrating the action into one episode) – throwing an interesting light on its particularly ambivalent intention to entertain and instruct – and the textual group with religious content on the other.[282]

If the features listed are grouped under three headings: pragmatic (presence of speakers of various kinds with possible audience relationship), those referring to the structuring of the subject of communication (deictic versus thematic) and those concerned with content, it will be seen that almost every textual type has at least one feature from all three groups. There are two exceptions: the medley, with its absence of any structuring of the subject of communication, and the dialogue ballad, which merely has two textual speakers. Their inclusion in the text corpus will be discussed at a later stage. All in all, out of the variety of separate procedures, a personalized speaker and a clear structuring, predominantly deictic in nature, can be established as recurrent features of the street-ballad text corpus.

5 Pragmatic genre definition of the street ballad and its cultural and historical position

In conclusion, we shall attempt to define the street ballad as a literary genre.[1] In line with recent theoretical debate, it is not only textual features which are of significance here but also communicative functions.[2] As with linguistics, literary criticism has become pragmatic in its approach. Since the main emphasis of this investigation has been on the communicative function of the street ballad and the functional nature of its structural procedures, a pragmatic genre definition can be drawn up on the basis of the literary and sociological components determining its production, distribution and reception which have thus far been established, and on a description of its textual constitution. A consideration of the close correlation between textual constituents and socio-cultural factors within the framework of the historical speech situation enables us at least tentatively to place this literary manifestation in its context from both the historical and the literary angle. At the same time, such a genre definition of the street ballad should not be regarded as final. This study has been limited to a description of macrostructural features and their pragmatic dimension. A microstructural analysis of stylistic phenomena would have to offer supplementary aspects and possibly indications relevant to genre. Furthermore, ballad content could be brought into a systematic genre description. In addition, the nature of the street ballad as distinct from other contemporary literary forms and genres, a factor which has here only been touched on, has yet to be investigated in detail. Finally, since our study is limited to the period 1550–1650 it is not possible to generalize. A cursory glance at the available texts of the eighteenth and nineteenth centuries does show, however, that essential characteristics are more or less retained, although from the literary point of view they often appear less convincing than in the heyday of the street ballad.

5.1 Genre characteristics: personalization of the message, and functional transparency as a procedure specific to the street ballad as a literary medium

In respect of its various contents, themes, traditionally based literary forms, and textual strategies, and its use of both the reporting and the performative speech situation, the English street ballad of our period of investigation appears to constitute a fairly heterogeneous text corpus. Of the quantity of verse texts printed on broadsides and distributed by means of performance and sale, a large proportion of those from the first half of the seventeenth century can be classed according to the criterion of the presenter level of communication. The importance of this criterion of difference lies not only in its frequent recurrence and its function as a more general speech criterion determining structure; it is also of supreme relevance for the process of communication typical of the street ballad. The potential, and individually applicable, partial congruence between the textual deictic and illocutionary features of the presenter speech situation on the one hand, and the actual situation of performance and sale on the other, serve to promote a communication of the textual message which is effective and familiar within the sphere of popular amusement. The presenter level of communication marks out the street ballad as to a certain extent belonging to the 'show business' of the time, which also embraced fairground showmen, conjurors, artistes, theatre clowns, and court jesters. The special feature of the street-ballad presenter consists in his orientation towards the textual message he has to convey – its communication being his primary concern – and may be described as a conversion of showmanship into the literary medium. This is seen not only in the presenter's function of conveying a – usually fictionalized – object through language, but also in the textual differentiation of presenter procedures. Such procedures are manifested in various forms of reference to self, appeals to the listener, and reference to the outside world, ranging in intention from entertainment and instruction to advertising techniques.

The dominance of an explicit speaker on the presenter level, often with correlating audience address, has its parallels on the other communication levels which are specific to textual type. The explicit narrator determines the way a story is communicated with his action-syntagmatic and action-semantic commentary; in the role-play fiction, conflict and expression of opinion are centred on the role-play figure; the discursive speaker personalizes the theme by conveying his own point of view. Because his functions can be transposed on to the empirical speech situation of street-ballad communication, the presenter can achieve only a small measure of fictionality. The other textual speakers, however, are a part of the respective textual fiction. There are often smooth transitions from presenter speech to the functions of explicit narrator, dramatic role-play figure, or discursive speaker. Here also it is clear that with the conversion of presenter functions into language, so prevant in the street ballad, a literary and artistic principle is evolved which cannot be explained by reference to economic factors of production and distribution alone.

Literary showmanship, that is, a functional personalization of the message which is specific to the situation, is also, in modified form, characteristic of such modern literary manifestations as the music-hall song, cabaret song, *chanson*, political song, commissioned poem, political speech, and advertising text. These share with the street ballad the integration of the two intentions to amuse and influence. An important difference, however, is that the modern forms do not share the bibliographical feature of the broadside and the concomitant immediate sale. Their traditional links with the street ballad have still to be systematically investigated.[3] As far as I can discover the presenter level of communication in its relationship to the various subjects of communication decreases in complexity during the further development of the street ballad in England, becoming fixed in a few set clichés, although even then its principle is still evident. However, in an assessment of the historical influence of the English street ballad, to be found mainly in the sphere of seventeenth- and eighteenth-century literary entertainment,[4] the humorous and parodistic literary ballad,[5] and the satirical political song, all the other characteristics of the street ballad must also be taken into account.

In addition to the presenter speech situation, supported by speakers specific to the textual type, our macrostructural analysis of the street ballad reveals a further characteristic – the principle of functional transparency (see esp. above, pp. 145–6 and pp. 220–1): from the repertoire of structural procedures already available within literary texts, in part specific to textual type, only one or two predominate in any one text, with complementary support from a few procedures having subordinate function. Where there is a choice between several structural procedures having similar function, the simplest is chosen. Thus, for instance, in narrative texts the chronological sequence is preferred for the conveying of time, and in the discursive ballad simple types of progression are used in the treatment of a theme. The feature matrix (see chapter 4, pp. 224–5) shows the alternating distribution of the most important structural procedures throughout the text corpus, thereby indicating the proportion of predominant features occurring within any one ballad type (and therefore also in the individual text). The coherence of the individual text can be attributed to a few easily distinguishable linking devices whose function is to clarify both the structure and the content of the textual message. Thus, for example, the iterative–durative conveying of events in the role-play ballad enables the listener to concentrate on the conflict situation of the speaker of the role; the absolute predominance of events in the news ballad excludes the possibility of motivational links, and therefore of individual psychological imponderables, in order to suggest factual authenticity and the exemplary function of prodigies. On the other hand, in the criminal ballad the psychological dimension is certainly taken into account, though it remains subordinate to the logic of the action in order to underline the didactic exemplary nature of the case in question. Congruence of chronology and logic of action in numerous narrative ballads suggests structurally a teleology which can be used through the content for conveying a link between guilt and atonement. In the discursive ballad the hierarchical ordering of semantic elements according to isotopic concrete examples and generalizing statements and instruction in the thematic progression of type 3 (see pp. 197–8) combines the everyday world of experience with didactic elements in a most plausible way.

The main structural procedures which we have established as occurring in the street ballad cannot be set up as distinguishing criteria, since taken on their own they also occur in other literary genres and types. What is characteristic for the street ballad is the preference for simple structural procedures and the predominance of one procedure in any one ballad type. This feature of selection and combination I have termed 'functional transparency'. It is intentionally applied as a structural principle in the various ballad types and in individual texts. Functional transparency is, however, such a comprehensive structural principle that it is not only characteristic of the street ballad but also of numerous other textual groups, primarily in the sphere of entertainment and instruction. It only becomes a distinguishing criterion when in correlation with the presenter speech situation, and as a structural principle of individual textual types characteristic of the street ballad.

The virtual absence of the presenter level of communication in the ballad types of the second half of the sixteenth century calls into question their inclusion in the street-ballad corpus. There is an obvious link here with the predominance of spiritual content which does not lend itself to presenter-type gestures. Since at the same time there seems to be very little documentary evidence of the method of distribution for this period (see appendix and chapter 6), it remains unclear whether it was anything like the situation of performance and sale which prevailed in the seventeenth century. If we take as a starting-point the unquestionable link between the presenter-type textual constitution and the performance situation, such a similarity is probably doubtful. The distribution of these texts on broadsides did however at least ensure their public character, which they share with later street ballads. One must also consider here the various possibilities of their use in the context of religious functions, such as sermons, processions, and church services. Texts between 1550 and 1650 also have in common the presence of a personalized speaker with communicative functions, whether it was a – perhaps not so predominant – explicit narrator, or the beginnings of a situational particularization of a fictional speaker in the martyr ballad, or a 'simple personalized speaker'.[6] Such speakers with clear appeal and presentation function should be regarded historically as essential for the development and evolution of a presenter-type speaker, who fulfils the potential of communicative functions specific to performance. With other procedures there are also similarities between earlier and later ballad types which can be subsumed under the criterion of functional transparency. On the whole the verse texts from the second half of the sixteenth century which are extant on broadsides can be assigned to the text corpus as early forms of the street ballad, as it were in a preparatory function.

Any genre definition must take into account diachronic and typological transitional forms and peripheral phenomena, for these can be seen to have historical and functional origins. The medley and the dialogue ballad can be described as borderline cases among seventeenth-century street ballads, since they correspond only slightly to the feature matrix we have drawn up. In spite of its lack of functional transparency, the medley must be assigned to the street-ballad genre on the basis of its particularly well-developed presenter speech situation which adequately corresponds to the lighthearted character of its subject of communication. At the same time the close links with the showmanship of the theatre clown and court jester are evident in this textual type. The dialogue ballad is a true borderline case: it is the only textual type with two separate speakers, preventing any presenter communication. Its origins in the jig do indicate, however, practical functional elements common to the street ballad, such as musical performance, theatricality, and its function as entertaining interlude.

The genre definition undertaken here of the street ballad and its further classification into street-ballad sub-genres and ballad types has been drawn up on the basis of feature combinations – for the most part structural features – and also of textually preformed practical function. It does of course extend far beyond the genre awareness of the period in question. The collective term 'ballad' (for the history of the term see above, p. 4) is nevertheless found frequently and regularly in the titles of the most diverse ballad types. Similarly, it is recurrently met with in contemporary documents as a mainly derogatory term to describe a literary form targeted at the lower end of the social scale and characterized by sung rendition, disturbingly widespread distribution, primitive style, and trivial, immoral, content (see appendix and chapter 6). Medial components and a global distinction between the street-ballad text corpus and others, especially the folk ballad, are intuitively present here. Within the communicative reference area between ballad producer and recipient, however, 'ballad' must have been understood as a label having positive value. Furthermore, the most common textual descriptions in the titles convey relevant information only to a very limited extent. The most reliable descriptions are the terms 'dialogue' (occasionally also 'discourse') and 'jig' for dialogue ballads, 'jest' for comic tales, and 'medley', although the two last are not used consistently for all the textual types which would merit such descriptions. 'Advice' (also 'counsel') and 'warning' frequently signal a corresponding textual intention, though without taking into account their explicit predominance and the respective structural principle (narrative, role-play fiction, or discursive). 'Lament' describes the basic tenor of a text, similarly independent of its type of deictic or thematic structure (usually a life history), and again it is not used at all consistently for all the texts which could be subsumed under the term. 'Song' and 'ditty', with their rather vague announcement function which at the same time connotes a higher literary stratum, are used quite arbitrarily.[7] On the whole these contemporary terms denoting textual types within the detailed announcements in the titles have their metatextual functions of attraction and information, reflecting attempts to latch on to existing traditions. Poetological awareness, however, is evident here only to a very limited degree.

Those features specific to the street-ballad genre which are summarised as 'personalization of the message' – primarily through the presenter – and 'functional transparency' have the effect not only of manipulating but also of easing reception. A clearly profiled speaker, who can be optically and acoustically particularized in a balladmonger in direct communication with his audience, attracts the listeners' attention and clarifies the textual message which in turn is rendered easily understandable through its functional transparency. Thus the constitution of the street-ballad text makes it possible to convey and process information in a way suited to an audience situation having the particular disturbance factors connected with street-ballad rendition. It also makes it possible to understand the text at a later point, that is, for those who join the audience when the performance is in full swing. Thus, for example, the predominantly action-logical link between guilt and punishment, with its chronological order and corresponding references to previous points in the text, gives the late arrival at least an approximate idea of the beginning of the ballad. The recurrent illustration of a conflict situation in the role-play ballad also makes reception considerably easier for the newcomer. It is especially easy to pick up the threads in the discursive ballad, where the theme is repeatedly explained and exemplified. The relatively high level of redundancy, manifested in the various forms of functional transparency, should in no way be judged negatively in this context. It is rather a procedure whereby the textual message is very much influenced by a concern for the particular conditions of street-ballad reception. As well as the components of the practical, external situation, these conditions of reception also include those of the social class of the audience (see above, p. 26). The latter's relatively low level of culture, literary awareness, and cognitive subtlety is accommodated by the phatic, psychological, and aesthetic devices for ease of reception which are found in the street ballad. The orientation towards a speaker, clear and urgent appeals to the listener, pleasant and acceptable presentation procedures, and contents which are largely familiar through their reference to everyday reality enable a predominantly middle- and lower-class audience to participate in fictional worlds and in the confrontation of reality through language.

The features specific to the genre of the English street ballad in our period of investigation, especially in the first half of the seventeenth century, show that in this text corpus the conditions of distribution and reception were taken into account to a substantial extent in the coding of the textual message. The pragmatically orientated determination of genre leads to the conclusion that what we are dealing with is a distinct form of literary medium. The term 'medium' has recently been extended to include any kind of vehicle for communication (see H. Schanze [1974], pp. 27–37, 44–7), and at the same time it has been recognized that a definition of the term 'medium' which limits its application to 'vehicle for news transmission' is not tenable, since the medium affects the form and content of the message. These shifts in attitude towards the term 'medium' make possible a better understanding of the medial functions of literature and also the placing of individual literary genres within the system of social communication. Broadside and public performance as medial conditions of distribution and reception, with their influencing of textual constitution, characterized the position of the street ballad in the contemporary sphere of literary activity.[8] It was integrated into the popular cultural and mercantile practices of the time, whereby its considerable independence of the forces regulating orthodox literature, and the concomitant readiness to take financial risks (see above, chapter 1.2.1), contributed to its low-class orientation and correspondingly widespread circulation.

The classification of the street ballad as a literary medium is based merely on the fact that textual procedures characteristic of this text corpus relate to the conditions surrounding its communication. This does not yet explain whether and to what extent the street ballad can be regarded as a journalistic medium. The features defined in mass-communication studies as characterizing journalistic media[9] can be established for the street ballad only in a modified form which is historically conditioned and genre-specific. Through the technological possibility of serial print production and its particular and effective system of distribution, the street ballad achieved what for that time would be a high degree of publicity. Its form of communication is 'indirect', that is, with distance in time and space between the communication partners, to the extent that the text written by the author was stored in print. In performance, however, through the introduction of the additional 'transmitter' in the person of the ballad-monger, it becomes direct. The 'one-sidedness' of communication as evidenced in modern mass media can be applied to the street ballad only to a limited extent, since the audience could participate directly at least in the refrain if not also in other forms of behaviour, which can now only be inferred. This audience is in no way 'scattered' to the same degree as the present-day mass-media audience; at the same time it is not limited to an elite, as is the case with the readership of orthodox literature. The specific and clear effects of institutional conditions of production in the manner of communication and the constitution of the message (see above, chapter 1.2.1; 1.2.2) can also be compared to the situation in the modern journalistic media. We may also mention as individual analogies the use of the trailer and the personalized communication of the message. All in all, the street-ballad communication situation contains, apart from genre-specific characteristics of a literary medium, components of a journalistic medium which are all the more significant in that they represent an innovation for that period. However, in settling the question of how far the street ballad should be regarded as a modified early form of journalism, its intended audience relationship has still to be taken into account.

5.2 Textual intention and audience expectation: entertainment, instruction, topicality

The difficulties involved in reconstructing a historical audience, its expectations, taste (see above, pp. 25–6) and reactions, especially when dealing with ah audience other than that of orthodox literature,[10] limit us mainly to an extrapolation of textual intention.[11] It would also be necessary to collect as many facts as possible regarding the everyday experience of the recipients of the time, and investigate existing contemporary value systems, in order to gain a more detailed understanding of the referential links in the texts. This has only occasionally been possible in the present study, and requires further investigation. In conclusion, therefore, entertainment, instruction, and audience relevance as evidenced specifically in the street ballad will be outlined merely as a framework for the latter's intentionality. The explicitness of presenter statements, and the tendency towards clarification in the structure and content of the street ballad, certainly provide pointers. The hypothesis of an orientation of textual intention towards audience expectation is supported by the nature of the street ballad as 'wares', its popularity and wide circulation, as well as by certain needs of the lower and middle classes which can be inferred from cultural and historical circumstances.

The term 'entertainment' comprises aspects of production and distribution as well as practical and functional textual and sociological characteristics which can be applied to the street ballad. It was printed and distributed on what was for that time a large scale, in order to reach a class of audience with, for the most part, little or no literary background. The intention to amuse, which can be defined sociologically in terms of audience requirements, can be historically most effectively demonstrated through reference to the literary showmanship evident in the street ballad. Explicit metatextual references to the intention to entertain are abundantly present in the title, trailer, and concluding formulas, whereby sensational, exciting, comic, moving, and realistic aspects are emphasized according to the nature of the respective textual content. 'Entertainment literature' should be read, listened to, and watched 'for pleasure', that is without any particular effort and with a compensatory effect for otherwise unfulfilled needs or unsatisfied interests.[12] A precondition for an entertaining effect of this kind is the presence of textual and functional devices for ease of reception such as are found in the street ballad on the presenter level of communication and in functional transparency.

The street ballad frequently also looks at social reality critically, humorously, and from diverse points of view, all of which can be combined with didactic intentions. The street-ballad intention to instruct is clearly recognizable in the recurrent illocutionary acts of warning and advice on the level of the presenter's communication with his audience, and implicitly present on the level of reference to the outside world. The subject of communication acquires didactic functionality through its explicit references and semantic correlation with the specific instruction intended. The didactic intention comprises religious exhortations based on biblical material, exemplary martyr stories, prodigies and political events; warnings against the path leading to crime, often spiced with sensational elements; everyday practical advice and the pointing out of social ills. The thematic orientation of the intention to instruct is dogmatically predetermined in religious ballads; in ballads with secular content, although hyperbolic to the point of cliché and highly recurrent in topic,[13] it is in principle not far removed from reality and relatively flexible with regard to norms. The procedures which promoted ease of reception, thereby also furthering the aim to entertain, were equally effective in serving didactic intentions. This is particularly true of the tendency towards clarification. The close combining of entertainment and instruction characteristic of the street ballad is only possible on the secular level. It is achieved through showmanlike presentation and the fictional establishment of the example's autonomy with its sensational, moving, or comic effects. The variation in the proportion of didactic intent in relation to entertainment ranges from mere pretext to prime concern. The intention to instruct in the street ballad should be seen in the context of the general demand that all literature should serve a useful purpose. It should provide culture, education and a model of social behaviour according to the ideas of Castiglione for the courtier, professional knowledge for the academic, edification for the Puritan, and factual information and everyday practical advice for the up-and-coming tradesman and businessman (see E. H. Miller [1959], pp. 25–6).

The street ballad's intention to instruct is a genre-specific form of that tendency to satisfy expectations which was a general feature of the writing of the time. From another standpoint, however, the street ballad must be seen as having considerable innovative status: in the choice of themes and the nature of their communication a tendency towards topicality can be observed. It is not so much topicality in the strict sense of proximity in time, which, although often announced, and signalled in particular by the epithet 'new', was seldom actually in evidence. Topicality of that kind is found primarily in early street ballads orientated towards religious politics, while the tradition-bound interpretations of prodigies tended rather to use sensational presentation to cover up their lack of topicality. Of more importance to literary history than the presenter's explicit claims to topicality is its presence as manifested in the relevance of the subject of communication for the immediate everyday world of the target group. For an urban middle class of tradesmen and businessmen, just beginning to assert itself socially and economically (for details see L. B. Wright [1963]), the fictionalized, superficially critical, and entertaining treatment of various aspects of everyday reality was likely to have encouraged a sense of identity. This is reinforced communicatively by the personalization of the message, especially as the ballad acquires an air of graphic and even vivid topicality through the presenter, conveying an impression of immediate relevance to the present. Claims to and tendencies towards topicality, audience orientation, quasi-serial production, and a high degree of publicity reaching a relatively wide audience are journalistic characteristics of the street ballad which in this early historical context certainly have precursory significance. The double function of the street ballad as both literary and journalistic medium lies in the overlapping of the two with regard to distinctive medium-specific procedures, the combining of entertainment and didactic influences, and the variety of the supply on offer.[14]

5.3 Changes within the genre 1550–1650: secularization of content and textual strategies; the speaker as a literary expression of contemporary individualism

Over the period from 1550 to 1650 there is an obvious change in the content of the English street ballad, from religious material and themes in the second half of the sixteenth century to the treatment of secular themes in the first half of the seventeenth century. This fact constitutes the starting-point for an examination of the history of the genre. An analysis and interpretation of numerous street-ballad texts from the aspects of speech and presentation structure has repeatedly shown, during the course of this investigation, that there is a definite link between the secularization of content and the emergence both of a presenter level of communication (see above, chapter 3.5.4 and feature matrix, pp. 224–5) and other textual speakers. The reason for this, from the point of view of textual intent, is to be found not only in the unsuitability of presenter communication practices for religious and theological moral themes, but more in the principal function of a speaker who assumes sole responsibility for conveying the subject of communication. Where this subject of communication is part of an unquestioned, fixed world view orientated towards salvation and redemption there is no necessity for a personalized statement. It was only during the process of secularization, which characterized the seventeenth century, where the abandonment of dogmatic safeguards made possible a plurality of opinion and choice of behaviour, that a personalization of the textual message proved useful if not vital. A source of information was created which was obliged to authenticate and justify the subject of communication. The concomitant specification in the audience addresses (see above, chapter 3.3.1) shows clearly the relevance of a theme for a particular audience group *hic et nunc*, whereas in earlier ballads the collective first-person plural or addressing of the whole of Christendom, as well as calls to prayer, appeal to the audience *sub specie aeternitatis*.

A selective presentation of everyday experience needs to be reinforced if it is to be communicated successfully. This is not only achieved on the presenter level of communication but is also supported by the fictional speech situations of the narrator, role-play figure, and discursive speaker, according to the specific type of text. The task of the speaker is here – as it were independently – to legitimize the existence of the fictionally portrayed individual case by means of realistic detail and place it in a contemporary social value system which is no longer firmly established. The productive activity of the explicit narrator finds expression in the action-syntagmatic and action-semantic commentary. In the distance between speaker and subject of communication, it can create a relationship between an individual fate and generalizatioons based on examples. Thus the narrative function signals responsibility for aesthetic aspects of production and at the same time a subjective perspective, a factor which is particularly true of the first-person narrative. This ambivalence of speaker authority and subjectivity, of generalization based on example and realistic particularization, is even more clearly in evidence in the role-play ballad. The predetermined exemplary value of biblical material and martyr stories, lamentations of sin and allegorical figures (see above, pp. 120–3, 181–7), requires only a minimum of narrative and role-play mediation respectively to establish the intended framework for communication. Finally, the discursive speaker shows his mediating responsibility in his showmanlike extolling and weighing up of a theme; in the early forms of the discursive ballad his function is restricted to exhortations.

The separation of the individual life history from the frame of reference of salvation and redemption, and its obligation towards norms and values which although still partly transcendental already had predominantly social relevance, can be understood in terms both of the nature and content of the speaker's mediating function and of the secularization of deictic detail.[15] The deterrent effect of the execution of the criminal takes the place of the reinforcement of Christian belief intended by accounts of the execution of martyrs. The impersonal lamentation of sin is replaced by the fictional role-play conflict situation within the system of social values, and the biblical narrative gives way to the comic tale. While serious misdeeds continue to be placed under divine jurisdiction, delegated to human agents, there are now also noticeably frequent portrayals of self-regulatory processes for those human errors and weaknesses which remain outside judicial sanction.[16] Such processes are intended for application both by groups and by individuals in private interaction. As subjects of communication they allow a humorous distance on the part of the speaker, and occasionally also moral ambivalence. The fictionalized portrayal of problems of immediate relevance to the audience, and the treatment of socially critical themes in the discursive ballad, show that it was no longer possible to rely solely on the intervention of a transcendental power, or postponement until the next world. Only the news ballad preserves the literary and philosophical traditional link with the metaphysical and oral–theological interpretation of prodigies. This could explain why this type of ballad appears with far less frequency within the predominantly secularized ballad production of the first half of the seventeenth century (see above, chapter 4.2.3, esp. p. 115).

The emergence of textual speakers and the isolation of the individual case provide the procedural conditions for a plurality of opinion within the text corpus, marking a clear diachronic change from the moral–theological conformity of the early ballads. The most striking example of direct and tangible debate between ballad authors is the answer ballad (see above, chapter 3.4.3). The further diversity in the opinion and presentation perspectives of recurrent themes and material has no direct relation to other ballads, but is manifested rather as the personal emotion, commitment and consternation of the particular speaker. Thus the same problem of role is portrayed now as a conflict, now as a resolution of cognitive dissonance (see above, pp. 173–5). Complementary and contrasting perspectives in the role-play ballad (see above, pp. 168–9) and the first-person narrative (see above, pp. 115–20) attach different opinions on similar experiences to different fictional experiencing subjects. The discursive dialogue ballad is structurally predestined for a contrasting of opinions within the same text. Finally, in the discursive ballad a variation of stand-point in different speech attitudes – predominantly instructional or pre-dominantly entertaining – is comprehensible in relation to recurrent themes and examples.

The history of the street-ballad genre over the period of our investi-gation can be understood in the light of certain changes: from religious to secular themes, from a speaker with only slight significance to a respon-sible position of mediation with the functions of presenter according to the specific textual type, from collective to target-group address, from examples with rigidly fixed significance to the portrayal of particular individual cases which are freely disposable as far as interpretation is con-cerned, and from dogmatic strictures to plurality of opinion. These changes indicate, not only as far as content is concerned but also struc-turally, a tendency towards secularization during the transition from the Middle Ages to the modern age. The aspects of genre change mentioned can be assigned to the criteria of historical philosophy which Blumenberg quotes as 'identifying the modern age'.[17] These are: 'secularization' as a historical process; a new self-awareness of the thinking subject which is increasingly based on a rational attitude towards safeguarding his existence and on creative independence; activity and responsibility of the individual which is unrelated to transcendental intervention and immut-able authorities; and a change in function of ideas, concepts, and experi-ences, which is more than a quantitative reduction of interest in the transcendental sphere. The textual processing of the changing character of everyday experience and its communication to the public, achieved with the limited means of the street ballad, should be seen as an emancipatory step within the secularization process of the transition from the Middle Ages to modern times which allowed the lower strata of the populace to participate in a general historical development of ideas, according to their level of culture and awareness.

From the linguistic point of view this development is manifested in the street-ballad text as socio-cultural presuppositions. The pragmatic genre definition deriving from a consideration of the situational context is thereby extended to the tentative inclusion of a comprehensive socio-cultural speech situation.[18] We have seen that the presenter as speaker, with his correlative audience address, derives primarily from the con-ditions surrounding performance, that is, from presuppositions relevant to the situation. Regardless of this observation, however, it must be stressed that his communicative function of mediation is also determined by the presupposition of 'individual independence without the security of a transcendental frame of reference'. This socio-cultural presupposition applies also to the fictional textual speaker, direct situational relevance being reserved for the presenter.

In order to describe more precisely the socio-cultural determining factors of speech acts in the English street ballad, with its changes from the sixteenth to the seventeenth centuries, we can single out one essential component of this gradual process of secularization which has frequently been the subject of historical research: the development of individualism, which is clearly analogous to the personalization of the textual message. From the philosophical viewpoint this individualism was founded on the central position of man in the Neoplatonist cosmic order (see E. Cassirer [1969]) which has taken its place in the history of ideas as the 'chain of being'.[19] Man's new self-assurance was based first and foremost on the cultural ideal of the *uomo universale*. The impulses towards individual initiative in shaping one's own destiny which were connected with this ideal stemmed not only from the humanist tradition of the Renaissance,[20] but also from the individualism of the Reformation, where the motives for a man's actions became the yardstick for judgement on him.[21] Combined with the complex conception of individualism we find both an idealized and a sceptical view of human nature, the one supported by, for example, Ficino and Pico and the other by Machiavelli and Hobbes.[22] Hobbes took an egocentric social and political individualism as the premise for his theory of the state which was certainly orientated towards seventeenth-century reality.[23] The egocentric and active component of individualism was very clearly discernible in the socio-economic sphere which, as humanist culture and political theory, would have had direct influence on the class of ballad producers and recipients. The gradual transition from the medieval economic system to that of modern times was generally characterized by a dissolution of corporate bonds and an increase in individualist tendencies.[24] Competition and the desire for profit became paramount in agriculture, business, and trade, going hand in hand with concentration of capital, division of labour, and more efficient manufacturing. Mercantile adventurism, focusing very much on this world, and successful enterprise had a determining influence on the self-assurance of the individual, as did isolation and the element of risk, where man had previously been thought of as being part of a community and assured of salvation in the next world.[25]

Despite the conceptual and methodological uncertainties attending brief surveys of historical change and definitions of epochs, we may safely describe the development of the English street-ballad genre between 1550 and 1650 as the literary expression of a far more extensive development in which, through their communication via the text, author and audience consciously participated.[26] The newly perceived growing secularization of man's view of the world, and the manifold philosophical, religious, political, social and economic forms of individualism are manifested in a change of outlook in the street-ballad speech situation. An individualist concept of the self as caught up between insecurity and self-assurance, together with a new flexibility and mobility, finds expression in the content and textual strategies of the street ballad. As a literary and journalistic medium the street ballad fulfilled its function in a socially definable cultural sector whose historical importance as an integrative force has been almost universally neglected.[27] Since it was directly related to the circumstances of its performance[28] and exerted general social and cultural influence, a pragmatic genre definition can determine the cultural–historical position of the street ballad more precisely than has so far been the case.

The subsequent history of the street ballad can be described on the basis of this genre definition. After the historical watershed of the Civil War (see above, pp. 24–5), certain changes could be expected in its usage and textual strategies. Also at this time, the street ballad was increasingly being removed from its unique performance context and transferred to chapbooks and anthologies purely as reading-matter.[29] This change of function is also shown in its transition to the spheres of theatre (i.e. where dialogue was interspersed with song) and entertainment at social gatherings in the form of songs or poems. At the same time early forms of journalistic publication were taking over as precursors of the newspaper, a role which up to the middle of the seventeenth century had been fulfilled by the street ballad. A comprehensive history of the street ballad must be concerned with its historical influence on poetry, especially on the literary ballad, and with the level of its literary innovation.[30]

6 Reputation of the street ballad: views of contemporary writers

We have described the English street ballad from 1550 to 1650 as a literary genre whose textual constitution is to a large extent pragmatically orientated within a distinct socio-cultural situation of communication. This definition requires the additional consideration of the question of its contemporary reception.[1] The ballad audience's level of expectation and reactions are more easily deduced from the text corpus itself, however. Historical documents relating to reception, although informative as to the degree of circulation and popularity of the street ballad, tend to reveal the biased perspective of the street ballad's critics rather than echo the sentiments of a wider public. We must therefore acknowledge that the street ballad had for the most part a poor reputation, at least in that area of its reception restricted to the assessments of contemporary writers: there is no documentary evidence from which we could deduce the effects of the street ballad on the public as a whole. We can assume that it was the literary–historical achievement of the street ballad, as a new genre-norm,[2] to change and emancipate the level of expectation,[3] but reception history provides only a fragmentary and distorted picture, leaving us rather to infer *ex negativo*.

No description or discussion of the literary phenomenon of the street ballad is to be found in late sixteenth- and seventeenth-century poetics, only occasional polemical references. That is to say, in contemporary orthodox criticism and discussions of literary theory, which operated from a normative concept of literature orientated towards that of the ancient world, the street ballad did not feature: it did not correspond to the demands of existing concepts of genre, ideal values, erudition, and lofty style. The street ballad was acknowledged in prose criticism, satirical verse, and drama only on the level of occasional and commissioned writing. In drama the balladmonger was portrayed or mentioned on stage as a popular, feared, despised, but also comic figure. In these reception documents too, invective predominates. At the same time, many of these documents provide accurate information regarding characteristics of the text corpus, its distribution, and its status in the cultural life of the time. It can be seen from the extant references giving indications of ballad reception that there is no question here of a systematic poetological or complex literary-critical analysis of this genre. It is necessary to build up a picture

242

of the street ballad's function, effectiveness and reputation from a large number of separate references. Some aspects of a level of ballad-audience expectation can similarly be established from these documents, although this is for the most part from the polemical standpoint of street-ballad critics who saw themselves either as defenders of the sacred cow of 'great' literature or at least as advocates of a strict puritanical morality. The level of expectation can always be deduced from the offer made to readers in the actual texts, an offer which we can assume, on the basis of their popularity and wide circulation, corresponded to certain expectations (see above, chapter 5.2).

There are over eighty documents relating to contemporary views on the street ballad during the period 1550 to 1700 in the appendix. A systematic analysis according to recurrent basic ideas is preferable to a historical presentation, since during that time only slight changes in criteria of judgement and opinion can be observed. It is significant that the term 'ballad' in the late sixteenth and the seventeenth centuries applied exclusively to the street ballad and not to the folk ballad.[4] The predominance of the street-ballad genre is seen not only in the wealth of comment on it but also in the similarity of the comment, which could almost be described as an opinion trend.

Literary criticism at the turn of the sixteenth century and during the seventeenth century already indicated very clearly an awareness of the distinction between accepted literature which was legitimized and hallowed by patronage and cultural institutions on the one hand, and an inferior level of popular literature on the other, even though critics lacked the appropriate terminology. This is particularly obvious in the case of the street ballad. Ben Jonson's dictum 'A poet should detest a ballad maker',[5] is a pithy formulation of the polarization. Many variations of this notion are found in contemporary comment. In 1570 Roger Ascham measured the mass production of hastily cobbled-together ballad texts against the cultural level of classical authors, who were content to respond less readily to the demands of their cultured audiences (appendix B 5; see also B 15 and B 20). Richard Stanyhurst argued similarly in 1582 (ibid., B 10), and Thomas Nashe (1592) derided ballad writers as 'poore latinlesse Authors' (ibid., B 18). In 1586 William Webbe compared the barley wreath of the bibulous author of trivia with the poet's laurels, citing the alehouse song as an example of street-ballad amusement, whose triviality was heightened by popular tunes and everyday usage (ibid., B 12). In 'The Tears of the Muses' (1591; ibid., B 12), Spenser lamented the demise of poetry, mentioning the street ballad as a representative example; although he does not refer to it explicitly, he describes its characteristics. Drayton saw ballad literature, with its wide circulation and popularity, as a pernicious attack on the Muses (ibid., B 52). The ballad author was seen as the prototype of the author of trivial literature and the tireless rhymester (ibid., B 15; B 23, B 31, B 56). John Earle's description of a 'Pot-Poet' in *Microcosmographie*, his collection of stylized character portraits (1628), is modelled on the features of the ballad author.[6] In 1641 an anonymous pamphleteer lamented the financial distress which forced some authors to earn their living writing 'penny-pamphlets' of no literary value, or even ballads, citing Martin Parker as a representative of this lowest of all literary levels (ibid., B 72). This erroneous literary verdict[7] shows that invective against the street ballad could also be motivated by professional envy or by hopes of enhancing the writer's own prestige. The latter becomes clear where the balladmonger is denounced as the antithesis of the true poet (appendix B 19, B 56). In 1615 Henry Parrot was so concerned for the status of his own modest literary work that he expressly instructed the publisher and bookseller to make sure that it could not be mistaken by the public for a collection of ballads.[8]

William Fulwood also used the ballad author as an effective negative antithesis, in his street ballad *A Supplication to Eldertonne* (c. 1570–1590; ibid., B 4), which is addressed to the first well-known ballad author. Under the pretext of excusing the literary attack on Elderton by Leach, an honourable, godfearing hosier and author of pious traces (see *BB*, fn, p. 143), he in turn attacks Elderton as the prototype of an author of trivial literature. Fullwood's reproving criticisms were also those of the subsequent period and developed into a tradition of literary-critical invective against the street ballad. The latter was accused of immorality (appendix B 4, vv. 2 and 5, B 9, B 24, B 26), lies and slander (ibid., B 4), sinful worldliness and lack of piety (ibid., vv. 9, 15, 18, 21), and a low intellectual level.

The street ballad was indeed frequently reproved for its lack of 'learning', a value concept which was central to contemporary poetological debate. Literary subjects had to be 'erudite', that is, part of a traditional cultural heritage of proven worth and therefore suitable for literary treatment. Such material was seldom used by the street ballad, whose innovative value consisted in precisely the opposite – a concern with present reality. 'Learning' also meant the instructional character of the content, however, in both the moral and informative sense. The street ballad also laid claim to 'learning' of this kind, although it was on the 'lower' level of practical, everyday instruction, humorous weighing up of possibilities and actions within the scope of human beings, and information of an entertaining nature. Finally, 'learning' also implied the use of a model form based on classical example. This was certainly not a feature of the street ballad with its brisk, sometimes jingling rhythm, simple verse forms, and colloquial style. Thus the criticism that the street ballad did not conform to the normative ideal of learning, made variously by R. Ascham in 1570 (ibid., B 5), W. Webbe in 1586 (ibid., B 12), T. Nashe in 1589 (ibid., B 15,

B 17) and R. Stanyhurst in 1582 (ibid., B 10), was well founded. Stanyhurst is even emphatic that a 'grammar schoole' education and a knowledge of Greek and Latin are essential for a good poet, a requirement which he noted was not fulfilled by the ballad author. Closely associated with this lack, according to Stanyhurst, were the ballad author's inadequate sense of form and casual attitude towards metre and rhyme. This repeated criticism[9] was certainly valid for a considerable number of street ballads, but it could also be applied to certain verse texts which were accepted as literature on the basis of the learning manifested in their content or style. Such phrases as 'base and rude rhyming' (ibid., B 10, B 15, B 16), 'babling Ballets' (ibid., B 16), 'ragged rhymes' (ibid., B 15) and 'verses running like the tap' (ibid., B 61) refer not only to the metrical form but also extend connotatively to the baseness of the street ballad *per se*, just as in poetics a discussion of versification is the tangible starting-point for global demands for decorum, inspiration, and the highest poetic and moral standards.

The low reputation of the street ballad and the criticism of the genre should be understood not least from within the general context of contemporary literary criticism. It was precisely during the period of intense invective against the ballad, between *c.* 1570 and 1620, that a desire for a national literature of quality was variously expressed in theoretical writings, especially where poetry was concerned. This desire was accompanied by severe criticism of any literature which did not conform to the high standard expected. It was above all the mass-produced literature of the ballads, pamphlets, chapbooks and the like which came under fire. Not only were they assigned a specific literary and social status, they were also made the scapegoat for any poetic failure. The polarization of high-status literature and trivial literature, the hackneyed disparagment of the balladmonger, and the correlation of lack of learning and 'base rhyming' all point in this direction.

I trust we shall haue Englishe Poetry at a higher price in short space: and the rabble of balde Rymes shall be turned to famous workes.[10]

The chief cause for the debasement of poetry, in the minds of Elizabethan critics, was to be found in the extensive and growing participation in the art of a multitude of low rimesters or 'poet-apes', as Sidney terms them. The problem involved in the invasion of the field of poetry by this horde of versifiers, who by their persistent and exasperating activity menaced the very life of the art, was to the critics a problem of tremendous concern and one that largely occupied their thought and energy and influenced the character of their criticism.   (G. A. Thompson [1914], pp. 9–10)

There are very few exceptions to the normative demands for poetics. One is provided quite early on in 1578, by Barnabe Rich, who advocated a 'homely style' (appendix B 6), and expressed his rejection of the classical conception of poetry and its later adherents via a code of mythological names and topographies. In 1653 Dorothy Osborne refers expressly to the ballad as representing popular poetry, in a letter to Sir William Temple enthusing about the idyll of the countryside and the singing of ballads (ibid., B 76). The only balanced view of ballad literature to emerge from the period of its early development, and the only one to show any critical subtlety, is expressed in a street ballad: *A new balade entituled as foloweth: To such as write in metres I write / Of small matters an exhortation* (between 1556 and 1571; ibid., B 3). It is an appeal to the authors of verses and to their printers and purveyors to show a sense of responsibility in their functions of selecting and supervising, and certainly accords with demands for quality as expressed in the poetics. The ballad's arguments focus mainly on printed matter hawked by pedlars, especially the ballad,[11] which is described as varying in quality according to content and versification. Some indeed are 'pithie', well formed and pleasant-sounding.[12]

A further criticism frequently levelled at the street ballad was its immorality and obscenity as opposed to the purity and piety expected of literature: 'filthy' versus 'godlie'. This should be seen in the wider context of the question of morality in poetry, as raised by, for example, William Baldwin in 1549 (appendix, B 1), Thomas Brice in a ballad *Against filthy writing / and such like delighting* (1561/2; ibid., B 2) or Thomas Lovell in 1581 (ibid., B 9). *The Gude and Godlie Ballates* (1567; see A. F. Mitchell's edition) is a collection of hymns, including some translations from the German, which saw itself as a campaign against verse of an entertaining, worldly nature, although this was not made explicit in the title until the edition of 1621: *with sundrie of other Ballates changed out of prophaine sanges, for avoyding of sinne and harlotrie.* This discussion did not revolve around the difference between literature, as accepted by men of letters, and trivial or entertainment literature, but concerned itself with functional literature only. The street ballad quickly became the main target for criticism, if not the scapegoat for anything in the poetry of the time which was profane or expressed enjoyment of worldly pleasures.

The polarization into edifying literature and frivolous entertainment, the latter possibly having an obscene emphasis, can be observed in practically every comment on this characteristic of the street ballad. It was expressed as 'lewdnes' and 'filthy rymes' versus 'scripture' by W. Fullwood in 1590 (appendix B 4, vv. 2, 5, and 18); 'rybaldry' and 'foolishe ballets' versus 'good and godly practises' by T. Lodge in 1579 (ibid., B 8); 'ballads and pamphletes full of ribaudrie and all scurrilous vanity, to the prophanation of God's name, and with-drawing people from Christian exercises' (ibid., B 24); and 'lascivious, idle, and unprofitable' versus 'the Word of God' in a petition supposed to have been signed by 150,000 citizens in

1640 (ibid., B 67). In 1624 (ibid., B 56) J. Davies used the expression 'filth' in connection with ballad literature, and in 1641 an anonymous critic has a ballad author indicate with regret that the text he has just written is 'not licenceable' (ibid., B 71) – whether for moral or political reasons, we are not told.

Erotic themes doubtless played a part in the advertising and selling of street ballads. In *A Song for Autolycus* (*c.* 1620; ibid., B 50) the speaker lures prospective customers with snippets of the erotic stories contained in the ballads he is selling. On the whole, however, the charge of obscenity is justified for only a very small proportion of the street-ballad text corpus: particular textual passages which either refer metaphorically to sexual activity or explicitly describe it. It is possible that the accusations also applied in a wider sense to those ballads admitting the occurrence of, or recommending, premarital and adulterous sexual relations, or those revealing any kind of enjoyment of eroticism. The general accusation of immorality may also have been directed, from a puritanical standpoint, against the street ballad's plurality of opinion, its predominantly secular themes and its entertainment value *per se*. Edifying and exhortational ballads, as also moralizing sensational ballads, were clearly ignored in this line of criticism. During the course of the seventeenth century, however, the position of entertainment literature *vis-à-vis* edifying literature was gradually being consolidated. This can be seen, for example, in a speech of one of the figures in Beaumont and Fletcher's *Monsieur Thomas* (1639; ibid., B 66), where the 'godly ballad' and similar works are associated with the moral coward, puritanical zealot, and unsociable stay-at-home.

The function of the street ballad as entertainment literature can be seen clearly in a series of contemporary opinions and accounts. It is primarily in drama that this aspect of ballad literature is dealt with. The Autolycus scene in *The Winter's Tale* (first performed *c.* 1609–10; see appendix B 37) portrays the reaction of a ballad audience from the lowest social class who know and appreciate the entertainment value of this kind of litera-ture: (apparent) factuality and news value, sensational excitement and merriment are expected, inducing Servant, Clown, Mopsa and Dorcas to buy several broadsides. Cokes's reaction also, at the appearance of the balladmonger Nightingale in the scene in Ben Jonson's *Bartholomew Fair* (1614; ibid., B 42–4) shows almost a craving for ballads which derives above all from a desire to be amused. The servants in William Cavendish's *The Triumphant Widow* (1677; ibid., B 83) show a similar happy excite-ment at the appearance of a pedlar whose biggest seller turns out to be ballads. The themes mentioned there reveal the entertaining character of these texts. In Shakespeare's *Coriolanus* (1623; ibid., B 54) a servant describes the boring, uneventful peacetime era as a breeding-ground for ballad production, thereby assigning to it the function of compensatory entertainment. On the other hand, in 1621 no less a writer than Robert Burton, without any sign of irony, was recommending ballads as an antidote to melancholy (ibid., B 51). Don Pedro, in the tragicomedy *The Court Secret* (1653; ibid., B 75), wants to cheer up his master and fellow sufferers, who are condemned to death, with a ballad – not only a hint that the drama will end happily but also an indication of the entertainment value of the 'good-night ballads' here referred to. By 1675 street ballads had long become institutionalized as entertainment literature, alongside the recently established 'drollery' and printed play, so that Mrs Pinchwife could expect and ask for them from the bookseller (ibid., B 81).

In connection with the entertainment function of the street ballad, themes were often announced which were obviously intended to attract an audience by their content. The type most frequently alluded to is the 'good-night ballad' (ibid., B 53, B 73, B 75, B 55, B 61). Although this type is considered representative of the sensational reporting of events, in the text corpus up to the mid-seventeenth century it occurs by no means as often as these allusions would seem to indicate. Other ballad titles, presumably invented but in successful imitation of those of the street ballad, refer to exciting events and accounts of miracles. Autolycus in *The Winter's Tale* offers his prospective customers an account of a fish that sings (ballads) (ibid., B 37), Nightingale offers what is clearly the story of the exposing of a swindler ('the ferret and the coney') and a report of a windmill being blown down by a witch's fart (ibid., B 43;, and the *Autolycus* of 1620 has a '*Sussex Serpent* to fright you' in his collection (ibid., B 50). J. Hall and J. Earle allude similarly to monster ballads (ibid., B 29 and B 61). Excitement and possibly social criticism are promised by the incredible tale of a 'Courtier that died rich', a ballad praised by its pedlar, Footpad (ibid., B 83). Responding to a plea for a 'melancholy Ditty', he suggests a ballad on 'a Virgin of thirteen or forteen that dy'd a Maid' (ibid.), and for a lewd ballad he suggests 'a very strange Ballet, of a lusty Widow' which he has in his collection. This selection of topic areas does not cover the actual spectrum in the text corpus, nor goes it give an accurate picture of the quantitative distribution. We have here rather an expression of the conception of the street ballad which had already become stereotyped and which fits into the context of general invective found elsewhere.

Closely related to the street ballad's thematic attraction for the audience is its allusion to the newness of its material or the topicality of the events described. This claim, characteristic of the intention of so many ballads, is also noted as a typical feature of the street ballad in documents of the time relating to reception (ibid., B 37, B 42, B 72, B 83, B 86), although the authenticity of street-ballad content is sometimes doubted (ibid., B 4, v. 9; B 16, B 83). There is remarkably frequent expression of a fear of gossip and defamation of character which might appear in ballads. The documents pertaining to reception are in this case always dramas, and it is figures in these who, finding themselves in awkward circumstances, express a fear of being exposed to public ridicule in street ballads sung on the street and in the alehouse.[13] It is not clear whether such comments refer to actual practice or merely to the public character of the street ballad and its possibilities as a means of political propaganda.[14] Biographical authenticity can only be established in the case of a few criminal ballads. John Selden, a well-known lawyer of the time (died 1654), describes the ballad in his *Table Talk* as an important vehicle of libel (appendix B 84, published posthumously).

Other stereotyped characteristics of the street ballad include sentimentality and banality of emotional effect, often reinforced by the tune. Such stereotyping ignores the considerable proportion of gaiety, humour, and satire in the text corpus. Shakespeare's Autolycus recommends a ballad's 'doleful tune' (ibid., B 37; see also B 35), the *Autolycus* of 1620 offers, in ballad jargon, 'a doleful ditty' (ibid., B 50), and the pedlar Footpad responds immediately to the request of his customer: 'Oh I love a melancholy Ditty, I can weep at a Ballet so sweetly – ' (ibid., B 83). J. Earle also expects this reaction from a naive audience (ibid., B 61).

In addition to contemporary literary-critical opinion,[15] there is an almost equal amount of material relating to such aspects as mass-production, methods of distribution, audience, and popularity and social status of the ballad author and balladmonger, which can be classified as literary-sociological comment. We can deduce from this that the age showed just as much awareness and interest in the ballad's socio-cultural function and effects as in its concrete textual form.[16]

References to the quantity of ballads produced usually relate at the same time to their correspondingly wide circulation.[17] Such comments are also frequently made in conjunction with complaints regarding a decrease in quality,[18] which in this connection are in principle justified. The method of street-ballad distribution is often vividly described and discussed from diverse points of view. A distinction is made between the professional balladmonger, hawking by pedlars, and distribution at second hand by members of the audience. Shakespeare's Autolycus and the speaker in the *Song of Autolycus* are professional balladmongers (ibid., B 37 and B 50). H. Chettle's *Anthonie Now Now* regards himself as belonging to the old guard of ballad-singers, and his criticism of the state of affairs after his death is correspondingly valid.[19] J. Earle's 'Pot-Poet' is aware of the connection between the mass-production of broadsides and their distribution by hired singers travelling from market to market (appendix B 61). The appearance of the balladmonger in the scene from *Bartholomew Fair*, mentioned above, is portrayed in vivid detail (ibid., B 43 and 44; see also above, chapter 1.1). In the general context of fairground amusements the showmanlike and market-crier aspects of ballad performance would have come into their own, as would the public's readiness to listen and buy. The listeners' fascination with the performance enabled the balladmonger (Nightingale) to liaise with a cutpurse (Edgworth). Robert Greene had already treated this aspect of street-ballad performance in detail in 1591, in a piece from his *Conny-Catching Tracts* (ibid., B 22). The pickpockets observe where listeners, having been persuaded to buy a broadside, replace their purses after paying. The criminals' success is short-lived, however, as the victims soon suspect the truth and set upon the balladmonger before handing over the thieves to the authorities.

Pedlars carried street-ballad broadsides amongst their wares, operating mainly in rural areas. This type of distribution received such frequent and casual mention that we can assume that the process was institutionalized (ibid., B 23, B 24, B 45, B 68). A scene from *The Triumphant Widow* (1677) conveys a vivid impression of the selling ploys, street-ballad wares and willing customers of a pedlar on his visit to a country nobleman's house (ibid., B 83). Audiences themselves would pass on ballads, a fact which also would have contributed to their wide circulation, and is recorded in contemporary documents. From comments by T. Lodge in 1579 (ibid., B 8), J. Hall in 1597 (ibid., B 32), an anonymous speaker in 1597 (ibid., B 31; see also B 80) and D. Osborne in 1653 (ibid, B 76) we can infer that ballads were on everyone's lips. For this to be possible it would be necessary for the audience to join in the singing of certain passages during ballad performance in order to retain the tune and the text, as described by Ben Jonson and W. Cavendish (ibid., B 44 and B 83); possession of the broadside would also serve as a memory aid and reminder of the performance. These broadsides were often preserved as wall decorations, as mentioned by Ben Jonson in 1614 (ibid., B 44), J. Davies in 1624 (ibid., B 57) and Isaac Walton between 1653 and 1655 (ibid., B 77).

From references to the massive circulation of the street ballad in public places[20] and in the private sphere we can deduce the immense popularity of these texts, which is indeed expressly if reluctantly confirmed by Drayton in 1621; 'Base Balatry is so belov'd and sought' (ibid., B 52). T. Lodge is similarly disparaging in 1579 (ibid., B 8), as are N. Breton in 1618 (ibid., B 49) and J. Earle in 1628 (ibid., B 61), while around the middle of the century we can discern an attitude of acceptance of the street-ballad phenomenon, with its wide circulation and popularity, as a fact of life.[21] The popularity of street ballads is always evident in fictional portrayals of the appearance of a balladmonger. Although the audience in such portrayals is always from the lower classes of society (ibid., B 37, B 41, B 42, B 50, B 83), there was at the same time an awareness of the different social levels of the ballad readership (ibid., B 46). It is very probable that the popularity of the street ballad and the resulting financial rewards (see above, chapter 1.2.1) helped to reinforce a disapproving and polemical attitude in an age when the majority of authors were scarcely able to earn a living from their writing (see E. H. Miller [1959]).

The balladmonger was not infrequently discredited on the grounds of his social status (see also H. Rollins [1919a], pp. 296–306). Idle youths (appendix B 24 and B 27), escaped convicts, and swindlers are mentioned (ibid., B 68 and B 22) as belonging to the class of beggars and musicians swarming around London (ibid., B 7). The professional balladmonger is portrayed in drama as a comic figure performing the function of entertainer.[22] The ballad author is categorized by literary critics in the first instance as a trivial author (see above, pp. 243–4) bent on making a quick profit. The only other social marker evident in the documents available is that of alcohol addiction (appendix B 16, B 17, B 61, B 79), where drunkenness is generally associated with an inferior literary product (ibid., B 12, B 32, B 72, B 73). Irresponsible occasional verses (see especially B 15) are contrasted with creations having divine inspiration.

Documents relating to contemporary reception show that the street ballad represented a very considerable component of cultural and social life. It was variously a bone of contention, much-sought-after entertainment for certain sections of the populace, a scapegoat for literary failure, and a deterrent example of frivolous diversion and profane worldliness. As a literary mass product it was sold and circulated everywhere. It was produced and distributed by individuals of dubious reputation, and presumably exerted a powerful influence on the imagination and behaviour of a large section of the populace. Defoe's elegy on the English street ballad in *Applebee's Journal* of 1722 (appendix, B 86) marks the point where important functions of this literary medium were already being taken over by journals and newspapers. The past importance of the street ballad is here conveyed only ironically, through the perspective of the speaker, a 'Ballad-Maker'. With the showman's overbearing manner and rhetorical verbosity, this figure argues for the preservation of an institution of such political and economic import which significantly contributed to the formation of public opinion. It is clearly only the immediately preceding phase of street-ballad development which he has in mind, in which it had become a predominantly party-political medium.[23]

Although contemporary literary-critical comment on the street ballad is of limited value, seen in its historical context it is highly revealing. The genre was classified, with polemical overtones, as what we would today term trivial or entertainment literature. The ballad author was judged accordingly, and there are repeated references to certain characteristics of this literary medium. These either apply only partially and in a very limited way to the text corpus, as for example poor versification, immorality, obscenity, and scandal; or they fail to take into account the fact that the street ballad was intended for a particular social sector. It is accused, for example, of a lack of 'learning', or of providing frivolous entertainment for a certain type of audience. Although such contemporary descriptions and evaluations should be understood from within the context of their literary-historical limitations, they in fact remained standard for scholars well into the twentieth century (see above, Introduction, p. 4). In contrast, our investigation has attempted to do justice to the literary procedures of the street ballad which, although simple, are often adequate to the communication of the intended message. In addition, we have been concerned to evaluate this genre, in its relation to the audience, as a vehicle of information, entertainment and instruction. The impressive quantity of contemporary references, partly humorous and partly polemical, reflects the literary and cultural function and widespread impact of the street ballad. In our investigation this was taken further and assumed to be a determining factor in the constitution of the text in its communicative frame of reference. The change in the street-ballad genre over our period of investigation has been shown to be the literary and aesthetic expression of a historical change in ideas, a change which was conveyed through this medium to a social class with minimal literary background.

Appendix: Documents relating to the street ballad: literary and cultural criticism between 1550 and 1700

The following documentation of contemporary comment on the street ballad makes no claims to completeness. It can however be regarded as representative, since the selection given shows numerous repetitions of opinion, in which prevailing views can be discerned. The order of the texts is chronological. The numbering of the documents is designed for easy reference in the main text. Details of sources refer to section 1.3 of the bibliography (see also the introductory remarks to this section). For street-ballad texts, the abbreviations for the editions given on pp. x–xi have been used.

William Baldwin, *The Canticles or Balades of Salomon* (1549)

B 1   Would god that suche songes myght once driue out of office the baudy balades of lecherous loue that commonly are indited and song of idle courtyers in princes and noble mens houses.

Thomas Brice, *Against filthy writing, and such like delighting* (1561/62)

B 2   What meane the rimes that run thus large in euery shop to sell?
With wanton sound, and filthie sense, me thinke it grees not well
We are not Ethnickes, we forsoth, at least professe not so
Why range we then to Ethnickes trade? come bak, where wil ye goe?
Tel me is Christ, or Cupide Lord? doth God or Venus reigne?
And whose are wee? whom ought wee serue? I aske it, answere plaine
If wanton Venus, then go forth, if Cupide, keep your trade
If God, or Christ, come bak the best, or sure you will be made
Doth God? is he the Lord in deed? and should we him obey?
Then his commaundement ought to guide, all that wee doo or say
But shew me his commaundement then, thou filthy writer thou
Let seet, I cease, if not, geue place, or shameles shew thee now.
                                          (*BB*, no. 13, lines 1–12, p. 36)

anon., *A new balade entituled as foloweth* ... (between 1556 and 1571)

B 3   ...
For when by writing men doe detect
   Their wysedome or els their follie in deede,
Yf it be foolish, they doe correct,
   Or ought that can, and that with speede,
   As *Horace* did, the vnskylfull breede
Of poets that wrote in his time, I say;

253

The workes of such, as ye may read,
Continue not long, but fall away.

Such spices and wares as come from the sea,
   They be good to vse from towne to towne, –
To the pedler they be a right good stay
   To put in his stuff, blacke, white or browne; –
   Good for the master, and good for the clowne;
So make – as ye know – the matter cleane,
   Good to take vp, and good to cast downe;
When ye haue doen, ye know what I meane.

Your balades of loue, not worth a beane,
   A number there be, although not all;
Some be pithie, some weake, some leane,
   Some doe runne as round as a ball; –
   Some verses haue such a pleasant fall,
That pleasure it is for any man,
   Whether his knowledge be great or small,
So that of a verse some skyll he can.

But some yf ye take in hand to skan,
   They lacke their grace, they lacke good sence;
The printer shoulde, therfore, with his fan
   Pourge chaff from corne, to avoyde offence;
   And not for lucre, vnder pretence
Of newes, to print what commeth to hand,
   But that which is meete to bring in pence
Let him print, the matter well scand.

                    (*AB*, no. 63, pp. 304–8, vv. 5–8, pp. 305–7)

William Fulwood, *A Supplication to Eldertonne, for Leaches vnlewdnes: Desiring him to pardone, his manifest vnrudenes* (c. between 1570 and 1590)

B 4   Good gentle maister Eldertonne,
          may I not you intrete?
       To pardō Leache yt he hath dōne,
          and not with him to frete?

       For I confesse and know the same,
          it was for lack of lewdnes:
       That he so blasde abrode your name,
          therfore forgiue his rudenes.   (vv. 1–2)

       Therefore though that your filthy rymes,
          he filthy name to bee:
       Accuse him not I say of crimes,
          you heare his qualitie.   (v. 5)

I may wel muse and meruel much,
   what might be your intent:
Sith that you proue your selfe one such,
   as truthe cannot content.   (v. 9)

Your harte is vaine and bent to euill,
   your toung also is naught:
How can it be then but the deuil,
   must rule both toung and thought.   (v. 15)

And if in deed you could him [Leach] cause,
   from scripture for to flie:
No doubt forsoth but clause by clause,
   much brauery should we see.   (v. 18)

A worthy worke it is doubtles,
   and ful of lerned skill:
Wherby appeareth your shameles,
   and wilful wicked will.   (v. 21)

Muche better then the witte to spend,
   a Parasite to play:
The bad to please, the good to offend,
   and play the foole all day.   (v. 27)

O wicked man darste thou be bolde,
   suche sinful seed to sowe?
And eke the same for to vpholde,
   in sinful hartes to growe?

O Lord shal whoredom thus preuaile?
   shal men thus sinne mainteine?
Is this a christen common weale,
   and can such filth susteine?   (vv. 33–34)

Repent (O wretche) and cal for grace,
   leaue of these wicked toyes:
Lest Sathan reache thee sower sauce,
   to these thy pleasant ioyes.   (v. 38)
                   (BB, no. 49, pp. 139–43)

Roger Ascham, *The Scholemaster* (1570)

B 5   For, as the worthie Poetes in *Athens* and *Rome* were more carefull to
satisfie the iudgement of one learned than rashe in pleasing the humor of
a rude multitude, euen so if men in England now had the like reuerend
regard to learning, skill, and iudgement, [. . .] surelie than rash ignorant
heads, which now can easely reckon vp fourten sillabes, and easelie
stumble on euery Ryme, either durst not, for lacke of such learnyng, or els
would not, in auoyding such labor, be so busie as euerie where they be;
and shoppes in London should not be so full of lewd and rude rymes, as
commonlie they are. But now the ripest of tong be readiest to write: And
many dayly in setting out bookes and balettes make great shew of

blossomes and buddes, in whom is neither roote of learning nor frute of
wisedome at all.   (G. G. Smith (ed.) (1964), I, p. 31)

Barnabe Riche, *Allarme to England* (1578)

B 6   But such is the delicacie of our readers at this time, that there are none
may be alowed of to write, but such as haue bene trained at schoole with
Pallas, or at the lest haue bene fostered vp with the Muses, and for my
parte (without vaunt be it spoken) I haue bene a trauayler, I haue sayled
in *Grauesende Barge* as farre as *Billings* gate. I haue trauayled from
Buckelers bery to *Basingstocke*, I haue gone from *S. Pankeridge* church
to *Kentish* towne by lande, where I was combred with many hedges,
ditches, and other slippery bankes, but yet I could neuer come to those
learned bankes of *Helicon*, neither was I euer able to scale *Parnassus* hyl,
although I haue trauailed ouer *Gaddes* hyll in *Kente*, and that sundrie
tymes and often.
No marueill then good reader, although I want such sugered sape,
wherwith to sauce my sense, whereby it might seeme delightfull vnto
thee: such curious Coxcombes therefore, which can not daunce but after
Apollos pype, I wish them to cease any further to reade what I haue
written: but thou which canst endure to reade in homely style of matters,
more behooueful and necessarie, then eyther curiouse or fyled, . . .
                                                              (Sig. III)

Stephen Gosson, *The Schoole of Abuse* (1579)

B 7   London is so full of vnprofitable Pipers and Fidlers, that a man can no
soner enter a tauerne, but two or three caste of them hang at his heeles,
to giue him a daunce before he departe; therefore let men of grauitie
examine the case, and judge vprightly, whether the sufferance of such idle
beggers be not a greuous abuse in a commonewealth.
                                              (E. Arber (ed.) (1868), p. 70

Thomas Lodge, *A Defence of Poetry* (1579)

B 8   Beleeue mee the magestrats may take aduise (as I knowe wisely can) to
roote out those odde rymes which runnes in euery rascales mouth,
sauoring of rybaldry. Those foolishe ballets that are admitted make poets
good and godly practises to be refused.
                                              (G. G. Smith (ed.) (1964), I, p. 76)

Thomas Lovell, *A Dialogue between Custom and Verity, concerning the use and abuse of dauncinge and minstralsye* (1581)

B 9   But this do minstrels clean forget:
         Some godly songs they have,
     Some wicked ballads and unmeet,
         As companies do crave.   (W. Chappell (1859), I, p. 107)

Richarde Stanyhurst, *Thee First Fovre Bookes of Virgil his Aeneis* ...
(1582). 'To thee Right Honovrable ... Lord Baron of Dunsayne'

B 10   Good God, what a frye of such *wooden rythmours* dooth swarme in
stacioners shops, who neauer enstructed in any grammar schoole, not
atayning too thee paringes of thee Latin or Greeke tongue, yeet lyke blynd
bayards rush on forward, fostring theyre vayne conceites wyth such ouer-
weening silly follyes, as they reck not too bee condemned of thee learned
for ignorant, so they been commended of thee ignorant for learned. Thee
reddyest way therefore too flap theese droanes from thee sweete senting
hiues of *Poetrye* is for thee learned too applye theym selues wholye (yf
they be delighted wyth that veyne) too thee true making of verses in such
wise as thee *Greekes* and *Latins*, thee fathers of knowledge, haue doone,
and too leaue too theese doltish coystrels theyre rude rythming and
balducktoom ballads . .   (G. G. Smith (ed.) (1964), I, p. 141)

Philip Stubbes, *The Anatomie of Abuses: Containing a Discoverie, or
briefe Summarie of such Notable Vices and Corruptions, as now raigne
in many Christian Countreyes of the Worlde* (1583)

B 11   Euery towne, Citie, and Countrye is full of these minstrelles to pype vp a
dance to the Deuill; but of dyuines, so few there be as they maye hardly
be seene.   (F. J. Furnivall (ed.) (1977), p. 172)

William Webbe, *A Discourse of English Poetie* (1586)

B 12   If I let passe the vncountable rabble of ryming Ballet makers and com-
pylers of sencelesse sonets, who be most busy to stuffe euery stall full of
grosse deuises and vnlearned Pamphlets, I trust I shall with the best sort
be held excused. For though many such can frame an Alehouse song of
fiue or sixe score verses, hobbling vppon some tune of a Northern Iygge,
or Robyn hoode, or La lubber etc., and perhappes obserue iust number of
sillables, eyght in one line, sixe in an other, and there withall an A to make
a iercke in the ende: yet if these might be accounted Poets (as it is sayde
some of them meanes to be promoted to the Lawrell) surely we shall
shortly haue whole swarmes of Poets: and euery one that can frame a
Booke in Ryme, though for want of matter it be but in commendations of
Copper noses or Bottle Ale, wyll catch at the Garlande due to Poets;
whose potticall, poeticall (I should say), heades I would wyshe at their
worshipfull comencements might in steede of Lawrell be gorgiously
garnished with fayre greene Barley, in token of their good affection to our
Englishe Malt. One speaketh thus homely of them, with whose words I
wyll content my selfe for thys time, because I would not bee too broade
wyth them in myne owne speeche.
      (G. G. Smith (ed.) (1964), I, pp. 246–7)

B 13   . . . I thinke wee may not onelie get the meanes, which wee yet want, to
discerne betweene good writers and badde, but perhappes also challenge
from the rude multitude of rusticall Rymers, who will be called Poets, the
right practise and orderly course of true Poetry.   (ibid., p. 227)

George Puttenham, *The Arte of English Poesie* (1589)

B 14   . . . for commonly who so is studious in th' Arte or shewes him selfe excellent in it, they call him in disdayne a *phantasticall*; and a light headed or phantasticall man (by conuersion) they call a poet.

(G. G. Smith (ed.) (1964), II, p. 19)

Thomas Nashe, *The Anatomie of Absurditie* (1589)

B 15   It were to be wished, that the acts of the ventrous, and the praise of the vertuous were, by publique Edict, prohibited by such mens merry mouthes to be so odiouslie extolde, as rather breedes detestation then admiration, lothing then lyking. What politique Counsailour or valiant Souldier will ioy or glorie of this, in that some stitcher, Weauer, spend-thrift, or Fidler, hath shuffled or slubbered vp a few ragged Rimes, in the memoriall of the ones prudence, or the others prowesse? It makes the learned sort to be silent, whē als they see vnlearned sots so insolent.

(R. B. McKerrow (ed.) (1904–10), I, p. 24)

B 16   Hence come our babling Ballets, and our new found Songs & Sonets, which euery rednose Fidler hath at his fingers end, and euery ignorant Ale knight will breath foorth ouer the potte, as soone as his braine waxeth hote. Be it a truth which they would tune, they enterlace it with a lye or two to make meeter, not regarding veritie, so they may make vppe the verse.

(ibid., pp. 23–4)

Thomas Nashe, *Strange Newes, of the intercepting of certaine Letters* (1592)

B 17   We are to vexe you migthely for plucking *Elderton* out of the ashes of his Ale, and not letting him inioy his nappie muse of ballad making to him-selfe, but now, when he is as dead as dead beere, you must be finding fault with the brewing of his meeters.
Hough *Thomas Delone, Philip Stubs, Robert Armin* & c. Your father *Elderton* is abus'd. Reuenge, reuenge on course paper and want of matter, that hath most sacriligiously contaminated the diuine spirit & quintessence of a penny a quart.

(R. B. McKerrow (ed.) (1904–10), I, p. 280)

idem, *Pierce Pennilesse His Svpplication to the Diuell* (1592)

B 18   Alas poore latinlesse Authors, they are so simple they know not what they doe; They no sooner spy a new Ballad, and his name to it that compilde it; but they put him in for one of the learned men of our time. I maruell how the Masterlesse men, that set vp their bills in Paules for seruices, & such as paste vp their papers on euery post, for Arithmetique and writing Schooles, scape eternity amongst them.

(ibid., I, p. 194)

Sir John Harington, *A Preface, or rather a Briefe Apologie of Poetrie*
(1591)

B 19   . . . the common sort that terme all that is written in verse Poetrie, and,
rather in scorne then in praise, bestow the name of a poet on eurie base
rymer and balladmaker.   (G. G. Smith (ed.) (1964), II, p. 197)

B 20   the men of greatest learning and highest wit in the auncient times did of
purpose conceale these deepe mysteries of learning, and, as it were, couer
them with the vaile of fables and verse for sundrie causes: one cause was
that they might not be rashly abused by prophane wits.   (ibid., p. 203)

Edmund Spenser, 'The Tears of the Muses' (1591)

B 21   They to the vulgar sort now pipe and sing,
And make them merrie with their fooleries,
They cherelie chaunt and ryme at random fling,
The fruitfull spawne of their ranke fantasies
They feede the eares of fooles with flattery
And good men blame, and losels magnify.
        (J. C. Smith and E. de Selincourt (eds.) (1912), p. 483, lines 319–24)

Robert Greene, *The Second part of Conny-catching* (1591)

B 22   Of late time there hath a certaine base kind of trade been vsed, who
though diuers poor men, & doubtles honest apply themselues to, only to
relieue their need: yet are there some notorious varlets to the same, beeing
compacted with such kind of people, as this present treatise manifesteth
to the worlde; and what with outward simplicity on the one side, and
cunning close trechery on the other, diuers honest Cittizens and day-
labouring men, that resort to such places as I am to speake of, onely for
recreation as opportunity serueth, haue bin of late sundry times deceiued
of their purses. This trade, or rather vnsufferable loytring qualitie, in
singing of Ballets and songs at the doores of such houses where plaies are
vsed, as also in open markets and other places of this Cittie, where is most
resort: which is nothing els but a sly fetch to draw many togeather, who
listning vnto an harmelesse dittie, afterward walke home to their houses
with heauie hearts: from such as are heereof true witnesses to their cost,
do I deliuer this example. A subtill fellow, belike imboldned by acquaint-
ance with the former deceit, or els béeing but a beginner to practise the
same, calling certaine of his companions together, would try whether he
could attaine to be maister of his art or no, by taking a great many of fools
with one traine. But let his intent and what els beside, remaine to abide
the censure after ẙ mater is heard, & come to Gracious stréet, where this
villanous pranke was performed. A roging mate, & such another with
him, were there got vpõ a stal singing of balets, witch belike was som
pretty toy, for very many gathered about to heare it, & diuers buying, as
their affections serued, drew to their purses, & paid the singers for thẽ.
The slye mate and his fellowes, who were dispersed among them that
stoode to heare the songes: well noted where euerie man that bought, put

vp his purse againe, and to such as would not buy, counterfeit warning was sundrie times giuen by the rogue and his associate, to beware of the cut-pursse, and looke to their pursses, which made them often feel where their pursses were, either in sléeue, hose, or at girdle, to know whether they were safe or no. Thus the craftie copesmates were acquainted with what they most desired, and as they were scattered, by shouldring, thrusting, feigning to let fall something, and other wilie tricks fit for their purpose: heere one lost his purse, their another had his pocket pickt, and to say all in briefe, at one instant, vpon the complaint of one or two that sawe their pursses were gone, eight more in the same companie, found themselues in like predicament. Some angrie, others sorrowfull, and all greatly discontented, looking about them, knewe not who to suspect or challenge, in that the villaines themselues that had thus beguiled them, made shewe that they had sustained like losse. But one angrie fellow, more impacient then al the rest, he falles vpon the ballade singer, and beating him with his fists well fauouredly sayes if he had not listened his singing, he had not lost his purse, and therefore would not be otherwise perswaded, but that they two and the cutpurses were compacted together. The rest that had lost their purses likewise, and saw that so ma[n]y complaine[d] togither: they iumpe in opinion with the other fellow, & begin to tug & hale the ballad singers, when one after one the false knaues began to shrinke awaie with ẙ pursses. By meanes of some officer then being there presēt, the two roges wer had before a Iustice, and vpon his discréete examination made, it was found that they and the Cutpurses were compacted together, and that by this vnsuspected villanie, they had deceiued many. The fine Foole-taker himselfe, with one or two more of that companie, was not long after apprehended: when I doubt not but they had their reward aunswerable to their deseruing: for I heare of their journey westward, but not of their returne: let this forewarne those that listen singing in the streets.

(A. B. Grosart (ed.) (1964), X, p. 161)

Henry Chettle, *Kind-Harts Dreame. Conteining Fiue Apparitions with their Inuectives against Abuses Raigning* (1592)

B 23   For such is the folly of this age, so witlesse, so audacious, that there are scarce so manye pedlars brag themselues to be printers because they haue a bundel of ballads in their packe, as there be idiots that think themselues artists because they can English an obligation, or write a true straffe to the tune of fortune.   (E. F. Rimbault (ed.) (1851), I)

The Friendly Admonition of Anthonie Now Now to Mopo and Pickering, Archouerseers of the Ballad Singers, in London or else-where

B 24   *Anthony Now now*, a God's blessing, to his louing and liuing bretheren Mopo and Pickering, greeting: whereas, by the daily recourse of infinit numbers to the infernall regions, whose plaintes to be heard are no lesse lamentable, then their paines to be felt intollerable, I am giuen to vnderstand that there be a company of idle youths, loathing honest labour and dispising lawfull trades, betake them to a vagrant and vicious life, in

euery corner of cities and market townes of the realme singing and selling
of ballads and pamphletes full of ribaudrie and all scurrilous vanity, to
the prophanation of God's name, and with-drawing people from
Christian exercises, especially at faires, markets and such publike meetings; I humbly desire ye that ye ioyne with another of your bretheren free
of one citie and profession, that, alwaies delighting in godly songes, is
now in his age betaken to his beads, and liueth by the dolefull tolling of
Deaths bell warning. Deere frendes, I beseech you ioyntly to agree to the
suppressing of the fore named idle vagabonds. And, that I right incite (as
I hope) your forward effectes, I will particularize the difference between
the abused times among you reputed, and the simplicity of the daies
wherein I liued. Withall I wish ye to expect no greater matter then
Anthonyes capacity can comprehend. When I was liked, there was no
thought of that idle vpstart generation of ballad-singers, neither was
there a printer so lewd that would set finger to a lasciuious line.

                                                              (ibid., pp. 13–14)

B 25   what is so lewd that hath not there [in London], contrary to order, beene
         printed, and in euery street abusiuely chanted!   (ibid., p. 14)

B 26   It were to be wisht, if they will not be warnd, that as well the singers as
         their supporters were burned in the tongue, that they might rather be euer
         utterly mute, then the triumphers of so many mischiefes. Neither are
         these two alone in fault, though they stand worthely formost as *Malorum
         Duces*, but besides them others, more then a good many, some as I haue
         heard say, taken to be apprentices by a worthlesse companion (if it proue
         true that is of him reported) being of a worshipful trade, and yet no
         stationer, who after a little bringing them vppe to singing brokerie, takes
         into his shop some fresh men, and trust his olde seruantes of a two
         months standing with a dossen groates worth of ballads. In which, if they
         prooue thrifty, hee makes them prety chapmen, able to spred more
         pamphlets by the state forbidden then all the bookesellers in London; for
         only in this citie is straight search; abroad, smale suspition, especially of
         such petty pedlars.   (ibid., pp. 16–17)

B 27   For, to sing publikely, is, by a kinde of tolleration, permitted only to
         beggars ... As vile it is that boyes, of able strength and agreeable capacity,
         should bee suffered to wrest from the miserable aged the last refuge in
         their life (beggery excepted) the poore helpe of ballad-singing.
                                                              (ibid., pp.18–19)

Kindharts Conclusion of his Dreame, and his Censure on the Apparitions
Seuerally.

B 28   For memories sake, let me see what conclusion we shall forme. Antthony
         tolde a long tale of runnagate song-singers, inueighing, especially against
         those lasciuious ballads that are by authority forbidden, priuily printed,
         and publikely solde. In whiche I finde no reason (as before I saide)
         because I beleeue none are so desperate to hazard their goods in printing

or selling any thing that is disallowed. Or, if there be some such, I
perswade my selfe the maiestrates diligence is so great they would soone
be weeded out. But now let mee sound a little into Anthonies meaning:
hee complaines not that these lasciuious songes howe ever in London they
beginne, are there continued, but thence they spread as from a spring;
and, albeit they dare not there be iustified, yet are they in every pedlers
packe sent to publike meetings in other places; where they are suffered
because the sellers sweare they are published by authoritie, and people
farre off thinke nothing is printed but what is lawfully tollerated. Such
knaues indeede would be lookt into that are not content with corrupting
the multitude but they must slaunder the maiestrates. If Mopo and his
mates bee such men that I may meete with, I will not onely deliver them
Anthonies minde, but vrge them to exasperate the matter.   (ibid., p. 55)

Joseph Hall, *Martin Mar-sixtus* (1592)

B 29   I lothe to speak it, every red-nose rhymester is an author; every drunken
man's dream is a book; and he, whose talent of little wit is hardly worth
a farthing, yet layeth about him so outrageously as if Helicon had run
through his pen: in a word, scarce a cat can look out of a gutter, but out
starts a halfpenny chronicler, and presently a proper new ballet of a
strange sight is indited.   (W. Chappell (1895), I, p. 106)

William Shakespeare, *Love's Labour's Lost* (first performed 1595,
Quarto 1598)

B 30   Armado and Moth:
ARM. Is there not a ballad, boy, of the King and the Beggar?
MOTH. The world was very guilty of such a ballad some three ages since;
        but I think now 'tis not to be found; or if it were, it would neither
        serve for the writing nor the tune.
                    (I, 2, lines 105–10; P. Alexander (ed.) (1964), p. 170)

anon., *The Pilgrimage to Parnassus with the two parts of the Return
from Parnassus* (between 1597 and 1601)

B 31   Who blurres fayer paper with foul bastard rimes,
Shall liue full many an age in latter times:
Who makes a ballet for an ale-house doore,
Shall liue in future times for euer more.
Then Bodenham thy muse shall live so long,
As drafty ballats to the paile are sung.   (W. D. Macray (ed.) (1836), p. 83)

Joseph Hall, *Satires* (1597)

B 32   Some drunken rhymer thinks his time well spent,
If he can live to see his name in print;
Who when he is once fleshed to the press,
And sees his hansel have such fair success,

Sung to the Wheel, and sung unto the pail,
He sends forth thraves of ballads to the sale.
(Book IV, Sat. VI; ed. (1837–39), XII, pp. 242–3)

W. Shakespeare, *King Henry the Fourth, Part I* (Quarto 1598)

B 33   Hotspur to Glendower:
I had rather be a kitten and cry mew
Than one of these same metre ballad-mongers;
I had rather hear a brazen canstick turn'd,
Or a dry wheel grate on the axle-tree;
And that would set my teeth nothing on edge,
Nothing so much as mincing poetry.
(III, 1, lines 127–33; P. Alexander (ed.) (1964), p. 497)

B 34   Falstaff to Henry, Prince of Wales:
And I have not ballads made on you all,
and sung to filthy tunes, let a cup of
sack be my poison.   (II, 1, lines 43–6, ibid., p. 488)

W. Shakespeare, *As You Like It* (first performed *c.* 1599)

B 35   Jacques [speech on the ages of man]:
And then the lover,
Sighing like a furnace, with a woeful ballad
Made to his mistress' eyebrow.   (III, 1, lines 146–8, ibid., p. 266)

George Chapman, *Monsieur d'Olive* (1606)

B 36   'I am afraid of nothing but I shall be balladed.'
(W. Chappell (1859), I, p. 253)

W. Shakespeare, *The Winter's Tale* (first performed *c.* 1609/10)

B 37 Servant, Autolycus, Clown, Mopsa:
CLO. What hast here? Ballads?
MOP. Pray now, buy some. I love a ballad in print a-life, for then we are
    sure they are true.
AUT. Here's one to a very doleful tune: how a usurer's wife was brought
    to bed of twenty money-bags at a burden, and how she long'd to eat
    adders' heads and toads carbonado'd.
MOP. Is it true, think you?
AUT. Very true, and but a month old.
DOR. Bless me from marrying a usurer!
AUT. Here's the midwife's name to't, one Mistress Taleporter, and five or
    six honest wives that were present. Why should I carry lies abroad?
MOP. Pray you now, buy it.
CLO. Come on, lay it by; and let's first see moe ballads; we'll buy the other
    things anon.
AUT. Here's another ballad, of a fish that appeared upon the coast on

Wednesday the fourscore of April, forty thousand fathom above
water, and sung this ballad against the hard hearts of maids. It was
thought she was a woman, and was turn'd into a cold fish for she
would not exchange flesh with one that lov'd her. The ballad is very
pitiful, and as true.

DOR. Is it true too, think you?

AUT. Five justices' hands at it; and witnesses more than my pack will hold.

CLO. Lay it by too. Another.

AUT. This is a merry ballad, but a very pretty one.

MOP. Let's have some merry ones.

AUT. Why, this is a passing merry one, and goes to the tune of 'Two maids
wooing a man'. There's scarce a maid westward but she sings it; 'tis
in request, I can tell you.

MOP. We can both sing it. If thou'lt bear a part, thou shalt hear; 'tis in
three parts.

DOR. We had the tune on't a month ago.

AUT. I can bear my part; you must know 'tis my occupation. Have at it
with you.

(IV, 4, lines 251–90; P. Alexander (ed.) (1964), pp. 399–400)

Gentleman:

B 38   2 GENT. . . . The oracle is fulfill'd: the King's daughter is found. Such a deal
of wonder is broken out within this hour that ballad-makers cannot
be able to express it.   (V, 1, lines 21–5; ibid., p. 409)

William Parkes, *The Courtaine-Drawer of the World* (1612)

B 39   Then were there not halfe so many puling Ballett-mongers, nor a quarter
of so many fashions, nor halfe a quarter of so many Taylors, Poets and
Taylors as they here stand within the length of a paire of sheares together,
so in their Arte & vse in the world, they differ not much. The Poet stands
all vpon invention: so doth the Taylor. The Poet first casts his plot, then
diuides his Sceane: so the Thaylor first his stuffe, then his fashion, then
diuides it into seuerall skirts and quarters, in the end knits it all together
in an equal proportion, so makes his garment. So likewise the Poet. Lastly
they onely, but greatly, differ in this, that the Taylor couers all secrets,
and the Poet layes all open.
Then was not I cloyed with so many Idle Pamphlets, nor Pamphlet
stitchers. If a search had been made neuer so curiously betwixt *Temple-
barre* and *Pauls*, was not aboue two to be found, now drawne to a large
multiplication.   (A. B. Grosart (ed.) (1876), p. 5)

W. Turner, *Turners dish of Lentten stuffe, or Galymaufery* (1612)

B 40   the world is ful of thredbare poets,
         that liue vpon their pen:
     But they will write too eloquent,
         they are such witty men.
     But the Tinker with his budget,
         the begger with his wallet,

And *Turners* turnd a gallant man,
   at making of a Ballet.   (*PG*, no. 5, v. 14, p. 34)

Henry Parrot, *Laquei ridiculosi: or Springes for Woodcockes* (1613)

B 41   To the Reader.
To the Courteous, Generous, and Scolasticke Readers: I cannot stoop too submissiue-low with that obseruance which to them belongeth. But to th'illiterat and home-spun-Peasants, proue I as harsh and indigestable as is their spite and ignorance vnreproueable. I know I shall be fowly censured of some *Slauonians* that scarce haue any taste or feeling of inuention, . . .   (no pagination)

Ben Jonson, *Bartholomew Fair* (1614)

B 42   CORN. Have you any corns in your feet and toes?
MOUSE. Buy a mousetrap, a mousetrap, or a tormentor for a flea?
TRASH. Buy some gingerbread?
NIGHT. Ballads, ballads! fine new ballads: −
    (II, 1; W. Gifford and F. Cunningham (eds.) (1897), II, p. 163)

B 43   NIGHT. 'Hear for your love, and buy for your money,
    A delicate ballad o'the ferret and the coney.
    A preservative again' the prunk's evil.
    Another of goose-green starch, and the devil.
    A dozen of divine points and godly garters:
    The fairing of good counsel, of an ell and three quarters.'
    What is't you buy?
    'The windmill blown down by the witch's fart
    Or Saint George, that, O! did break the dragon's heart.'
                    (ibid., pp. 163–4)

B 44   *Enter* Edgworth, Nightingale, *and People, followed, at a distance, by* Overdo.
OVER. I cannot beget a project, with all my political brain yet: my project is how to fetch off this proper young man from his debauched company. I have followed him all the Fair over, and still I find him with this songster, and I begin shrewdly to suspect their familiarity; and the young man of a terrible taint, poetry! with which idle disease if he be infected, there's no hope of him in a state-course. *Actum est* of him for a commonwealth's man, if he go to't in rhyme once.
                            [*Aside.*]
EDG. [*To* Nightingale.] Yonder he is buying of gingerbread; set in quickly, before he part with too much of his money.
NIGHT. [*Advancing and singing.*] 'My masters and friends, and good people draw near' −
COKES. [*Runs to the ballad-man.*] Ballads! hark, hark! pray thee, fellow, stay a little; good Numps, look to the goods. What ballads hast thou? let me see, let me see myself.
WASPE. Why so! he's flown to another lime-bush, there he will flutter as

long, more; till he have ne'er a feather left. Is there a vexation like this, gentlemen? will you believe me now, hereafter shall I have credit with you?

QUAR. Yes, faith shalt thou, Numps, and thou art worthy on't, for thou sweatest for't. I never saw a young pimperrant and his squire better matched.

WINW. Faith, the sister comes after them well too.

GRACE. Nay, if you saw the justice her husband, my guardian, you were fitted for the mess, he is such a wise on his way –

WINW. I wonder we see him not here.

GRACE. O! he is too serious for this place, and yet better sport then than the other three, I assure you, gentlemen, wherever he is, though it be on the bench.

COKES. How dost thou call it? *A caveat against curpurses!* a good jest, i' faith, I would fain see that demon, your cut-purse you talk of, that delicate-handed devil; they say he walks hereabout; I would see him walk now. Look you, sister, here, here – [*He shews his purse boastingly*] – let him come, sister, and welcome. Ballad-man, does any cut-purse haunt hereabout? pray thee raise me one or two; begin, and shew me one.

NIGHT. Sir, this is a spell against them, spick and span new; and 'tis made as 'twere in mine own person, and I sing it in mine own defence. But 'twill cost a penny alone, if you buy it.

COKES. No matter for the price; thou dost not know me, I see, I am an odd Bartholomew.

MRS. OVER. Has it a fine picture, brother?

COKES. O, sister, do you remember the ballads over the nursery chimney at home o' my own pasting up? there be brave pictures, other manner of pictures than these, friend.

WASPE. Yet these will serve to pick the pictures out of your pockets, you shall see.

COKES. *So I heard them say!* Pray thee mind him not, fellow; he'll have an oar in everything.

NIGHT. It was intended, sir, as if a purse should chance to be cut in my presence, now, I may be blameless though; as by the sequel will more plainly appear.

COKES. We shall find that in the matter: pray thee begin.

NIGHT. To the tune of Paggington's pound, sir!

COKES. [*sings*] *Fa, la la la, la la la la, fa la la la!* Nay I'll put thee in tune and all! mine own country dance! pray thee begin.

NIGHT. It is a gentle admonition, you must know, sir, both to the purse-cutter and the purse-bearer.

COKES. Not a word more out of the tune, an thou lov'st me: *Fa, la la la, la la la, fa, la la la.* Come, when?

NIGHT. [*sings.*] 'My masters, and friends, and good people, draw near.
And look to your purses, for that I do say;'

COKES. Ha, ha, this chimes! Good counsel at first dash.

NIGHT. 'And tho' little money in them you do bear,
It cost more to get, than to lose in a day.'

COKES. Good!

NIGHT. 'You oft have been told,
 Both the young and the old,
 And bidden beware of cut-purse so bold;'

COKES. Well said! he were to blame that would not, i' faith.

NIGHT. 'Then if you take heed not, free me from the curse,
 Who both give you warning, for, and the cut-purse.
 Youth, youth, thou hadst better been starved by thy nurse,
 Than live to be hanged for cutting a purse.'

COKES. Good i' faith; how say you, Numps, is there any harm in this?

NIGHT. 'It hath been upbraided to men of my trade,
 That oftentimes we are the cause of this crime;'

COKES. The more coxcombs they that did it, I wusse.

NIGHT. 'Alack and for pity, why should it be said?
 As if they regarded or places, or time!
  Examples have been
  Of some that were seen
 In Westminster-hall, yea, the pleaders between;
 Then why should the judges be free from this curse,
 More than my poor self, for cutting the Purse?'

COKES. God a mercy for that! why should they be more free indeed?

NIGHT. 'Youth, youth, thou hadst better been starved by thy nurse,
 Than live to be hanged for cutting a purse.'

COKES. That again, good ballad-man, that again. [*He sings the burden
 with him.*] O, rare! I would fain rub mine elbow now, but I dare not
 pull out my hand. Oh, I pray thee; he that made this ballad shall be
 poet to my masque.

NIGHT. 'At Worc'ster 'tis known well, and even in the jail,
 A knight of good worship did there shew his face,
 Against the foul sinners, in zeal for to rail,
 And lost *ipso facto* his purse in the place.'

COKES. Is it possible?

NIGHT. 'Nay, once from the seat
  Of judgment so great,
 A judge there did lose a fair pouch of velvéte.'

COKES. I' faith?

NIGHT. 'O Lord for thy mercy, how wicked or worse,
 Are those that so venture their necks for a purse!
 Youth, youth, thou hadst better been starved by thy nurse,
 Than live to be hanged for cutting a purse.'

COKES. [*Sings after him.*] Youth, youth, & c. – Pray thee stay a little,
 friend. Yet o' thy consience, Numps, speak, is there any harm in
 this?

WASPE. To tell you true, 'tis too good for you, less you had grace to follow
 it.

OVER. It doth discover enormity, I'll mark it more: I have not liked a paltry
 piece of poetry so well a good while.   [*Aside.*

COKES. *Youth, youth,* & c.; where's this youth now? a man must call
 upon him for his own good, and yet he will not appear. Look here,

here's for him; [*Shews his purse.*] handy dandy, which hand will he have? On, I pray thee with the rest; I do hear of him, but I cannot see him, this master youth, the cutpurse.

NIGHT. 'At plays, and at sermons, and at the sessions,
'Tis daily their practice such booty to make;
Yea, under the gallows at executions,
They stick not the stare-abouts' purses to take.
    Nay, one without grace,
    At a [far] better place,
At court, and in Christmas, before the king's face;'

COKES. That was a fine fellow! I would have him now.

NIGHT. 'Alack then for pity must I bear the curse,
That only belongs to the cunning cutpurse?'

COKES. But where's their cunning now, when they should use it? they are all chained now, I warrant you. [*Sings.*] *Youth, youth, thou hadst better* – The rat-catchers' charms are all fools and asses to this; a pox on them, that they will not come! that a man should have such a desire to a thing, and want it!

QUAR. 'Fore God I'd give half the Fair, and 'twere mine, for a cut-purse for him, to save his longing.

COKES. Look you, sister, [*Shews his purse again.*] here, here, where is't now? which pocket is't in, for a wager?

WASPE. I beseech you leave your wagers, and let him end his matter, an't may be.

COKES. O, are you edified, Numps!

OVER. Indeed he does interrupt him too much: there Numps spoke to purpose.   [*Aside.*

COKES. Sister, I am an ass, I cannot keep my purse! [*Shews it again, and puts it up.*] On, on, I pray thee, friend.

NIGHT. 'Youth, youth, thou hadst better been starved by thy nurse,
Than live to be hanged for cutting a purse.'
    [*As Nightingale sings, Edgworth gets up to Cokes and tickles him in the ear with a straw twice to draw his hand out of his pocket.*]

WINW. Will you see sport? look, there's a fellow gathers up to him, mark.

QUAR. Good, i' faith! O, he has lighted on the wrong pocket.

WINW. He has it! 'fore God, he is a brave fellow; pity he should be detected.

NIGHT. 'But O, you vile nation of cutpurses all,
Relent and repent, and amend and be sound,
And know that you ought not, by honest men's fall,
Advance your own fortunes, to die above ground;
    And though you go gay,
    In silks, as you may,
It is not the highway to heaven (as they say).
Repent then, repent you, for better, for worse,
And kiss not the gallows for cutting a purse.
Youth, youth, thou hadst better been starved by thy nurse,
Than live to be hanged for cutting a purse.'

ALL. An excellent ballad! an excellent ballad!

EDG. Friend, let me have the first, let me have the first, I pray you.
    [*As Nightingale reaches out the ballad,*
    Edgworth slips the purse into his hand.]
COKES. Pardon me, sir; first come first served; and I'll buy the whole
    bundle too.
WINW. That conveyance was better than all, did you see't? he has given the
    purse to the ballad-singer.
QUAR. Has he?
EDG. Sir, I cry you mercy, I'll not hinder the poor man's profit; pray you,
    mistake me not.
COKES. Sir, I take you for an honest gentleman, if that be mistaking; I met
    you to-day afore: ha! humph! O Lord! my purse is gone, my purse,
    my purse, my purse!
WASPE. Come, do not make a stir, and cry yourself an ass through the Fair
    afore your time.
COKES. Why, hast thou it, Numps? good Numps, how came you by it, I
    marle?
WASPE. I pray you seek some other gamester to play the fool with; you may
    lose it time enough, for all your Fair wit.
COKES. By this good hand, glove and all, I have lost it already if thou hast it
    not; feel else, and Mistress Grace's handkerchief too, out of t'other
    pocket.   (II, 1, ibid., pp. 176–9)

Henry Parrot, *The Mastive, Or Young-Whelpe of the Old-Dogge.*
Epigrams and Satyrs (1615)

B 45   Ad Bibliopolam
Printer or Stationer, or what ere thou prooue,
Shalt mee record to Times posteritie:
Ile not enioyne thee, but request in loue,
Thou so much deigne my Booke to dignifie;
As first it bee not with your Ballads mixt,
Next, not at Play-houses, mongst Pippins solde:
Then that on Posts by the 'Eares it stand not fixt,
For euery dull-Mechanicke to beholde.
Last, that it come not brought in Pedlers packs,
To common Fayres, of Countrey, Towne, or Cittie:
Solde at a Booth mongst Pinnes and Almanacks;   (Sig. A 4ᵛ)

B 46   Trahit sua quemque Voluptas
First comes a Statesman to the *Stationer*,
And many better Bookes hee passing ouer,
By chaunce findes this, whereon he reades a while,
Then bytes the lippe, then frownes, then giues a smile,
And to the *Seller* sayes such fiery braines,
Should warme the prison to reward their paines,
Becomes it any man of his profession,
Reproue vs of our manners or transgression?
Away goes hee; Next comes my gallant Dycer,

His ordinarie stomacke is more nicer,
Who asks for new Books; this the *Stationer* showes him,
Streight sweares t'is nought vnles the Poet knows him,
Nor will hee read a Line: this *Fortunes* Mynion,
Likes forsooth nothing but his owne opinion,
The mending Poet takes it next in hand,
Who hauing oft the Verses ouer-scand'.
O filching streight, doth to the *Stationer* say,
Heer's foure lines stolne from forth my last New-play.
And that hee'l swere euen by the *Printers* Stall,
Although hee knowes tis false hee speakes in all.
Then com[e]s my *Innes-of-Court-Man*, in his Gowne,
Cryes *Mew*, what *Hackney*, brought this wit to towne,
But soone againe my gallant Youth is gon,
Minding the *Kitchin* more then *Littleton*.
Tut, what cares hee for Law, shall haue inough,
When's Father dyes, that Cankard *Miser* Chuffe.
Put him a *Case* in *Ploydon* then who will,
That being his, plod you on Law-Bookes still.
Next comes by my *Familiar*, yet no Spirit,
Who forceth me his Friendship to i[n]herit:
He sees my Booke in Print, and streight hee knowes it,
Then asketh for the Booke, and the Boy showes it.
Then reades a while and sayes, I must commend it,
But sure, *Some Frend of his* for him hath pend it.
He cannot write a Booke in such a fashion,
For well I wote 'twas nere his Occupation.
Besides by *Checquer Clarks*, that oft haue seene him,
I nere could heare of Schollership was in him.
Twere good to poze him but to haue it knowne,
Or 'tis no matter, let it euen alone.
Next after him, your Countrey-Farmer viewes it,
It may be good (saith hee) for those can vse it.
Shewe me King *Arthur*, *Beuis*, or *Syr Guye*,
Those are the Bookes he onely loues to buye.
Well, that he likes and walkes. Then comes a Diuell,
With sober countenance, and Garments ciuill.
A *Puritane*, or pure one, choose you whether,
(For both as one makes selfe-same sense together.)
He lookes on some, and finding this the next,
With very sight therof his minde is vext.
Fye on't (saith he) that any man should buye,
Such Bookes prophane of fained Poetrie,
That teacheth vice, worse then your Playes on Stages,
And is a shame to olde and future Ages.
To louing Brother-hoods Communitie,
That are defilde by such impuritie.
Away retires my fained *Publican*,
And after him next comes my Seruing-man.

Who calls for new Bookes, heres one sayes the Boy,
He reads, and tells him, tut, this is a toy,
And nere will please our Maides that take delight,
In bookes of Ladies or some valiant Knight.
Those wittie workes buyes hee, and thence he passes,
Next him comes my *Scholaris*, mongst those *Asses*;
Who scarce vouchsafes his eyes thereon to glance,
Or reading but a line or two by chance.
Must on it streight way striue to breake a iest,
(As who shall know hee's wiser then the rest.)   (Sig. H 4 – I)

John Fletcher, *The Queen of Corinth* (between 1616 and 1619)

B 47   Euphanes:
        and whate'er he be
Can with unthankfulness assoil me, let him
Dig out mine eyes, and sing my name in verse
in ballad verse, at every drinking house.
                                  (A. Dyce (ed.) (1843–46), V, p. 395)

Henry Fitzgeffrey, *Satyres and Satyricall Epigrams* (London, 1617)

B 48   Who'd not at venture *Write*? So many waies
A man may proue a *Poet* now a daies?
Does Nature witt afford to break a Iest?
This is a *Poet*: and his friends protest
He is to blame he *Writes* not: when (indeed,)
Th' Illiterate Gull can neither *write* nor *read*.   (Satyra prima, Sig. A 5)

Let Natures causes (which are too profound
For euery blockish sottish *Pate* to sound.)
Produce some *monster*: some rare *spectacle*:
Some seauen yeares *Wonder*: Ages *miracle*:
Bee it a worke of nere so slight a waight,
It is recorded vp in *Metre* straight,
And counted purchase of no small renowne,
To heare to *Praise* sung in a Market-toune.
    How many *Volumes* lye neglected thrust
In euery Bench-hole? euery heape of dust?
Which from some *Gowries* practice, *Powder* plot,
Or *Tiburne Lectur's*, all their substance got:
Yet tosse our Time-stalles youll admire the rout
Or carelesse fearlesse *Pamphlets* flye about.
    Bookes, *made* of Ballades: Workes: *of* Playes,
Sights, *to be* Read: *of my* Lo: Maiors *day's*:
Post's *Lately set forth*: Bearing (*their Backe at*)
Letters *of all sorts: An intollerable Packet.*
Villains discouery, by *Lanthorn and Candle-light*:
(*strange if the author should not see it to handle right*)
A Quest of Inquirie: (Iacke a Douer's)

The Iests of Scoggin: *and diuers others*
(*which no man Better the* Stationer *knowes*)
Wonderfull Writers; Poets *in* Prose.
What poste pin'd *Poets* that on each base *Theame*,
With Inuocations vexe *Apollo's* Name.   (Sigs. A 7ᵛ – A 8 ᵛ)

Let not each *Pesant*, each *Mecannick* Asse,
That neer knew further then his *Horn-booke* crosse.
Each rauin-*Rusticke*: each illiterate *Gull*:
Buy of my *Poesie*, by pocket full.
Bookes like Made-Dishes may for Daintyes goe.
Yet will not euery *pallate* taste 'em so: (Sig. G 4ᵛ)

Nicholas Breton, *The Court and Country* (1618)

B 49   COURTIER. But yet let me tell you, had you seene but one of our showes in
our Triumphs, heard one of our Songs in our solemne dayes, and
tasted one of our dishes, in our solemne feasts, you would never
looke more on a Maygame, listen more to a louzy Ballad, nor ever be
in love with beefe and pudding . . .

COUNTRYMAN. [. . .] Now for Songs, a plaine ditty well expressed, is
better with us, then a fine conceit, as faigned in the voyce as the
matter.   (*A mad World* (1929), I, p. 218)

anon., *A Song for Autolycus* (c. 1620)

B 50   Will you buy a new merry booke,
Or a dolefull ditty, then looke?
     Here's a proper ballet,
     Most fit for the pallet
     Of a chamber-maid,
     That was over laid,
     Which she ru'th,
     'Tis call'd *A Warning for Youth*:
He took her bout the middle so small,
He threw her downe, but that was not all,
I should howl out right to tell of the rest,
How this poor maid was over prest.
Therefore quickly come and buy, and read for your penny,
Come, my hearts, 'tis as good a bargain as e're you had any;
     Here's no *Sussex Serpent* to fright you here in my bundle,
     Nor was it ever printed for the widdow *Trundle*.
                         (E. F. Rimbault (ed.) (1840), p. 157)

Robert Burton, *The Anatomy of Melancholy* (1621)

B 51   A carman's whistle, or a boy singing some ballad early in the street, many
time alters, revives, recreates a restless patient that cannot sleep.
                         (W. Chappell (1819), p. 254)

Michael Drayton, 'To Master George Sandys' (1621)

B 52   This very time, wherein we two now live,
Shall in the compasse, wound the Muses more,
Then all the old *English* ignorance before;
Base Balatry is so belov'd and sought,
And those brave numbers are put by for naugth,
Which rarely read, were able to awake
Bodyes from the graves . . .

(lines 76–82; J. W. Hebel (ed.) (1932–42), III, p. 208)

John Fletcher, *The Pilgrim* (1622)

B 53   Alphonso:
    I shall be taken
For their commander now, their General,
And have a commanding gallows set up for me
As high as a May pole, and nasty songs made on me,
Be printed with a pint pot and a dagger.

(III, 4; A. Dyce (ed.) (1843–46), VIII, p. 49)

W. Shakespeare, *Coriolanus* (1623)

B 54   2 Servingmen:
    2 SERV. This peace is nothing but to rust iron, increase tailors, and breed ballad-makers.
    1 SERV. Let me have war, say I; . . . Peace is a very apoplexy, lethargy; mull'd, deaf, sleepy, insensible; a getter of more bastard children than war's a destroyer of men.

(IV, 6, lines 215–25; P. Alexander (ed.) (1964), p. 858)

Philip Massinger, *The Parliament of Love* (1624)

B 55   Chamont:
    I will have thee
Pictured as thou art now, and thy whole story
Sung to some villainous tune in a lewd ballad,
And make thee so notorious in the world,
That boys in the street shall hoot at thee.

(W. Chappell (1859), I, p. 253)

John Davies, *A Scovrge for Paper-Prosecutors, or Papers Complaint, compil'd in ruthfull Rimes, Against the Paper-spoylers of these Times* (1624)

B 56   What heart so hard, that splits not when it heares,
What ruthlesse Martyrdome my Body beares
By rude *Barbarians* of these latter Times,
Blotting my spotlesse Brest with *Prose* and *Rimes*,
That *Impudence*, it selfe, whould blush to beare;
It is such shamelesse Stuffe and irksome Geare?

. . .

Yea Ballet-mongers make my sheets to shake,
To beare Rimes-doggrell making Dogs perbrake;
Whereto (ay me) grosse Burthens still they adde,
And to that put againe, light Notes and sad:
O Man in desperation, what a dewce
Meanst thou such *filth* in my white face to sluce?   (pp. 1–2)

B 57   A generall Folly reigneth, and harsh Fate
Hath made the World it selfe insatiate:
It hugges these Monsters and deformed things,
Better than what *Johnson* or *Drayton* sings:
As in North-Villages, where euery linne
Of *Plumpton* Parke is held a work diuine.
If o're the Chymney they some Ballad haue
Of *Chevy-Chase*, or of some branded slaue
Hang'd at Tyborne, they their Mattins make it
And Vespers too, and for the Bible take it.   (ibid., p. 4)

B 58   But to behold the wals
Butter'd with weekely Newes compos'd in Pauls,
By some *Decaied Captaine*, or those *Rooks*,
Whose hungry braines compile prodigious *Books*,
Of *Bethlem Gabors* preparations, and
How termes betwixt him and th'*Emperor* stand:
Of *Denmarke*, *Swede*, *Poland*, and of this and that,
Their Wars, Iars, Stirs, and I wrote not what:
The *Duke of Brunswicke*, *Mansfield*, and *Prince Maurice*,
Their Expeditions, and what else but true is,
Yea of the *Belgique state*, yet scarcely know,
Whether *Brabant* be in *Christendome* or no:
To see such *Batter* euerie weeke besmeare
Each publike post, and Church dore, and to heare
These *shamefull lies*, would make a man in spight
Of Nature, turne *Satyrist*, and write
Reuenging lines, against these *shamelesse men*,
Who thus torment both *Paper*, *Presse*, and *Pen*.   ibid., pp. 6–7)

W. Browne, 'Britannia's Pastorals' (1625)

B 59   *Ballad-mongers* on a *Market-day*
Taking their stand, one (with as harsh a noyse
As euer Cart-wheele made) squeakes the sad choice
Of *Tom* the *Miller* with a golden thumbe,
Who crost in loue, ran mad, and deafe, and dumbe,
Halfe part he chants, and will not sing it out,
But thus he speakes to his attentiue rout:
Thus much for loue I warbled from my brest,
And gentle friends, for money take the rest:

So speake I to the ouer-longing eare,
That would the rest of her description heare,
Much haue I sung for loue, the rest (not common)
Martial will shew for coine, in's crabbed woman.
                              (W. C. Hazlitt (ed.) (1868), I, p. 176)

John Fletcher, *The Humorous Lieutenant* (1625)

B 60   Lieutenant:
        Now shall we have damnable ballads out against us,
        Most wicked Madrigals; and ten to one, Colonel,
        Sung to such lamentable tunes.
                              (II, 2; A. Dyce (ed.) (1843–46), VI, p. 447)

John Earle, *Micro-cosmographie* (1628)

B 61   A Pot-Poet
Is the dregs of wit; yet mingled with good drink may have some relish. His inspirations are more real than others'; for they do but feign a God, but he has his by him. His verses run like the tap, and his invention as the barrel ebbs and flows at the mercy of the spigot. In thin drink he aspires not above a ballad, but a cup of sack inflames him and sets his must and nose afire together. The Press is his Mint, and stamps him now and then a sixpence or two in reward of the baser coin his pamphlet. His works would scarce sell for three half-pence, though they are given oft for three shillings, but for the pretty title that allures the country Gentleman: and for which the printer maintains him in ale a fortnight. His verses are like his clothes, miserable centos and patches, yet their pace is not altogether so hobbling as an Almanac's. The death of a great man or the burning of a house furnish him with an argument, and the Nine Muses are out straight in mourning gown, and Melpomene cries, 'Fire, Fire.' His other poems are but briefs in rhyme, and like the poor Greeks' collection to redeem for captivity. He is a man now much employed in commendations of our Navy, and a bitter inveigher against the Spaniard. His frequentest works go out in single sheets, and are chanted from market to market, to a vile tune and a worse throat; whilst the poor country wench melts like her butter to hear them. And these are the stories of some men of Tyburne, or a strange monster out of Germany: or sitting in a bawdy-house, he writes God's judgements. He ends at last in some obscure painted cloth, to which himself made the verses, and his life like a can too full spills upon the bench. He leaves twenty shillings on the score, which my Hostess loses.   (H. Osborne (ed.) (1933), pp. 65–6)

William Rowley, *A New Wonder, A woman never Vext* (1632)

B 62   Old Forster:
And I'll proclaim thy baseness to the world;
Ballads I'll make, and make 'em tavern music
To sing thy churlish cruelty.   (I, 1; C. W. Dilke (ed.) (1815), p. 243)

John Forde, *Loues Sacrifice* (1633)

B 63   Nibrassa:
Get from me, strumpet, infamous whore, leprosie of my blood, make thy
moane to Ballad singers, and Rimers, they'll ligge out thy wretchednesse
and abominations to new tunes; as for me, I renounce thee.   (III, Sig. F 3)

B 64   Fioromonda:
Th' hadst better, Duke, thou hadst bin borne a peasant;
Now boyes will sing thy scandall in the streets,
Tune ballads to thy infamy.   (ibid., IV, Sig. H 2ᵛ)

Thomas Heywood, *A Challenge for Beautie* (1636)

B 65   Valladaura:
She has told all; I shall be balladed –
Sung up and down by minstrels.   (W. Chappell (1859), I, p. 253)

Beaumont and Fletcher, *Monsieur Thomas* (1639)

B 66   Sebastian:
thou hast marr'd him,
Thou, and thy prayer-books: I do disclaim him.
Did not I take him singing yesternight
A godly ballad, to a godly tune too,
And had a certain catechism in's pocket, damsel?
One of your dear disciples, I perceive it.
When did he ride abroad since he came over?
What tavern has he us'd to? what things done
That shew a man and mettle? When was my house
At such a shame before, to creep to bed
At ten o'clock, and twelve, for want of company?
No singing, nor no dancing, nor no drinking?
Thou think'st not of these scandals. When and where,
Has he but shew'd his sword of late?
                    (A. Dyce (ed.) (1843–46), VII, pp. 361–2)

Pennington, et al., 'Alderman Pennington, with some hundreds following
him, presented the Citizens Petition, subscribed by 15 000, against the
Discipline, and Ceremonies of the Church.' (11 Dec. 1640)

B 67   The swarming of lascivious, idle, and unprofitable Books and Pamphlets,
Playbooks, and Ballads, as namely . . . *Parkers* Ballads in disgrace of
Religion, to the increase of all vice, and withdrawing of people from
reading, studying, and hearing the Word of God, and other good Bookes.
(H. E. Rollins (1919c), p. 123; see Bibliography: 2 Secondary literature)

anon., *The Dovvnefall of Temporizing Poets, unlicenst Printers, upstart
Booksellers, trotting Mercuries, and bawling Hawkers. Being a very
pleasant Dialogue between* Light-foot *the Mercury, and* Suck-bottle *the*

Hawker, Red-nose *the Poet being Moderator between them; the corruption of all which is plainly described* (1641)

B 68   *Light-foot:*
You may well call your selves wandring Stationers, for there was scarce one of you that could say, at such a house I will lodge to night: one of you came out of a hedge, another out of New-gate, a third out of the New-prison, and the fourth, not beeing above a moneth out of Bedlam, roundly, profoundly and soundly cries out with a voyce made of cannon proofe, *Come buy a new Booke, a new Booke, newly come forth*; these are the most admirable proprieties which belong to your most admired Corporation.   (p. 2)

B 69   *Suck-bottle:*
. . . the Regent Master of all Ballad-singers, [Red-nose the Poet] he who thinkes his Muse came from *Helicon,* when as it is well knowne the first originall of it was taken out of a Tar-pit.   (p. 38)

B 70   *Light-foot:* [to Red-nose]
[. . .] You have an indifferent strong Corporation: 23 of you sufficient writers, besides *Martin Parker.*   (p. 4)

B 71   *Poet:*
Money? I wonder when you ever see Poets have money two dayes together, I sold a copy last night, and have spent the money, and now have another copy to sell, but a pox on't, no body will buy it because it is not licenceable . . .   (p. 5)

anon., *The Actors Remonstrance, or complaint for the silencing of their profession, and banishment from their severall play-houses* (1643)

B 72   For some of our ablest ordinarie Poets, in stead of their annuall stipends and benificiall second-dayes, being for meere necessitie compelled to get a living by writing contemptible penny-pamphlets in which they have not so much as poetical licence to use any attribute of their profession; but that of *Quid libet audendi?* and faining miraculous stories, and relations of unheard of battles. Nay, it is to be feared, that shortly some of them; (if they have not been enforced to do it already) will be encited to enter themselves into *Martin Parkers* societie, and write ballads. And what shame this is, great *Phoebus,* and you sacred Sisters; for your owne Priests thus to be degraded of their ancient dignities. Be your selves righteous Judges, when those who formerly have sung with such elegance the acts of Kings and Potentates, charming like *Orpheus* the dull and brutish multitude, scarce a degree above stones and forrests into admiration, though not into understanding with their divine raptures, shall be by that tyrant Necessitie reduced to such abject exigents, wandring like grand children of old *Erra Paters,* those learned Almanack-makers, without any *Macenas* to cherish their loftie conceptions, prostituted by the mis-fortune of our silence, to inexplicable miseries, having no heavenly Castalian Sack to actuate and informe their spirits almost confounded

with stupiditie and coldnesse, by their frequent drinking (and glad too
they can get it) of fulsome Ale, and hereticall Beere, as their usuall
beverage.   (pp. 7–8)

John Fletcher, *The Bloody Brother* (1648)

B 73   Master Cook:
        Good Master Sheriff, your leave too;
        This hasty work was ne'er well done: give us so much time
        As but to sing our own ballads, for we'll trust no man,
        Nor no tune but our own; 'twas done in ale too,
        And, therefore, cannot be refus'd in justice;
        Your penny-pot poets are such pelting thieves,
        They ever hang men twice.   (II, 2; A. Dyce (ed.) (1843–46), X, p. 428)

Sir Francis Wortley (1648)

B 74   Bless the printer from the searcher
           And from the Houses' takers.
        Bless Tom from the slash; from Bridewell's lash,
           Bless all poor ballad-makers.
        Those who have writ for the King, for the good King,
           Be it rhime or reason,
        If they please but to look through Jenkins his book
           They'll hardly find it treason.   (W. Chappell (1859), II, p. 417)

James Shirley, *The Court Secret* (1653)

B 75   MEN: What's that?
        PEDRO: A ballad sir,
           Before I die, to let the people know
           How I behav'd myself upon the scaffold;
           With other passages, that will delight
           The people, when I take my leave of the world,
           Made to a pavin tune. – Will you hear it?
                                  (V, 1; W. Gifford (ed.) (1833), V, p. 500)

Dorothy Osborne, *The Letters of Dorothy Osborne to William Temple*
(June 1653)

B 76   . . . the heat of the day is spent in reading or working and about sixe or
        seven a Clock, I walke out into a Common that lyes hard by the house
        where a great many young wenches keep Sheep and Cow's and sitt in the
        shade singing of Ballads; I go to them and compare theire voyces and
        Beauty's to some Ancient Sheperdesses that I have read of and finde a
        vaste difference there, but trust mee I think these are as innocent as those
        could bee. I talke to them, and finde they want nothing to make them the
        happiest People in the world, but the knowledge that they are soe.
                       (Letter 24, 2–4 June 1653; G. C. Moore (ed.) (1928), pp. 51–2)

Izaak Walton, *The Compleat Angler* (1653–55)

B 77   An honest ale-house where we shall find a cleanly room, lavender in the windows, and twenty ballads stuck about the wall.

(J. Bartlett (1968), p. 326a)

anon. (1658)

B 78   A Ballet, a ballet! let every Poet,
           A ballet make with speed:
       And he that has wit, now let him shew it;
           For never was greater need:
       And I that never made ballet before;
       Will make one now, though never make more.

(*Wit Restor'd* (1658), p. 39)

anon., 'The Ex-Ale-tation of Ale' (1661)

B 79   The *Poet* Divine, that cannot reach Wine,
           Because that his money doth many times faile,
       Will hit on the vein to make a good strain,
           If he be but *inspir'd* with a *pot of good ale.*

       For *ballads* Elderton never had Peer;
           How went his wit in them, with how merry a Gale,
       And with all the Sails up, had he been at the Cup
           And washed his beard with a *pot of good ale.*

(J. W. Ebsworth (ed.) (1876), p. 118)

anon., *A Garland for the New Royal Exchange* (1669)

B 80   Mr. Lovesong:
       I buy every [one] of them that is printed, so soon as it comes abroad, and I hear it cried; and I promise you that they have cost me more money than I'll say. And I can sing them all, too, . . . with the very air and tune of your most exquisite ballad singers o' the streets.
       (H. E. Rollins (1919a), p. 332; see Bibliography: 2 Secondary literature)

William Wycherley, *The Country Wife* (1675)

B 81   Mrs. Pinchwife and Bookseller:
       MRS. PINCH. Pry, have you any ballads? give me sixpenny worth.
       BOOKSELLER. We have no ballads.
       MRS. PINCH. Then give me 'Covent Garden Drollery', and a play or two –
           Oh, here's 'Tarugo's Wiles', and 'The Slighted Maiden'; I'll have
           them.   (II, 1; E. Gosse (ed.) (1962), pp. 133–4)

George Etherege, *The Man of Mode* (1676)

B 82   Dorimant and Shoemaker:
       DOR. Sirrah, I'll have you stand i' the pillory for this libel.
       SHOEM. Some of you deserve it, I'm sure; there are so many of 'em that our

journeymen nouadays, instead of harmless ballads, sing nothing but your damned lampoons.   (I, 1; E. Gosse (ed.) (1962), p. 443)

William Cavendish, *The Triumphant Widow, or the Medley of Humors* (1677)

B 83   CICELY. I thank you, *Gervas*; but what must I give you again?

GERVAS. A little thing that shall cost thee nothing, *Cicely*, Oh for a blessed Pedler, if it be thy will; for there are more Wenches won, with their Trinkets, than with any we have about us; mass wish and have. Look where he is, peace.

Enter Footpad *like a Pedler.*

>   Footpad sings.
>   *Come, Maids, what is it that you lack?*
>   *I have many a fine knack*
>   *For you in my Pedler's Pack.*
>   *Your Sweet hearts then kindly smack,*
>   *If they freely will present you,*
>   *And with Trinkets wil! content you.*

CICELY.Oh rare, how rarely he sings!
>   [Three or four Maids and Men come running,
>   crying, Oh Here's the Pedler, the Pedler.

>   Footpad sings.
>   *Brushes, Combes of Tortoise shell*
>   *For your money I will sell,*
>   *Cambrick, Lawn as white as milk,*
>   *Taffata as soft as silk,*
>   *Garters rich, with silver Roses,*
>   *Rings with moral divine Posies.*

1 MAID. Oh what brave things he has got!

2 MAID. Peace, peace, let him troll it away, he sings curiously.

>   Footpad sings.
>   *Rainbow-Ribbands of each colour,*
>   *No walking Shop yet e're was fuller,*
>   *Various Points and sev'ral Laces*
>   *For your Boddies straight embraces,*
>   *Silver Bodkins for your hair,*
>   *Bobs, which Maidens love to wear.*

1 MAN. Oh this is a rare Fellow, I warrant he's pure Company.

2 MAN. I warrant you he is very ingenious, peace.

>   Footpad sings.
>   *Here are various Pick-tooth Cases,*
>   *And the finest Flanders Laces,*
>   *Cabinets for your fine Doxies,*
>   *Stoppers and Tobacco Boxes,*

> *Crystal* Cupids *Looking glasses*
> *Will enamour all your Lasses.*

CICELY. Sure, *Gervas*, this is the Kings Pedler, he has such rare things
about him, and he sings like a Nightingal.

GERVAS. I Believe he's the Kings Pedler indeed.

>   Footpad sings.
> *Fine gilt Pray'r Books, Catechism,*
> *What is Orthodox, or Schisms.*
> *Or for loyal Faith defendant*
> *Presbyter, or Independent;*
> *Ballads fresh, all singing new,*
> *And all those Ballets too are true.*

GERVAS. That's rare, come let's see 'em.

1 MAN. Let me see.

2 MAN. Stand away, let me come.

GERVAS. You come! stand away, you Puppy, you have no judgment.

CICELY. Oh pray let *Gervas* see, he has a notable vein this way.

1 MAID. Ay, pray let *Gervas* see.

GERVAS. Oh Ballets, fine Ballets, Oh I love a Ballet but e'ne too well,
Heaven forgive me, for being so given to the love of Poetry. What are
the Contents of this, for I scorn to read.

FOOTPAD. Marry, Sir, a most lamentable business.

GERVAS. Oh it's no matter, so it be a fine Ditty.

CICELY. Oh I love a melancholy Ditty, I can weep at a Ballet so sweetly –

FOOTPAD. Why it is of a Virgin of thirteen or fourteen that dy'd a Maid,
that's the truth on't.

GERVAS. Nay I'le be hang'd then, thirteen or fourteen, and die a Maid? it
cannot be now a days.

1 MAN. What a scandalous World this is, to abuse a poor G[i]rl so.

GERVAS. Ay, and after her death too.

CICELY. Methinks they should have more conscience, than to speak ill of
the dead.

GERVAS. First and formost, I hope she had more Grace than to die so, I
speak like a Christian.

2 MAN. If she did die so, mercy of her say I, that's charitable, I'm sure.

GERVAS. If she did die so, let it be a warning to you Maids, to shun such
abominable ways.

CICELY. I hope it will, *Gervas*, be a warning, an' we had but Grace.

1 MAID. Yes we should lay it to heart, and take warning.

2 MAN. Look here, what fine Ballet's this?

FOOTPAD. This is a very strange Ballet, of a lusty Widow.

GERVAS. A lusty Widow is no strange thing.

FOOTPAD. Yes a lusty Widow, that lives and dies chastly.

GERVAS. Is't possible a lusty Widow live and die chast?

2 MAN. Lord, Lord, what lying things these Ballets are, and to be in print
too!

FOOTPAD. All the Parish Hands are to the Certificate to confirm it.

2 MAN. Puh, 'twas plain malice in 'em, to asperse a lusty Widow so.

GERVAS. The Parish should have had a lusty young Vicar, and he'd have converted her i'faith. Maids have a care; for you hope to be Widows, have a care I say of dying chast.

CICELY. Well, we'l think on't; but pray let's see his Ware.

GERVAS. How now, *Cicely*, you are a Wag, have patience, and he will shew you all. Oh vile Flesh and Blood! Oh corrupt Nature, to despise the edification of Ballets; but what's this?

FOOTPAD. A Ballet of a Courtier that died rich.

GERVAS. That's a miracle indeed, I warrant he cozen'd many a pour body for't.

FOOTPAD. No, Sir, he scorn'd to meddle with the poor.

GERVAS. That shew'd he had some conscience; but Oh *Cicely*, here's the brave Ballet you and I use to sing, I know it by the Picture.

CICELY. Oh pray let's sing it.

        They sing.

GERVAS. *To Fayrs and Markets I did go*

CICELY. *And I did follow you, you know.*

GERVAS. *As I return'd, I threw you down.*

CICELY. *Upon the Grass.*

GERVAS. *My sweetest Lass;*

        And so did give you a green Gown.

CICELY. *But if it chance my Belly swell,*

GERVAS. *Then will Marriage hide it well.*

CICELY. *Your Son and Heir, or Daughter fair,*

        If you'l not stay,

GERVAS. *But run away,*

        Is left unto the Parish care.

        Enter a Servant in haste.

SERV. Oh, Sirs, my Lady wants ye, there are a great sort of strangers that are to come to dine here, and none of ye in the way to receive Orders, come away.   (I, 1, pp. 4–7)

John Selden, *Table Talk* (1689)

B 84   Though some make slight of libels, yet you may see by them how the wind sits: as, take a straw and throw it up into the air, you shall see by that which way the wind is, which you shall not do by casting up a stone. Solid things do not show the complexion of the times so well as ballads and libels.   (F. Pollock (ed.) (1927), p. 72)

Andrew Fletcher, 'Letter to the Marquis of Montrose' (1703)

B 85   I knew a very wise man ... [who] believed that ... if a man were permitted to make all the ballads, he need not care who should make the laws of a nation. And we find, that most of the antient legislators thought they could not well reform the manners of any city without the help of a lyric, and sometimes of a dramatic poet.   (*Works* (1749), p. 266)

Daniel Defoe, 'The Ballads-maker's Plea' (1722)

B 86   A. J., Oct. 13. – Sir, I am very much discontented in my Spirit, and am afraid if you do not find me out some Remedy, I shall Plot and Rebel, and what not, *not against the* KING *tho', pray Mark that!* I am, Sir, by Trade a British Manufacturer, and I have often heard wise Men say, that all our Manufactures should be encouraged; for that it is by the Success of our Manufactures that our Nation is made happy, rich, powerful and great, and our Trade carry'd on.

I need not run out here in a long Dissertation concerning the Excellence of our Manufactures; their Value abroad, and how they are of a Universal Usefulness in the World. The Manufacture indeed that I am Master of, is generally for a home Consumption, and yet I will appeal to you whether it is not as useful in its kind, as any Manufacture of them all; in a Word, I am a very useful Person in my Place, I am a *Ballad-Maker*.

No I find this ancient Art and Mystery of *Ballad-Making* has suffer'd deeply in the Calamities of the Times, and is of late very much, and more than ever discourag'd, and under a sensible Decay at present. The Business is to have you be first convinc'd of its Necessity and Usefulness, and then to be prevail'd upon to set your helping Hand to the Work of raising its drooping Condition for the Publick Good.

The first Work I have upon me is to prove the Usefulness of this noble Manufacture or Invention; for if that be secured, I would hope it would be easy to find Friends to espouse it. To this Purpose, I have many Things to propose; but previous to the rest, and before I proceed upon the Merit of the Manufacture itself, you are to understand, that there is another Thing belongs to it, as most Manufactures have their Dependants, and this is the great numerous Corporation of *Ballad-Singers*; this, tho'it be a Lingua-facture, rather than a Manufacture, yet employs a very great Number of Poor, who, *may it please your Honour*, are like to be utterly undone, if this Manufacture be not supported, and must of Necessity be maintain'd by the Parish; *that is to say*, in the Gaols or the Houses of Correction. But I hasten to the merit of the Case, and to give an Account of myself in the Capacity of a Manufacturer, and of the Usefulness of my Manufacture.

And, first, Saving to myself the Liberty (due to me as an Englishman,) of bringing any other or further Argument in Defence of the Manufacture of *Ballad-Making*, and of that great Lingua-facture of *Ballad-Singing*, as above, I must say, that I am a Whig *Ballad-Maker*. And I crave leave to add, that the Whigs have as much Reason to favour the Masters in these Arts, as any Set of Party Men whatsoever; and I think I may say a great deal more. *For Example*: Did not the famous Ballad of *Lilly-burlero* sing King *James* out of his three Kingdoms? And, speaking of remote Causes, did it not form the Revolution of Blessed Memory? I hope that is a service the Whigs ought never to forget.

Nor have the other Societies, or Parties of Men in this Nation, been without their several and particular Advantages from this useful Society. Who can forget of what Universal Benefit that important Song (tho' since turn'd to an ill use,) was at the Restoration of King *Charles II.*, viz., *The*

K-- shall enjoy his own again. I say nothing of the ill Use made of it since, but that it has generally turn'd to a dull Account to those that have been so foolish as to try it; in the Days of General *Monk*, it was the *Lilly-burlero* of that Time; and General *Monk's* Musick (they say) play'd that Tune every Morning after his coming to *London*, till the King came himself, and then, you know, there was no more Occasion for it.

How many Operations have since been wrought by the Force of *Ballad-Singing*, I need not go far to recollect. The Riots in Scotland were usher'd in with a Song, call'd *AWA, Whigs, AWA.* The Mobs of Dr. *Sacheverell's* Time had *Down with the Round Heads*, an old Ballad reviv'd. The Hurries of the late Reign had the reviv'd Ballad of Chevy Chase; nay, even the Solicitations for the late *Callico Bill* were introduced with the Ballad of a *Callico Madam.*

But now, alas! We not only have no Ballad, but are in great Danger of Losing that useful incentive (to Mischief) the Manufacture itself; and, I hear, the greatest Merchant in that kind of Goods has been taken up lately for something done *in his Way*, a little out of the Way, &c.

As to what he has done, and whether it be in his Way, or out of his Way, 'tis not much to our Purpose to enquire. But why must the Trade of *Ballad-Making* sink upon this Occasion? Why must we have no new Song to make our Hearts full glad on the approach of the new Parliament, or upon the Plot, or upon anything in which the Useful Faculty of *Ballad-Making* has been used to be exercised? This is really, in my Opinion, a National Grievance, and I hope it will be complain'd of in Publick, and I recommend it to you, Sir, to acquaint the World with it accordingly.

What! do you think I am so exhausted that I have not one Song in my Budget for King George? Do you think I cannot make one Stanza, for all the merry Times of Bite and Bubble that are past? Can I produce nothing worth while, do ye think, upon the Plot? And shall the jolly Fellows that may chance to Swing upon this Occasion, have never a *Passing Song* for them, as well as they have a *Passing Bell* at *St. Sepulcher's?*

Never fear it, I can furnish you with something suitable to every Occasion, and you shall perhaps have a Test of my Performance very speedily.

Your Humble Servant,
Jeffery Sing-Song.

(*Applebee's Journal*, 13 Oct. 1722; W. Lee (ed.) (1889), III, pp. 57–60)

Notes

Introduction: survey of research to date and delineation of study area

1 Both are often subsumed under the term 'balladsheet', see L. Shepard (1962), pp. 23–4. The sheets were between 30 × 20 cm and 40 × 25 cm in size (ibid., p. 58). For collections they were often cut to a certain size, so that their original form is no longer apparent.

2 It is probable that in the very early stages handwritten sheets containing ballad texts were also sold (see Shepard [1962], p. 51).

3 See R. B. McKerrow (1927), pp. 297–8. 'Black-letter' is equivalent to Gothic script.

4 See W. Chappell, RB, I, p. xi; Shepard (1962), pp. 58 and 65. 'White-letter' is also called 'roman type'.

5 Also referred to as the 'George Daniel Collection', after its first owner. The bibliographical fate of this amateur collection led to its break-up into separate publications. See BB, pp. xi–xiii; AB, pp. xi–xii and RB, pp. viii–ix.

6 See bibliography for complete titles; for the most important editions, see also list of abbreviations, p. x–xi.

7 Some of the texts in this edition appear again, with more precise bibliographical information, in H. L. Collmann and other editions.

8 H. E. Rollins (1919b), pp. 340–51, sees the MS. as a copy of broadsides with which he can prove similarities. D. C. Fowler (1968), pp. 96–102, agrees with T. Wright that this is a 'minstrel book' which is particularly typical because of its large number of singable and unsingable pieces, and which served as a model for broadsides.

9 It contains approximately 1,800 ballads, 1,376 of which are in black-letter. It was begun by John Selden (d. 1654) and finished by Samuel Pepys, and is now located in Magdalene College, Cambridge.

10 'this Garland reprints the most interesting seventeenth century ballads . . . none of them later than 1639' (PG, p. ix).

11 Produced 1600–3 and 1609–16; for details see the introduction to the edition, pp. 1–3.

12 The collection was begun by Robert Harley (d. 1711) and named after its fourth owner, the Duke of Roxburghe, who bought it in 1788. In 1845 it was acquired by the British Museum. For the history of the Roxburghe Collection see W. Chappell, Introduction, RB, I (1888), pp. i–iv and J. W. Ebsworth, Introduction to The Bagford Ballads, 2 vols. (Hertford 1878), I, pp. v–viii.

13 The other volumes contain mainly texts from the last third of the seventeenth century.

14 See W. Chappell, Introduction, RB, I, p. xvi.

15 Only the first text is dated (approximately) 1535. The time gap between vols. I and II is filled by Rollins's *CP*.

16 Further texts of this type can be found in *RB* and *SHB*.

17 As far as I can ascertain, the following collections have not yet been sufficiently taken into account (disregarding those which duplicate the collections already mentioned): Wood Collection (totalling 279 texts, Bodleian); Douce (877 texts, Bodleian); Rawlinson (Bodleian); Halliwell Phillips (Chetham Library, Manchester); an unnamed collection in Manchester Free Reference Library (usually quoted as such); broadsides in the possession of the Library of the Society of Antiquaries (Lemon's Catalogue). See also W. Chappell's survey of smaller collections: Introduction to *RB*, I, p. x.

18 In contrast to German street ballads, which for reasons of (apparent) topicality and increased sales were usually undated and without imprint; see K. V. Riedel (1963).

19 In this connection see the reference works of E. G. Duff (1905), R. B. McKerrow (1910) and H. R. Plomer (1907), also the list of 'Publishers of Black-Letter Ballads in the Seventeenth Century', by W. Chappell, *RB*, I, 2nd part, pp. xvii–xxiii.

20 H. E. Rollins (1924), also in *SP*, 21 (1924), pp. 1–324.

21 In the case of German street ballads, K. V. Riedel (1963) considers this impracticable, maintaining that most of the broadsides cannot be dated and the number of extant texts is relatively small.

22 See A. B. Friedmann (1961), p. 35; Rollins, Preface to *PG*, pp. ix–x.

23 The English balladmonger used neither bench nor display board. Occasionally he would stand on something to raise his position. Probable textual differences need to be examined in more detail from the Germanist angle. See also L. Petzoldt (1974).

24 Apart from editorial preservation of the material, only three contributions to research are of central importance: H. E. Rollins (1919a) still provides the best introduction, with information about the format, printing, distribution and price of the street ballad as well as its relationship to the audience, and the reputation of the authors and of ballad production in general; one or two literary features are mentioned, but only in passing. A. B. Friedmann (1961), in his history of the ballad's reception and influence, gives the broadside ballad appropriate consideration and includes contributions from individual scholars. His orientation towards content, and the biased value judgements underlying his description and classification, do not go beyond the traditional approach in ballad research. L. Shepard (1962) summarizes research on the English street ballad in a popularist survey of its history, from its beginnings to the present day, whereby bibliographical aspects and a rather sweeping historical approach to its impact predominate. I have not listed individual articles and references which use single ballads as historical documents, since they are irrelevant to our particular investigation.

25 D. C. Fowler (1968) refutes this idea and shows that most of the texts, owing to their late transition from oral tradition to written form, were considerably influenced by the language of the eighteenth and nineteenth centuries.

26 This does not only apply to the history of the German ballad, but can already be discerned in the comments of A. Phillips, T. Percy, T. Evans and J. Ritson on their ballad editions in the eighteenth century.

27 For disparaging comment on the street ballad as opposed to the folk ballad, see F. J. Furnivall (1868–72) I, p. v; F. B. Gummere (1907), pp. 4–16; H. L. Collmann, *BB*, p. ix; W. E. Richmond (1951), p. 159; H. Grierson and J. C. Smith (1956), p. 44. Even A. B. Friedmann (1961) comments: 'no one will dispute the general superiority of traditional balladry' (p. 220).

28 A. Clark, in 1907, feels it necessary to justify the fact that in his textual reproductions indecent words and themes have not been toned down or omitted: 'All of them are eloquent as to the baseness of popular taste in Shakespeare's time' (*SHB*, p. 3). Ebsworth (1878), too, makes sure that his readers will not misunderstand his intentions: 'Let it be understood that we have endeavoured to faithfully give these *historical documents* in their entirety. When offensive words occur, they are retained, to the shame of the past writers and singers, not of ourselves, the merely antiquarian students' (p. iii). Chappell's commentary on the *Roxburghe Ballads* also contains expressions of moral outrage at certain texts, and even Rollins is not completely free from such sentiments.

29 W. Chappell: 'Comparatively few of high merit are to be found among printed ballads, for they are chiefly the productions of the people's special rhymesters' (Introduction to *RB*, I, p. viii); J. P. Collier: 'It will be found that they all possess some features of interest, while only few, it must be owned, are worthy of preservation for their own separate and poetical merits' (Introduction to *BBLB*, p. i); Ebsworth: 'Rough and clumsy as is the workmanship in many of them'; 'often irregular in rhyme and rhythm, always uncertain in spelling, vague in chronology, dubious in morals, questionable in taste, and generally untrustworthy in statements' (Introduction to *Bagford Ballads* (1878), I, pp. ii and xiii); H. V. Rowth (1909): 'doggerel fragmentary verses' (p. 363); L. B. Wright (1935): 'The vogue of broadside ballad, dreadful as its verses usually are, can easily be accounted for' (p. 419); Rollins: 'Ballads were not written for poetry' (Preface to *PG*, p. xi). H. C. Baker's comments (1939) in his search for 'classical material' in the street ballads typify the application of cultural prestige with classical content as a value criterion: 'there survives a considerable body of broadsides that were obviously written by cultured men' (p. 982).

30 J. W. Ebsworth emphasizes the value of the street ballad as a 'historical document', see Introduction, *Bagford Ballads*, p. iii and n. 1 and *passim*. 'Our political ballads, being supplemented by others of a miscellaneous character, help us to see the England of Stuart days without disguise' (p. iv). A. Clark, *SHB* (1907) sees his task as a historical contribution and is gratified at being able to confirm the 'historical accuracy of these ballads' (p. 3) through examination of sources. C. Firth used ballads as source material in several lectures to the Royal Academy, see L. B. Wright (1964), p. 418, n. 1. It is known that Macaulay also used street ballads as sources.

31 See e.g. *PB*, I, pp. 47, 51, 109, 148, 200, 214, 218, 232; *PB*, II, pp. 43, 47, 219, 234.

32 *PB*, I, p. ix; in what follows (pp. ix–xiii), Rollins also tries to arouse above all the cultural and historical interest of the reader; in the introductions to his other editions, too, this aspect predominates.

33 J. W. Ebsworth's crude division according to topic areas in the postscript to the nine-volume edition of the *Roxburghe Ballads* (*RB*, VIII (1897), pp. ix–

civ) is representative. See also Rollins (1919a), p. 274 and *passim*, and the introductions to his editions; A. Clark, Introduction to *SHB* (1909), pp. 7–8; Ebsworth, *Bagford Ballads*, I, pp. xiv–xix.

34 'Street Ballads, forerunners of Newspapers', Ebsworth, *RB*, VIII (1897), p. xvii; Rollins (1919a), p. 265 and variously in his editions; A. Clark, *SHB*, pp. 7–8; A. B. Friedmann (1961), p. 49 and *passim*; V. de Sola Pinto, Introduction to *CM*, p. 17.

35 Ebsworth, *RB*, p. xxx: 'Love rules the Courth, the Camp, the Grove'.

36 Ebsworth differentiates between fictionally narrative, pseudo-biographical, and critical ballads concerned with immediate reality.

37 This does not of course apply to all texts; sentimentality, exaggerated and inappropriate pathos and clumsy borrowings from standard literature are not infrequent.

38 Pinto (1947), p. 45; see in this connection also A. J. Walker (1935).

39 See H. E. Rollins (1919a), p. 261; L. Shepard (1962), pp. 49–52, A. B. Friedmann (1958): 'Broadsides of whatever description have proved the most ephemeral products of the early press; we have very few of them which antedate the reign of Elizabeth' (p. 107). H. L. Collmann, *BB*: 'The Registers for the first forty years of the Stationers' Company abound with licenses for ballads, fourpence being the usual fee charged for each item . . . by far the greater number are not to be found in any of our older libraries, and must therefore be regarded as irrevocably lost, and to this fate they were by reason of their form and popularity particularly exposed' (p. x).

40 See in this connection H. Huth. An expert on early prints and their time, Huth has established that in the largest and most varied collection of broadsides, in the possession of the Society of Antiquaries and catalogued by Robert Lemon, not a single ballad is to be found (*AB*, p. xviii). The earliest street ballad is generally considered to be *A Ballad of Luther, the Pope, a Cardinal, and a Husbandman* (*c.* 1530), *PB*, I, pp. 3–7. Extant texts dating from before the 1570s are rare, however.

41 We have very little information on performance and sale during this period. The unsingability of some of the early texts (see A. B. Friedmann [1961], p. 45) indicates a partly untypical distribution.

42 The second research area to do with street-ballad impact, which Pinto mentions, cannot be covered in this investigation.

43 Editions which have so far appeared include a major proportion of extant ballads and are therefore to some extent representative. The editions to date which are only selective are the Euing Collection, Douce and Wood; these often contain duplications from *Roxburghe* and *Pepys*.

44 A more precise description of plot and scene, such as became usual in German broadsides at a very much earlier date, is almost completely absent. See A. B. Friedmann (1961), p. 47.

45 See e.g. J. P. Collier, *BBLB*, pp. v–vii: the picture of a noisy, drunken company of animals, among which the boar is vomiting, accompanies the farewell dialogue of two lovers.

46 See the relevant handbooks for the tunes: W. Chappell (1859 and 1855–9); C. M. Simpson (1966).

47 See Chappell (1855–9), I, p. 162; Simpson (1966), pp. 225–31, 233, 285, 565, 622.

48 Rollins (1919a), p. 314: 'The Tunes themselves are often attractive; yet by the literary men of the period they are almost invariably spoken of as vile, perhaps because these men felt an instinctive repugnance to countenancing anything connected with the ballad trade.'
49 See Rollins (1919a), p. 268; Ebsworth (1878), I, pp. xvi–xix; Shepard (1962), p. 33.
50 See A. C. Baugh (1948); W. Schirmer (1954); C. Ricks (1956); D. Daiches (1960); E. Mertner and K. Standop (1967).
51 See A. W. Ward and A. R. Waller (eds.), vol. IV (1909), pp. 362–3; D. Bush (1962), pp. 48–9.
52 The literary ballad was of far less significance in English literature than in German literature. See W. Kayser (1936).
53 The street ballad was taken as a model by e.g. Wordsworth, Thackeray and W. S. Gilbert in a large number of ballads. The majority of ballad imitators in the eighteenth century were orientated towards the folk ballad, however, as was Swinburne. The entertainment verse of the Restoration is also worth investigating from the point of view of street-ballad influence.

1 Literary and social conditions for the rise, distribution and textual structure of the street ballad

1 Most of the references in contemporary documents describe only the ballad-monger's vocal and gestural efforts to attract an audience: see appendix, B 44, B 59, B 80. There is however also mention of such aids as 'stall', and 'pitch': see B 22. In this connection see also H. E. Rollins (1919a), p. 320; A. B. Friedmann (1961), p. 48.
2 See above, p. 9 and p. 45. For the situation as regards the German street ballad, see K. V. Riedel (1963): 'The presenter stands outside and above the action, directing the attention through his words and pictorial display' (p. 39). L. Petzoldt (1974), pp. 57–8.
3 See H. E. Rollins (1919a), pp. 306–11; also below, pp. 18–21.
4 For the distribution of the street ballads by pedlars, see also documentary references in the appendix: B 3, B 23, B 45, B 68, B 83.
5 *True Wonders, and strange news* (c. 1670–5), POA, no. 32, pp. 191–4; v. 1,1–2, p. 192.
6 *The Worlds Wonder* (1677), POA, no. 33, pp. 195–9, v. 1,1–1,2, p. 196.
7 *A Pleasant new Ballad you here may behold* (1630), RB, II, pp. 366–71, v. 1,1–7, p. 367.
8 *Euery Mans condition* (1627), PG, no. 47, pp. 270–5, v. 11,1–3, p. 274. My italics.
9 *A songe of foure Preistes that suffered death at* Lancaster (1601), OEB, no. 11, pp. 70–8, v. 14,3–4, p. 74.
10 *Terrible News from* Brainford (1661), POA, no. 13, pp. 75–80; v. 1,1–6, p. 77.
11 *Faire fall all good Tokens!* (between 1624 and 1640), RB, I, pp. 341–6; v. 1,5–8, p. 342.
12 *A Pleasant new Ballad you here may behold* (1630), RB, II, pp. 366–71; v. 1,1–4, p. 367.
13 PG, no. 78, pp. 443–8; title, p. 444.

14 First performed *c.* 1609 or 1610; see appendix B 37 and 38.
15 See appendix B 42–4. The closeness to reality of this scene is confirmed by Robert Greene's earlier (1591/2) description of the teamwork between rogues and balladmongers; see appendix B 22.
16 For more detail see the evaluation of all documentary evidence below, pp. 242–5.
17 See also H. E. Rollins (1919a), p. 310 and W. Chappell (1859), II, p. 484.
18 See appendix B 16, B 60, B 61.
19 See appendix B 33, B 39, B 61.
20 Preface to *PB*, I, p. xiii, see quotation above, p. 5.
21 R. Weimann (1967), p. 20. Where stage play and audience are no longer indivisible in the ritual, an attempt is made to bridge the developing separation with the newly established audience relationship (ibid., pp. 33–47). H.-J. Diller (1973): see esp. '*Die Zuschaueranrede*', pp. 148–216.
22 Quoted after R. B. McKerrow (1910).
23 Day had the privilege of printing the catechism, Tottel, that of printing all legal documents and Jugge printed all the Bibles. See F. A. Mumby (1956), pp. 66–7.
24 'It is remarkable how soon after its invention the art of printing became an instrument of popular amusement and instruction – an active agent in the development of the mind of the people', remarks the private collector of old MSS and prints, Henry Huth (Introduction, *AB*, xv).
25 See ibid., pp. 76–7 and E. H. Miller (1959), pp. 94–136.
26 F. A. Mumby (1956), p. 90. C. Bladgen (1954) modifies the meaning of 'Ballad Stock' along the lines that this group of printers, in comparison with the other 'Stocks', were not so specialized in what they produced (p. 163).
27 P. M. Handover (1960) shows how the Company's monopoly and financial security stifled initiative in the printing trade (p. 50).
28 For the periodical press, see ibid., p. 98.
29 These dates are derived from McKerrow (1910) and H. R. Plomer (1907); dates given refer to verifiable activity.
30 F. Coles, H. Gosson, J. Grismand, H. Kirkham (1570–93), J. Trundle (1603–26), C. Wright (1613–39), J. Wright. For the hierarchical structure of the Company and conditions for membership, see McKerrow (1910), Introduction, pp. xvii–xxii.
31 W. M. Chappell's list of ballad-printers, *RB*, I, pp. xvii–xxii, contains numerous names not mentioned by McKerrow and Plomer. Such printers are therefore documented only in their inclusion in the Stationers' Register and not through their membership of the Company.
32 See F. A. Mumby (1956), p. 93. A ballad or short published work earned the author the same amount as the translation of a whole book – a few pounds (see H. S. Bennett [1970], p. 229).
33 The popularity of the street ballad is amply confirmed in secondary literature (see V. de Sola Pinto, *CM*, Introduction; H. E. Rollins [1919a], pp. 260–1; and others), and can be discerned in the contemporary comment of actual opponents of this literary form (see below, chapter 6).
34 In contrast to the sale of books, which was stationary and could count on a traditional type of customer.
35 See E. H. Miller (1959), pp. 75–7. H. E. Rollins (1919a) points out the fact

that well-known and popular ballad authors at least were highly rated by publishers as commercial successes (pp. 304–5). Interest in the ballad business can be clearly seen in the competition for privileges.

36 P. Sheavyn (1909) talks of a 'large, ready sale for ballads . . . proven by the very large numbers of "ballets" and broadsides registered by the stationers' company' (p. 39).

37 He usually received a single, one-off fee; see H. E. Rollins (1919a), pp. 296–7.

38 See E. H. Miller (1959), pp. 94–136: 'Like the concept of order and the moralistic hostility toward usury, patronage was in conflict with a world moving from an agricultural economy and closed society to a capitalistic system and open society' (p. 94). See also G. A. Thompson (1914), pp. 26–35. For the following period there has to my knowledge been no research undertaken. L. L. Schücking deals with patronage from the aspect of the development of literary taste (1961), pp. 18–21.

39 'With the notable exception of Shakespeare and Spenser, the lives of Elizabethan authors comprise case histories of poverty' (E. H. Miller [1959], p. 12).

40 See E. K. Chambers (1923), I, pp. 308–18; H. Castrop (1972), pp. 106–12.

41 See Ben Jonson's portrayal, appendix B 44 and B 22.

42 H. E. Rollins (1919a), pp. 318–19, surmises that the balladmonger frequently earned a fair amount, in spite of his minor sales role, through tips.

43 For this see E. K. Chambers (1954), I, pp. 1–88; E. Faral (1910).

44 See E. K. Chambers (1954), I, p. 69.

45 In *The Actors' Remonstrance* (1643) there is an indication that many actors who became destitute through the closing of the theatres went over to the ballad trade (see H. E. Rollins, *CP*, p. 14).

46 First verifiable ballad in 1624/25; last entry in the Stationers' Register in 1660.

47 Even a comprehensive investigation such as that of F. S. Siebert (1952) makes only occasional mention of the street ballad.

48 See W. W. Greg (1956), pp. 45–6 and 51. The Master of the Revels was responsible for the theatre, and after the beginning of the seventeenth century this position was in the gift of the Lord Chamberlain.

49 Captain Francis Bethen, appointed on 13 September 1648 and particularly strict in pursuing prose pieces and ballads, practically succeeded in banning the sale of ballads from the streets (see H. E. Rollins, *CP*, p. 40).

50 E. H. Miller (1959) maintains that there are no sources relating to this (p. 181).

51 See ibid., pp. 171–202. The case of John Stubbes, whose right hand was severed on 27 September 1579, led earlier scholars to overestimate censorship in Elizabethan times.

52 See R. B. McKerrow (1910), pp. x–xix, E. H. Miller (1959), pp. 171–202, W. W. Greg (1956), pp. 41–52, H. E. Rollins, *CP*, pp. 3–74, F. S. Siebert (1952), pp. 21–41.

53 F. S. Siebert (1952), p. 21; R. Fraser (1970) on the other hand maintains that it was precisely owing to the decrease in power that censorship measures became stricter.

54 F. S. Siebert (1952), pp. 143–6; H. S. Bennett (1970), pp. 45–58.

55 See H. E. Rollins (1919a), pp. 292–4; from 1557–1640, ballad titles com-

prised approximately half of the entries in the Stationers' Register (Rollins [1924], p. 1).

56 See L. B. Wright (1964), pp. 81–118; E. H. Miller (1959), pp. 63–93.

57 In this connection, see literary–sociological investigations by H. N. Fügen (1963), esp. pp. 169–76, and R. Escarpit (1961), esp. p. 83.

58 See H. E. Rollins (1919a), pp. 329–33; he also points out, however, that members of the higher ranks of society also read and listened to ballads. E. H. Miller (1959): 'Ballads were the common man's delight – and sometimes, but of course surreptitiously, the nobleman's too . . . The reasons for their popularity were obvious enough. Ballads were brief, farcically humorous, or sentimentally tragic, frequently bawdy, almost always topical and "new", poetic in the mechanical singsong fashion that the uncultivated admire, and generally set to a popular tune. In addition, they were inexpensive' (pp. 75–6).

59 'To one person who visited the book-stalls there were of course hundreds who heard ballads sung' (H. E. Rollins 1919a, p. 295).

60 'Ballad jig', 'farce jig' and 'stage jig' are terms which describe the possible transitions. C. R. Baskervill (1929) gives the following assessment, based on his knowledge of the field: 'a number of other ballads on one score or the other give evidence of dramatic presentation' (p. 164).

61 Rollins (1919a) recognized, at least to a certain extent, that this applied to the street ballad: 'Ballad singing affected ballad writing. Responding quickly to the exigencies of the trade, writers would insert lines or even whole stanzas, to help the singers, and many of these insertions eventually became part of the ballad-technique. For one thing, all ballads were made to insist upon their newness' (p. 315).

2 Preliminary investigation of the interrelation between street-ballad text and socio-cultural environment: description of textual structure

1 For a basic exposition see K. Baumgärtner (1971), esp. pp. 371–80; also K. Baumgärtner et al. (eds.) (1973), pp. 27–83; R. Jakobson (1971); W. Kallmeyer et al. (1974), I, pp. 26–60; for application to literary texts: D. Janik (1973); R. Fieguth (1973); D. Breuer (1974).

2 It is based on an explication of speech functions derived from Jakobson (1971), via Bühler (1965) and used by K. Baumgärtner (1971), p. 373, who transposes Sebeok's model on to literary communication.

3 See K. Bühler (1965). The relationship of 'expression' to 'speaker', of 'appeal' to 'listener' and of 'presentation' to the object referred to is not made explicit in Sebeok's representation of his model.

4 See below, chapter 3.

5 U. Eco (1972), modifying the Ogden–Richards diagram, points out that the relationship between signifier and signified is historically determined and can therefore only be understood in historical terms as a particular interpretation of the referent (esp. pp. 69–81).

6 This term defines the text as a speech phenomenon in its various manifestations as song, broadside, journal, book etc. See D. Breuer (1974), p. 53 and *passim*.

7 See J. L. Austin (1963); J. R. Searle (1971); S. J. Schmidt (1973); D. Wunder-

lich (1971) and (1973); K. Baumgärtner *et al.* (1973); W. Kallmeyer *et al.* (1974), pp. 15–24.

8 Fieguth calls this position 'reader'; it also includes textual preformations of 'listener' and 'onlooker', however.

9 This will be dealt with in more detail in chapter 4.

10 Speech-act theory defines speech as an act in the sense that it is intentional, socio-communicative behaviour which through its performance establishes meaning and intends certain effects. The division of the speech act into various components makes possible a more precise description of the relationship between expression (phonetic and phatic act), meaning (propositional act) and intention (illocutionary act), in their relation to the speech situation. A consideration of the effect intended and possibly achieved in the speech act (perlocutionary act and effect) should relate, over and above the spoken expression, to listeners' reactions which correlate to the intention of the speaker. For varying explicitness of illocutions see V. Ehrich and G. Saile (1972); A. Davison (1975); J. R. Searle (1975).

11 In the sense of assumptions which a speaker makes and also expects from the listener if he wishes to perform a successful speech act; they are already implicitly contained in the spoken expression; see S. J. Schmidt (1973), pp. 92–106; see also the 'rules' for the 'success' of speech acts, J. R. Searle (1971), pp. 96–113.

12 This corresponds to the 'situational' presupposition (similarity of perception and assessment of the communication situation) and the 'action-semantic' presupposition (concerning the socio-communicative relevance of the communication).

13 The narrator level does not apply in the dramatic text, although narrative functions can be taken over by a figure. In a discursive text the speaker and the 'message of the text as a whole' are very often congruous.

14 H. Link (1976) gives a survey of the diverse terminology of various theoreticians such as W. Iser (1970), J. Anderegg (1973) and R. Fieguth (1973).

3 Procedures of the presenter and his relationship to his audience

1 See above, chapter 1, for the literary and sociological conditional components of the street ballad.

2 This definition of 'juggler' is documented by the *OED* up to 1557.

3 H. Chettle, *Kind-Harts Dreame. Conteining Fiue Apparitions with their Inuectives against Abuses Raigning* (1592), ed. Rimbault (1851), p. 45.

4 Until the end of the sixteenth century, 'pass' meant the juggler's manipulation of objects (see *OED*, section IV.2); 'hey-pass' and 're-pass' are also cries and incantations from the repertoire of the juggler and the conjuror (see *OED*, *Hey*, Phr. and *repass*, v.b.). The variations 'bypasse' and 'compasse' refer to the jugglers' competitiveness.

5 For a detailed account of the distinction between these sub-genres of the street ballad, see below, chapter 4.1.

6 *A Maruellous Murther, Committed* ... (1638), *POA*, no. 3, pp. 15–20; v. 1, p. 16.

7 *A Noble Dewel* (1660), *POA*, no. 9, pp. 52–7; vv. 1,1–5, p. 53. I shall occasionally be taking an example from the period after 1650, as ballads of sensational nature and treating of marvels and miracles are better documented then.

8 *The cryes of the Dead* (*c.* 1625), *PG*, no. 39, pp. 222–5; v. 1, p. 223.

9 *BBLB*, pp. 118–24; *RB*, I, pp. 51–6; between 1624 and 1640 by Martin Parker; quoted from *BBLB*, four verses of the text are missing in the Roxburghe version.

10 *RB*, II, pp. 339–44; between 1601 and 1640.

11 *RB*, I, pp. 341–6; between 1624 and 1640.

12 *The Constant VVife of Sussex* (1632), *PB*, no. 85, II, pp. 229–33; 1,1; p. 230.

13 *The Golden Age: Or, An Age of plaine-dealing* (1662), *PB*, no. 34, I, pp. 207–13; 1,1–2; p. 208.

14 *The merry Old Woman* (1633), *RB*, II, pp. 163–9; 1,1–1,3, p. 164.

15 *A Pleasant new Ballad you here may behold* (1630), *RB*, II, pp. 366–71; 1,1–1,4; p. 367.

16 From the title of *The Essex man coozened by a VVhore* (1631), *PB*, no. 78, II, pp. 191–5, p. 192.

17 *The Pedler opening of his Packe* (*c.* 1620), *PG*, no. 19, pp. 116–20; 2,1–2,4, p. 116.

18 'The Humours of Bertholomew Fair'. The text is not documented until 1681 in a song collection, but we can presume its previous existence in oral tradition. *LBSB*, pp. 160–1, 1,1–2. For further examples see below under 'presenter's appeals to the listener', pp. 54–61.

19 Cf. also street-cries and similar.

20 *The praise of Nothing* (between 1601 and 1640), *RB*, II, 14, 1–4, lines 105–8, p. 344. On asking for money, see below, chapter 3.3.2.

21 See P. Teigeler (1968), pp. 11–12, 16–17, 82, *passim*; N. Macoby (1971), pp. 55–70, esp. p. 60, and R. A. Bauer (1973).

22 For more on this topic see below, chapter 3.4, ballad introduction.

23 *A Bill of Fare* (1637), by Martin Parker, *RB*, I, pp. 70–4, 1,1–1,2, p. 70.

24 *A Pleasant new Ballad you here may behold* (1630); *RB*, II, pp. 366–71; 1,5–1,6, p. 367.

25 *A Lamentable List, of certaine Hidious, Frightfull, and Prodigious Signes.* (1638), *POA*, no. 4, pp. 21–5; 1,1–1,2, p. 22.

26 *Here begins a pleasant song of a Mayden faire.* (1630?), *PB*, no. 72, II, pp. 157–61; 14,1–14,2.

27 *A pretty new Ditty: Or, A Young Lasses Resolution* (between 1601 and 1640), *RB*, II, pp. 289–94; 1,1–1,4, p. 290.

28 *The merry Old Woman* (1633), *RB*, II, pp. 163–9; 1,3.

29 *The Honest Age* (1632), *PG*, no. 71, pp. 406–9; 1,3.

30 *Leanders loue to loyall Hero* (1614), *PG*, no. 8, pp. 49–53; 1,7–1,8.

31 See examples of performance practice given above, p. 15.

32 *The Winter's Tale*, IV.4, lines 251–2, Shakespeare, *Works* (1964), pp. 399–400.

33 Ben Jonson, 'News from the New World discovered in the Moon' (1620), ed. H. Morley (1890), pp. 242–3.

34 The word 'news' already had the modern meaning of a very recent happening of special interest.

35 See C. H. Firth (1950), the chapter entitled 'Folklore and Superstition'; J. Brand (1848), esp. on belief in marvels and witches, pp. 1–90; M. St Clare Byrne (1957): 'For simple folk the marvellous lay all around them' (p. 245); 'The remote, as always, was matter for wonder but so in those days was actuality' (p. 246). E. M. W. Tillyard (1966) points out the adherence of the Elizabethans to medieval thought (p. 2 and *passim*). L. C. Knights (1951) emphasizes that 'vigour' and persuasive powers were more effective in this period than logical argument.

36 *The four Wonders of this Land* (between 1672 and 1695), RB, I, pp. 353–9, 25, 1–3, lines 97–9, p. 357.

37 *The Divils cruelty to Mankind. Being a true Relation of the Life and Death of George Gibbs* (1663), POA, no. 20, pp. 122–5; 10,5–10,6, p. 125.

38 AB, no. 65, pp. 321–7. The word 'description' here is not meant to indicate that the speaker was an eyewitness, but should be understood in the late medieval sense.

39 *The desperate Damsell's Tragedy: or, the faithlesse young Man* (1627), RB, I, pp. 264–70 (after 1615), v. 1, lines 1–10, by Martin Parker.

40 *The woful complaint of a Love-sick Maid* (between 1626 and 1681), RB, II, pp. 202–8; 1,1–1,4, p. 203. A further example of a girl's lament with this opening topos is *The lovely Northerne Lasse. Who in this ditty, here complaining, shewes / What harme she got milking her dadyes Ewes* (between 1626 and 1681), RB, I, pp. 587–92; 1,1–1,4, p. 588. Another example is *A Penny-worth of Good Counsell* (between *c.* 1624 and 1660), RB, II, pp. 294–9; 1,1–1,17, pp. 295–6.

41 *The Batchelor's Feast, or The difference betwixt a single life and a double;* (between 1628 and 1667), RB, I, pp. 46–51; 1,1–1,8, p. 47.

42 *Love in a Maze; Or, The Young Man put to his Dumps; being a gallant Discourse on May-day last between two witty Lovers* (between 1641 and 1674), RB, II, pp. 41–8, v. 1, p. 42.

43 *A Pleasant new Dialogue; Or, The discourse between the Serving-man and the Husband-man* (1626), RB, I, pp. 299–305; v. 1, p. 300.

44 *The tvvo inseparable brothers* (1639), POA, no. 2, pp. 7–14, v. 2.

45 BBLB, pp. 42–7, by Philip Stubbes, esp. v. 4,1–4,4, p. 43.

46 *The Essex man coozened by a VVhore* (1631), PB, no. 78, II, pp. 191–5; v. 2, p. 192.

47 POA, no. 3, pp. 15–20. 'Neere *Chesterfield* in Darbysheire, / In Brampton parish (as I heare)', 2,1–2,2, p. 16. See also 'of late I mette with one did tell me' in *A Balade of a Preist that loste his nose* (probably end of the sixteenth century), AB, no. 38, pp. 206–11; 1,1–1,2, p. 206.

48 'The truth of which is known both far and wide / And hath by many men been justified', *The Disturbed Ghost* (*c.* 1775), POA, no. 29, pp. 172–8; 2,1–2,2, p. 175.

49 PG, no. 54, pp. 309–15, by Martin Parker.

50 For a consideration of the affective area in persuasion strategies, see P. Teigeler (1968), p. 17 and *passim*; N. Macoby (1971), pp. 67–9.

51 See E. R. Curtius (1965), p. 183; p. 441 for the function of *adtestatio rei visae* as a means of arousing pathos.

52 The ballad is based on a historically documented occurrence; see H. E. Rollins, PG, n. pp. 276–7.

53 *A pleasant history of a Gentleman in Thracia* (1633), *RB*, II, pp. 262–7; 1,1–1,2, p. 263.

54 'The existence of a source was more important for that tradition-bound civilisation than was the specification of the particular source', L. Spitzer (1942), p. 416, n. 3; P. A. Christensen (1927), pp. 67–77, mentions only this type of claim to authenticity.

55 See also: *A most notable example of an ungracious Son* (between 1601 and 1640), *RB*, II, pp. 73–9; 1,1–1,4, p. 74. *The Map of Mock-begger hall, with his scituation in the spacious Countrey called Anywhere* (between 1633 and 1652), *RB*, II, pp. 132–6; 1,1, p. 132. Reference to a biblical source, *A proper New Balad of the Bryber Gehesie. Taken out of the fourth booke of Kinges, the V. chapter* (1566/7), *AB*, no. 13, pp. 61–5; see also 1,3–1,5, p. 61 and 8,3, p. 63.

56 On this topic see also *Warning* and *Advice* below, chapter 3.3.3.

57 For a more detailed account, see below under 'presenter's reference to the outside world', chapter 3.4.1.

58 *The Tragedy of Hero and Leander* (*c.* 1649), *RB*, VI, pp. 556–9; 1,1–1,4, p. 558.

59 See above, pp. 35–7, where this is explained.

60 See e.g. *The Wooing Maid*, pp. 165–7 below.

61 *The* Frenchmens *VVonder* (1621), *PG*, no. 26, pp. 161–5; 1,1, p. 162.

62 *The Mad Man's Morrice* (1637), *RB*, II, pp. 153–8; v. 14, line 111, p. 158.

63 *PG*, no. 45, pp. 256–62; 13, 1–4, p. 260.

64 *The cryes of the Dead. Or the late Murther in South-warke* (*c.* 1625), *PG*, no. 39, pp. 222–5; v. 6, pp. 224–5.

65 Types of public address in the Middle English verse romance tend, however, to be stereotyped, having little thematic relevance. The greeting 'Lordings' recurs, though this did not necessarily imply a noble audience (see P. A. Christensen (1927), pp. 37–8). In addition, forms of general address are used such as 'old and young', 'good men', 'wives', 'maidens', 'all men' (ibid., p. 39), which are also used in the street ballad. We can assume that there was some personal contact between the late medieval minstrel and the balladmonger (see above, pp. 22–3), which may account for the adopting of individual formulas. What is indisputable is the further differentiation and expansion of the presenter's various functions in the forms of address of the street ballad. Comparisons can be made with later forms of address in prologues and epilogues, as for instance in Dryden, which are directed at certain groups: 'Critics', 'Cits', 'Sparks', 'Fops', 'Punks', 'Gallants', 'Wits', 'Ladies'. See H. Castrop (1972).

66 On the generally limited development of the presenter communication level in the early street ballads, see below, chapter 3.5.4 and chapter 5.3.

67 *The songe of the death of mr.* Thewlis (1616), *OEB*, no. 13, pp. 87–100; v. 29, p. 100.

68 *The songe mr.* Thewlis *writ him selfe* (1616), *OEB*, no. 12, pp. 79–86; 1,1–4, p. 80.

69 *A proper newe sonet declaring the lamentation of Beckles* (1586), *AB*, no. 21, pp. 118–23, 10,1–2, p. 121.

70 *An excellent Ditty made vpon the great victory, which the French king obtayned against the Duke de Maine* (1590), *BB*, no. 53, pp. 156–8, 1,1–1,4,

p. 156. For further examples of this form of address, see *A Complaynt agaynst the wicked enemies of Christ* (1664), BB, no. 16, pp. 46–9, 1,1–4, p. 46. *A Ballad reioysinge the sodaine fall, Of rebels that thought to deuower vs all* (between 1570 and 1593), AB, no. 79, pp. 392–7. 'Aryse and wak, for Christis sake' (*c.* between 1550 and 1560), SB, no. 52, pp. 168–9, lines 1–8, p. 168.

71 *A ninuectyue agaynst Treason* (1553), OEB, no. 1,1–7; 1,1–2, p. 2.

72 *Remember Death, and thou shalt neuer sinne* (1569), BB, no. 2, 3–4; 1,1–2, p. 3.

73 (From the reign of Queen Elizabeth, not later than 1576), OEB, no. 51, pp. 281–4. See also *God doth blesse this realme* (*c.* 1570), OEB, no. 26, pp. 180–3, where the national community is apostrophized as 'England' (10, 1–3, p. 182).

74 For a comparatively differentiated and thematically relevant address, see also *A Ballad intituled, Prepare ye to the plowe* (1669/70); AB, no. 50, pp. 259–63; 1,1–4, p. 259. *A warning vnto repentaunce and of* christes *comming vnto Judgement* (probably between 1586 and 1595), OEB, no. 42, pp. 240–4, where princes, dukes, bishops and all men and women are warned about the Last Judgement.

75 *A godly ditty or prayer to be song vnto God* (between 1557 and 1575), AB, no. 32, pp. 176–9, 1,1, p. 177.

76 *The Refuge of a Sinner* (1565), BB, no. 15, pp. 44–5; 1,1–2, p. 44.

77 *The songe of the death of mr.* Thewlis (1616), OEB, no. 13, pp. 87–100; v. 30, p. 100; see also v. 1, p. 88. Other prayer-like ballads: *The prayer of the Prophet Daniel* (*c.* 1553), BBLB, pp. 6–8; *A prayer and also a thanksgiving* (1577), BBLB, pp. 16–20. *A godly and vertuous songe or Ballade* (end of the sixteenth century), OEB, no. 8, pp. 47–53; vv. 21–2, p. 52. *O blessed God, O Sauiour sweete* (*c.* 1616), OEB, no. 16, pp. 114–18; v. 1, p. 114; v. 12, p. 116; v. 21, p. 118. *A godly ballad declaring by the Scriptures* (1566), AB, no. 26, pp. 149–53, vv. 2–4, p. 149; vv. 5–6, p. 150.

78 Various forms of prayer also form a fixed introductory convention in the Middle English verse romance (see P. A. Christensen [1927], pp. 47–61), whereby the minstrel was looking to secure the most harmonious relationship with a religious audience which was orientated towards the hereafter, and to justify his narrative intention (ibid., pp. 57–9).

79 Poems in praise of Queen Mary: *An* AVE MARIA *in Commendation of our most Vertuous Queene* (between 1553 and 1558), OEB, no. 3, pp. 13–18; in praise of music: *A songe in praise of musique* (1603), OEB, no. 21, pp. 142–6; in praise of the Holy City: *A song made by F.B.P.* (end of the sixteenth century?), OEB, no. 24, pp. 163–9; in praise of Calvary: *Caluarie mount is my delight* (*c.* 1616), OEB, no. 22, pp. 147–51.

80 See below, chapter 3.3.3.

81 See above, chapter 3.2.2, where examples have already been given.

82 See P. A. Christensen (1927), pp. 38–9, 45.

83 *The life and death of M.* Geo: Sands (1626), PG, no. 44, pp. 248–55; 1,1–1,2, p. 250.

84 *The Cooper of Norfolke* (between 1625 and 1660), RB, I, pp. 98–104; 1,1–1,2, p. 99.

85 *A famous Sea-fight* (1639), POA, no. 5, 26–30; 1,1–1,2, p. 27.

86 *A most wonderful and sad judgement of God upon* . . . (1661), *POA*, no. 11, pp. 62–7; 1,1–1,2, p. 64.
87 *A Warning-peice for Ingroosers of Corne* (1643), *POA*, no. 6, 31–5, 1,1–4, p. 32.
88 *The Constant VVive of Sussex* (1632), *PB*, no. 85, II, pp. 229–33; 1,1 and 1,4, p. 230.
89 *A Warning for all Murderers* (1638), *RB*, III, pp. 136–43; 1,1–4, II, 1–4, p. 137.
90 *John Spenser a Chesshire Gallant* (c. 1626), *PG*, no. 45, pp. 256–62; 1,1–4, p. 257.
91 This element of the showman's procedure is also largely absent in the early street ballad.
92 *A new merry Ballad I haue here to shew,* / *Come pence a peece for them,* / *I tell you but so* (1629), *PB*, no. 66, II, pp. 116–23; v. 26, pp. 122–3.
93 L. B. Wright (1964) gives a detailed account of the didactic claims of the 'low literature' of the time and remarks at one point 'Pamphlets describing murders and other crimes were recommended as warning pieces and were so interpreted by their readers' (p. 100). He does not, however, attempt a genre-specific terminology of the period, let alone of the street ballad, which he examines along with other forms of literature of instruction and entertainment.
94 See Wright (1964), pp. 91–105, 293–6, 376–8, 383, 401–2, 607–8; 'utilitarian qualities and virtues were attributed to much Elizabethan literature that might otherwise have been damned as idle and frivolous' (p. 102). See also Sheavyn (1909), p. 180.
95 The position of the street ballad, especially within the context of the tradition of didactic justification of literature, is a subject which is worth investigating in detail: in relation to the verse romance, for instance, where a story from the past is praised as a model; or to mirrors for princes; or the *Refutatio* (for instance in Chaucer's *Troilus and Criseyde* or his 'Balada de Bon Conseyl'); or religious songs in the Ashmolean MS 48 and the collection 'The Gude and Godlie Ballatis' (1567).
96 For a more detailed examination of the presenter's methods of referring to the content, see below, chapter 3.4.2.
97 The following are isolated examples: *A warnyng to Englan[d], let London begin: To repent their iniquitie, & flie from their sin* (1564/5) by William Birch, *BB*, no. 9, pp. 25–6. The immediate occasions of this exhortation to repent and reform were the collapse of the tower of St Paul's in 1561, the defeat against France at Le Havre in 1563 and the outbreak of the plague. *A warning to all false Traitors By Example of 14. Whereof VI were executed in divers places neere about London, and 2 neere Braintford, the 28. day of August, 1588, BBLB*, pp. 57–62. Interestingly enough these ballads already contain the specific terminology, in contrast to general religious exhortations.
98 *The father hath beguil'd the sonne* (1629), *PG*, no. 54, pp. 309–15; v. 16, pp. 314–15. By offering a large inheritance, the ageing father persuades his son's bride to marry him instead of his son. The son stabs himself to death, whereupon the father is driven mad with remorse and the unfaithful girl drowns herself in a well.
99 *A warning for wiues, By the example of one* Katherine Francis, *alias* Stoke,

who for killing her husband, Robert Francis *with a paire of Sizers, on the 8. of Aprill at night, was burned on* Clarkenwell-greene, *on Tuesday, the 21 of the same moneth, 1629* (1629), by Martin Parker, *PG*, no. 52, pp. 299–304; v. 15, p. 304.

100 *A new merry Ballad I haue here to shew* (1629), *PB*, no. 66, II, pp. 116–23; 1,5–1,8, p. 117. The ballad describes a series of political and social ills; the appeal in the refrain reinforces the didactic intention.

101 'Aryse and wak . . .' (between *c.* 1550 and 1565), *SB*, no. 52, pp. 168–9; lines 1–8, p. 168. The song exhorts listeners to remorse and repentance of sins with the appropriate vocabulary: *confes* (line 29), *repent* (lines 200; 34), *vengence* (lines 12; 46), *God's rod* (line 45), *mercy* (line 41), *Christes blod* (line 29).

102 'Take hede in tyme' (between *c.* 1550 and 1565), *SB*, no. 10, pp. 29–31; v. 1, p. 29. There follow reflections on the transitoriness and frailty of earthly life, accompanied by the appeal in the refrain 'Therfor take hede', which the later street ballad adopted as a formula.

103 'Awak, rych men' (between 1550–65), *SB*, no. 33, pp. 111–14; v. 1, p. 111. The appeal to the rich to help the poor is well within the tradition of the Christian–ethical hymn, while later street ballads were much more concrete in their treatment of socially critical topics.

104 Further examples: 'Say weill is gude, bot do weill is better' (mid-sixteenth century, A. F. Mitchell [1897], pp. 207–8). *Seeke wisdome cheefly to obteine* (*c.* 1616), *OEB*, no. 38, pp. 226–8. *A warning vnto repentaunce and of* christes *comming vnto Judgement* (*c.* 1586–95), *OEB*, no. 42, pp. 240–4. A ballad by Laurence Price stands at the close of this tradition. It is noticeable that he already takes a story as an example, namely that of Job, in order to link his exhortations to it: *Bee Patient in Trouble; or the Patient Man's Counsell* (1636), *RB*, III, pp. 174–8.

105 *A proper new balade expressyng the fames, / Concerning a warning to al London dames* (1570/71), *BB*, no. 71, pp. 206–8. The admonitory voice in this ballad first praises beauty and virtue, courtly behaviour and the taste of the titled ladies of London, only to remind them later, in an anticlimax, of death and transitoriness.

106 Other examples are: *The lamentable fall of Queen El[li]nor; who for her pride and wickednesse, by God's judgement, sunke into the ground at Charing-crosse and rose up at Queene Hive* (between 1619 and 1629), *RB*, II, pp. 67–73; esp. v. 20, lines 153–60, p. 73. *The Woful Lamentation of Mrs Jane Shore, a Gold-smith's Wife of London, some-time King Edward the Fourth's Concubine, who for her Wanton Life came to a Miserable End* (1603), *RB*, I, pp. 479–92; esp. v. 37, pp. 147–52, p. 488 and *The second part*: v. 21, lines 273–8, p. 492. *John Spenser a Chesshire Gallant, his life and repentance* (*c.* 1626), *PG*, no. 45, pp. 256–62; esp. vv. 21–2, pp. 261–2. *The life and death of M. Geo: Sands, who after many enormous crimes by him committed, with* Iones *and* Gent *his confederates, was executed at Tyburne on Wednesday the 6 of September, 1626* (1626), *PG*, no. 44, pp. 248–55; esp. v. 17, p. 254. *A most excellent new Ballad of an Olde Man and his Wife, in their olde age and misery, which sought to their owne Children for succour, by whom they were disdained* (end of sixteenth century and seventeenth century), *RB*, II, pp. 347–52; esp. v. 13,5–6, lines 114–15, p. 351. *The desperate Damsells Tragedy, or the Faithlesse Young Man* (1627), *RB*, I, pp. 264–70

(after 1615), esp. v. 13, p. 107. *A fearefull and terrible Example of Gods iuste iudgement executed vpon a lewde Fellow* (between 1591 and 1603), *BBLB*, pp. 42–7; esp. vv. 13–14, p. 46. *A Maruellous Murther, Committed vpon the Body of one* George Drawnfield (1638), *POA*, no. 3, pp. 15–20; esp. vv. 29–30, p. 20. *A Warning for all Murderers. A most rare, strange, and wonderfull accident, which by God's just judgement was brought to passe* (1638), *RB*, III, pp. 136–43. *The Mad Man's Morrice: wherin you shall finde / His trouble and grief, and discontent of his minde; / A warning to young men to have a care, / How they in love intangled are* (1637), *RB*, II, pp. 153–8.

107 *A merry Jest of John Tomson and Jakaman his wife, / Whose jealousie was justly the cause of all their strife* (1586), *RB*, II, pp. 136–42; esp. v. 18, 4–18,8, lines 164–7, p. 142.

108 *A goodfellowes complaint against strong beere, Or Take heed goodfellowes for heere you may see / How it is strong beere that hath vndone me* (c. 1630), *PG*, no. 63, pp. 361–4; v. 1, p. 361.

109 *The Cruell Shrow: Or, The Patient Man's Woe* (between 1601 and 1640), *RB*, I, pp. 93–8; v. 1, lines 1–8, p. 94; by Arthur Halliarg. See also *The Batchelor's Feast, or The difference betwixt a single life and a double* (between 1628 and 1667), *RB*, I, pp. 46–51; esp. v. 12, lines 106–17, p. 51; by Laurence Price.

110 *A Warning for Maides; / Or, The false dissembling, cogging, / Cunning, cozening young man: / Who long did try and use his skill / To wo[o] a coy young maid to his will; / And when he had obtain'd her love, / To her he very false did prove* (between 1634 and 1667), by Richard Climsall, *RB*, III, pp. 41–6; esp. vv. 22–3, lines 85–92, p. 46. *Here begins a pleasant song of a Mayden faire, / To purchase her desire, her Coine she did not spare, / And shee most freely parted with her money / To a Youngman, the which shee call'd her dearest Honey* (c. 1630), *PB*, no. 72, II, pp. 157–61; esp. v. 24, p. 161.

111 *A Prouerbe old, yet nere forgot / Tis good to strike while the Irons hott* (between 1625 and 1650), *PG*, no. 40, pp. 229–33; vv. 1, 2 and 4, pp. 229–30.

112 *A merry Song of a rich Widdowes wooing, / That married a young man to her owne vndoing* (c. 1625), *PB*, no. 43, I, pp. 257–61, v. 16, p. 261.

113 *A new merry Ballad I haue here to shew, / Come pence a peece for them, / I tell you but so* (1629), *PB*, no. 66, II, pp. 116–23. *The Virgin's A, B, C; Or, An Alphabet of vertuous Admonitions for a chaste, modest, and well-governed Maid* (between 1626 and 1681), *RB*, II, pp. 650–4. As opposed to practical, worldly advice, religious exhortation is comparatively rare in the seventeenth-century street ballad. *An excellent Song, wherein you shall finde / Great consolation for a troubled minde* (between 1619 and 1629), *RB*, I, pp. 325–30. *Good Admonition Or To al sorts of people this counsell I sing, / That in each ones affaire, to take heed's a faire thing* (1633), *PB*, no. 87, II, pp. 239–43.

114 *A Table of Good Nurture. Wherin is contained a Schoolemaster's admonition to his Schollers to learne good manners, the Father to his Children to learne vertue; and the Housholder to his Servants to learne godlinesse* (1624), *RB*, II, pp. 569–75.

115 Empirical research on advertising provides illustrations on this point. See N. Macoby (1971), p. 61; P. Teigeler (1968), p. 93.

116 *Good Counsell for young Wooers* (1633), RB, I, pp. 422–7; 2,1, line 19, p. 423.

117 *Nobody his Counsaile to chuse a Wife* (c. 1626), PG, no. 46, pp. 263–9; 15,2, p. 269. *The Cucking of a Scould* (c. 1615), PG, no. 12, pp. 72–7; 5,5, p. 74.

118 *Good Counsell for young Wooers*, RB, I, 10,4, line 80, p. 426. *A Prouerbe old, yet nere forgot. / Tis good to strike while the Irons hott* (between 1625 and 1650), PG, no. 40, pp. 229–33; as refrain.

119 'To be jealous', see F. P. Wilson (1970), p. 925. *A merry Jest of John Tomson* (1586), RB, II, pp. 136–42.

120 *A Caueat or VVarning* (c. 1620), PB, no. 20, I, pp. 128–32; 1,2–1,3, p. 129.

121 *I Smell a Rat* (c. 1630), PB, no. 69, II, pp. 139–44. See *The Oxford Dictionary of Quotations* (London, 1966), 110, no. 25 and 407, no. 8.

122 *O yes! If any man or woman any thing desire* (between 1620 and 1629), RB, II, pp. 352–7; 2,5–2,6, lines 15–16, p. 354.

123 Ibid., 5,7–5,8, lines 44–5, p. 354; again a proverbial expression.

124 *A Ditty delightfull of mother Watkins ale* (c. 1590), AB, no. 76, pp. 370–5, 8,9, p. 375. For this ballad see also above, p. 70.

125 *The praise of Nothing* (between 1601 and 1640), RB, II, pp. 339–44; 14,5–14,7, lines 109–11, p. 344. 'Flea in one's ear': 'a stinging reproof, which sends one away discomfited'; see F. P. Wilson (1970), p. 267.

126 I have confined myself here to a few selected examples. The street-ballad colloquial element will be referred to again several times in other contexts: see under discursive street ballad: *Come, buy this new Ballad*, below, pp. 203–4. *The XXV orders of Fooles*, below, pp. 218–19; also street-ballad 'Medleys', below, pp. 208–12.

127 Of the 80 texts in total in the edition: *A Pepysian Garland*, ed. H. E. Rollins (1922), 19 for instance have a refrain: PG, nos. 10, 12, 37, 41, 42, 52, 55, 56, 59, 62, 64, 69, 70, 72, 73, 76, 77, 78, 80.

128 For 'Refrain der broadside-ballads', see W. Weiss (1964), pp. 34–8.

129 *The vnnaturall Wife* (1628), PG, no. 49, pp. 283–7, v. 2, p. 284.

130 *The Cucking of a Scould* (c. 1615), PG, no. 12, pp. 72–7; on this ballad, see also below, p. 111, p. 130, p. 139.

131 RB, I, pp. 136–41; see also below, pp. 175–6.

132 PG, no. 55, pp. 316–22; for this ballad see also above, pp. 44–5, and below, p. 205.

133 PG, no. 40, pp. 229–33.

134 *A merry Ballad, both pleasant and sweete, . . .* (1661), RB, II, pp. 126–31.

135 This can be deduced from contemporary documents; for more detail, see under 'Reception and effect', pp. 250–2 below.

136 This frequently has a brief announcement of theme: see P. A. Christensen (1927), pp. 61–6.

137 *Leanders loue to loyall Hero* (1614), PG, no. 8, pp. 49–53; v. 1, pp. 49–50.

138 *Damnable Practises Of three Lincoln-shire Witches* (c. 1615), PG, no. 16, pp. 96–103; v. 1, p. 97.

139 *The life and death of M. Geo: Sands, who after many enormous crimes by him committed, with Iones and Gent his confederates, was executed at Tyburne on Wednesday the 6 of September, 1626* (1626), PG, no. 44, pp. 248–55; v. 2, p. 251.

140 This also applies to book titles of the time, which were usually extensive. Dif-

ferences between these and street-ballad titles, both in style and intention, would be worth investigating. The opening verse as trailer is specific to the street ballad.

141 See above, p. 61, with relevant quotations.

142 *[Dice, Wine and Women] /, or, The vnfortunate Gallant gull'd at London* (*c.* 1625), PB, no. 39, I, pp. 237–41; v. 1, p. 238.

143 *A merry Jest of John Tomson and Jakaman his wife / Whose jealousie was justly the cause of all their strife* (1586), RB, II, pp. 136–42; 1,1–8, p. 137.

144 *A merry Progresse to London to see Fashions, by a young Country Gallant, that had more Money then Wittz* (*c.* 1620), PB, no. 23, I, pp. 148–55; v. 1, p. 151.

145 *A Batchelers Resolution* (1629), PB, no. 65, II, pp. 110–15; v. 1, p. 111.

146 *The XXV orders of Fooles* (1569/70), AB, no. 23, pp. 128–36; 1,1–2, p. 128.

147 See also Primary texts, pp. 323–39.

148 See *The Honor of the Inns of Court Gentlemen* (between 1633 and 1643), BBLB, pp. 112–17; 1,1–1,6, p. 113. *The songe of the death of mr.* Thewlis (1616), OEB, no. 13, pp. 87–100; v. 36, p. 94. *Whipping Cheare* (*c.* 1612), PG, no. 6, pp. 39–43; and others.

149 For this topic see L. L. Schücking (1961), pp. 18–20. There is a possible link here between the street-ballad presenter's trailer and the 'presenter' of the strolling players, though the latter's activities can only be guessed at. See R. Weimann (1967), pp. 55, 139–40, 164, 174–5, 181, 249.

150 E.g. interview, letter, telephone conversation etc. See B.Sandig (1972) who includes this procedure in her catalogue of features determining types of text; see also R. Harweg (1968).

151 PB, no. 72, II, pp. 157–71; (*c.* 1630?).

152 *A New Medley, Or, A Messe of All-together* (between 1624 and 1660), RB, II, pp. 239–45; 16,1; line 121, p. 245; by Martin Parker.

153 *Friendly Counsaile* (1633), RB, I, pp. 65–9; 21,1, line 127, p. 69. Also similar in formulation: *This Maide would giue tenne Shillings for a Kisse* (*c.* 1615), PG, no. 13, pp. 78–83; 23,1, p. 83.

154 *Turners dish of Lentten stuffe* (1612), PG, no. 5, pp. 30–8; 27,5, p. 38.

155 *The life and death of M. Geo. Sands, who after many enormous crimes by him committed, . . . was executed at Tyburne . . .* (1626), PG, no. 44, pp. 248–55; 17,1–17,2, p. 255.

156 *A most excellent new Ballad of an Olde Man and his Wife . . .* (end of the sixteenth century and seventeenth century), RB, II, pp. 347–52; 13,5–13,6; lines 115–16, p. 351.

157 *An excellent Ballad of the Mercer's Son of Midhurst and the Cloathier's Daughter of Guilford* (seventeenth century), RB, II, pp. 189–97; 20,1–20,2, lines 153–4, 194.

158 *The vnnaturall Wife . . .* (1628), PG, no. 49, pp. 283–7; 14,1, p. 287.

159 *Natures Wonder? OR, [A True acc]ount how the Wife of one* John Waterman *an Ostler in the Parish of* Fisherton-Anger, *near* Salisbury, *was Delivered of a strange Monster* (1664), POA, no. 23, pp. 139–45, vv. 1–2, pp. 141–2. See also below, pp. 155–6, for presenter's comments in other monster ballads.

160 See *A new merry Ballad I haue here to shew* (1629), PB, no. 66, II, pp. 116–23, also v. 1, p. 117. *The Cruell Shrow* (between 1601 and 1640), RB, I, pp. 93–8; 1,3–1,4, lines 3–4, p. 94; and several others.

161 In the archaic sense of 'neighbourliness'.
162 Ibid., v. 12, lines 45–8, p. 128.
163 Ibid., v. 16, lines 61–4, p. 129. See *Brewer's Dictionary*, ed. I. H. Evans (1970), p. 89.
164 Ibid., v. 26, lines 100–4, p. 130.
165 Ibid., v. 15, lines 57–60, p. 129. See *Brewer's Dictionary* (1970), p. 543.
166 Ibid., v. 31, lines 125–8, p. 130.
167 'Quite clear, obvious, and unmistakable', see *Brewer's Dictionary* (1970), p. 834. v. 17, lines 65–8, p. 129.
168 V. 21, lines 81–4, p. 129. See *Brewer's Dictionary* (1970), p. 442: 'One course in a race; that part of a race run as "instalment" of the main event. One, two or more heats make a race.'
169 V. 19, lines 73–6, p. 129.
170 V. 35, lines 141–4, p. 131. See also *Brewer's Dictionary* (1970), p. 411.
171 This is the earliest extant version of the text; see W. Chappell, II, p. 126.
172 See *The Praise of Brotherhood*, quoted above, pp. 92–3.
173 See *The Praise of Nothing*, quoted above, pp. 94–5.
174 See H. E. Rollins (1919a), pp. 292–3.
175 *RB*, I, pp. 417–21 and *PB*, no. 65, II, pp. 110–15. For a more detailed interpretation see below, pp. 170–1.
176 'The Blazing Torch'; see W. Chappell's commentary, *RB*, I, p. 417.
177 *RB*, III, pp. 237–42 and ibid., pp. 242–8.
178 *CM*, no. clx, pp. 315–17 and *CM*, no. clxi, pp. 317–19.
179 *PG*, no. 71, II, pp. 406–9 and *PG*, no. 72, II, pp. 410–14. For interpretations see below, pp. 196–8.
180 See especially the varying form of the refrain. For an example of two narrative ballads which are linked to each other in their similarity of theme (seduction of two and three girls respectively by the same man) see *Newes from the Tower-hill: Or, A gentle warning to Peg and* Kate / *To walke no more abroad so late* (1631), *PG*, no. 66, pp. 376–9, and *A good throw for three Maidenheads* (1631), *PG*, no. 67, pp. 380–5.
181 H. E. Rollins does make some preliminary remarks on this topic: (1919a), pp. 288–9.
182 On this topic see also individual ballads which show presenters' attitudes and activities regarding their subject in the figure of the (market-)crier: *O, yes! If any man or woman any thing desire, Let them repaire forthwith unto the Cryer* (between 1620 and 1629), *RB*, II, pp. 352–7; in the figure of the salesman, *The Pedler opening of his Packe* (c. 1620), *PG*, no. 19, pp. 116–20; in the figure of the rat-catcher, *The Famous Ratketcher* (c. 1615, *PG*, no. 10, pp. 60–5; and in the reproduction of street-cries, *Turners dish of Lentten stuffe* (1612), *PG*, no. 5, pp. 30–8.
183 Ibid., vv. 1–2, pp. 55–6; 'impes', abbreviation of 'imperial'; the present power of the Devil is meant here.
184 *A proper newe sonet declaring the lamentation of Beckles [a market towne in] Suffolke, which was in the great winde vpon S. Andrewes eue last past most pittifully burned with fire* (1586), *AB*, no. 21, pp. 118–23; 1,5–8, p. 118. The devastated town is personified as the narrator.
185 *Franklins Farewell to the World* (1615 or 1616), *AB*, no. 22, pp. 124–7; lines 17–18, p. 125.

4 Sub-genres of the street ballad

1 See K. W. Hempfer (1973), esp. pp. 155–64.
2 To my knowledge there has so far been no adequate classification of types of text belonging to this category.
3 'Discourse' denotes, in textual linguistics, a sequence of sentences or utterances showing certain coherence factors. See Z. S. Harris (1952); I. Bellert (1970).
4 Only in the didactically orientated literature of roguery and in Nashe's *The Unfortunate Traveller* do we find a more evolved level of explicit narrator.
5 *A feareful and terrible Example* (between 1591 and 1603), *BBLB*, pp. 42–7; 2,2-4; 3,1–3; p. 43.
6 *AB*, no. 27, pp. 154–62. 'Pining' without the double 'n' is likely to be misunderstood by the modern reader.
7 (Recorded in second half of the seventeenth century, but probably older; see bibliography); *RB*, II, pp. 391–8.
8 *A Caueat or VVarning. For all sortes of Men both young and olde, to auoid the Company of lewd and wicked Woemen* (*c.* 1620), *PB*, no. 20, I, pp. 128–32, 1,3–4, p. 129.
9 *RB*, I, pp. 479–92; see also below, pp. 132–4.
10 A change of narrative perspective is also found in *An excellent Ballad of the Mercer's Son of Midhurst and the Cloathier's Daughter of Guilford* (seventeenth century), *RB*, II, pp. 189–97.
11 See further examples below, pp. 139–40
12 See also a ballad from the second half of the seventeenth century, *The Fox-Chace* (*RB*, I, pp. 359–64), where the narrator is first witness to the foxhunt, then active participator.
13 The refrain contains an explicit appeal to the audience.
14 *RB*, v. 5, lines 49–57, pp. 138–9. The colour yellow is used symbolically as a sign of jealousy.
15 The description of the healing of Naaman's leprosy, nature of the rewards, etc.
16 See Book of Jonah, chapter 4; the following lines are taken verbatim from the Authorized Version: 1,2; 1,7; 2,1–2; 2,4; 3,1; p. 67 and elsewhere.
17 *OEB*, no. 13, v. 11, p. 90; cf. the verse 'What stedfastnes . . .', quoted above.
18 *AB*, no. 17, pp. 88–93. For the treatment of the motif 'wife hides lover in chest or similar' in German and English ballads, see K. Roth (1977), p. 95; for this ballad see pp. 376–7 (could not be analysed in detail).
19 *RB*, I, 2,1–4, lines 7–10, p. 99. For the motif of the hidden lover see also the 10th story of the 5th book of the *Decameron*.
20 *RB*, II, pp. 366–71; see also above, pp. 113–14. For the same motif, see also Child no. 278.
21 See the standard work on this topic by R. Wehse (1979), where over 500 types of content of comic street ballads are given.
22 For a hierarchical description of isotopic levels (syntagmatic dimension, level of specification and complexity), see W. Kallmeyer *et al.* (1974), I, pp. 143–61. A study of isotopes as an analytical starting-point for 'readings' of a text has been made by A. J. Greimas, ibid., vol. 2, pp. 126–52 and F. Rastier, ibid., pp. 153–90.

23 *PG*, no. 12, pp. 72–7; see above, pp. 111.

24 See vv. 4–5, lines 31–48, *RB*, II, p. 138.

25 See vv. 7–10,7, lines 58–96, ibid., pp. 139–40.

26 See v. 11, lines 97–105, ibid., p. 140.

27 See J. M. Lotman (1972), pp. 340–68; M. Pfister (1977), pp. 220–64.

28 See pp. 111 and 130 above for more on this ballad.

29 *PG*, no. 39, pp. 222–5. See pp. 130–1 above for more on this ballad.

30 See pp. 115–16 and p. 132 above for more on this ballad.

31 *John Spenser a Chesshire Gallant* (c. 1626), *PG*, no. 45, pp. 256–62; vv. 2–3, p. 257.

32 *A Pleasant new Ballad* (1630), *RB*, II, pp. 366–71; see above, p. 128.

33 (Between 1586 and 1618), *RB*, II, pp. 86–95; see above, pp. 126 and 135.

34 (Between 1601 and 1640), *RB*, II, pp. 73–9; see also above, p. 125 for this ballad.

35 See vv. 5–11, lines 41–96, *RB*, II, pp. 75–7.

36 See also *The* Essex *man coozened by a* VV*hore* (1631), *PB*, no. 78, II, pp. 191–5, esp. v. 4, p. 192; v. 7,5, p. 193; v. 9, p. 193. *A merry Progresse to London* (c. 1620), *PB*, no. 23, I, pp. 148–55, where the explicit self-characterization is found mainly at the beginning.

37 This title is a logical emendation of the subtitle given: OR *The vnfortunate Gallant gull'd at London* (c. 1625), *PB*, no. 39, I, pp. 237–41.

38 See textual examples, p. 111 and p. 138 above.

39 *The Cooper of Norfolke* (between 1625 and 1660), *RB*, I, pp. 98–104; see also above, pp. 127–8, and Martin Parker's ballad showing a similar procedure: *The father hath beguil'd the sonne*, pp. 136–7 above.

40 *A merry Jest of John Tomson and Jakaman his wife* (1586), *RB*, II, pp. 136–42; see also pp. 119–20 above.

41 (1633), *PG*, no. 75, pp. 425–30, by Martin Parker.

42 Ibid., v. 5,2, p. 426; see also v. 8,2, p. 427; v. 13,2, p. 428, and the opening verse, p. 425.

43 *The Marchant's Daughter of Bristow* (between 1586 and 1618), vv. 5–6, lines 17–24, *RB*, II, p. 87.

44 *A pleasant history of a Gentleman in Thracia*, *RB*, II, pp. 262–7.

45 *A most notable example* (between 1601 and 1640), vv. 6–9, lines 47–72, *RB*, II, pp. 75–7. *The Cobler of Colchester* (between 1589 and 1603), v. 2, *BBLB*, 32. *The Marchant's Daughter*, v. 52, lines 205–8, *RB*, II, p. 93.

46 *A merry Jest of John Tomson* (1586), v. 9,1–9,4, lines 88–91, *RB*, II, p. 140.

47 *The father hath beguil'd the sonne* (1629), vv. 10–11, *PG*, pp. 312–13.

48 *A merie newe Ballad intituled, the Pinnyng of the Basket* (between 1570 and 1593), vv. 6,1–6,4 and 7,6–7,9, *AB*, pp. 155–6.

49 *The Cobler of Colchester*, *BBLB*, v. 6,1–6,8, pp. 33–4.

50 H. E. Rollins (1919a) makes the sweeping statement: 'and perhaps the best way in which to judge the broadside ballad as a whole *is* frankly to compare it with the modern newspaper' (p. 265).

51 See A. B. Friedmann (1961), pp. 49–53. Rollins (1919), p. 333 uses for this the somewhat misleading term 'lyrics' (as opposed to 'news ballad' or 'journalistic ballad'), which Friedmann uses more precisely as a sub-category of the 'literary ballad', assigning to it the highest status in this group

(pp. 51–3), V. de Sola Pinto (1957) contrasts ballads which he describes as 'popular journalism of the day' with other groups, without making value distinctions.

52 See Rollins (1919a), p. 333; Friedmann (1961), pp. 49–50.

53 The year 1622 is generally pinpointed as marking the beginning of the rise of the newspaper. That year saw the (irregular) publication of a journal with no fixed title but which went down in the history of newspapers as the *Weekly Journal*. M. A. Shaaber (1966) has extensively investigated the period from the introduction of printing in England to 1620. J. Frank (1961) investigates the subsequent period, giving an account of the rise of the newspaper.

54 Both chapbooks and pamphlets are unbound, uncut 'booklets'. The chapbook consists of one sheet, folded at varying intervals and therefore differing in format. The pamphlet is thicker. The book on the other hand is bound, and also usually thicker. See L. Shepard (1973), pp. 224–5.

55 For a bibliographical and content classification, see Shaaber (1966). 'Personal news', 'official news', 'news published under partisan auspices' and 'popular news' are further sub-categorized. Pre-journalistic printed material and authors are also taken into account as further investigatory and classificatory aspects.

56 See J. Frank (1961), pp. 17, 214, 242, 271; he makes only ocasional and cursory mention of the street ballad, and clearly does not regard it as being relevant to the history of the newspaper.

57 A survey of the tables of contents and full titles in the extant ballad editions shows the relatively high frequency of the label 'new' – largely irrespective of content – while 'true relation' etc. is usually reserved for sensational and miraculous reports. See also above, pp. 47–9.

58 See e.g. the *POA* collection of texts.

59 These would be news-type publications in chapbooks and pamphlets; see M. A. Shaaber (1966), pp. 196–7, 224. H. E. Rollins (1919a), pp. 272–3, however, cites instances of the use of ballads as historical sources by historians.

60 See M. A. Shaaber (1966), pp. 193–4.

61 In the present debate on the concept of fiction, a pragmatic definition has been arrived at. See J. Landwehr (1975), esp. pp. 157–99; N. Würzbach (1984), pp. 1105–11.

62 See above, chapter 1.2.3, esp. pp. 24–5. Rollins draws attention to the small number of ballad entries in the Stationers Register for the years 1641–7, attributing this to the circumvention of the compulsory registration and the forging of licences, although it was precisely during this period that the political ballad must have exerted enormous influence on public opinion (*CP*, pp. 11–14).

63 Neither Rollins, Chappell nor Ebsworth gives any opinion on this. Shaaber (1966) shows no interest in a diachronic differentiation regarding this aspect in the case of the news ballad.

64 See summary of these below, chapter 5.3.

65 In this ballad it is a courier who travels from London to Ware, 20 miles distant in Hertfordshire. See Rollins, *PG*, p. 139. The term 'post' ('post-boy' did not become common until somewhat later) derives from the use of riders posted

on a stretch of road for purposes of carrying royal letters and news (see *OED*).

66 'Current news'; see M. A. Shaaber (1966), pp. 311–18.

67 'Taylors' are taken as examples; see *PG*, v. 1,9–1,11, p. 140.

68 For the role-change between presenter and narrator see above, chapter 4.1, pp. 107–8; for the presenter as guarantor of the truth see above, pp. 47–9.

69 For historical details see Rollins, *PG*, p. 144.

70 *PG*, v. 1, p. 145; 1.3 should presumably read 'Whereat'.

71 *A famous dittie of the joyful receauing of the Queens moste excellent maiestie by the worthy citizens of London* (1584), AB, no. 52, pp. 270–5. For full titles, and also of the following ballads, see bibliography (primary texts).

72 *The Honor of the Inns of Court Gentlemen Or a briefe recitall of the Magnificent and Matchlesse Show* (between 1633 and 1643), BBLB, pp. 112–17.

73 *A briefe description of the triumphant show made by the Right Honourable Aulgernon Percie, Earle of Northumberland* (1635), RB, III, pp. 219–24.

74 *The Honor of the Inns of Court Gentlemen*, v. 1, BBLB, p. 113.

75 See e.g. *A Monstrous shape* (1640), PG, no. 79, v. 12, p. 454; *A description of a strange . . . Fish* (between 1632 and 1636), PG, no. 77, v. 1,6, p. 438 and v. 3,5 f., p. 439; *The tvvo inseparable brothers* (1639), POA, no. 2, v. 2, p. 11; *A Lamentable List* (1638), POA, no. 4, v. 2,3, p. 22; *Strange Newes from Brotherton* (c. 1648), POA, no. 7, v. 1,7–8, p. 40.

76 There is to my knowledge no comprehensive survey of English prodigy literature. From the numerous source references to miracle and monster ballads given by Rollins it is clear how closely such ballads follow prose literature of similar content. Investigations of French and German prodigy literature show that this was a phenomenon apparent throughout Europe, presumably of a fairly homogeneous nature; see R. Schenda (1961; 1962).

77 See the comprehensive historical survey by L. Thorndyke (1941), vols. V and VI; (1958), vols. VII and VIII.

78 See Thorndyke (1958), vol. VII, p. 325; (1958), vol. VIII, p. 13, also the relevant Register entries, ibid.

79 See R. Plott, *The Natural History of Staffordshire* (1686), in which 'all along many monsters and lusus naturae are described' (quoted from Thorndyke [1958], vol. VIII, p. 490).

80 This is Thorndyke's assessment of the sixteenth century (1941), vol. V, p. 10. His portrayal of the seventeenth century makes it clear that this description indicates a gradually decreasing tendency which also applies to the seventeenth century.

81 See Thorndyke (1941), vol. VI, pp. 406–9; (1958), vol. VIII, pp. 627–8; Bernard Connor, *Evangelium medici seu medicinia mystica: de suspensis naturae legibus sive de miraculis* (1697).

82 For this recurrent debate on the classification of prodigies see Thorndyke (1941), vol. V, pp. 236, 399; (1941), vol. VI, pp. 408, 416, 434, 439, 534, 540; (1958), vol. VII, pp. 57, 303, 371, 432; (1958), vol. VIII, pp. 563, 576.

83 See Thorndyke (1941), vol. V, pp. 108, 399, 567; (1941), vol. VI, pp. 134, 367, 496; (1958), vol. VII, p. 432.

84 See Marcus Frytschius, *A Catalogue of Prodigies and Portents divinely*

Manifested in Heaven and Earth in Punishment of Crimes and Signification of Great Changes in the World (1563), quoted from Thorndyke (1941), vol. VI, p. 490.

85 See above, pp. 47–9; also K. Tetzeli von Rosador (1970): 'Magic and witchcraft for the Elizabethans were not a manifestation of a fairy-tale, mythical world but fearful, tangible reality' (p. 31). See also: P. Meissner (1952), pp. 494–514.

86 This needs to be investigated in more detail with regard to style and content.

87 *The Anatomie of Absurdities* (1589), in *The Works of Thomas Nashe*, ed. R. B. McKerrow, 6 vols. (London, 1904–10), vol. I, pp. 1–59.

88 The anthology on this thematic area: *The Pack of Autolycus (POA)* conveys the impression of a consistency of content and interpretation practice.

89 See Rollins, *POA*, p. 21. Exceptionally, the term 'warning' occurs here, though not as an explicit illocution but as the definition of the moral-theological value of the phenomena as signalling the threat of punishment.

90 See *A Lamentable List*, v. 4,3–4, *POA*, p. 23; *The lamentable Burning of the Citty of* Corke (1622), *PG*, no. 25, v. 3, p. 156; also Rollins's source details for the last-mentioned ballad, *POA*, pp. 150–1.

91 *The lamentable Burning of the Citty of* Corke (1622), *PG*, no. 25, pp. 155–60; see vv. 16–26, pp. 158–60. The exhortation to repent appears as late as 1666 in a street-ballad account of the Great Fire of 1666 in the final verse of *London mourning in Ashes* (1666?), *PB*, no. 91, III, pp. 3–10.

92 *SHB*, no. 47, pp. 203–7; see also vv. 1–2, p. 204 and vv. 16–17, p. 207. The time-lapse between the lightning-bolt as the immediate cause of the tower's collapse, accompanied by a thunderstorm, and the fire which started later serves as proof of the miraculous nature of the event.

93 *A proper newe sonet declaring the lamentation of Beckles [a market towne in] Suffolke, which was in the great winde vpon S. Andrewes eue last past most pittifully burned with fire, to the losse by estimation of twentie thousande pound and vpwarde, and to the number of foure score dwelling houses, 1586.* (1586?), *AB*, no. 21, pp. 118–23, possibly by Thomas Deloney ('T.D.'). *A briefe sonet declaring* (1586?); the title is practically identical, but not the text; *BB*, no. 87, pp. 261–3.

94 *POA*, no. 7, pp. 36–43; see also Rollins's detailed commentary, ibid., pp. 36–9.

95 See L. Thorndyke (1941), vol. VI, p. 408. The idea of divine retribution predominated in popular belief: see C. H. Firth, ed. (1950), vol. I, p. 529.

96 See *AB*, nos. 8, 14, 18, 58, 59, 61, 65, 74. Where there is a division into a prose account and a verse section, the verse is reserved for the moral and didactic appeal to the audience (nos. 8, 14, 53, 59, 74).

97 It is only after the middle of the century that they once more appear with any frequency, as Rollins's anthology *POA* shows.

98 On the use of medical compendia for prodigy literature see R. Schenda (1961), pp. 52–7. In this ballad the workings of God are depicted as being manifested through nature.

99 *A discription of a monstrous Chylde* (1592?), *AB*, no. 62, pp. 299–303.

100 *PG*, no. 77, pp. 437–42; v. 4,3–4,6, p. 439; see also v. 9,6, p. 440.

101 *POA*, no. 2, pp. 7–14; v. 18,4–18,6, p. 14; see also v. 19, p. 14. The material was well known at this period; see Rollins (1919c), p. 121 and n. 1.

102 *The tvvo inseparable brothers*, v. 3, *POA*, p. 11.
103 *A description of a strange (and miraculous) Fish*, v. 2, *PG*, pp. 438–9.
104 *A Monstrous shape. Or A shapelesse Monster* (1640), *PG*, no. 79, pp. 449–54; see also Rollins's commentary, pp. 449–50.
105 See vv. 1 and 2, p. 452; Leda is wrongly described as having been changed into a swan herself.
106 *A famous dittie*, *AB*, no. 52, vv. 7–14, pp. 272–5.
107 *The Honor of the Inns of Court Gentlemen*, *BBLB*, pp. 112–17, refrain and v. 13, p. 117; *A briefe description of the triumphant show*, *RB*, III, pp. 219–24, vv. 2–3, lines 10–25, p. 221 and v. 15, lines 105–13, p. 224; *An Exact Description Of the manner how his Maiestie*, *CP*, no. 1, pp. 77–82, v. 2, p. 78 and v. 15, p. 82.
108 *A true discou[r]se of the winning of the towne of* Berke *by Grave Maurice, who besieged the same on the 12 day of June 1601, and continued assaulting and skirmidging there vntill the last day of July, at which time the towne was yeelded* (1601), *SHB*, no. 57, pp. 271–6; see also v. 16, p. 276.
109 *Rochell her yeelding to the obedience of the French King, on the 28. of October 1628. after a long siege by Land and Sea, in great penury and want.* To the tune of *In the dayes of old*, Martin Parker, *PG*, no. 51, pp. 293–8.
110 See titles already quoted, also: *A description of a strange . . . Fish*, v. 1, *PG*, p. 438; *The tvvo inseparable brothers*, vv. 1–2, *POA*, pp. 10–11; *A Monstrous shape*, v. 3, *PG*, p. 452; *The Honor of the Inns of Court Gentlemen*, v. 8, *BBLB*, p. 115.
111 See *The Honor of the Inns of Court Gentlemen*, v. 4, *BBLB*, p. 114; *An Exact Description Of the manner how his Maiestie and his Nobles went to the Parliament*, v. 9, *CP*, p. 80; *A briefe description of the triumphant show made by the Right Honourable Aulgernon Percie*, v. 6, lines 40–6, *RB*, III, p. 221.
112 *A famous dittie of the joyfull receauing of the Queens moste excellent maiestie*, v. 3,1–3,4, *AB*, p. 271.
113 *The deserued downfall of a corrupted conscience*, v. 9, *PG*, p. 148.
114 See *The lamentable Burning of the Citty of* Corke, v. 11, *PG*, p. 157; *A proper newe sonet declaring the lamentation of Beckles*, v. 6, *AB*, p. 120; *Rochell her yeelding to the obedience of the French King*, v. 4, *PG*, p. 295.
115 See *A battell of Birds*, v. 6,5–6, *PG*, p. 152; *Miraculous Newes from the cittie of* Holdt, v. 13,7–8, *SHB*, p. 79.
116 See above, pp. 146–8, esp. the summarizing assessment of M. A. Shaaber.
117 This will become clear from the textual examples in 4.3.1 and 4.3.3 below.
118 It is common for early monster ballads to be divided into a predominantly discursive verse section and a prose section giving a detailed description of the abnormalities. See *The true reporte of the forme and shape of a monstrous Childe*, *AB*, pp. 38–42.
119 *The tvvo inseparable brothers*, see vv. 5–13, *POA*, pp. 11–13.
120 *A newe Ballad of the most wonderfull and strange fall of* Christ's Church *pinnacle*, see vv. 3–7, *SHB*, pp. 204–5 and the commentary, pp. 203–4.
121 *A briefe sonet declaring the lamentation of Beckles*, v. 4,3–4,8; *BB*, p. 262.
122 *The deserued downfall*, *PG*, no. 23, pp. 144–9.
123 See e.g. R. Browning: *Fra Lippo Lippi, The Laboratory, Andrea del Sarto, My last Duchess* and others. On the popularity of this genre in the nineteenth century, see E. Faas (1969) and (1974).

124 See v. 8,1, line 39, ibid., p. 55; v. 11, lines 54–8, p. 55.
125 See v. 8,4, line 42, p. 55; v. 13,4; line 67, p. 55.
126 There was no recognized and acceptable way of life for the unmarried woman apart from dependence on the family and the ridiculed state of spinsterhood; see R. Thompson (1974), pp. 114–15 and *passim*.
127 Ibid., v. 12,4, line 67, p. 55 and v. 13, lines 69–74, pp. 55–6.
128 See ibid., v. 1,1, p. 53; 10,1–10,3, lines 54–6, p. 55; v. 12, lines 64–8, p. 55.
129 See ibid., v. 3,1–3,3, lines 13–15, p. 53; 4,1, line 18, p. 53; 6,1–2, lines 28–9, p. 54.
130 See ibid., v. 1,2, line 2, p. 53; 3,4, line 16, p. 53; 4,3, line 19, p. 53; 5,3, line 25, p. 53; 7,4, line 37, p. 54; 10,4, line 57, p. 55.
131 See ibid., vv. 1,3–4, lines 3–4, p. 53; 2,1–2,3, lines 7–9, p. 53; 4, 2, line 18, p. 53; 5,1, line 23, p. 53; 7,3, line 36, p. 54; 8,1–8,3, lines 39–41, p. 55; v. 9, pp. 49–53, p. 55.
132 See ibid., v. 2,4, line 10, p. 53; 4,4, line 21, p. 53; 5,4, line 26, p. 53; 6,4, line 31, p. 54; 7,1–2, lines 34–5, p. 54; 7,4, line 42, p. 55; 8,4, line 47, p. 55.
133 See refrain and v. 5,4, line 26, p. 53; 6,3, line 30, p. 54; 9,2 and 9,3, lines 50 and 51, p. 55; v. 11, lines 59–63, p. 55; 12,4, line 67, p. 55.
134 This theme is also treated in the narrative street ballad; see the examples above, pp. 128–9; p. 130; pp. 134–5.
135 See *OED*: 'Usu. qualified as *bad*, *cheap*, *dear*, *good*, etc.'.
136 Ibid., p. 295. The first verse constitutes a narrative observer's standpoint with the introductory topos 'as I was walking . . .' (see above, pp. 49–50), which scarcely matches the rest of the role-play text.
137 See v. 8, quoted above, also v. 7,1–7,4, lines 61–4, p. 298.
138 See v. 3, lines 21–30; the refrain stresses this point of criticism as all-important and does not have here a summarizing function for the textual message of the ballad as a whole.
139 See v. 6,1–2, lines 51–2, p. 297; 8,3–4, lines 73–4, p. 298.
140 See v. 3,1–3,3, lines 21–3, p. 296; v. 5, lines 41–50, pp. 296–7.
141 Ibid., vv. 3–4, lines 19–32, p. 95. Further episodic portrayals: vv. 5–9, lines 33–72, pp. 95–7; v. 11, lines 81–8, p. 97.
142 See v. 5,5–5,8, lines 37–40, p. 95; vv. 6–7, lines 41–56, pp. 95–6.
143 See v. 8, lines 57–64, pp. 96–7; v. 11, lines 81–8, p. 97. On the characteristics mentioned, see F. L. Utley (1970), p. 49; on gossiping in particular: 'gossips' songs' (ibid., p. 50); on the 'shrew' (bad moods, quarrelsomeness, assertion of authority): pp. 49–50 and nos. 7, 50, 66, 70, 157, 184, 200, 227, 289 of the bibliographical index.
144 See v. 4,8, line 32, p. 95; v. 7,7–8, lines 55–6, p. 96; v. 10, lines 73–80, p. 97; v. 12,5–6, lines 93–4, p. 97.
145 Ibid., v. 1, lines 1–8, p. 94; see also v. 15, lines 113–20, p. 98.
146 See F. L. Utley's summary (1970), p. 49, also on 'wantonness' (p. 50, with example references to the bibliographical index), on drinking, see 'alewife poems' (ibid., p. 50 with examples) and on the shrew's assertion of authority see pp. 25 and 49–50, with numerous examples.
147 For this medieval tradition see Utley (1970), pp. 43, 46 and *c.* fifty examples in the bibliographical index.
148 See v. 5,1, p. 51. The street is now called Worship Street 'on the w. side of Norton Folgate, leading to Bunhill Field', see E. H. Sugden (1969), p. 251.

The word 'hog' is used in its metaphorical meaning: 'to arch (the back) upward like that of a hog' (until 1769), see OED.

149 See L. Festinger (1962); he starts from the premise that cognitive dissonance, as for example the contradiction between one's own conviction and cultural norms or between earlier and recent experience, is perceived by the individual as unpleasant and therefore where possible avoided or reduced.

150 See v. 7, lines 49–58, p. 292; v. 14, lines 105–12, p. 294.

151 The presenter-type trailer (see sub-title and opening verse) announces that she will find the husband of her choice. The role-play figure herself goes through various possible professions (v. 13, lines 97–104, p. 293) and names (v. 15, lines 113–20, p. 294), remaining equivocal with her declaration: 'I love with my heart A *handsome young man*' (v. 12,7–8, lines 95–6, p. 293).

152 See vv. 3–4, lines 17–32, p. 291; v. 10, lines 73–80, p. 293; v. 12, lines 89–96, p. 293.

153 See v. 6, p. 366; v. 7, p. 367; v. 10, p. 367; v. 14, p. 368.

154 See v. 9, p. 367; v. 11, p. 368; v. 13, p. 368.

155 See v. 1, p. 365; v. 13, p. 368; v. 15, pp. 368–9.

156 This ballad enjoyed particular popularity right into the eighteenth century (see Chappell's commentary, RB, I, pp. 165–6). It went to the same tune as H. Carey's 'Sally in our Alley', and a traditional link with Addison's 'Merry Milkmaid' cannot be ruled out.

157 Natural beauty, simplicity of dress, cheerfulness, health, innocence, modesty and honesty.

158 The refrain 'Downe, downe, derry, derry downe', taken over from the folk ballad, connotes – in addition to Robin Hood's Greenwood atmosphere – social justice for the lower classes.

159 RB, I, pp. 129–36, attributed to Martin Parker; the title, obliterated in the original, was formulated by Chappell (see ibid., p. 129).

160 See *The Jew of Malta* and Shylock, to name but the most prominent examples. The motif of squandering an inheritance is an essential component of the 'Prodigal Son Plays'; the action comprises in all the conferring of the inheritance, a dissolute life and the impoverished and repentant son's being received back into the parental home. See F. P. Wilson (1969), pp. 96–101 and A. W. Ward and A. R. Waller (1909), pp. 109–14. For other ballads using this material: A New Ballad; Declaring the Excellent Parable of the Prodigal Child (second half of seventeenth century) see above, pp. 11–12; A new Ballad, intituled, A Warning to Youth (beginning of seventeenth century?) see above, pp. 124–5; A goodfellowes complaint against strong beere (c. 1630), see above, p. 134.

161 See L. C. Knights (1951), p. 127; pp. 164–8. The arguments used against usury are that God has forbidden it and that it is unnatural for dead money to increase.

162 See A goodfellowes complaint against strong beere (c. 1630), PG, no. 63, pp. 361–4, above, p. 134; Dice, Wine, and Women (c. 1625), PB, no. 39, I, pp. 237–41, above p. 113.

163 See Heres to thee kind Harry (1627), PB, no. 61, II, pp. 88–93, v. 10,9–10,14, p. 93; Good Ale for my money (c. between 1628 and 1680), RB, I, pp. 411–17, v. 14, lines 127–34: 'Thus to conclude my verses rude'.

164 Heres to thee, v. 1,1, PB, II, p. 89.

165 *A very pleasant new Ditty* (c. 1625), *PB*, no. 42, I, pp. 251–6. For a ballad which is similarly specific to the situation see *Good Ale for my money*, v. 8, lines 67–78, *RB*, I, p. 415.

166 See *Roaring Dick of Douer* (1632), *PB*, no. 86, II, pp. 234–8.

167 See *A very pleasant new Ditty*, vv. 5–6, *PB*, I, p. 253 and vv. 8–13, pp. 254–5.

168 See *Roaring Dick of Douer*, v. 2, *PB*, II, p. 235; v. 5, p. 236; v. 13, p. 238; *Heres to thee kind Harry*, vv. 4–9, *PB*, II, pp. 90–2.

169 *Roaring Dick of Douer*, v. 2, *PB*, II, p. 235.

170 See further drinking-songs: *A Messe of Good Fellowes* (1634), *RB*, II, pp. 142–8, by Martin Parker; *Mondayes Worke* (between 1623 and 1661), *RB*, II, pp. 149–53.

171 See F. L. Utley (1970), p. 50 and examples with text index numbers 79, 107, 172, 193, 195, 251, 252, 277 (John Skelton's 'The Tunning of Elynour Rumming') pp. 336, 368.

172 See also the further clarification of the contrast through the differing sound effects in significant rhymes: 'those drowsie sots, / . . . tosse the pots' (v. 3,5 and 3,7, *PB*, II, p. 176), 'merry' / 'sherry' (ibid., v. 7,2 and 7,4, p. 176); 'But little does our husbands thinke / . . . drinke' (4,1 and 4,3, p. 176); beer is 'loathsome', sack on the other hand is 'wholesome' (6,6 and 6,8, p. 176).

173 A surplus of women was caused by the predominantly male emigration to the newly discovered colonies and greater male mortality during plague epidemics. See R. Thompson (1974), pp. 21–59.

174 See ibid., pp. 8–9. The shrew topos is well documented in the medieval satire; see F. L. Utley (1970), p. 50 and the examples given, also references to the text index.

175 See above, chapter 3.3.1. Early forms of audience address, see p. 57, 58.

176 *OEB*, no. 12, pp. 79–86; see the narrative treatment of the same material: *The songe of the death of mr. Thewlis* (1616), *OEB*, no. 13, pp. 87–100; v. 1 quoted, p. 80 and v. 14, p. 84.

177 *OEB*, no. 11, pp. 70–8; the battle song of faith is put into the mouths of the four priests Robert Nutter, Edward Thwing, Robert Middleton and Thurston Hunt, who were executed on 26 July 1600 and 3 March 1601.

178 See v. 22, p. 75; a figure considered realistic by Rollins (*OEB*, p. 70).

179 This notional construct can also, from the titles and criteria of arrangement of his material, be seen as the determining factor in J. Foxe's *Book of Martyrs*, that is, *Actes and Monuments of these latter perilous times touching matters of the Church* (1563).

180 *RB*, I, pp. 29–34. Anne Askewe was burnt at the stake for her faith, at the age of 24, in Smithfield in 1546, after being tortured without disclosing any information concerning her fellow believers. She herself wrote a religious song during her imprisonment in Newgate.

181 John Foxe's documentation and report on Anne Askewe only gives an account of her steadfastness of faith. The modification in the ballad may have been occasioned by the unexplained question of her ambiguous addition to the text of her recantation (see *The Actes and Monuments of John Foxe*, ed. G. Townsend, 8 vols. [1843–9], vol. v, pp. 542–3). In a different text, not extant as a broadside: 'The Balade whych Anne Askewe made and sange when she was in Newgate' (1547), *RB*, I, p. 30, this motif is also absent.

182 The bishop of Winchester, whose name was Gardiner and who persuaded her, appears as the gardner of her soul.
183 *I might haue liued merelie* (1564/65), *OEB*, no. 35, pp. 216–18; v. 1, p. 216.
184 See this text; also other lamentations of sin.
185 *OEB*, no. 59, pp. 306–11. See also *The complaint of a sinner, vexed with paine,* / *Desyring the ioye, that euer shall remayne* (1562/63), *BB*, no. 7, pp. 19–21.
186 See the text corpus of carols, ed. R. L. Greene (1977), esp. 'Carols of Repentance', 'Carols of the Passion', 'Carols of the Saints'; connections with tradition need to be investigated in more detail.
187 *OEB*, no. 45, pp. 257–61; see the similar figure in *The triumphe of death* (c. 1588), *OEB*, no. 46, pp. 262–4.
188 *Deth with houreglasse*, vv. 1–2, pp. 257–8 and v. 7, p. 259.
189 I have used as a basis the definition and description of this genre given by R. L. Greene (1977).
190 Greene (1977): 'All evidence combines to show, therefore, that the carol as a genre in written English is popular, that is, one degree removed from traditional folksong, and yet lower in the scale of education and refinement than the courtly lyric or scholarly Latin poem. This does not imply that there are not considerable variations in the tone and style of the carols, marking what might be called "degrees of popularity"' (p. 133).
191 Their originally very widespread religious and secular use became increasingly confined to the rural lower class in the late fifteenth century and the sixteenth century; see Greene (1977), p. 78.
192 This applies mainly to songs of religious edification as early forms of the street ballad (see below, pp. 216–20).
193 This type of poem is characterized by a combination of narrative and dramatic procedures by which a narratively conveyed frame is used in the deictic realization of the utterances of one or several speakers in monologue or dialogue form. The frame situation is fixed by means of the topos of a traveller who unexpectedly becomes the eyewitness of a scene. See H. E. Sandison (1913). This type of poem is also found amongst carols.
194 See *A Penny-worth of Good Counsell* (above, p. 71); *The Batchelor's Feast* (above, p. 174); *The Cruell Shrow* (above, pp. 169); *A pretty new Ditty; Or, A Young Lasses Resolution* (see above, pp. 173–4). The narrative introductory topos is, however, also used within the street ballad for those texts, see pp. 49–50.
195 R. L. Greene (1977), no. 406, pp. 240–1: *burden* and emendations in italics to vv. 1 and 2 are not given here, as italics in the street-ballad text have a different typographical function, namely that of emphasis. On this text see also F. L. Utley (1970), no. 20, p. 106: fifteenth century.
196 See Greene (1977), no. 405, p. 240; no. 451, p. 275, vv. 2–3; no. 469, p. 288, vv. 5–6.
197 See ibid., no. 417, p. 247; no. 418.1, p. 248. Greene points to dramatic models for this example of a 'strutting and boastful dandy' (ibid., notes, p. 463).
198 See ibid., no. 468 (in all versions), pp. 286–8; the speaker's defensive attitude

('But I am as I am') in this text is certainly comparable to that of the role-speaker of the street ballad where there is resolution of cognitive dissonance.

199 This is usually already determined by the subject, e.g. in 'Carols of the Nativity', 'Carols of the Epiphany', 'Carols of the Annunciation' and those concerned with martyrs and saints. See Greene's classification (1977).

200 On this see C. R. Baskervill (1929); H. E. Rollins: 'A jig may be defined as a miniature comedy or farce, written in ballad-measure, which, at the end of a play, was sung and danced on the stage to ballad tunes' (PG, p. xiv).

201 See Baskervill (1929), pp. 14–16; W. Chappell defines ballads marked as 'jigs' solely in terms of their rhythm and tune: 'easy tunes of strongly marked metre', 'the tune . . . a tripping one' (RB, I, n. p. 628).

202 R. Weimann (1967) sees in the jig the continuance of the village saturnalia of the 'Lord of Misrule' with their burlesque satire of church ritual and inversion of social rank; the satirical, burlesque and parodistic elements remain (pp. 65, 239).

203 See Baskervill (1929), pp. 90–105. The discursive ballad *A prettie newe Ballad, intytuled: The Crowe sits vpon the wall* (1592), *AB*, no. 77, pp. 377–82 is attributed to Tarlton; see below, pp. 214–15. *Frauncis new Jigge* (1595), *PG*, no. 1, 1–10, a particularly typical jig ballad, was written by G. Attowell. We can only guess at the extent to which other actors were active as authors or singers in the ballad trade; see above, chapter 1.2.2; also Baskervill (1929), pp. 164–5.

204 'Nay doe not frown, good Dickie' (v. 10,4–5, p. 4); 'But here he comes' (v. 12,9–10, p. 5); see also directions for entries and exits.

205 E.g. the reference to Daphne, Piramus and Thisbe, Juno and Zeus in *The Louers Guift*, *PB*, I, pp. 163–7; and to Hero and Leander, Penelope and Venus in *A most pleasant Dialogue*, *PB*, II, p. 228.

206 For further examples see: *A mad kinde of wooing* (between 1619 and 1629), *RB*, II, pp. 121–6; *The two Kinde Lovers* (between 1620 and 1642), *RB*, II, pp. 617–20; *A Paire of Turtle Doves* (between 1633 and 1643), by Martin Parker, *RB*, II, pp. 317–22; *Love in a Maze* (between 1641 and 1674), *RB*, II, pp. 42–8; also references in Baskervill (1929), pp. 188–93.

207 *PG*, no. 42, pp. 239–43; this is an answer ballad to Martin Parker's *The wiuing age* (between 1621 and 1625), *PG*, no. 41, pp. 234–8.

208 See F. L. Utley (1970), p. 50; also alewife poems, ibid.

209 Ibid., vv. 3–4, lines 13–24, p. 184. A ballad with a similar schematic procedure, on a different theme: *A Pleasant new Dialogue: Or, The discourse between the Serving-man and the Husband-man* (1626), *RB*, I, pp. 299–305; a dialogue between a well-to-do farmer and a servant in a town household who vie with each other in representing their respective life-styles and views.

210 *RB*, I, pp. 122–5. See also *The Honest Wooer* (1632), *RB*, I, pp. 463–8.

211 See the corresponding self-portrayal in the role-play poem, above, pp. 184–5.

212 See the examples quoted by Rollins, n. in ibid., p. 270.

213 See *Man's Felicity*, v. 21, lines 121–6, *RB*, II, p. 188; *The Louers Guift*, v. 12, *PB*, I, p. 167.

214 See *mother Watkins ale*, v. 8, *AB*, pp. 374–5, see quotation above, p. 70. *A Wench for a VVeauer*, vv. 16–17, *PB*, II, pp. 167–8.

215 See *A Country new Jigge*, v. 18, *PG*, p. 138.

216 See *A merry Dialogue*, v. 1, lines 1–6, *RB*, II, p. 159, and v. 14, lines 79–84, p. 162; *Clod's Carroll*, v. 23, lines 155–61, *RB*, I, p. 206.

217 See *Man's Felicity*, v. 21, lines 121–6, *RB*, II, p. 188.

218 See *A Wench for a VVeauer*, v. 17, *PB*, II, p. 168.

219 See *A Wench . . .* , vv. 16 and 17, *PB*, II, pp. 167–8.

220 See *Man's Felicity*, as above; *A Country new Jigge*, as above; *mother Watkins ale*, as above; *A merry Dialogue*, as above; *Clod's Carroll*, v. 23, lines 155–61, *RB*, I, p. 206.

221 For heuristic reasons only this part of the concept of 'functional sentence perspective' has been singled out, in simplified form, and is limited to the procedure developed by F. Daneš (1970 and 1976).

222 'Theme and rheme represent two complementary functions in the communication of the different semantic components of a statement: in almost every statement one can distinguish between the thing about which something is said (*theme*) and that which is said about it (*rheme*), the statement in its particular, narrow sense'. F. Daneš (1970), pp. 72–3.

223 For the delimitation of the presenter and other textual speech principles, see above, chapter 4.1.

224 For the answer ballad see above, chapter 3.4.3.

225 Exceptions are the medley and related forms, which raise lack of organization to the level of a structural principle.

226 This schematic progression can in a sense be seen as a mixed form showing characteristics from Daneš's types 3 and 4; with type 4 it shares 'The development of a split rheme' and the inclusion of 'two (or several) independent subprogressions' (Daneš [1970], p. 77), and with type 3 the presence of a hypertheme and the parallel derivation of sub-themes from it. A multiple-theme model with varying rhemes is not envisaged by Daneš. Since the macrostructural predominance of the hypertheme (not included in type 4) with a clearly recognizable derivation of sub-themes is such a determining factor in discursive ballads, I have decided on type 3, with appropriate modifications, for the schematic presentation.

227 See as a further example: *The Poore Man Payes for All* (1630), *RB*, II, pp. 334–8.

228 A fifth sub-theme, addiction to court cases (v. 18), is hardly integrated into the structure, being mentioned once only.

229 *I smell a Rat* (c. 1630), *PB*, no. 69, II, pp. 139–44.

230 *RB*, II, pp. 339–44; for this ballad see also above, pp. 42–3, p. 62, pp. 94–5.

231 See the opening verse, in which the speaker establishes himself as a representative of this tradition, *RB*, p. 340.

232 See *PG*, vv. 11–13, lines 81–104, pp. 343–4, which contain moral exhortations.

233 *PG*, v. 1,1–1,3, p. 271. 'Mind' here in the sense of 'purpose, intention, wish' (*OED*).

234 W. Chappell characterizes the medley as 'made out of the titles, burdens, and subjects of other ballads, intermixing them with popular sayings' (*RB*, II, p. 239), regarding this primarily from the bibliographical aspect: 'Medleys . . . made up from crossreadings of old ballads and interspersed with proverbs, show us the immense proportion of ballads that have perished, while they

supply dates of current popularity for the few that now remain' (*RB*, I, p. 51). J. H. Long (1970) defines the medley as follows: 'a mixture of nonsense, half-sense, and foolery occasionally laced with a dash of satire. The resulting conglomeration is set to the most common ballad tunes' (p. 505).

235 In this context J. H. Long (1970) points to the influence of the ballad medley on Shakespeare and the drama of his time, when heterogeneity of speech, often also referred to as 'motley' and 'patch', was used functionally for the fool and for the depiction of madness.

236 See 'The tune is *Tarleton's Medley*', *BBLB*, p. 118; 'To the Tune of *Tarleton's Medley*', *RB*, I, p. 52 and *RB*, II, p. 240. *A prettie newe Ballad, intytuled: The Crowe sits vpon the wall. / Please one and please all* (1591/92), *AB*, no. 77, pp. 377–82, a humorous and parodistic advice ballad (see below, pp. 214–15), is attributed to Tarlton.

237 Cf. the saying, 'Fame is but the breath of people', see F. P. Wilson (1970), p. 243.

238 *The Woful Lamentation of . . .* (1603), *RB*, I, pp. 479–92; see above, pp. 117–18. On the widespread familiarity with this material in the ballad world, see E. von Schaubert (1926). The allusion can be found in *A New Medley*, v. 5,3–4, lines 33–4, *RB*, II, p. 241, and also in *An excellent new Medley*, v. 3,2, line 18, *RB*, I, p. 53.

239 See *This Maide would giue tenne Shillings for a Kisse* (*c*. 1615), *PG*, no. 13, pp. 78–83; see above, p. 167. 'Sweetheart, Ile give thee eighteen pence / to kisse thee', *A New Medley*, v. 10,7–8, lines 79–80, *RB*, II, p. 244.

240 See 'The Fair Flower of Nurthumberland', Child, no. 9, *A New Medley*: 'The fairest lasse that ere was seene: / that was the flower of Kent'; v. 6,3–4, lines 43–4, *RB*, II, p. 241.

241 Ibid., v. 6,2, line 42, p. 241. See above, pp. 49–50, *A New Medley*, v. 6,2, line 42, *RB*, I, p. 241.

242 Ibid., v. 1,1–2, lines 1–2, p. 240; v. 4,3–4, lines 27–8, p. 241.

243 Ibid., v. 7,1–7,4, lines 49–56, p. 242; v. 11, lines 81–8, p. 244; v. 13,5, line 101, p. 244. Other ballads thematicizing this kind of nostalgia: *A Balade declaryng how neybourhed, loue, and trew dealyng is gone* (1561), *AB*, no. 36, pp. 196–201; *Churchyardes Lamentacion of Freyndshyp* (1565/66), *BB*, no. 29, pp. 85–8; *Turners dish of Lentten stuffe, or a Galymaufery* (1612), *PG*, no. 5, pp. 30–8; *The Honest Age* (1632), *PG*, no. 71, pp. 406–9; *Knauery in all Trades* (1632), *PG*, no. 72, pp. 410–14.

244 E.g. completely out of the blue: 'He oft thinkes most that says the least' (*A New Medley*, v. 5,7, line 39, *RB*, II, p. 241); or contextualized by brief references to the sins of youth: 'Who touches Pitch shall be defil'd' (*An excellent new Medley*, v. 9,6, *PG*, no. 71, pp. 406–9; *Knauery in all Trades* (1632), *PG*, no. 72, pp. 410–14).

245 Allusions to the anal region belong to the repertoire of popular entertainment, for example, *A New Medley*, v. 3,1, line 17, *RB*, II, p. 241. The reference to the prostitute district of Wood Street (see. E. H. Sugden 1969, p. 570) is combined with the ambiguous term 'mace' (musk), meaning 'aphrodisiac' and 'swindler' (E. Partridge 1963, p. 227) (*An excellent new Medley*, v. 1,6, lines 6–7, *RB*, I, p. 52), 'W,men are ships and must be man'd', ibid., v. 10,2, line 74, p. 55.

246 See *A New Medley*: v. 2, lines 9–16, *RB*, II, p. 241, where reference is made to Turnbull Street, one of the most disreputable streets of London at that time, and subject areas connected with it are mentioned. See further ibid., v. 10, lines 73–80, p. 244; v. 6, lines 57–64, p. 242.

247 *A New Medley*, v. 6, lines 41–8, p. 241.

248 *Ben Jonson*, ed. H. Morley (1890), pp. 280–2; see also H. E. Rollins (1919c), p. 120. The text was not printed until 1640, the same time as the publication of Parker's *Bill of Fare*.

249 'A rich fat usurer stewed in his marrow. / And by him a lawyer's head and green sauce'; (v. 6,12, *Ben Jonson*, ed. H. Morley [1890], p. 218): 'Two roasted sheriffs came whole to the board'; (ibid., v. 8,1, p. 281).

250 *A Bill of Fare*, v. 15, lines 113–20, *RB*, I, p. 73.

251 *A New Medley*, v. 16, lines 121–8, *RB*, II, p. 245.

252 See also the 'juggling with words' above, pp. 92–5.

253 *A Bill of Fare*, v. 1,1, *RB*, I, p. 70.

254 Ibid., v. 7,3, line 51, p. 71; see also v. 10,2, line 74, p. 72.

255 *An excellent new Medley*, v. 3,4, line 20, *RB*, I, p. 53.

256 Ibid., in the version of *BBLB*, v. 4,3–4, p. 119.

257 *A New Medley*, v. 2,3–4, lines 11–12, *RB*, II, p. 241.

258 *PG*, no. 46, pp. 263–9. As long as the examples remain subordinated to the thematic progression, an advice ballad may be described as a form of discursive ballad. There are also texts, however, which announce 'advice' in the title, but in fact illustrate this with the figure's own life story in narrative or semi-dramatic form; see above, p. 71; p. 72; p. 73.

259 See the request for attention, the reference to the speaker's function of communication, the naming of the theme in the first verse. *PG*, p. 264; *captatio benevolentiae* and self-presentation in the last verses, ibid., p. 269.

260 *RB*, I, pp. 422–7; by Martin Parker; for the full title see bibliography.

261 *AB*, no. 77, pp. 377–82. The title can be interpreted as an allusion to various proverbial sayings concerning the conceit of a bird of humble status who gives itself airs. See 'A Crow is never the whiter for washing herself often'; 'The Crow thinks her own bird(s) fairest'; 'Like a Crow in a gutter'; see F. P. Wilson (1970), p. 156.

262 The broadside has the initials 'R.T.'; H. Huth supports this attribution of authorship, see Introduction, *AB*, p. xviii.

263 *RB*, I, pp. 427–34; for the numerous printings see n., ibid., pp. 427–8.

264 Examples can be found mainly in the MS Ashmole (see *SB*); the priority of the latter's texts over corresponding broadsides is disputed (see above, p. 2). As a further example see *Behold our saviour crucifide* (c. 1616), *OEB*, no. 17, pp. 119–26, where the exhortations to lead a Christian life are based on Christ's sacrifice and the details of His suffering.

265 See e.g. *A proper newe Ballad sheweing that philosophers learnynges are full of good warnynges* (1568/69), *AB*, no. 37, pp. 202–5 by William Elderton. He supports his exhortations to self-knowledge, duty, moderation, purity of conscience and patience in suffering with references to the authorities of the ancient world, 'that these pagans may counsel good Christians' (esp. v. 7,3, p. 205) and by the same author, *A Ballad intituled, Prepare ye to the plowe* (between 1581 and 1592), *AB*, no. 50, pp. 259–63.

266 *OEB*, no. 52, pp. 285–90. See also *Against nigardie and riches* (1560), *OEB*, no. 15, pp. 106–13.

267 See ibid., v. 5,7–8, p. 287; v. 6, p. 287; v. 7,1–3, p. 287; v. 14,1–14,4, p. 289.

268 See ibid., v. 7,4–7,8, p. 287; v. 13,4–13,8, p. 289; v. 14,4–14,6, pp. 289–90.

269 The individual misdemeanours range from bad table manners via pessimistic complaining and garrulousness to dissipation, selfishness and deception.

270 See above, pp. 101–2, pp. 120–3, pp. 180–7.

271 v. 1, *AB*, p. 128, 'A hood for this foole, to kepe him from the rayne' became a popular saying through Barclay's *Ship of Fools* (1509): 'To kepe you from the rayne, ye shall haue a foles hode' (line 38), quoted from F. P. Wilson (1970), p. 383.

272 *OEB*, no. 1, pp. 1–7; 'ninuectyve' should presumably read 'an invective'.

273 The crimes of the Duke of Gloucester, the treason of Sir Richard Empson and Edmund Dudley against Henry VIII and the praise of Edward VI and Queen Mary are placed in general metaphysical relation to each other.

274 Ibid., two lines of trailer and v. 1,1–1,4, p. 2.

275 *AB*, no. 9, pp. 43–6; the text has no imprint, so that an approximate dating cannot be made on the basis of the printer's period of activity. H. Huth is probably correct in assuming that the ballad was written in homage to Queen Elizabeth at the beginning of her reign (see *AB*, p. xxxix).

276 See H. Huth, *AB*, Introduction, pp. xl–xlii.

277 See ibid., v. 4,1–4,4, p. 356; v. 5,8–5,12, pp. 356–7; v. 7,11–12, p. 358; vv. 8 and 9, 358–9.

278 *BB*, no. 41, pp. 114–16. On the same theme see *AB*, no. 1, pp. 1–6, also by William Elderton, and *AB*, no. 31, pp. 176–9 and *AB*, no. 71, pp. 338–42 by other authors.

279 See *Sure my Nurse was a witch*, above, p. 206; *The praise of Nothing*, above, pp. 206–71.

280 The variation in the extent of presenter communication in the individual texts has not been taken into account in the matrix.

281 Motivational links are also occasionally evident in other narrative types, and in 'martyr figures' and the action-orientated dialogue ballad.

282 The religious aspects of some news-ballad content derive mainly from the tradition of prodigy interpretation.

5 Pragmatic genre definition of the street ballad and its cultural and historical position

1 By 'literary genre' I mean here of course a sub-category of the main genres of speech structure ('primary styles'), that is, 'reporting' and 'performative', although the street ballad uses both.

2 See E. Gülich and W. Raible (1972); W.-D. Stempel (1972); K. W. Hempfer (1972; 1973), and above, chapter 4.1.

3 Traditional links between modern forms of street balladry in German-speaking countries since 1900 – *chanson*, political or socially critical song (F. Wedekind, A. Holz, B. Brecht), cabaret song (K. Tucholsky, Erich Kästner) and nonsense verse (C. Morgenstern, H. C. Artmann) – and the German street ballad, have been highlighted by K. Riha (1965). The presenter

component was overlooked, however. See also L. Petzoldt (1974), pp. 112–33. The connection between the nineteenth-century street ballad and other literary genres, such as the drawing-room ballad, music-hall song, etc., has been examined by J. S. Bratton (1975).

4 For example T. D'Urfey, H. Carey, M. Prior, J. Gay and others.

5 W. M. Thackeray's ballads written for *Punch* and W. S. Gilbert's 'Bab Ballads' clearly show characteristics of the street ballad in modified form.

6 In this connection see again the schematic survey in the feature matrix, pp. 224–5.

7 For example in comic tales: *A merry new Song how a Bruer meant to make a Cooper cuckold* (*c.* end of sixteenth century), AB, no. 17, pp. 88–93; *The Cobler of Colchester. A merry new Song* (between 1589 and 1603), BBLB, pp. 31–5; in a news ballad: *A famous dittie of the joyful receauing of the Queens moste excellent maiestie* (1584), AB, no. 52, pp. 270–5; in a narrative text described at the same time as a 'warning': *A Ditty delightfull of mother Watkins ale / A warning wel wayed, though counted a tale* (*c.* 1590), AB, no. 76, pp. 370–5.

8 The work of G. Ecker (1981) confirms the relevance of a medium-orientated textual analysis and genre definition, using a related example from a German-speaking country.

9 See H. Bessler and F. Bledjan (1967); G. Maletzke (1972), esp. pp. 35–6; H. Schanze (1974), pp. 28–9.

10 Documents relating to the history of reception can be used as source material here.

11 This approach has been largely adopted in reception research to date.

12 See M. Dahrendorf (1972), p. 270; L. Löwenthal (1964), p. 97; G. Waldmann (1972), pp. 248–50; H. D. Zimmermann (1972), pp. 389, 406.

13 See the treatment of marriage, competition on the marriage-market, parental duties and children's obedience, the dangers of a life of pleasure, honesty and deceit in trade and business, and murder.

14 See also J. W. Ebsworth (1897): 'They [the ballads] furnished the favourite reading among people whose only libraries were these roughly adorned sheets. The study and remembrance of them, with few exceptions, did far more humanizing good than all the polemical disputes and exhortations of the day' (*RB*, VIII, p. lxi). This double function as both literary and journalistic medium renders impossible a distinction between the two in individual ballads. Such a division is attempted by A. B. Friedmann (1961), pp. 49–53, with his contrasting of 'literary ballad' and 'journalistic ballad', his scale of values being obviously orientated towards 'high poetry'. The texts of early German broadsides clearly made more extensive use of the medium's capacity for swift reaction in its processing of topical events; see G. Ecker (1981) and R. W. Brednich (1974), esp. on 'Historisches Ereignislied' (pp. 133–84) and 'Zeitungslied' (pp. 184–243).

15 For particularly instructive examples, see above, pp. 67–9; chapter 3.5.3.

16 Typical themes are courtship and marriage, marital quarrels and adultery, wasteful extravagance and bibulousness in either narrative or role-play form. With all the stylization of figure, dominance of events and relative paucity of motivational links, the temporal nature of the action is extremely apparent here.

17 See H. Blumenberg (1966), esp. pp. 11–74. For the tendency towards a secularization of world view, and similar in English literatuɪe from 1600 to 1660, see also D. Bush (1962), p. 1 and *passim*.

18 For the application of the concept of presupposition to the street ballad, see above, pp. 33–4. The extension and application of the concept of presupposition to the conditions and circumstances of the relationship between text and socio-cultural context are more likely to clarify linguistic and communicative links than are structural analogies, as for example those drawn by P. Bourdieu (1970), p. 197.

19 See A. O. Lovejoy (1936); E. M. W. Tillyard (1966).

20 See E. Cassirer (1969), pp. 77–82. The combination of modern individualism and initiative in England was explored by P. Meissner (1952): 'Im Anfang war die Tat' (pp. 286–314), 'Der politische Aktivismus' (pp. 315–83), 'Der wirtschaftliche und soziale Aktivismus' (pp. 384–408).

21 C. Hill (1961) sees in the consequent strengthening of self-confidence the psychological basis for economic enterprise and the rise of early capitalism.

22 H. Haydn (1950) calls this opposition the 'Counter-Renaissance'.

23 See C. B. Macpherson (1967), pp. 21–125. His analysis of Hobbes's theory of the State shows that his social model corresponded closely to seventeenth-century English reality and that Hobbes, starting from the construct of the 'state of nature', was concerned to reduce the 'struggle of all against all' to a sensible, civilized level.

24 In his detailed exposition of the economic history of the sixteenth and seventeenth centuries, E. Lipson (1956) sees 'the rise of individualism and the advent of capitalism'(p. xiii) as closely connected. Symptomatic for this are, among other factors, the functional division between the acquisition of raw materials, manual work and distribution; the credit system, rapid circulation of money, shareholdings in large enterprises, increased production and price rises, and far-reaching trade relations – all essential factors in promoting both a readiness to take risks and successful enterprise.

25 See H. Craig (1960), pp. 1–18; E. Lipson (1956) *passim*, from the economic historical standpoint.

26 See above, chapter 2.1, esp. the communication model for an aesthetic placing as regards reception and socio-cultural placing of the street ballad, p. 31.

27 Accounts of cultural history are almost always concerned with the educated, socially prominent classes. L. B. Wright (1964) is an exception. Histories of literature, of course, virtually ignore the trivial and entertainment literature of past ages.

28 Economic individualism as a situational presupposition is seen most clearly here in the producers' readiness to take risks and eagerness for profit, which have an effect on the textually preformed attitude of the balladmonger. See chapter 1.2.

29 See L. Shepard (1962), pp. 69–70; H. E. Rollins, *CP*, Introduction, pp. 32–74.

30 See the genre typology for the ballad (folk ballad, street ballad, literary ballad) outlined by N. Würzbach (1983).

6 Reputation of the street ballad: views of contemporary writers

1 See the communication model, p. 31, which also includes this dimension of investigation.

2 The main change here is the displacing of the folk ballad by the street ballad, with a consequent shift in audience expectations.

3 For a thorough investigation see H. R. Jauss (1970).

4 Sidney's famous praise of the folk ballad: 'Chevy-Chase', in his *Defence of Poesie* (1595), is a special case, and refers to a specific text. It is not described as a ballad but as the 'old Song of *Percy* and *Duglas*' (A. Feuillerat, ed., III, p. 24). See also A. B. Friedmann (1958), pp. 95–110 and (1961), p. 35.

5 'Conversations with Drummond of Harthornden', W. Gifford, ed., IX, p. 404.

6 Appendix B 61; the features listed there will be examined in detail below.

7 It is precisely the ballad texts of Martin Parker which display the highest quality in their use of every possibility available to the genre. Some of his texts would long ago have taken their place in anthologies of English verse alongside, for example, Matthew Prior, John Philips, John Gay and Henry Carey in the eighteenth century, if the same prejudice did not determine selections even today.

8 Appendix B 45. There is a general demand for a critical distinction between good and bad poetry: see B 13 and B 14.

9 R. Ascham 1570, B 5; R. Stanyhurst 1582, B 10; W. Webbe 1586, B 12; T. Nashe 1589, B 15 and 1592, B 17; J. Harrington 1591, B 19; Spenser 1591, B 21; Shakespeare 1598, B 33; J. Earle 1628, B 61.

10 W. Webbe, *A Discourse of English Poetry* (1586); G. G. Smith, ed. (1964), I, p. 301.

11 It is reasonable to suppose that the figure of the 'pedler', who offers all kinds of spices for sale to various prospective customers (social levels of audience: 'master' and 'clowne'; v. 6), was linked to the ballad discussed in the following verse; the novelty of its content (v. 7) also implies this. Whether 'black' and 'white' already allude to the printing techniques of black-letter and white-letter must remain open.

12 See appendix B 3, v. 7: 'pithie', and 'some doe runne as round as a ball', where 'round' also has the connotation of perfection. See also W. Turner's self-praise: appendix B 40.

13 Shakespeare: B 34; G. Chapman: B 36; J. Fletcher: B 47, B 53 and B 60; P. Massinger: B 55; W. Rowley: B 62; J. Forde: B 63 and B 64; G. Etherege: B 82.

14 In editors' commentaries on the ballads of our period of investigation there is no reference to any veiled scandal.

15 The documents given here could certainly be supplemented by others. There is, however, a clear trend in those quoted which would presumably not be greatly contradicted by additional finds in contemporary literary criticism.

16 This is an approach which is entirely appropriate to the subject, and one which was also adopted in the present investigation.

17 Appendix B 24–6; H. Chettle 1592, B 28; J. Hall 1592, B 29; W. Parkes 1612, B 39; H. Fitzgeffrey 1617, B 48; J. Davies 1624, B 56; anon. 1658, B 78.

18 Ibid., R. Ascham 1570, B 5; W. Webbe 1586, B 12; J. Earle 1628, B 61.

19 Ibid., B 24–7; according to the fiction of Chettle's *Kind-Harts Dreame* he is
    speaking from beyond the grave.
20 Ibid., B 11; B 16; B 25; B 27; B 28; B 39; B 44; B 45; B 57; B 58; B 59; B 80.
21 J. Shirley 1653, B 75; D. Osborne 1653, B 76; anon. 1658, B 78.
22 Ibid., B 37; B 42–4; B 75; B 83; see also B 50.
23 See also B 74, where censorship measures are alluded to; also B 85 for the
    ballad as a means of influence.

Bibliography

1 Primary texts

1.1 Street ballads treated in the main text

The bibliography of street-ballad texts treated or mentioned in this investigation is based on the editions listed in section 1.2 of the bibliography. For reasons of space, titles quoted merely as additional examples have not been included in the bibliography. As the authors are for the most part unknown, the ballads have been arranged according to title, in word order. I have used modern English orthography as a guide, which means that the inconsistencies of sixteenth- and seventeenth-century spelling have not affected the alphabetical order; e.g. 'ballad, ballat, ballade, balad' = 'ballad'; 'cryes' = 'cries'; 'faulcon' = 'falcon'; 'Jone' = 'Joan'.

The following information has been given:

Title   All ballads verifiable as extant broadsides are regarded as individual texts and printed in italics, although the texts have been taken from editions and not from broadside collections. All other titles are in quotation marks. Typographical variation within a title cannot be reproduced; 'long s' is printed as 's'; all other orthographical peculiarities of the time have been retained. In verse titles, lines are indicated by '/'. The name of the tune used is also contained in the title.

Publication date   I have taken the dates of texts, where they are given, from the various editions (especially Rollins); otherwise the text is dated according to the known period of activity of the printer whose imprint it bears; see E. G. Duff (1905), R. B. McKerrow (1910) and H. R. Plomer (1907). In the case of an entry in the Stationers' Register, see H. E. Rollins (1924). Other clues are found in the naming of a well-known ballad author, whose period of publication or birth and death dates provide the *termini post quem* and *ante quem*.

Author   The majority of texts were published anonymously. Mention of the few writers who were well known as ballad authors is of primary relevance for us: William Elderton (d. 1592?), Thomas Deloney (1543–1600?), Martin Parker (first verifiable ballad: 1624/5, last entry in the Register of the Stationers' Company: 1660) and Laurence Price (first verifiable ballad: 1628). The other authors are for the most part not even biographically traceable in the *DNB*.

Editions   See list of abbreviations at the beginning of this study, and information there as to methods of reference; also bibliography, 1.2.

323

Verification of tune   I have taken the tune from the editions, if it is mentioned there, otherwise from Chappell (*PMO*) and Simpson (*BBBM*). In titles where no tune is indicated, or where it is not verifiable, reference to the tune has been omitted.

Provenance of texts from collections of broadsides   I was concerned here to give only the respective collection, not the exact provenance which in many cases has still to be established. I have therefore omitted any information if the text is from *RB* or *PB*, since it is obvious from the titles of the editions that the respective text is from the *Roxburghe Ballads* or *Pepys Ballads* collections. The provenance of the text is given in the editions. In *PG* also, most of the texts come from Pepys's collection; I have therefore only given added information where this is not the case. (For the most important ballad collections see above, pp. 2–3; in all other cases, information regarding the location or origin of collections which also contain texts other than ballads has been omitted.)

An Admirable New Northern Story, Of two Constant Lovers, as I understand, / Were born near Appleby in Westmoreland; / The Lad's name Anthony, Constance the Lass, / To Sea they went both, and great dangers did pass; / How they suffer'd shipwrack on the coast of Spain; / For two years divided, and then met again, / By wonderfull fortune and case accident, / And now both live at home with joy and content. The Tune is, *I would thou wer't in Shrewsbury* (1st half of 17th cent.; *RB*, I, pp. 24–9

Against filthy writing, / and such like delighting. (1561/62); Thomas Brice; *BB*, no. 13, pp. 36–7; *OB*, Part I, 49–52; Suffolk Collection

Against nigardie and riches (1560); *OEB*, no. 15, pp. 108–13; Addit. MS., 15, 225 fols. 7ᵛ–9ᵛ

An [Anne] Askew. Entituled, I am a Woman Poor and Blind (between 1546? and 1675); *RB*, I, pp. 29–34

Any thing for a quiet life; Or the Married mans bondage to a curst Wife. To the tune of *Oh no, no, no, not yet;* or *Ile neuer loue thee more* (c. 1625); *PB*, no. 49, II, pp. 16–21; M: *PMO*, I, pp. 182, 193, 378 and *BBBM*, pp. 356, 740

'Aryse and wak, for Cristis sake' (between c. 1550 and 1565); *SB*, no. 52, pp. 168–9; M: *PMO*, I, pp. 93–4; MS Ashm. 48

An AVE MARIA *in Commendation of our most Vertuous Queene* (between 1553 and 1558); Leonard Stopes; *OEB*, no. 3, pp. 13–18; only copy: Library of the Soc. of Antiquaries, London (see Lemon's Catalogue of Broadsides, p. 12)

A Ballad against Slander and Detraction (between 1560 and 1582); [John?] Haywood; *AB*, no. 3, pp. 12–18; Suffolk Collection

A ballad concernynge the death of mr. Robart glover, *wrytone to maystrys* marye glover, *his wyf, of a frend of heres* (1555); Robert Bott; *OEB*, no. 7, pp. 33–46; Stowe MS. 958, fols. 8ᵛ–17

A ballat intituled Northomberland newes, / Wherin you maye see what Rebelles do vse (1569/70); William Elderton; *BB*, no. 41, pp. 114–16; Suffolk Collection

A Ballad intituled, Prepare ye to the plowe. To the tune of *Pepper is blacke* (between 1581 and 1592);[1] William Elderton; *AB*, no. 50, pp. 259–63; M: *PMO*, I, p. 121 and II, p. 627; Suffolk Collection

---

[1] The year 1592 is presumed to be that of Elderton's death.

A Ballad without title, having a large cut representing five figures, that of Death with his dart pursuing them, with legends underneath each, as follows: [. . .]² (2nd half of 16th cent.);³ AB, no. 25, pp. 143–8; Suffolk Collection

The Batchelor's Feast, or The difference betwixt a single life and a double; being the Batchelor's pleasure, and the married Man's trouble. To a pleasant new Tune called, *With a hie dildo, dill* (between 1628 and 1667);⁴ Laurence Price; RB, I, pp. 46–51

A Batchelers Resolution. Or Haue among you now, Widowes or Maydes, / For I come woing as Fancie perswades. / I must haue a Wife, be she Older or Younger, / For I cannot, nor will not lye alone any longer. To the tune of, *The Blazing Torch* (1629), PB, no. 65, II, pp. 110–15

A battell of Birds Most strangly fought in Ireland, vpon the eight day of September last, 1621. where neere vnto the Citty of Corke, by the riuer Lee, weare gathered together such a multytude of Stares, or Starlings, as the like for number, was neuer seene in any age. To the tune of *Shores wife.* Or to the tune of *Bonny Nell* (1622), PG, no. 24, pp. 150–4; M: *BBBM,* pp. 548, 121

The Beggers Intrusion, Or the worlds Illusion. To the tune of *Sallingers Rownde* (c. 1628); William Hockom; PB, no. 62, II, pp. 94–8; M: *PMO,* I, pp. 69–71

Behould our saviour crucifide (c. 1616), OEB, no. 17, pp. 119–26; Addit. MS. pp. 15, 225, fols. 20–22ᵛ

A Bill of Fare: For a Saturday night's Supper, A Sunday morning Breakfast, and A Munday Dinner, Described in a pleasant new merry Ditie. To the tune of *Cooke Laurell,* or *Michaelmas Terme* (1637); Martin Parker; RB, I, pp. 70–4; M: *PMO,* I, p. 161

A briefe description of the triumphant show made by the Right Honourable Aulgernon Percie, Earle of Northumberland, at his Installation and Iinitiation into the Princely Fraternitie of the Garter, upon the 13 of May, 1635. To the Tune of *Quell the pride, etc.* (1635); Martin Parker, RB, III, pp. 219–24

A briefe sonet declaring the lamentation of Beckles, a Market Towne in Suffolke, which was in the great winde vpon S. Andrewes eue pitifully burned with fire, to the value by estimation of tweentie thousande pounds. And to the number of fourescore dwelling houses, besides a great number of other houses, 1586. To the tune of *Labandalshotte.* (1586); D. Sterrie; BB, no. 87, pp. 261–3; AB, no. 20, pp. 133–7; Suffolk Collection; M: *BBBM,* pp. 418–20, 534

Caluarie mount is my delight (c. 1616), OEB, no. 22, pp. 147–51; Addit. MS. 15, p. 225, fols. 2ᵛ–3

A Caueat or VVarning. For all sortes of Men both young and olde, to auoid the Company of lewd and wicked Woemen. To the tune of *Virginia. c.* 1620; PB, no. 20, I, pp. 128–32.

Charles Rickets *his recantation. Warning all good Fellowes to striue, / To learne with him the way to thriue.* To the Tune of his lamentation, or *Ile beat my wife no more* (1633?); PG, no. 74, pp. 420–4

'The Children in the Wood', see *The Norfolke Gentleman* . . .

---

² The ballad was given this title by the editor, H. Huth.
³ There is similarly no imprint here.
⁴ The first ballad by L. Price was printed in 1628; J. Wright jun. ceased printing in 1667.

'Cleane witheowt feare truthe dothe me constrene' (between 1550 and 1565); Thomas Watertoune; *SB*, no. 4, pp. 9–11; MS. Ashm. 48

The Cobler of Colchester. A merry new Song, wherein is shewed the sorowfull cudgelling of the Cobler of Colchester by his Wife, for the eating of her Apple Pye. To a pleasant new Tune called Trill lill (between 1589 and 1603); *BBLB*, pp. 31–5.

Come, buy this new Ballad, before you doe goe: / If you raile at the Author, I know what I know. To the Tune of Ile tell you but so (1620), *RB*, I, pp. 115–21

The complaint of a sinner, vexed with paine, Desyring the ioye, that euer shall remayne (1562/63); William Birch; *BB*, no. 7, pp. 19–21; Suffolk Collection

A Complete Gentle-woman Described by her feature; Her person slender, her beauty admirable, her wit excellent, her carriage modest, her behaviour chast, with her constancie in love. To the tune of Sabina (1633); L. P.; *RB*, I, pp. 196–200; M: *BBBM*, pp. 624–6

The Constant VVife of Sussex. / Unto you here I will declare, / A story wonderfull and rare, / Of a wife to preuent her husbands shame, / Vpon her selfe tooke all the blame. To the tune of, I haue for all good wiues a song (1632), *PB*, no. 85, II, pp. 229–33

The Cooper of Norfolke: or A pretty Jest of a Brewer and the Cooper's Wife: And how the Cooper served the Brewer in his kind. To the tune of The Wiuing Age (between 1625 and 1660); Martin Parker; *RB*, I, pp. 98–104; M: *PMO*, I, p. 208 and II, p. 774

The Countrey Lasse, To a dainty new note: Which if you cannot hit, / There's another tune which doth as well fit. That's the Mother beguiles the Daughter (1620 or 1621); Martin Parker?; *RB*, I, pp. 165–70; M: *PMO*, I, pp. 306, 375 and II, p. 647

A Country new Jigge betweene Simon and Susan, to be sung in merr[y] pastime [by] Bachelors and Maydens. To the tune of I can nor will no longer lie alone. Or, Falero lero lo (c. 1620); *PG*, no. 21, pp. 132–8

The cryes of the Dead. Or the late Murther in South-warke, committed by one Richard Price Weauer, who most vnhumaynly tormented to death a boy of thirteene yeares old, with two others before, which he brought to vntimely ends, for which he lyeth now imprissoned in the White-Lyon, till the time of his triall. To the tune of Ned Smith (c. 1625); *PG*, no. 39, pp. 222–5; M: *PMO*, II, p. 517

The Cruell Shrow: Or, The Patient Man's Woe. Declaring the misery, and the great paine, / By his vnquiet wife he doth dayly sustaine. To the Tune of Cuckolds all arowe (between 1601 and 1640); Arthur Halliarg; *RB*, I, pp. 93–8; M: *PMO*, I, p. 341

The Cucking of a Scould. To the tune of, The Merchant of Emden (c. 1615?); *PG*, no. 12, pp. 72–7; M: *PMO*, I, p. 381

Cuckold's Haven, Or, The marry'd man's miserie, who must abide / The penaltie of being hornify'd: / Hee unto his neighbours doth make his case knowne, / And tels them all plainely, The case is their owne. To the tune of The Spanish Gipsie (1638); Martin Parker; *RB*, I, pp. 148–53; M: *PMO*, I, pp. 46–7

The cunning Age. Or A re-married Woman repenting her Marriage, / Rehearsing her Husbands dishonest carriage. / Being a pleasant Dialogue between a re-married Woman, a Widdow, and a young Wife. To the Tune of The Wiuing

Age (between 1624 and 1626); John Cart; *PG*, no. 42, pp. 239–43; M: *PMO*, I, p. 208

The cunning Northerne Begger, Who all the By-standers doth earnestly pray / To bestow a penny upon him to day. To the tune of *Tom of Bedlam* (between 1626 and 1681); *RB*, I, pp. 136–41; M: *PMO*, I, pp. 335–6

Damnable Practises Of three Lincoln-shire Witches, Joane Flower, and her two Daughters, Margret and Phillip Flower, against Henry Lord Rosse, with others the Children of the Right Honourable the Earle of Rutland, at Beauer Castle, who for the same were executed at Lincolne the 11. [of] March last. To the tune of *the Ladies fall* (c. 1615); *PG*, no. 16, pp. 96–103; M: *PMO*, I, pp. 196–8; *BBBM*, pp. 96–101, and *passim*

Deth with houreglasse in the one hand and speare in the other threatneth all estates (probably c. 1580) *OEB*, no. 45, pp. 257–61; Sloane MS. 1896, fols. 51ᵛ–52ᵛ

A declaration of the death of Iohn Lewes, a most detestable and obstinate hereticke, burned at Norwich, the XVII daye of September, 1583. About three of the clocke in the after noone. To the tune of *Iohn Carelesse* (1583); Thomas Gilbart; *OEB*, no. 9, pp. 54–61; only copy: Library of the Soc. of Antiquaries, London (see Lemon's *Catalogue of Broadsides*, p. 26)

A discription of a monstrous Chylde, borne at Chychester in Sussex, the XXIII, daye of May (1592); *AB*, no. 62, pp. 299–303; Suffolk Collection

A description of a strange (and miraculous) Fish, cast upon the sands in the meads, in the Hundred of Worwell, in the County Palatine of Chester (or Chesshiere). The certainty whereof is here related concerning the said most monstrous Fish. To the tune of *Bragandary* (1636); Martin Parker; *PG*, no. 77, pp. 437–42; M: *BBBM*, pp. 743–4; Wood 401 (127)

The deserued downfall of a corrupted conscience, degraded from all Authority and titles of Knighthood, censured in the high Court of Parliament, and executed at the Kings Bench barre vpon the 20. day of June last, 1621. in the presence of foure great Peeres of this Kingdome. To the tune of *The humming of the Drone* (1621?); *PG*, no. 23, pp. 144–9

The desperate Damsells Tragedy, or the Faithlesse Young Man. To the tune of *Dulcina* (1627); Martin Parker; *RB*, I, pp. 264–70 (after 1615); M: *BBBM*, pp. 201–5; Suffolk Collection

A Dialogue betwene Christe and the pore oppressed synner (1586); *OEB*, no. 48, pp. 270–1; Sloane MS. 1896, fols. 25–25ᵛ

A dialogue betwene death and youthe (1563/64); *OEB*, no. 44, pp. 252–6; Sloane MS. 1896, fols. 6ᵛ–8

[Dice, Wine, and Women], Or, The vnfortunate Gallant gull'd at London. To the tune of *Shall I wrastle in despaire* (c. 1625); *PB*, no. 39, I, pp. 237–41; M: *PMO*, I, pp. 315–16 and *BBBM*, pp. 653–4

The Discourse betweene A Souldier and his Loue. Shewing that she did beare a faithfull minde, / For Land nor Sea could make her stay behinde. To the tune of *Vpon a Summer time* (1640); *PB*, no. 90, II, pp. 253–7; M: *PMO*, I, pp. 254–5

A Ditty delightfull of mother Watkins ale, / A warning wel wayed, though counted a tale (c. 1590); *AB*, no. 76, pp. 370–5; M: *BBMB*, pp. 745–6; Suffolk Collection

Doctor Doogood's Directions, To cure many diseases in body and minde, lately

written and set forth to the good of infected persons. To the tune of *The Golden Age* (between 1633 and 1652); *RB*, I, pp. 234–8; M: *PMO*, I, p. 266 and II, p. 774; *BBBM*, pp. 779–80

A dolefull dittye of five vnfortunat persons that were drowned in their drunknes in crossing over the Thames *neere* Iuy Bridge, *vpon sundaye night the* 15 *of* October *last,* 1616: *set forth for an example for all such prophaners of the Lord's Sabaoth daye.* To the tune of *Essex good-night* (1616?); Shirburn Fol. 126ᵛ; *SHB*, no. 14, pp. 67–71; M: *BBBM*, p. 206

Englands Lamentation For the late Treasons conspired against the Queenes Maiestie by Frances Throgmorton: who was executed at Tyborne, on the 10 *day of July, Anno* 1584. *To the tune of Weepe, weepe* (1584); *BBLB*, pp. 21–8; M: *BBBM*, p. 660.

The Essex *man coozened by a* VVhore. *Or a fine and merry new Ditty,* / *That lately was done neere* London *City,* / *And if you please to stay a while,* / *You shall heare how th'* Whore th' Essex *man did beguile.* To the tune of, *Gallants come away* (1631); Richard Climsall; *PB*, no. 78, II, pp. 191–5

Euery Mans condition, O euery Man has his seuerall opinion, Which they doe affect as the Welchman *his* Onion. To the tune of *two Slips* (1627); Llewellyn Morgan; *PG*, no. 47, pp. 270–5

An Exact Description Of the manner how his Maiestie and his Nobles went to the Parliament, on Munday, the thirteenth day of Aprill, 1640, *to the comfortable expectation of all Loyall Subiects.* To the tune of *Triumph and Ioy, etc.* (1640); Martin Parker; *CP*, no. 1, pp. 77–82; Wood 401 (139); M: *BBBM*, p. 270

An excellent Ballad of the Mercer's Son of Midhurst and the Cloathier's Daughter of Guilford. To the Tune of *Dainty come [thou] to me.* (17th cent.);[5] *RB*, II, pp. 189–97; M: *PMO*, I, p. 517

An excellent new Medley. Which you may admire at (without offence), For euery line speaks a contrary sence. To the Tune of *Tarleton's Medley* (between 1624 and 1640);[6] Martin Parker, *BBLB*, pp. 118–24 (Suffolk Collection) and *RB*, I, pp. 51–6

Faire fall all good Tokens! Or, A pleasant new Song, not common to be had, / *Which will teach you to know good tokens from bad.* To a pleasant nevv tune (between 1624 and 1640); Martin Parker?; *RB*, I, pp. 341–6

A famous dittie of the joyfull receauing of the Queens moste excellent maiestie by the worthy citizens of London, *the* XII. *Day of Nouember,* 1584, *at her graces comming to Saint James.* To the tune of Wigmores Galliard (1584); Richard Harrington; *AB*, no. 52, pp. 270–5; M: *PMO*, I, p. 242; Suffolk Collection

The famous Ratketcher, with his trauels into France, and of his returne to London. To the tune of *the iouiall Tinker* (c. 1615); *PG*, no. 10, pp. 60–5; M: *PMO*, I, p. 333 and II, p. 779

The father hath beguil'd the sonne. Or, a wonderfull Tragedy, which lately befell in Wiltshire, as many men know full well. To the tune of *Drive the cold Winter away* (1629); *PG*, no. 54, pp. 309–15; M: *BBBM*, pp. 197–8

---

⁵ The imprint shows 'A.M.'; these initials could denote any of several printers active between 1633 and 1697.

⁶ The imprint 'H.G.' frequently stands for the ballad printer Henry Gosson, active until 1640; Martin Parker's first published ballad appeared in 1624/25.

A fearful and terrible Example of Gods iuste iudgement executed vpon a lewde Fellow, who vsually accustomed to sweare by Gods Blood: which may be a caueat to all the world. That they blaspheme not the name of their God by Swearing (between 1591 and 1603); Philip Stubbes; *BBLB*, pp. 42–7; Suffolk Collection

A Fooles Bolt is soone shot. / Good Friends beware, I'me like to hit yee, / What ere you be heer's that will fit yee; / Which way soeuer that you goe, / At you I ayme my Bolt and Bowe. To the Tune of, *Oh no no no not yet* (1629);[7] T.F.; *PG*, no. 55, pp. 316–22; M: *PMO*, I, p. 378

Fowre wittie Gossips disposed to be merry / Refused muddy Ale, to drinke a cup of Sherrie. / Their Husbands did their Iudgements spend / strong Ale was best who did intend to try it. / Their Wiues reply to euery man / that Sacke is best and no man can deny it. To the tune of *the Mother beguilde the Daughter* (c. 1630); *PB*, no. 75, II, pp. 174–9; M: *PMO*, I, pp. 306, 356–7, 275–6

Frauncis new Jigge, betweene Frauncis a Gentleman, and Richard a Farmer. To the tune of *Walsingham* (1595); George Attowell *PG*, no. 1, pp. 1–10; *SHB*, no. 61, pp. 244–54; M: *PMO*, I, p. 121

Franklins Farewell to the World. With his Christian Contrition in Prison, before his Death (1615 or 1616); *AB*, no. 22, pp. 124–7

Friendly Counsaile. Or, Here's an answer to all demanders, / The which I'le declare to all by-standers, / Thereby to teach them how to know / A perfect Friend from a flattering Foe. To the Tune of, *I could fancy pretty Nancy* (1633); *RB*, I, pp. 65–9; M: *BBBM*, p. 95

A generall discourse vpon Covetousnesse (1560); *OEB*, no. 52, pp. 285–90; Sloane MS. 1896, fols. 33–5

God doth blesse this realme for the receyving of straungers being persecuted for the gospell, although some do repine therat (c. 1570); *OEB*, no. 26, pp. 180–3; Sloane MS. 1896, fols. 56ᵛ–8

A godly and vertuous songe or Ballade, made by the constant member of Christe, John Carelesse, being in prison in the kinges benche for professing his word; whoe, ending his dayes therin, was throwen out and buryed most Ignominiously vpon a donghill, by the aduersaryes of godes worde (c. 1580); *OEB*, no. 8, pp. 47–53; Sloane MS. 1896, fols. 1–12ᵛ

A godly ballad declaring by the Scriptures the plagues that haue insued whoredome (1566); A.J.; *AB*, no. 26, pp. 149–53; Suffolk Collection

Good Ale for my money. The Good-Fellowes resolution of strong Ale, / That cures his nose from looking pale. To the Tune of *The Countrey Lasse* (c. between 1628 and 1680); Laurence Price; *RB*, I, pp. 411–17; M: *PMO*, II, p. 647

Good Counsell for young Wooers: Shewing the Way, the Meanes, and the Skill, / To wooe any Woman, be she what she will: Then all young men that are minded to wooe, / Come, heare this new Ballad, and buy't ere you goe. To a dainty new tune, or else it may be / Sung to the tune of *Prettie Bessee* (1633); *RB*, I, pp. 422–7

The Good-fellowe's Advice: Shewing what favour a man shall have, while he hath meanes, But, being in want, then all Friendship ends. To the tune of *Upon a Summer time* (between 1601 and 1640); *RB*, III, pp. 261–7; M: *PMO*, I, p. 254

---

[7] Rollins suggests that copies were printed as early as 1614; see fn., ibid., p. 316.

A goodfellowes complaint against strong beere, Or Take heed goodfellowes for heere you may see / How it is strong beere that hath vndone me. To the Tune of *a day will come shall pay for all* (c. 1630); *PG*, no. 63, pp. 361–4

A good throw for three Maiden-heads. Some say that mayden-heads are of high price, / But here are three maids that haue lost theirs at dice. To the tune, *Of Ouer and Vnder* (1631); Martin Parker; *PG*, no. 67, pp. 380–5; M: *PMO*, I, p. 190

Here begins a pleasant song of a Mayden faire, / To purchase her desire, her Coine she did not spare, / And shee most freely parted with her money / To a Young-man, the which shee call'd her dearest Honey. To a pleasant new tune (c. 1630?); *PB*, no. 72, II, pp. 157–61

Heres to thee kind Harry. Or The plaine dealing Drunkard. To the tune of *Heres to thee good Fellow* (1627); *PB*, no. 61, II, pp. 88–93

The historie of the Prophet Ionas. The repentance of Niniuie that great Citie, which was 48. miles in compasse, hauing a thousand and fiue hundred Towers about the same, and at the time of his preaching there was a hundred and twenty thousand Children therein. To the tune of *Paggingtons round* (c. 1615?); *PG*, no. 11, pp. 66–71; M: *PMO*, I, p. 123 and II, p. 771; *BBBM*, p. 566

The Honest Age, Or There is honesty in all Trades; / As by this Ditty shall appeare, / Therefore attend and giue good eare. To the tune of *the Golden Age* (1632); Laurence Price; *PG*, no. 71, pp. 406–9; M: *PMO*, I, p. 208 and II, p. 774; *BBBM*, pp. 777–80

The honest plaine dealing Porter: / VVho once was a rich man, but now tis his lot, To proue that need will make the old wife trot. To the tune of The Maids A.B.C. (1630), *PG*, no. 64, pp. 365–9

The Honor of the Inns of Court Gentlemen, Or a briefe recitall of the Magnificent and Matchlesse Show, that passed from Hatton to Ely house in Holborne to Whitehall, on Monday night being the third of February, and the next day after Candlemans. To the tune of *our noble King in his Progresse* (between 1633 and 1643); Martin Parker; *BBLB*, pp. 112–17; Suffolk Collection

How every vice crepeth in vn[der] the name and shew of a vertue (1594); *OEB*, no. 49, pp. 272–6; Sloane MS. 1896, fols. 26–7^v

How happy and assured they are, in all stormes, that firmely depend vpon god (before 1576; *OEB*, no. 59, pp. 306–8; Sloane MS. 1896, fols. 49^v–50^v

An Hundred Godly Lessons, That a Mother on her Death-Bed gave to her Children, whereby they may know how to guide themselves towards God and Man, to the benefit of the Commonwealth, joy of their Parents, and good to themselves. To the Tune of *Dying Christian's Exhortation* (numerous copies circulated between c. 1640 and end of 17th cent., *RB*, I, pp. 427–8); *RB*, I, pp. 427–34; M: *BBBM*, p. 784

I might haue liued merelie (1564/65); *OEB*, no. 35, pp. 216–18; Addit. MS. 15, p. 225, fols. 18–18^v

I Smell a Rat, To the Tune of, Vpon a Summer tide, OR, *The Seminary Priest* (c. 1630), *PB*, no. 69, II, pp. 139–44; M: *PMO*, I, p. 254, and *BBBM*, pp. 730–1

'In an arber of honor' (between c. 1550 and 1565); John Walles; *SB*, no. 40, pp. 136–9; MS. Ashm. 48

'In a sartayn place' (between c. 1550 and 1565); John Walles; *SB*, no. 39, pp. 133–6; MS. Ashm. 48

It is not god but we our selves seke the euersion of our own countrey (between 1558 and 1576); *OEB*, no. 51, pp. 281–4; Sloane MS. 1896, fols. 30ᵛ–31ᵛ

John Spenser a Chesshire Gallant, his life and repentance, who for killing of one Randall Gam: was lately executed at Burford *a mile from* Nantwich. To the tune of *in Slumbring Sleepe* (*c.* 1626); Thomas Dickerson; *PG*, no. 45, pp. 256–62; M: *PMO*, I, p. 94 and *BBBM*, p. 614

Jone is as good as my Lady. To the tune of *What care I how faire she be* (*c.* 1620); *PB*, no. 24, I, pp. 156–61; M: *PMO*, I, p. 315 and *BBBM*, p. 654

Knauery in all Trades, OR *Here's an age would make a man mad*. To the tune of *Ragged and torne and true* (1632); Martin Parker; *PG*, no. 72, pp. 410–14; M: *PMO*, I, pp. 265–7 and *BBBM*, pp. 547–8

The lamentable Burning of the Citty of Corke *(in the Prouince of* Munster *in* Ireland*) by Lightning: which happened the Last of May, 1622. After the prodigious Battell of the* Stares, *which Fought most strangely ouer and neere that Citty, the 12. and 14. of May. 1621*. To the tune of *Fortune my foe* (1622); *PG*, no. 25, pp. 155–60; M: *PMO*, I, p. 162 and *BBBM*, XIII, pp. 169, 170, 225–31

A Lamentable List, of certaine Hidious, Frightfull, and Prodigious Signes, which have bin seene in the Aire, Earth, and Waters, at severall times for these 18. yeares last past, to this present: that is to say, Anno. 1618. *untill this instant.* Anno. 1638. *In* Germany, *and other Kingdomes and Provinces adjacent; which ought to be so many severall warnings to our Kingdome, as to the said* Empire. To the tune of *Aime not to high* (1638); *POA*, no. 4, pp. 21–5; M: *PMO*, I, pp. 162–7 and *BBBM*, pp. 100, 170, 229–31; Wood 402 (67)

Leanders loue to loyall Hero, To the tune of *Shackley hay* (1614); William Meash; *PG*, no. 8, pp. 49–53; M: *PMO*, I, p. 367 and *BBBM*, pp. 647–51; Percy Folio MS., ed. W. Hales, III, p. 295

The life and death of M. Geo: Sands, *who after many enormous crimes by him committed, with* Iones *and* Gent *his confederates, was executed at* Tyburne *on* Wednesday the 6 of September, 1626. To the tune of *Flying Fame* (1626); *PG*, no. 44, pp. 248–55; M: *PMO*, I, p. 198 and *BBBM*, pp. 96–9, and *passim*

The Louers Guift, Or a Fairing for Maides: Being a Dialogue betweene Edmund *and* Prisilly. To a pleasant new tune (*c.* 1620); *PB*, no. 25, I, pp. 162–7

A Mad Crue: Or, That shall be tryde. To the tune of, *Pudding-Pye Doll* (*c.* 1620); *PB*, no. 31, I, pp. 190–4

The Mad Man's Morrice: wherein you shall finde / his trouble and grief, and dis-content of his minde; / A warning to young men to have a care, / how they in love intangled are. To a pleasant new tune (1637); Humphrey Crouch; *RB*, II, pp. 153–8; M: *PMO*, I, p. 334

Man's Felicity and Misery: Which is, a good Wife and a bad; or, the best and the worst, discoursed in a Dialogue betweene Edmund *and* David. To the Tune of, *I have for all good wives a song* (1632); Martin Parker?, *RB*, II, pp. 182–8

The Marchant's Daughter of Bristow. To the tune of *The Mayden's Joy* (between 1586 and 1618); *RB*, II, pp. 86–95; M: *PMO*, I, pp. 117–18 fn.

The Married-womans Case: / OR / Good Counsell to Mayds, to be carefull of hastie Marriage, by the example of other Married-women. To the tune of *The Married-mans Case* (*c.* 1630); Martin Parker, *PB*, no. 74, II, pp. 169–73

A Maruellous Murther, Committed upon the Body of one George Drawnefield *of* Brempton, *Two Miles from* Chesterfield, *in* Darbyshire, *who (for Lucre of his wealth) was most cruelly murthered in his bed, on* Whitsunday *at night, by certaine bloody Villaines whereof Three are in* Darby Jayle, *One fled, and the rest bound ouer to the Asizes.* To the tune of *My bleeding heart* (1638?);[8] POA, no. 3, pp. 15–20; M: PMO, I, p. 377 and BBBM, p. 230; Manchester II, p. 1

The merry carelesse Lover; OR, *A pleasant new Ditty, called I love a Lasse since yesterday, and yet I cannot get her.* To the tune of, *The mother beguilde the daughter* (1634); Robert Guy; RB, II, pp. 105–10; M: PMO, II, p. 647 and BBBM, pp. 134–6

A merry Dialogue betwixt a married man and his wife, concerning the affaires of this carefull life. To an excellent Tune (between 1619 and 1629); RB, II, pp. 158–63

A merry Jest of John Tomson and Jakaman his wife / Whose jealousie was justly the cause of all their strife. To the tune of *Pegge of Ramsey* (1586); RB, II, pp. 136–42; M: PMO, I, p. 118 and BBBM, pp. 570–1, and *passim*

A merry new Ballad, both pleasant and sweete, / In praise of the Black-smith, which is very meete. To the tune of *Greene sleeves* (1661); RB, II, pp. 126–31; M: BBBM, pp. 268–78 and *passim*

A merie newe Ballad intituled, the Pinnyng of the Basket: and is to bee songe to the tune of the doune right Squire (between 1570 and 1593); T. Rider; AB, no. 27, pp. 154–62; Suffolk Collection

A merry nevv catch of all Trades. To the tune of *The cleane Contrary way* (c. 1624); PG, no. 34, pp. 196–9; M: PMO, II, p. 435 and BBBM, pp. 109, 254, 306, 778

A merry new Song how a Bruer meant to make a Cooper cuckold, and how deere the Bruer paid for the bargaine. To the tune of, *In Somer time* (c. end of 16th cent.);[9] AB, no. 17, pp. 88–93; M: PMO, II, pp. 392–3, 541 and BBBM, p. 751; Suffolk Collection

The merry Old Woman; Or, This is a good Old Woman, / This is a merry Old Woman; / Her counsell is good, Ile warrant, / For shee doth wish ill to no Man. To the tune, *This is my Grannam's deedle* (1633); Robert Guy; RB, II, pp. 163–9

A merry Progresse to London to see Fashions, by a young Country Gallant, that had more Money then Witte. To the tune of, *Riding to Rumford* (c. 1620); PB, no. 23, I, pp. 148–55; M: PMO, I, p. 111 and BBBM, p. 221

A merry new Song of a rich Widdowes wooing, That married a young man to her own vndooing. To the tune of, *Stand thy ground old Harry* (c. 1625); PB, no. 43, I, pp. 257–61; M: PMO, I, pp. 365–6

A Messe of Good Fellowes; Or, The generous spark, who roundly / doth call, and sayes for his part, / Tush, we haue, and shall have, abundance, / come, fill us the other odd quart. To the tune of *Ragged and torne* (1634); Martin Parker; RB, II, pp. 142–8; M: PMO, I, pp. 265, 267 and BBBM, pp. 547–8

---

[8] Rollins suggests that this refers to a true incident, on the basis of a verifiable execution which took place in 1638.

[9] There is no imprint; in 1624 a ballad was registered under the title alluded to by the tune (see Rollins, Index, no. 1238); the Suffolk Collection, however, contains almost without exception ballads from the second half of the sixteenth century.

Miraculous Newes from the cittie of Holdt *in* Germany, *where there were three dead bodyes seene to rise out of their Graues vpon the twentieth day of September last 1616, with other strange things that hapend.* To The Tune of *The ladye's fall* (1616?); *SHB,* no. 16, pp. 75–80; M: *PMO,* pp. 148, 196 and *BBBM,* pp. 369–71

A Monstrous shape. Or A shapelesse Monster. A Description of a female creature borne in Holland, / compleat in every part, save only a head like a swine, / who hath travailed into many parts, and is now to be seene in LONDON, / *Shees loving, courteous, and effeminate, / And nere as yet could find a loving mate.* To the tune of *the Spanish Pavin* (1640); Laurence Price; *PG,* no. 79, pp. 449–54. M: *PMO,* I, pp. 240–1 and *BBBM,* pp. 678–81

A most delicate, pleasant, amorous, new Song, made by a Gentleman that enioyes his Loue, shewing the worth and happinesse of Content, and the effects of loue, called, All Louers Ioy. To the tune of *New Paradise* (c. 1638); *PB,* no. 89, II, pp. 250–2

A most excellent new Ballad of an Olde Man and his Wife, in their olde age and misery, which sought to their owne Children for succour, by whom they were disdained, and scornfully sent away succourless; and how the vengeance of God was justly shewed upon them for the same. To the tune of *Priscilla* (end of 16th cent. and 17th cent.);[10] *RB,* II, pp. 347–52.

A most notable example of an ungracious Son, who in the pride of his heart denyed his owne Father, and how God for his offence turned his meat into loathsome toades. To the tune of *Lord Darley* (between 1601 and 1640); *RB,* II, pp. 73–9 and *BB,* no. 86, pp. 256–9

A most pleasant Ballad of Patient Grissell. to the tune of The Bride's Goodmorrow. (17th cent.);[11] *RB,* II, pp. 268–74; M: *BBBM,* pp. 66–7

A most pleasant Dialogue: OR *A merry greeting betweene two louers, / How* Will and Nan *did fall at strife, / And at the last made man and wife.* To the tune of *Lusina* (1632); Charles Records: *PB,* no. 84, II, pp. 224–8; M: *PMO,* I, pp. 269–70, 185; and *BBBM,* pp. 40, 448

A most wonderful and sad judgement of God upon one Dorothy Mattley *late of* Ashover *in the County of* Darby, *within fourteen miles of the said Town of Darby; who for so small a thing as two single pennies which she was charged with the taking of from a boy, did most presumptuously with sad imprecations wish and desire, that if she had taken or stole the same, that the ground might open and she sink therein, which by her neighbours relation was an expression very common with her, but so it pleased God to deal, that upon the same words the ground did open, and she with a Tub which she was washing Lead-Oare in sunk into the ground, to the amazement of the beholders, and the ground closed again upon her, as here underneath it is more fully declared; and this was done upon the 23 of March 1660. All which may well serve for an example to all wretches of this age whatsoever, who to advance themselves by falshood, or for the trifles of this world, take to themselves assumptions, and imprecations, nay will not at all stand to forswear themselves to compass*

---

[10] Rollins establishes 1675 as the date of the *RB* text; it is, however, already included in the Suffolk Collection (*BB,* no. 60) and was thus presumably already extant at the end of the sixteenth century (see H. Huth for the dating of this collection, Preface to *AB,* pp. xi–xiii.

[11] Chappell has here collated various seventeenth-century versions.

their own ends, as if there was no God or judgment to be expected; but they may hereby take notice that some time God will punish such creatures even in this life for example sake; yet if not here, their reward will be according to their works hereafter, and none shall be able to let it. The tune is, *Fortune my Foe* (1661); POA, no. 11, pp. 62–7; M: PMO, I, p. 162 and BBBM, pp. 225–31, *passim*; Wood 401 (177)

Natures Wonder? OR, *[A True acc]ount how the Wife of one* John Waterman *an Ostler in the Parish of* Fisherton-Anger, *near* Salisbury, *was Delivered of a strange Monster upon the 26th of* October 1664, *which lived untill the 27th of the same Moneth. It had two Heads, foure Armes, and two Legs. The Heads standing contrary each to the other; and the Loines, Hipps, and Leggs Issueing out of the middle, betwixt both. They were both perfect to the Navell, and there joyned in one, being but one Sex, which was the Female. She had another Child born before it (of the Female Sex) which is yet living, and is a very comely Child in all proportions. This is Attested for truth, by several Persons which were eye witnesses.* The Tune is, *London Prentice*; Or, *Jovial Batchelor* (1664); POA, no. 23, pp. 139–45; M: PMO, I, pp. 151, 265 and BBBM, pp. 16, 240; Euing, no. 237

A new Ballad against Unthrifts (between 1560 and 1582); W.F.; p. 29; AB, no. 44, pp. 226–9, Suffolk Collection

A new Ballad, Containing a communication between the carefull Wife and the comfortable Hus[band] touching the common cares and charges of Household (between 1620 and 1640); RB, I, pp. 122–5

A New Ballad; Declaring the Excellent Parable of the Prodigal Child. To the tune of The Wanton Wife (2nd half of 17th cent.);[12] RB, II, pp. 391–8; M: BBBM, pp. 743–4

A newe ballad (2nd half of 16th cent.); AB, no. 9, pp. 43–6

A new Ballad, intituled, A Warning to Youth, shewing the lewd life of a Marchant's Sonne of London, and the miserie that at the last he sustained by his rioutousnesse. To the tune of The Lord Darley (beginning of 17th cent.?);[13] RB, III, pp. 35–41

A newe Ballad of the most wonderfull and strange fall of Christ's Church *pinnacle in* Norwitch, *the which was shaken downe by a thunder-clap on the 29 of* Aprill 1601, *about 4 or 5 a'clocke in the after-noone: with a discription of a miraculous fire, which the verye next morninge consumed and burnt downe a great part of the cloyster. To The Tune of Flyinge fame* (1601?); Shirburne fol. 196; SHB, no. 47, pp. 203–7; M: PMO, I, p. 198 and BBBM, pp. 96–9, 588–9, *and passim*

A New Medley, Or, A Messe of All-together. To the tune of Tarleton's Medley (between 1624 and 1660);[14] Martin Parker; RB, II, pp. 239–45; M: BBBM, p. 680

A new merry ballad I haue here to shew, / Come pence a peece for them, / I tell you but so (1629); PB, no. 66, II, pp. 116–23

Newes from the Tower-hill: Or, a gentle warning to Peg and Kate, / *To walke no*

---

[12] Chappell assumes that the text, in this or similar form, goes back to the last third of the sixteenth century, when ballads on this theme were registered; see RB, II, pp. 391–2.

[13] See Chappell, n. RB, III, p. 35.

[14] This is Martin Parker's period of known publication; the ballad bears no imprint.

more abroad so late. To the tune of *the North countrey Lasse* (1631); Martin Parker; *PG*, no. 66, pp. 376–9; M: *PMO*, II, p. 457

A ninuectyue agaynst Treason (1553); Thomas Watertoune?; *OEB*, no. 1, pp. 1–7; British Mus. C. 18.e. I. (88)

Nobody his Counsaile to chuse a Wife: Or, The difference betweene Widdowes and Maydes. To the Tune of *the wanton Wife of Westminster* (c. 1626); *PG*, no. 46, pp. 263–9; M: *BBBM*, pp. 773–4

No body loues mee. To the tune of *Philliday* (c. 1625); *PB*, no. 51, II, pp. 29–35; M: *PMO*, I, pp. 182–4 and *BBBM*, pp. 576–8

No naturall Mother, but a Monster. Or, the exact relation of one, who for making away her owne new borne childe, about Brainford *neere* London, *was hang'd at* Teyborne, *on Wednesday the 11. of December, 1633.* To the tune of, *Welladay.* Martin Parker; M: *PMO*, I, p. 176; Manchester, II, p. 2; *PG*, no. 75, pp. 425–30

The Norfolke Gentleman, his last Will and Testament:[15] *And how hee committed the keeping of his children to his owne brother, who dealt most wickedly with them: and how God plagued him for it.* To the Tune of *Rogero* (between 1610 and 1675); *RB*, II, pp. 214–21; M: *PMO*, I, pp. 200–1 and *BBBM*, pp. 103–5

O blessed God, O Sauiour sweete (c. 1616); *OEB*, no. 16, pp. 114–18; Addit. MS. 15, 225, fols. 11ᵛ–13

O, yes! If any man or woman any thing desire, / Let them repaire forthwith unto the Cryer. To the tune of *The Parrator* (between 1620 and 1629); *RB*, II, pp. 352–7

The Pedler opening of his Packe, / To know of Maydes what tis they lacke. To the tune of, *Last Christmas 'twas my chance* (c. 1620); *PG*, no. 19, pp. 116–20; M: *BBBM*, p. 427

A peerelesse Paragon: Or, Few so chast, so beautious or so faire, / For with my love I think none can compare. To the tune of *The mother beguil'd the daughter* (1633); *RB*, II, pp. 299–304

A Penny-worth of Good Counsell. / To Widdowes, and to Maides, / This Counsell I send free; / And let them looke before they leape, / Or that they married be. To the Tune of *Dulcina* (between 1624 and 1660),[16] Martin Parker; *RB*, II, pp. 294–9; M: *PMO*, I, p. 143 and II, p. 771; and *BBBM*, pp. 201–5

A pleasant ballad of the iust man Jobe, *shewing his patience in extremitie* (1564/ 65); *OEB*, no. 33, pp. 209–12; Addit. MS. 15, 225, fols. 16ᵛ–17

A pleasant history of a Gentleman in Thracia, which had foure Sonnes, and three of them none of his own; shewing how miraculously the true heire came to enjoy his inheritance. To the tune of *Chevy Chase* (1633); Martin Parker; *RB*, II, pp. 262–7; M: *PMO*, I, pp. 196–9 and *BBBM*, pp. 96–101, and *passim*

A Pleasant new Ballad you here may behold, / How the Devill, though subtle, was gul'd by a Scold. To the tune of *The Seminary Priest* (1630); *RB*, II, pp. 366–71; M: *BBBM*, p. 731

The Poore Man Payes for All. This is but a dreame which here shall insue, / But the Author wishes his words were not true. To the tune of *In slumbring sleepe I lay* (1630); *RB*, II, pp. 334–8 and *CM*, no. 37, pp. 102–5; M: *BBBM*, p. 614

---

[15] Later well known under the title, 'The Children in the Wood'.

[16] No imprint; the first documented ballad by Martin Parker dates from 1624; a further copy of this text in the Pepys Collection dates from the reign of James I.

'The Post of the Signe' (1645);[17] *Wits Recreations*, anon. ed. (London, 1817), 2 vols., II, pp. 401–4

The Post of Ware: With a Packet full of strange Newes out of diuers Countries. To a pleasant new Tune (1620 or 1621); *PG*, no. 22, pp. 139–43

The Praise of Brotherhood; Or, A description of Hoodes, writ in Verse, not in Prose, / Shewing which best becomes the Nose. To the Tune of, *Abington Fayre* (1634); *RB*, II, pp. 361–6

The praise of Nothing: Though some doe wonder why I write in praise / of Nothing, in these lamentable daies, / When they have read, and will my counsell take, / I hope of Nothing Something they may make. To the Tune of *Though I have but a marke a yeare, etc.* (between 1601 and 1640); *RB*, II, pp. 339–44; M: *PMO*, I, p. 356 and *BBBM*, p. 263

A prettie newe Ballad, intytuled: The Crowe sits vpon the wall, / Please one and please all. To the tune of, *Please one and please all* (1591/92); R. T. (probably Richard Tarlton); *AB*, no. 77, pp. 377–81; Suffolk Collection

A pretty new Ditty; Or, A Young Lasses Resolution, / As her mind I truly scan, / Who shews in conclusion, / She loves a handsome young man. To the tune of *I Know what I Know* (between 1601 and 1640); *RB*, II, pp. 289–94; M: *BBMB*, p. 453

A proper New Balad of the Bryber Gehesie. Taken out of the fourth booke of Kinges, And songe to the tune of my Lorde Marques Galyarde, or the firste traces of Que passa, pp. 61–5; Suffolk Collection

A proper newe Ballad sheweing that philosophers learnynges are full of good warnynges. And songe to the tune of my Lorde Marques Galyarde, or the firste traces of *Que passa* (1568/69); William Elderton?; *AB*, no. 37, pp. 202–5

A proper newe sonet declaring the lamentation of Beckles [a market towne in] Suffolke, which was in the great winde vpon S. Andrewes eue last past most pittifully burned with fire, to the losse by estimation of twentie thousande pound and vpwarde, and to the number of foure score dwelling houses, 1586. To Wilson's Tune (1586); Thomas Deloney; *AB*, no. 21, pp. 118–23; M: *BBBM*, p. 792; Suffolk Collection

A Prouerbe old, yet nere forgot, / Tis good to strike while the Irons hott. / Or, / Counsell to all Young men that are poore, / To Marry with Widowes now while there is store. To the Tune of, *Dulcina* (between 1625 and 1650); Martin Parker; *PG*, no. 40, pp. 229–33; M: *PMO*, I, p. 143 and *BBBM*, pp. 201–5

A Quip for a scornfull Lasse. Or, Three slips for a Tester. To the tune of *Two slips for a Tester* (1627); *PB*, no. 60, II, pp. 82–7

Remember Death, and thou shalt neuer sinne (1569); Joh. Awd; *BB*, no. 2, pp. 3–4; Suffolk Collection

Roaring Dick of Douer: OR, *The Jouiall good fellow of Kent, / That ne'r is willing to giue ouer, / Till all his money be spent.* To the tune of *Fuddle, roare and swagger* (1632); *PB*, no. 86, II, pp. 234–8

Rochell her yeelding to the obedience of the French King, on the 28. of October 1628. after a long siege by Land and Sea, in great penury and want. To the

---

[17] First appeared in *Wit's Recreations* (1645); not extant as a single broadsheet.

tune of *In the dayes of old*; Martin Parker; *PG*, no. 51, pp. 293–8; M: *PMO*, I, p. 179; II, p. 773; and *BBBM*, p. 141

Roome for Companie, heere comes Good Fellowes. To a pleasant new tune (1614); *PB*, no. 8, I, pp. 51–7

Round boyes indeed. / Or / The Shoomakers Holy-day. / Being a very pleasant new Ditty, / To fit both Country, Towne and Citie, / Delightfull to peruse in every degree, / Come gallant Gentlemen, hansell from you let me see. To a pleasant new Tune (1637); Laurence Price; *PG*, no. 78, pp. 443–8; M: *PMO*, I, pp. 277–8

A songe of foure Preistes that suffered death at Lancaster. To the Tune of *Daintie, come thou to me* (1601); *OEB*, no. 11, pp. 70–8; M: *PMO*, II, p. 517 and *BBBM*, pp. 15, 16, 577, 578

The songe mr. Thewlis writ him selfe (1616); John Thewlis?; *OEB*, no. 12, pp. 79–86; Addit. MS. 15, 225, fols. 22–5

The songe of the death of mr. Thewlis. To the Tune of *Daintie, come thou to mee* (1616); *OEB*, no. 13, pp. 87–100; Addit. MS. 15, 225, fols. 25–7ᵛ; M: *PMO*, II, p. 517 and *BBBM*, pp. 15, 16, 577, 578

The Spanish Tragedy; Containing the lamentable Murders of Horatio and Bellimperia: with the pitifull Death of old Hieronimo. To the tune of *Queene Dido* (between 1599 and 1638); *RB*, II, pp. 453–9; M: *PMO*, I, pp. 370–2 and *BBBM*, pp. 587–90

Strange Newes from Brotherton in Yorke-shire, being a true Relation of the raining of Wheat on Easter day last, to the great amaizment of all the Inhabitants; It hath rained Wheate more or lesse every day since, witnessed by divers persons of good ranke and quality, as the Lady Ramsden *who gethered some her selfe, some of it was sent to Judge* Green, *and M.* Hurst *dwelling at the* Fountaine Taverne *in Saint* Anns *Lane neere* Aldersgate *in* London. To the Tune of *The rich Merchant man* (c. 1648); *POA*, no. 7, pp. 36–43; M: *PMO*, I, p. 382 and *BBBM*, pp. 602–4; Manchester II, p. 39

Sure my Nurse was a witch, / OR, / The merry Night-wench. / Who when her child doth cry, merry to make him, / Doth sing unto it, Come take him beggar, take him. To the tune of *See the golding*, or *Watton townes end* (c. 1626); *PB*, no. 57, II, pp. 63–9; M: *PMO*, I, p. 218; II, pp. 774–5 and *BBBM*, p. 461

A Table of Good Nurture. Wherin is contained a Schoolemaster's admonition to his Schollers to learne good manners, the Father to his Children to learne vertue; and the Housholder to his Servants to learne godlinesse. To the tune of *The Earle of Bedford* (1624); *RB*, II, pp. 569–75

'Take hede in tyme' (between c. 1550 and 1565); *SB*, no. 10, pp. 29–31; MS. Ashm. 48

This Maide would giue tenne Shillings for a Kisse: To the Tune of *Shall I wrastle in despaire* (c. 1615); *PG*, no. 13, pp. 78–83; M: of the first part of the ballad: *PMO*, I, pp. 315–16 and *BBBM*, pp. 653–4

A Triumph for true Subiects, and a Terrour vnto al Traitours: By the example of the late death of Edmund Campion, Ralphe Sherwin, *and* Thomas Bryan, *Jesuites and Seminarie priestes: Who suffered at* Tyburne, *on Friday, the first Daye of December. Anno Domini 1581* (1581); William Elderton?; *OEB*, no. 10, pp. 62–9

The true description of two monsterous children, laufully begotten betwene George Steuens *and* Margerie *his wyfe, and borne in the parish of* Swanburne *in Buckynghamshyre the iiij. of Aprill, Anno Domini 1566; the two children hauing both their belies fast ioyned together, and imbracyng one another with their armes: which children wer both alyue by the space of half an hower, and wer baptized and named the one John, and the other Joan* (1566); AB, no. 65, pp. 321–7; Suffolk Collection

A true discou[r]se of the winning of the towne of Berke *by Grave Maurice, who besieged the same on the 12 day of June 1601, and continued assaulting and skirmidging there vntill the last day of July, at which time the towne was yeelded.* To the Tune of *All those that are good fellowes* (1601?); Shirburne fol. 229, SHB, no. 57, pp. 271–6; M: BBBM, p. 14

The true reporte of the forme and shape of a monstrous Childe borne at Muche Yorkesleye, a village three myles from Colchester, in the Countye of Essex, the xxi daye of Apryll in this yeare 1562 [. . .] (1562?); AB, no. 8, pp. 38–42

Turners dish of Lentten stuffe, or a Galymaufery. To the tune of *Watton Townes end* (1612); W. Turner; PG, no. 5, pp. 30–8; PMO, I, pp. 219–20 and BBBM, pp. 460–2

The XXV. orders of Fooles (1569/70); T.Gr.?; AB, no. 23, pp. 128–36; Suffolk Collection; and BBBM, pp. 460–2

The tvvo inseparable brothers. OR *A true and strange description of a Gentleman (an Italian by birth) about seventeene yeeres of age, who hath an imperfect (yet living) Brother, growing out of his side, hauing a head, two armes, and one leg, all perfectly to be seen. They were both baptized together; the imperfect is called* Iohn Baptist, *and the other* Lazarus. *Admire the Creator in his Creatures.* To the tune of *The wandring Iewes Chronicle* (1639); Martin Parker; POA, no. 2, pp. 7–14; Manchester, II, p. 46

The vnnaturall Wife: Or, The lamentable Murther, of one goodman Dauis, *Locke-Smith in Tutle-streete, who was stabbed to death by his Wife, on the 29. of Iune, 1628. For which fact, She was Araigned, Condemned, and Adiudged, to be Burnt to Death in* Smithfield, *the 12. of Iuly 1628.* To the tune of *Bragandary* (1628); PG, no. 49, pp. 283–7; M: BBBM, p. 743

[The usurer and the Spendthrift].[18] *Come, worldlings, see what paines I here do take, / To gather gold while here on earth I rake [. . .]* To the Tune Of *To drive the cold winter away* (between 1625 and 1640);[19] Martin Parker, RB, I, pp. 129–36; M: BBBM, p. 198

A Warning for all Murderers. A most rare, strange, and wonderfull accident, which by God's just judgement was brought to passe, not farre from Rithin in Wales, and showne upon three most wicked persons, who had secretly and cunningly murdered a young gentleman named David Williams, that by no meanes it could be knowne, and how in the end it was revenged by a childe of five yeeres old, which was in his mother's wombe and unborne when the deed was done. To the Tune of *Wigmore's Galliard* (1638); RB, III, pp. 136–43; M: PMO, I, p. 242 and BBBM, pp. 783–5

A Warning-peice for Ingroosers of Corne; BEING *a true Relation how the* Divell *met with one Goodman* Inglebred *of Bowton, within six miles of* Holgay in *Norfolk; as he was comming from* Linn *Market, and Bargain'd for a great*

---

[18] Title interpolated by Chappell.
[19] The year 1625 was the beginning of Martin Parker's publication span; 1641 was the end of Henry Gossen's printing activity (imprint).

quantity of Barly for eight shillings a Bushell and gave earnest; and when he came to fetch it, brought Carts and Horses (to their thinking) and while 'twas measuring the Divell *vanished, and tore the Barne in pieces, and scattered all the Corne with such Windes and Tempest, which hath done such great harme both by Sea and Land, the like was never heard of before; the Farmer now lyeing destracted.* To the Tune of, *In Summer time*, etc. (1643); *POA*, no. 6, pp. 31–5; M: *PMO*, I, pp. 392–3 and *BBBM*, pp. 373–5 and *passim*; Wood 401 (162); Euing, no. 379

A Wench for a VVeauer. A Wench for a Weauer here you shall finde, / In defending his trade brought her to his minde. To the tune of *hang vp my Shuttle* (*c.* 1630); *PB*, no. 73, II, pp. 162–8; M: *PMO*, I, pp. 364–5

'When I do cawll to mynd' (between *c.* 1550 and 1565); *SB*, no. 15, pp. 40–4; MS. Ashm. 48

Whipping Cheare. Or the wofull lamentations of the three Sisters in the Spittle when they were in new Bride-well. To the tune of *hempe and flax* (*c.* 1612); *PG*, no. 6, pp. 39–43

The wiuing age. / Or / A great Complaint of the Maidens of London, / Who now for lacke of good Husbands are vndone, / For now many Widowes though neuer so old, / Are caught vp by young men for lucre of gold. To the tune of *the Golden age* (between 1621 and 1625); Martin Parker; *PG*, no. 41, pp. 234–8; M: *PMO*, I, p. 208 and *BBBM*, pp. 779, 780

The Woful Lamentation of Mrs. Jane Shore, a Gold-smith's Wife of London, sometime King Edward the Fourth's Concubine, who for her Wanton Life came to a Miserable End. Set forth for the Example of all wicked Livers. To the Tune of *Live with me* (between 1603 and 1675); *RB*, I, pp. 479–92; M: *PMO*, I, p. 215

The Wooing Maid; / Or, / A faire maid neglected, / Forlorne and rejected, / That would be respected: / Which to have effected, / This generall summon / She sendeth in common; Come tinker, come broomman: / She will refuse no man. To the Tune of *If 'be the dad on't* (1636); Martin Parker; *RB*, III, pp. 52–6 and *CM*, no. CLIX, pp. 313–15

Youth's Warning-peice. In a true Relation of the woefull Death of William Rogers, of Cranbroke, in Kent, an Apothecary, who, refusing all good counsell, and following lewd company, dyed miserably since Christmas last, 1635. To the tune of *Doctor Faustus* (1636); *RB*, III, pp. 1–4; M: *PMO*, I, p. 162 and *BBMB*, pp. 228, 534

1.2 Editions of street-ballad texts

The following editions of street-ballad texts and tunes are listed under the names of their editors. They are also referred to as such in the main text and notes, unless abbreviations have been used. Where two or more works are listed under one editor (or one author in the following sections) they are arranged in alphabetical order. Also see p. x for the list of abbreviations, which at the same time provides an alphabetical list of the most important titles.

Bell, R. (ed.), *Ancient poems ballads and songs of the peasantry of England taken down from oral Recitation and transcribed from private manuscripts rare broadsides and scarce publications* (London, 1857).

Chappell, W. (ed.), *The Ballad Literature and Popular Music of Olden Time*, 2 vols. (London, 1859).

(ed.), *Old English Popular Music . . . A new edition, with a preface and notes, and the earlier examples entirely revised by H. E. Wooldridge*, 2 vols. (London, 1893).

(ed.), *Popular Music of the Olden Time; a Collection of Ancient Songs, Ballads and Dance Tunes, illustrative of the National Music of England*, 2 vols. (London, 1855–59).

Chappell, W., and Ebsworth, J. W. (eds.), *The Roxburghe Ballads*, 9 vols. (Hertford, 1869–99, repr. New York, 1966).

Clark, A. (ed.), *The Shirburn Ballads 1585–1616* (Oxford, 1907).

Collier, J. P. (ed.), *Broadside Black-letter Ballads, Printed in the Sixteenth and Seventeenth Centuries; chiefly in the Possession of J. Payne Collier* (priv. print 1868).

(ed.), *Old Ballads from Early Printed Copies of the utmost Rarity*, vol. I (London, 1840).

Collmann, H. L. (ed.), *Ballads and Broadsides chiefly of the Elizabethan Period And Printed in Black-Letter Most of which were formerly in the Heber Collection and are now in the Library at Britwell Court Buckinghamshire* (Oxford, 1912).

Ebsworth, J. W. (ed.), *The Bagford Ballads. Illustrating The Last Years of the Stuarts*, 2 vols. (Hertford, 1878).

(ed.), *The Roxburghe Ballads*, see Chappell, W., and Ebsworth, J. W. (eds.).

Farmer, J. S. (ed.), *Merry Songs and Ballads prior to the Year A.D. 1800*, 5 vols. (1897, repr. New York, 1964).

Fawcett, F. B. (ed.), *Broadside Ballads of the Restoration Period from the Jersey Collection Known as the Osterley Park Ballads* (London, 1930).

Huth, H. (ed.), *Ancient Ballads and Broadsides Published in England in the Sixteenth Century, chiefly in the Earlier Years of the Reign of Queen Elizabeth* (London, 1867).

Johnson, R. B. (ed.), *A Book of British Ballads* (London, 1966).

Lilly, J. (ed.), *A Collection of Seventy-nine Black-letter Ballads: 1559–1597* (London, 1870).

Mitchell, A. F. (ed.), *A Compendious Book of Godly and Spiritual Songs commonly known as 'The gude and godlie ballatis.' Reprinted from the Edition of 1567* (Edinburgh, 1897).

Rimbault, E. F. (ed.), *A Little Book of Songs and Ballads, gathered from ancient musick book MS. and printed* (London, 1851).

Rollins, H. E. (ed.), *Cavalier and Puritan. Ballads and Broadsides Illustrating the Period of the Great Rebellion 1640–1660* (New York, 1923).

(ed.), *Old English Ballads: 1553–1625. Chiefly from Manuscripts* (Cambridge, 1920).

(ed.), *The Pack of Autolycus or Strange and Terrible News of Ghosts, Apparitions, Monstrous Births, Showers of Wheat, Judgements of God, and other Prodigies and Fearful Happenings as told in Broadside Ballads of the years 1624–1693* (Cambridge, Mass., 1927, repr. 1969).

(ed.), *The Pepys Ballads*, 8 vols. (Cambridge, Mass., 1929–32).

(ed.), *A Pepysian Garland. Black-letter Broadside Ballads of the Years 1595–1639. Chiefly from the Collection of Samuel Pepys* (Cambridge, 1922).

Simpson, C. M. (ed.), *The British Broadside Ballad and Its Music* (New Brunswick, 1966).

Sola Pinto, V. de (ed.), *The Common Muse. An Anthology of Popular British Ballad Poetry XVth–XXth Century* (London, 1957).

Wright, T. (ed.), *Political Ballads published in England during the Commonwealth* (London, 1841).

— (ed.), *Political Poems and Songs relating to the English History composed during the period from the accession of Edw. III to that of Ric. III*, 2 vols. (London, 1859–61).

— (ed.), *The Political Songs of England, from the Reign of John to that of Edward II* (London, 1839).

— (ed.), *Songs and Ballads, with Other Short Poems, chiefly of the Reign of Philip and Mary. Edited from a Manuscript in the Ashmolean Museum* (London, 1860).

1.3 Source material for reception history

This section provides a survey of texts containing contemporary comment on the street ballad. They are therefore listed with their original titles and with publication dates. If later editions are quoted in the relevant part of the appendix, these are placed after the title. Only those texts which in the appendix are quoted from G. G. Smith's anthology (1964) or from W. Chappell (1859) are given an abbreviated reference to their provenance after the original title, including volume number; the date of the relevant passage is given in the appendix. G. G. Smith and W. Chappell are listed in the following as editors of source material for reception history. Texts published anonymously are listed under their title.

The Actors Remonstrance, or complaint for the silencing of their profession, and banishment from their severall play-houses [. . .] (1643).

Ascham, R., *The Scholemaster* (1570); G. G. Smith, ed. (1964), I.

Baldwin, W., *The Canticles or Balades of Salomon* (1549).

'A Ballet, a ballet! . . . ' (1658) *Wit Restor'd In severall Select Poems Not formerly publish't* (London, 1658), p. 39.

Beaumont, F. and J. Fletcher, *Monsieur Thomas* (1639); A. Dyce, ed., *The Works of Beaumont & Fletcher*, 11 vols. (London, 1843–6).

'Bless the printer from the searcher . . . ' (1648); in W. Chappell (1859), II.

Breton, N., *The Court and Country* (1618); in *A mad World my Masters and other Prose Works by Nicholas Breton*, 2 vols. (London, 1929).

Brice, T., *Against filthy writing, and such like delighting* (1561/62); BB, no. 13, pp. 36–7.

Browne, W., 'Britannia's Pastorals' (1625); W. C. Hazlitt, ed., *The Whole Works of William Browne*, 3 vols. (London, 1868; repr. New York, 1970).

Burton, R., *The Anatomy of Melancholy* (1621); quoted from W. Chappell, ed., *Old English Music* (London, 1819).

Cavendish, W., *The triumphant Widow or the Medley of Humours* (1677).

Chapman, G., *Monsieur d'Olive* (1606).

Chappell, W., *The Ballad Literature and Popular Music of Olden Times*, 2 vols. (London, 1859).

Chettle, H., *Kind-Harts Dreame. Conteining Fiue Apparitions with their*

Inuectives (1592); E. F. Rimbault, ed., Percy Soc., *Early English Poetry, Ballads, and Popular Literature of the Middle Ages*, vol. 5 (London, 1841).

Davies, J., *A Scovrge for Paper-Persecutors, or Papers Complaint, compil'd in ruthfull Rimes, Against the Paper-spoylers of these Times* (1624).

Defoe, D., 'The Ballad-maker's Plea' (1722); W. Lee, ed., *Daniel Defoe: His Life and Recently Discovered Writings*, 3 vols. (London, 1869), III.

The Dovvnefall of Temporizing Poets, unlicenst Printers, upstart Booksellers, trotting Mercuries, and bawling Hawkers. Being a very pleasant Dialogue between Light-foot *the Mercury, and* Suck-bottle *the Hawker,* Red-nose *the Poet being Moderator between them, the corruptions of all which is plainly described* (1641).

Drayton, M., 'To Master George Sandys' (1621), J. W. Hebel, ed., *The Works of Michael Drayton*, 5 vols. (Oxford, 1932–42).

Earle, J., *Micro-cosmographie* (1628); H. Osborne, ed. (London, 1933).

'The Ex-Ale-tation of Ale' (1661), *Choyce Drollery*, J. W. Ebsworth, ed. (Boston, Lincs., 1876).

Fitzgeffrey, H., *Satyres and Satyricall Epigrams* (London, 1617).

Fletcher, A., *The Political Works of Andrew Fletcher, Esq., of Saltoun* (Glasgow, 1749).

Fletcher, J., *The Bloody Brother* (1648); A. Dyce, ed., *The Works of Beaumont & Fletcher*, 11 vols. (London, 1843–46), IV.

    The Humorous Lieutenant (1625); A. Dyce, ed. (1834–46; see above), VI.

    Monsieur Thomas (1639); A. Dyce, ed. (1843–46; see above), VII.

    The Pilgrim (1622); A. Dyce, ed. (1843–46, see above), VII.

    The Queen of Corinth (between 1616 and 1619); A. Dyce, ed. (1843–46, see above), V.

Forde, J., *Loues Sacrifice* (1633).

Fullwood, W., *A Supplication to Eldertonne, for eaches vnlewdnes* (*c.* between 1570 and 1590); BB, no. 49, pp. 139–43.

A Garland for the New Royal Exchange (1669).

Gosse, E. (ed.), *Restoration Plays* (London, 1962).

Gosson, S., *The Schoole of Abuse, Conteining a pleasaunt inuective against Poets, Pipers, Plaiers, Jesters and such like Catterpillers of a Commonwealth* (1579); E. Arber, ed. (English Reprints, London, 1868).

Greene, R., *The Second part of Conny-catching. Contayning the discouery of certaine wondrous Coosenages, either superficiallie past ouer, or vtterlie vntouch in the first* (1591); A. B. Grosart (ed.), *The Life and Complete Works in Prose and Verse of Robert Greene, M.A.*, 15 vols. (New York, 1881–86; repr. 1964), X.

Hall, J., *Martin Mar-sixtus* (1592).

    Satires (1547); J. Pratt and P. Hall, eds., *The Works of Joseph Hall*, 12 vols. (Oxford, 1937–39), XII.

Harington, J., *A Preface, or rather a Briefe Apologie of Poetrie* (1591); G. G. Smith, ed. (1964), II.

Heywood, T., *A Challenge for Beautie* (1636).

Jonson, B., *Bartholomew Fair* (1614); W. Gifford and F. Cunningham, eds., *The Works of Ben Jonson*, 3 vols. (London, 1897), II.

Lodge, T., *A Defence of Poetry* (1579); G. G. Smith, ed. (1964), I.

Lovell, T., *A Dialogue between Custom and Verity, concerning the use and abuse of dauncinge and minstralsye* (1581).

Massinger, P., *The Parliament of Love* (1624).

Nashe, T., *The Anatomie of Absurditie* (1589); R. B. McKerrow, ed., *The Works of Thomas Nashe*, 6 vols. (London, 1904–10), I, pp. 1–59.

Pierce Pennilesse His Svpplication to the Diuell (1592); R. B. McKerrow, ed. (1904–10; see above), I, pp. 137–45.

Strange Newes of the Intercepting of Certaine Letters (1592); R. B. McKerrow, ed. (1904–10; see above), I, pp. 247–51.

A new balade entituled as foloweth . . . (between 1556 and 1571); AB, no. 63, pp. 304–8

Osborne, D., *The Letters of Dorothy Osborne to William Temple*, G. C. Moore Smith, ed. (Oxford, 1928).

Parkes, W., *The Courtaine-Drawer of the World* (1612); A. B. Grosart, ed., *Occasional Issues of Unique and Very Rare Books*, vol. III (Manchester, 1876).

Parrot, H., *Laquei ridiculosi: or Springes for Woodcocks* (1613).

The Mastive, Or Young-Whelpe of the Olde-Dogge. Epigrams and Satyrs (1615).

Pennington, *et al.*, 'Alderman Pennington, with some hundreds following him, presented the Citizens Petition, subscribed by 15 000, against the Discipline, and Ceremonies of the Church' (11 Dec. 1640).

The Pilgrimage to Parnassus with the two parts of the Return from Parnassus. Three Comedies performed in St. John's College Cambridge. A.D. MDXCVII–MDCI; W. D. Macray, ed. (Oxford, 1886).

Puttenham, G., *The arte of English Poesie* (1589); G. G. Smith, ed., II.

Riche, B., *Allarme to England foreshewing what perilles are procured, where the people liue without regarde of Martiall lawe* (1578).

Rimbault, E. F. (ed.), *A Little Book of Songs and Ballads* (London, 1851).

Rowley, W., *A New Wonder, A Woman never Vext* (1632); C. W. Dilke, ed., *Old English Plays*, vol. 5 (London, 1815).

Selden, J., *Table Talk* (1689), F. Pollock, ed. (London, 1927).

Shakespeare, W., *As You Like It* (first performed *c.* 1599); P. Alexander, ed., *William Shakespeare. The Complete Works* (London, 1964), pp. 254–83.

Coriolanus (1623); P. Alexander, ed. (1964; see above), pp. 827–69.

King Henry the Fourth, Part I (Quarto 1598); P. Alexander, ed. (1964; see above), pp. 480–513.

Love's Labour's Lost (first performed *c.* 1595; Quarto 1598); P. Alexander, ed. (1964; see above), pp. 166–97.

The Winter's Tale (first performed *c.* 1609/10); P. Alexander, ed. (1964; see above), pp. 377–413.

Shirley, J., *The Court Secret* (1653); W. Gifford, ed., *The Dramatic Works of James Shirley*, 6 vols. (London, 1833), V.

Smith, G. G. (ed.), *Elizabethan Critical Essays*, 2 vols. (Oxford, 1964; 1st edn 1904).

A Song for Autolycus (*c.* 1620); E. F. Rimbault, ed. (1851), pp. 156–7.

Spenser, E., 'The Tears of the Muses' (1591); *The Poetical Works of Edmund Spenser*, J. C. Smith, E. de Selincourt, eds. (London, 1972), pp. 480–6.

344   Bibliography

Stanyhurst, R., *Thee First Fovre Bookes of Virgil his Aeneis* (1582); G. G. Smith, ed. (1964), I.

Stubbes, P., *The Anatomie of Abuses: Containing A Discoverie, or brief Summarie of such Notable Vices and Corruptions, as now raigne in many Christian Countreyes of the Worlde* (1583); F. J. Furnivall, ed., Shakespeare Soc., 1877.

Turner, W., *Turners dish of Lentten Stuffe, or Galymaufery* (1612), PG, no. 5, pp. 30–8.

Walton, I., *The Compleat Angler* (1653–55); quoted from J. Bartlett, *Familiar Quotations* (London, 1968), 326 a.

Webbe, W., *A Discourse of English Poetrie* (1586); G. G. Smith, ed. (1964), I.

1.4 Further primary texts

Collections of texts are listed under their editor, and works by single authors under the author's name.

Aristotle, *Poetik*, trans. Olog Gigon (Stuttgart, 1964).

Black, M. W. (ed.), *Elizabethan and Seventeenth-Century Lyrics* (Chicago, 1938).

Brook, G. L. (ed.), *The Harley Lyrics. The Middle English Lyrics of MS Harley 2253* (2nd edn, Manchester, 1956).

Chaucer, G., *The Works of Geoffrey Chaucer*, F. N. Robinson, ed. (2nd edn, London, 1957).

Child, F. J. (ed.), *The English and Scottish Popular Ballads*, 5 vols. (1882–98; repr. New York, 1965).

D'Urfey, T. (ed.), *Wit and Mirth: or Pills to Purge Melancholy; being a Collection of the best Merry Ballads and Songs, Old and New. Fitted to all Humours, having each their proper Tune for either Voice, or Instrument: Most of the Songs being new Set*, 6 (London, 1719–20).

Earle, J., *Microcosmography or a Piece of the World discovered in Essays and Characters*, H. Osborne, ed. (London, 1933).

Farmer, J. S. (ed.), *Musa Pedestris. Three Centuries of Canting Songs and Slang Rhymes (1536–1896)* (New York, 1964).

Fischer, H. (ed.), *Englische Barockgedichte. Englisch/Deutsche* (Stuttgart, 1971).

Foxe, J., *The Actes and Monuments of John Foxe*, G. Townsend, ed., 8 vols. (London, 1843–9).

Greene, R. L. (ed.), *The Early English Carols*. Second edition revised and enlarged (Oxford, 1977).

Jonson, Ben, *Masques and Entertainments*, H. Morley, ed. (London, 1890).

The Works, W. Gifford and F. Cunningham, eds., 3 vols. (London, 1897).

Lydgate, J., *Falls of the Princes*, H. Bergen, ed., EETS, pp. 121–4 (London, 1934).

McClure, N. E. (ed.), *Sixteenth-Century English Poetry* (New York, 1954).

Ricks, C. (ed.), *English Poetry and Prose 1540–1674* (London, 1956).

Rollins, H. E. (ed.), *A Handful of Pleasant Delights (1584)* (Cambridge, Mass., 1924, repr. New York, 1965).

(ed.), *Tottel's Miscellany (1557–1587)* (Cambridge, Mass., 1928–9, 2nd edn, 1966).

Rollins, H. E. and Baker, H. (eds.), *The Renaissance in England. Non-dramatic Prose and Verse of the Sixteenth Century* (Boston, 1954).

Shakespeare, W., *The Complete Works*, P. Alexander, ed. (London, 1964).

Sidney, P., *The Prose Works of Sir Philip Sidney*, A. Feuillerat, ed., 4 vols. (Cambridge, 1963).

2 Secondary literature

In order to facilitate quick reference, since titles in the main text and notes are given under author and publication date only, secondary literature has not been divided into areas of research.

Abbreviations

CL   *Comparative Literature*
DU   *Der Deutschunterricht*
DVJS   *Deutsche Vierteljahresschrift für Literaturwissenschaft und Geistes-geschichte*
GRM   *Germanisch-Romanische Monatsschrift*
LiLi   *Zeitschrift für Literaturwissenschaft und Linguistik*
MLN   *Modern Language Notes*
MLR   *Modern Language Review*
MP   *Modern Philology*
NLH   *New Literary History*
SP   *Studies in Philology*
STZ   *Sprache im Technischen Zeitalter*
WW   *Wirkendes Wort*

Albrecht, M. C., 'The Relationship of Literature and Society', *American Journal of Sociology*, 59 (1953/54), pp. 425–36.

Anderegg, J., *Fiktion und Kommunikation. Ein Beitrag zur Theorie der Prosa* (Göttingen, 1973).

Apel, K.-O., 'Szientistik, Hermeneutik und Ideologiekritik. Entwurf einer Wissenschaftslehre in erkenntnis-anthropologischer Sicht', *Hermeneutik und Ideologiekritik*, K.-O. Apel, et al. (Frankfurt, 1971), pp. 7–44.

Ashley, M., *England in the Seventeenth Century* (London, 1952).

Atkins, J. W. H., *English Literary Criticism: The Medieval Phase* (Gloucester, Mass., 1961).

Austin, J. L., 'Performative–Constative', *Philosophy and Ordinary Language*, C. Caton, ed. (Urbana, 1963), pp. 22–54.

Baker, E. A., *The History of the English Novel*, vols. 1–3 (New York, 1929, 3rd edn, 1957).

Baker, H. C., 'Classical Material in Broadside Ballads 1550–1625', *PMLA*, 54 (1939), pp. 981–9.

Baldensperger, F., 'Ist die Literatur Ausdruck der Gesellschaft?', *DVJS*, 7 (1929), pp. 17–28.

Baldwin, C. S., *Renaissance Literary Theory and Practice. Classicism in the Rhetoric and Poetic of Italy, France, and England* (Gloucester, Mass., 2nd edn, 1959).

Bartenschlager, K., 'Die Situation des Sprechers im Gedicht. Wyatt, Sidney, Spenser. Ein historisch-typologischer Versuch' (thesis, Munich, 1970).

Baskervill, C. R., *The Elizabethan Jig and Related Song Drama* (Chicago, 1929).

Bauer, J., 'Zum Gebrauchswert der Ware Literatur', *LiLi*, 1 (1971), 1/2, pp. 47–57.

Bauer, R. A., 'Das widerspenstige Publikum. Der Einflussprozess aus der Sicht sozialer Kommunikation', *Massenkommunikationsforschung. 2. Konsumtion*, D. Prokop, ed. (Frankfurt, 1973), pp. 152–66.

Baugh, A. C., ed., *A Literary History of England* (London, 1948).

Baumgärtner, K., 'Der methodische Stand einer linguistischen Poetik', in *Literaturwissenschaft und Linguistik*, 2: 2, ed. J. Iwre (Frankfurt, 1971), pp. 371–402.

Baumgärtner, K. *et al.*, *Funk-Kolleg Sprache. Eine Einführung in die moderne Linguistik*, 2 vols. (Frankfurt, 1973).

Bausinger, H., 'Wege zur Erforschung der trivialen Literatur', *Studien zur Trivialliteratur*, H. O. Burger, ed. (Frankfurt, 1968), pp. 1–33.

Bellert, I., 'On a Condition of the Coherence of Texts', *Semiotica*, 2 (1970), pp. 335–63.

Bennett, H. S., *English Books and Readers 1603 to 1640. Being a Study of the History of the Book Trade in the Reign of James I and Charles I* (Cambridge, 1970).

Bessler, H. and Bledjan, F., *Systematik der Massenkommunikationsforschung* (Munich, 1967).

Bierwisch, M., 'Poetik und Linguistik', *Literaturwissenschaft und Linguistik*, J. Ihwe, ed., vol. II/2 (Frankfurt, 1971), pp. 568–86.

Bladgen, C., 'Notes on the Ballad Market in the Second Half of the Seventeenth Century', *Studies in Bibliography*, 6 (1954), pp. 161–80.

Blumenberg, H., *Die Legitimität der Neuzeit* (Frankfurt, 1966).

Blumensath, H., ed., *Strukturalismus in der Literaturwissenschaft* (Cologne, 1972).

Booth, W. C., *The Rhetoric of Fiction* (Chicago, 1961).

Bourdieu, P., *Zur Soziologie symbolischer Formen* (Frankfurt, 1970).

Brand, J., *Observations on Popular Antiquities of Great Britain*, vol. III (London, 1848).

Bratton, J. S., *The Victorian Popular Ballad* (London, 1975).

Brednich, R. W., *Die Liedpublizistik im Flugblatt des 15. bis 17. Jahrhunderts*, vol. I, *Abhandlungen* (Baden-Baden, 1974), vol. II, *Katalog der Liedflugblätter des 15. und 16. Jahrhunderts* (Baden-Baden, 1975).

Breuer, D., *Einführung in die pragmatische Texttheorie* (Munich, 1974).

Bühler, K., *Sprachtheorie. Die Darstellungsfunktionen der Sprache*, 2nd edn (Stuttgart, 1965).

Burger, H. O., ed., *Studien zur Trivialliteratur* (Frankfurt, 1968).

Burke, T., *The Streets of London through the Centuries* (London, 1940).

Bush, D., *English Literature in the Early Seventeenth Century 1600–1660. The Oxford History of English Literature*, vol. V (Oxford, 1945, 2nd edn, 1962).

Campbell, B. G., 'Toward a Workable Taxonomy of Illocutionary Forces, and its Implication to Works of Imaginative Literature', *Language and Style*, vol. 8/1 (1975), pp. 3–20.

Carter, H., *A View of Typography* (Oxford, 1969).

Cassirer, E., *Individuum und Kosmos in der Philosophie der Renaissance* (Darmstadt, 2nd edn, 1969).

Castrop, H., 'Das elisabethanische Theater', *Shakespeare Handbuch*, I. Schabert, ed. (Stuttgart, 1972), pp. 73–123.

'Die Satire in Drydens Prologen und Epilogen', *Archiv*, 123 (1972), pp. 267–85.

Chambers, E. K., *The Elizabethan Stage*, 4 vols. (Oxford, 1923).

The Medieval Stage, 2 vols. (Oxford 1954).

Chappell, W., Introduction, *The Roxburghe Ballads*, vol. I (London, 1877), pp. i–xvi.

'Publishers of Black-Letter Ballads in the Seventeenth Century', *The Roxburghe Ballads*, vol. I, part 2 (London, 1888), pp. xvii–xxiii.

Christensen, P. A., 'The Beginnings and Endings of the Middle English Metrical Romances' (thesis, Stanford, 1927).

Collison, R., *The Story of Street Literature* (London, 1973).

Craig, H., *English Religious Drama of the Middle Ages* (Oxford, 2nd edn, 1960).

Curtius, E. R., *Europäische Literatur und lateinisches Mittelalter* (Bern, 5th edn, 1965).

Dähne, R., *Die Lieder der Maumariée seit dem Mittelalter*, Romanistische Arbeiten, 20 (Halle, 1933).

Dahrendorf, M., 'Literaturdidaktik und Trivialliteratur', *STZ*, 44 (1972), pp. 269–77.

Daiches, D., 'Literature and Society', *Critical Approaches* (London, 1967), pp. 358–75.

A Critical History of English Literature, vol. I (New York, 1960).

Daneš, F., 'Zur linguistischen Analyse der Textstruktur', *Folia Linguistica*, 4 (1970), pp. 72–8.

'Zur semantischen Struktur des Kommunikats', *Probleme der Textgrammatik* (Studia Grammatica XI), F. Daneš and D. Viehweger, eds. (Berlin, 1976), pp. 29–40.

Davison, A., 'Indirect Speech Acts and What To Do With Them?', *Syntax and Semantics, Volume 3: Speech Acts*. P. Cole and J. L. Morgan, eds. (New York, 1975).

Diller, H.-J., *Redeformen des englischen Misterienspiels* (Munich, 1973).

Dreitzel, H. P., *Die gesellschaftlichen Leiden und das Leiden an der Gesellschaft. Vorstudien zu einer Pathologie des Rollenverhaltens* (Stuttgart, 1972).

Dubois, J. et al., *Allgemeine Rhetorik* (Munich, 1974).

Duff, E. G., *A Century of the English Book Trade: Short Notices of all Printers, Stationers, Book-Binders, and others connected with it from the Issue of the first dated book in 1457 to the Incorporation of the company of stationers in 1557* (London, 1905).

Ebsworth, J. W., Introduction, *The Bagford Ballads. Illustrating The Last Years of the Stuarts*, 2 vols. (Hertford, 1878), pp. i–xlix.

Introduction to the Final Volume, *The Roxburghe Ballads*, W. Chappell and J. W. Ebsworth, eds., vol. VIII, pp. ix–civ.

Ecker, G., *Einblattdrucke von den Anfängen bis 1555. Untersuchungen zu einer Publikationsform literarischer Texte*, 2 vols. (Stuttgart, 1981).

Eco, U., *Einführung indie Semiotik* (Munich, 1972).

Ehrich, V. and Saile, G., 'Über nicht-direkte Sprechakte', *Linguistische Pragmatik*, D. Wunderlich, ed. (Frankfurt, 1972), pp. 255–87.

Entwistle, W. J., *European Balladry* (2nd edn, Oxford, 1951).

Escarpit, R., *Das Buch und der Leser. Entwurf einer Literatursoziologie* (Cologne, 1961).

Evans, I. H., ed., *Brewer's Dictionary of Phrase and Fable* (London, 1970).

Faas, K. E., 'Dramatischer Monolog und dramatisch-monologische Versdichtung', *Anglia*, 87 (1969), pp. 338–66.
Poesie als Psychogramm. Die dramatisch-monologische Versdichtung im viktorianischen Zeitalter (Munich, 1974).
Faral, E., *Les Jongleurs en France au Moyen Age* (Paris, 1910).
Festinger, L., *A Theory of Cognitive Dissonance* (2nd edn, Stanford, Calif., 1962).
Fieguth, R., 'Zur Rezeptionslenkung bei narrativen und dramatischen Werken', *STZ*, 47 (1973), pp. 186–201.
Firth, C., ed., *Shakespeare's England*, vol. I (5th edn, Oxford, 1950).
Fowler, D. C., *A Literary History of the Popular Ballad* (Durham, N.C., 1968).
Frank, J., *The Beginnings of the English Newspaper 1620–1660* (Cambridge, Mass., 1961).
Fraser, R., *The War against Poetry* (Princeton, 1970).
Friedmann, A. B., 'Ballad', *Encyclopedia of Poetry and Poetics*, A. Preminger, ed. (Princeton, 1965), pp. 62–4.
'Broadside Ballad', *Encyclopedia of Poetry and Poetics*, A. Preminger, ed. (Princeton, 1965), p. 86.
'The Late Medieval Ballade and the Origin of Broadside Balladry', *Medium Aevum*, 17 (1958), pp. 95–100.
The Ballad Revival. Studies in the Influence of Popular on Sophisticated Poetry (Chicago, 1961).
Fügen, H. N., *Die Hauptrichtungen der Literatursoziologie* (3rd edn, Bonn, 1963).
(ed.), *Wege der Literatursoziologie* (Neuwied, 1968).
Furnivall, F. J., ed., *Ballads from Manuscripts. Ballads on the Condition of England in Henry VII's and Edward VI's Reigns*, 2 vols., vol. I (London, 1868–72), vol. II (Hertford, 1873).
Greg, W. W., *Some Aspects and Problems of London Publishing between 1550 and 1650* (Oxford, 1956).
Grierson, H. and Smith, J. C., *A Critical History of English Poetry* (London, 1956).
Grose, F., *A Classical Dictionary of the Vulgar Tongue*, E. Partridge, ed. (3rd edn, London, 1963).
Gülich, E. and Raible, W., eds., *Textsorten. Differenzierungskriterien aus linguistischer Sicht* (Frankfurt, 1972).
Gummere, F. B., *The Popular Ballad* (1907; repr. New York, 1959).
Habermas, J., 'Der Universalitätsanspruch der Hermeneutik', *Hermeneutik und Ideologiekritik*, K.-O. Apel, et al. (Frankfurt, 1971), pp. 120–59.
'Vorbereitende Bemerkungen zu einer Theorie der kommunikativen Kompetenz', *Theorie der Gesellschaft oder Sozialtechnologie – Was leistet die Systemforschung?* J. Habermas and N. Luhmann (Frankfurt, 1971), pp. 101–42.
Hamburger, K., 'Die Ballade und ihr Verhältnis zu Bild- und Rollengedicht', *Die Logik der Dichtung* (Stuttgart, 1957), pp. 209–20.
'Zwei Formen literatursoziologischer Betrachtung. Zu Erich Auerbach "Mimesis" und Georg Lukács "Goethe und seine Zeit"', *Orbis Litterarum*, 7 (1949), pp. 142–60.
Handover, P. M., *Printing in London from 1476 to Modern Times* (London, 1960).
Hantsch, I., 'Zur semantischen Strategie der Werbung', *STZ*, 42 (1972), pp. 93–114.

Harris, Z. S., 'Discourse Analysis', *Language*, 28 (1952), pp. 1–30.

Harweg, R., 'Textanfänge in geschriebener und gesprochener Sprache', *Orbis*, 17 (1968).

Hastings, J., ed., *Encyclopaedia of Religion and Ethics*, 13 vols. (Edinburgh, 1908–26).

Hauser, A., *Sozialgeschichte der Kunst und Literatur* (Munich, 1972).

Haydn, H., *The Counter-Renaissance* (New York, 1950).

Hempfer, K. W., *Gattungstheorie* (Munich, 1973).

Tendenz und Ästhetik. Studien zur französischen Verssatire des 18. Jahrhunderts (Munich, 1972).

Hill, C., 'Protestantism and the Rise of Capitalism', *Essays in the Economic and Social History of Tudor and Stuart England*, F. J. Fisher, ed. (Cambridge, 1961), pp. 15–39.

Puritanism and Revolution. Studies in the Interpretation of the English Revolution of the 17th Century (London, 1969).

Society and Puritanism in Pre-Revolutionary England (London, 1966).

Ihwe, J., ed., *Literaturwissenschaft und Linguistik. Ergebnisse und Perspektiven*, 3 vols. (Frankfurt, 1971–2).

Iser, W., *Die Appellstruktur der Texte. Unbestimmtheit als Wirkungsbedingung literarischer Prosa* (Constance, 1970).

Jakobson, R., 'Der Doppelcharakter der Sprache. Die Polarität zwischen Metaphorik und Metonymik', *Literaturwissenschaft und Linguistik*, J. Ihwe, ed., vol. I (Frankfurt, 1971a), pp. 323–33.

'Linguistik und Poetik, *Literaturwissenschaft und Linguistik*, J. Ihwe, ed., vol. II/1 (Frankfurt, 1971b), pp. 142–78.

Janik, D., *Die Kommunikationsstruktur des Erzählwerks. Ein semiologisches Modell* (Bebenhausen, 1973).

Jauss, H. R., *Literaturgeschichte als Provokation* (Frankfurt, 1970).

Kallmeyer, W., et al., *Lektürekolleg zur Textlinguistik:* vol. 1: *Einführung*, vol. 2: *Reader* (Frankfurt, 1974).

Kallweit, H. W. Lepenies, 'Literarische Hermeneutik und Soziologie', *Ansichten einer künftigen Germanistik*, J. Kolbe, ed. (Munich, 1969), pp. 131–42.

Kayser, W., *Geschichte der deutschen Ballade* (Berlin, 1936).

Ker, W. P., 'On the History of the Ballads 1100–1500', *Proceedings of the British Academy*, vol. IV (1909–10), pp. 179–205.

Knights, L. C., *Drama and Society in the Age of Jonson* (2nd edn, London, 1951).

König, R., ed., *Soziologie*, Fischer Lexikon (Frankfurt, 1969).

Köster, R., *Ullstein Lexikon der deutschen Sprache* (Frankfurt, 1969).

Koszyk, K. and Pruys, K. H., eds., *DTV Wörterbuch zur Publizistik* (Munich, 1969).

Kuhn, H., 'Eine Sozialgeschichte der Kunst und Literatur, Kritische Reflexionen zu Arnold Heuser, Sozialgeschichte der Kunst und Literatur, München 1953', Kuhn, *Text und Theorie* (Stuttgart, 1969), pp. 59–79.

'Soziale Realität und dichterische Fiktion am Beispiel der höfischen Ritterdichtung Deutschlands', *Dichtung und Welt im Mittelalter* (Stuttgart, 1959), pp. 22–40.

Lämmert, E., *Bauformen des Erzählens* (Stuttgart, 1955).

Landwehr, J., *Text und Fiktion. Zu einigen literaturwissenschaftlichen und kommunikationstheoretischen Grundbegriffen* (Munich, 1975).

Lewis, C. S., *English Literature in the Sixteenth Century. Excluding Drama.* The Oxford History of English Literature, III (Oxford, 1959).

Link, H., 'Rezeptionsforschung', *Eine Einführung in Methoden und Probleme* (Stuttgart, 1976).

Lipson, E., *The Economic History of England, Volume II: The Age of Mercantilism* (6th edn, London, 1956).

Lockyer, R. W., *Tudor and Stuart Britain 1471–1714* (London, 1964).

Long, J. H., 'The ballad medley and the fool', *SP*, 67 (1970), pp. 505–16.

Lotman, J. M., *Die Struktur literarischer Texte* (Munich, 1972).

Lovejoy, A. O., *The Great Chain of Being* (Cambridge, Mass., 1936).

Löwenthal, L., *Literatur und Gesellschaft. Das Buch in der Massenkultur* (Neuwied, 1964).

McKerrow, R. B., *A Dictionary of Printers and Booksellers in England, Scotland and Ireland, and of Foreign Printers of English Books 1557–1640* (London, 1910).

An Introduction to Bibliography for Literary Students (Oxford, 1927).

Macoby, N., 'Die neue wissenschaftliche Rhetorik', *Grundfragen der Kommunikationsforschung*, W. Schramm, ed. (4th edn, Munich, 1971), pp. 55–70.

Macpherson, C. B., *The Political Theory of Possessive Individualism. Hobbes to Locke* (Oxford, 1962); transl. W. Wittekund: *Die politische Theorie des Besitzindividualismus von Hobbes bis Locke* (Frankfurt, 1967).

Maletzke, G., *Einführung in die Massenkommunikationsforschung* (Berlin, 1972).

Maser, S., *Grundlagen einer allgemeinen Kommunikationstheorie* (Stuttgart, 1971).

Meissner, P., *England im Zeitalter von Humanismus, Renaissance und Reformation* (Heidelberg, 1952).

Mertner, E. and Standop, E., *Englische Literaturgeschichte* (Heidelberg, 1967).

Miller, E. H., *The Professional Writer in Elizabethan England. A Study of Nondramatic Literature* (Cambridge, Mass., 1959).

Muir, E., *Essays on Literature and Society* (London, 1965).

Mumby, F. A., *Publishing and Bookselling. A History from the Earliest Times to the Present Day* (4th edn, London, 1956).

Muscatine, C., *Chaucer and the French Tradition* (2nd edn, Berkeley, 1965).

'The Canterbury Tales: Style of the Man and Style of the Work', *Chaucer and Chaucerians. Critical Studies in Middle English Literature*, D. S. Brewer, ed. (London, 1966), pp. 88–113.

Neuburg, V. E., *Popular Literature, A History and Guide* (Harmondsworth, 1977).

Nöth, W., *Semiotik. Eine Einführung mit Beispielen für Reklameanalysen*, Anglistische Arbeitshefte, 8 (Tübingen, 1975).

Nutz, W., 'Trivialliteratur', *Fischer Lexikon: Literatur II/2*, W.-H. Friedrich and W. Killy, eds. (Frankfurt, 1965), pp. 571–81.

Ohmann, R., 'Instrumental Style: Notes on the Theory of Speech as Action', *Current Trends in Stylistics*, B. Karu and H. Stahlke, eds. (Edmonton/Champaign, 1972), pp. 115–41.

'Speech Acts and the Definition of Literature', *Philosophy and Rhetoric*, 4 (1971), pp. 1–19.

'Speech, Literature and the Space between', *NLH*, 4 (1972), pp. 47–63.

Partridge, E., ed., *A Classical Dictionary of the Vulgar Tongue by Captain Grose* (London, 1963).

Petzoldt, L., *Bänkelsang. Vom historischen Bänkelsang zum literarischen Chanson* (Stuttgart, 1974).

Pfister, M., *Das Drama. Theorie und Analyse* (Munich, 1977). English translation published as *The Theory and Analysis of Drama* (Cambridge, 1988).

Studien zum Wandel der Perspektivenstruktur in elisabethanischen und jakobäischen Komödien (Munich, 1974).

Plett, H. F., *Textwissenschaft und Textanalyse. Semiotik, Linguistik, Rhetorik* (Munich, 1975).

Plomer, H. R., *A Dictionary of Booksellers and Printers who were at Work in England, Scotland and Ireland from 1641 to 1667* (London, 1907).

A Dictionary of the Printers and Booksellers who were at Work in England, Scotland and Ireland from 1668 to 1725 (Oxford, 1907).

Prokop, D. (ed.), *Massenkommunikationsforschung 1: Produktion* (Frankfurt, 1972).

(ed.), *Massenkommunikationsforschung 2: Konsumtion* (Frankfurt, 1973).

Riedel, K. V., *Der Bänkelsang. Wesen und Funktion einer volkstümlichen Kunst* (Hamburg, 1963).

Riha, K., *Moritat, Bänkelsang, Protestballade* (Frankfurt, 1975).

Moritat, Song, Bänkelsang (Höttingen, 1965).

Rollins,, H. E., *An Analytical Index to the Ballad-Entries (1557–1709) in the Register of the Company of Stationers of London* (Chapel Hill, N.C., 1924).

'The Black-Letter Broadside Ballad', *PMLA*, 34 (1919a), pp. 258–339.

'Concerning Bodleian MS Ashmole 48', *MLN*, 34 (1919b), pp. 340–51.

Introduction, *Cavalier and Puritan. Ballads and Broadsides Illustrating the Period of the Great Rebellion 1640–1660* (New York, 1923), pp. 3–74.

'Martin Parker. Famous Balladist', *MP*, 16 (1919c), pp. 113–38.

'William Elderton: Elizabethan Actor and Ballad-Writer', *SP*, 17 (1920), pp. 199–245.

Roth, K., *Ehebruchschwänke in Liedform. Eine Untersuchung zur deutsch- und englischsprachigen Schwankballade* (Munich, 1977).

Rowse, A. L., *The Elizabethan Renaissance. The Cultural Achievement* (London, 1972).

The Elizabethan Renaissance. The Life of the Society (London, 1971).

The England of Elizabeth. The Structure of Society (London, 1964).

Rowth, H. V., 'London and the Development of Popular Literature', *Cambridge History of English Literature*, vol. 4 (Cambridge, 1909), pp. 316–63.

St Clare Byrne, M., *Elizabethan Life in Town and Country* (London, 1957).

Saintsbury, G., *A History of Criticism and Literary Taste in Europe from the Earliest Texts to the Present Day*, 3 vols. (7th edn, Edinburgh, 1961).

Sandig, B., 'Zur Differenzierung gebrauchssprachlicher Textsorten', *Textsorten, Differenzierungskriterien aus linguistischer Sicht*, E. Gülich and W. Raible, eds. (Frankfurt, 1972), pp. 113–34.

Sandison, H. E., *The 'Chanson d'aventure' in Middle English*. Bryn Mawr College Monographs, 12 (Bryn Mawr, 1913).

Schabert, I. (ed.), *Shakespeare Handbuch. Die Zeit. Der Mensch. Das Werk. Die Nachwelt* (Stuttgart, 1972).

Schanze, H., *Medienkunde für Literaturwissenschaftler* (Munich, 1974).

Schaubert, E. v., 'Zur Geschichte der Black-Letter Broadside Ballad', *Anglia, 50* (1926), pp. 1–61.

Schenda, R., 'Die deutschen Prodigiensammlungen des 16. und 17. Jahrhunderts', *Archiv für Geschichte des Buchwesens*, 4 (1962), pp. 637–710.

Die französische Prodigienliteratur in der zweiten Hälfte des 16. Jahrhunderts, Münchner Romanistische Arbeiten, 16 (Munich, 1961).

Volk ohne Buch. Studien zur Sozialgeschichte der populären Lesestoffe 1770–1910 (Frankfurt, 1970).

Schirmer, W., *Geschichte der englischen und amerikanischen Literatur*, vol. I (Tübingen, 1954).

Schlieben-Lange, B., 'Perlokution. Eine Skizze', *STZ*, 48 (1974), pp. 319–34.

Schmidt, S. J. *Texttheorie. Probleme einer Linguistik der sprachlichen Kommunikation* (Munich, 1973).

Schmidt-Henkel, J., 'Die Trivialliteratur im Kanon der Literaturwissenschaft', *STZ*, 44 (1972), pp. 258–69.

(ed.), *Trivialliteratur. Literarisches Kolloquium* (Berlin, 1964).

Schramm, W. (ed.), *Grundfragen der Kommunikationsforschung* (Munich, 1964).

Schücking, L. L., 'Literaturgeschichte und Geschmacksgeschichte. Ein Versuch zu einer neuen Problemstellung', *GRM*, 5 (1913), pp. 561–77.

Soziologie der literarischen Geschmacksbildung (3rd edn, Munich, 1961).

Schulte-Sasse, J., 'Literarischer Markt und ästhetische Denkform. Analysen und Thesen zur Geschichte ihres Zusammenhanges', *LiLi*, 2, 6 (1972), pp. 11–31.

Searle, J. R., 'A Classification of Illocutionary Acts' (MS. UC Berkeley, 1973).

'Indirect Speech Acts', *Syntax and Semantics, Volume 3: Speech Acts*, P. Cole and J. L. Morgan, eds. (New York, 1975), pp. 59–82.

Sprechakte. Ein sprachphilosophischer Essay (Frankfurt, 1971). Originally published as *Speech Acts* (Cambridge, 1969).

Sebeok, T., 'Six Species of Signs: Some Propositions and Structures', *Semiotica*, 13 (1975), pp. 233–60.

Seemann, E., 'Bänkelsang', *Reallexikon der deutschen Literaturgeschichte*, W. Kohlschmidt and W. Mohr, eds., 2nd edn, vol. I (Berlin, 1958), p. 1280.

Shaaber, M. A., *Some Forerunners of the Newspaper in England 1476–1622* (New York, 1929, 2nd edn, 1966).

Sheavyn, P., *The Literary Profession of the Elizabethan Age* (Manchester University Press, 1909).

Shepard, L., *The Broadside Ballad. A Study in Origin and Meaning* (London, 1962).

The History of Street Literature (London, 1973).

Siebert, F. S., *Freedom of the Press in England 1476–1776* (Urbana, Ill., 1952).

Silbermann, A. (ed.), *Reader. Massenkommunikation*, vol. I (Bielefeld, 1969).

Skalička, V., 'Text, Context, Subtext', *Slavica Pragensia III* (Prague, 1961), pp. 73–8.

Sola Pinto, V. de, Introduction, *The Common Muse. An Anthology of Popular British Ballad Poetry XVth–XXth Century* (London, 1957), pp. 1–29.

'The Street Ballad and English Poetry', *Politics and Letters*, 2, 3 (1947), pp. 34–45.

Spitzer, L., 'Notes on the Poetic and Empirical "I" in Medieval Authors', *Traditio*, 4 (1942), pp. 414–22.

Standop, E., 'Die Bezeichnung der poetischen Gattungen im englischen und im deutschen', *GRM*, n.s. 6 (1956), pp. 382–94.

Stanley, H., *English Books and Readers 1475–1557. Being a Study in the Book Trade from Caxton to the Incorporation of the Stationers' Company* (Cambridge, 1952).

Stanzel, F. K., *Die typischen Erzählsituationen im Roman. Dargestellt an Tom Jones, Moby Dick, The Ambassadors, Ulysses* (Vienna, 1955).

Stempel, W.-D., 'Erzählung, Beschreibung und historischer Diskurs', *Geschichte, Ereignis und Erzählung. Poetik und Hermeneutik*, V. R. Kosellek and W.-D. Stempel, eds. (Munich, 1973), pp. 325–46.

'Gibt es Textsorten?', *Textsorten. Differenzierungskriterien aus linguistischer Sicht*, E. Gülich and W. Raible, eds. (Frankfurt, 1972), pp. 175–9.

Stow, J., *A survey of London, contayning the originall, antiquity, increase, moderne estate, and a description of that citie, written in the year 1598*, ed. Henry Monley (London, 1890).

Sugden, E. H., *A Topographical Dictionary to the Works of Shakespeare and his Fellow Dramatists* (New York, 1969).

Teigeler, P., *Verständlichkeit und Wirksamkeit von Texten*, vol. 1, *Effektive Werbung* (Stuttgart, 1968).

Tetzeli von Rosador, K., *Magie im elisabethanischen Drama* (Brunswick, 1970).

Thompson, G. A., *Elisabethan Criticism of Poetry* (Chicago, 1914).

Thompson, R., *Women in Stuart England and America* (London, 1974).

Thorndyke, L., *A History of Magic and Experimental Science: Volumes V and VI: The Sixteenth Century* (New York, 1941); *Volumes VII and VIII: The Seventeenth Century* (New York, 1958).

Tillyard, E. M. W., *The Elizabethan World Picture* (Harmondsworth, 1966).

Trevelyan, G. M., *English Social History* (London, 1942, 2nd edn, 1965).

History of England (London, 1926).

A Shortened History of England (Aylesbury, 1960).

Trier, J., 'Alltagssprache', *Die Deutsche Sprache im 20. Jahrhundert*, P. Hartmann *et al.*, eds. (Göttingen, 1966), pp. 110–33.

Utley, F. L., *The Crooked Rib. An Analytical Index to the Argument about Women in English and Scots Literature to the End of the Year 1568* (New York, 1970).

Voretzsch, K., *Introduction to the Study of Old French Literature*, authorized translation of the third and last German edition (Halle, 1931).

Waldmann, G., *Kommunikationsästhetik I. Die Ideologie der Erzählform. Mit einer Modellanalyse von NS-Literatur* (Munich, 1976).

'Der Trivialroman als literarisches Zeichensystem. Modellanalyse eines Frauenschickals-Adels-Heftroman', *WW*, 22 (1972), pp. 248–67.

Walker, A. J., 'Popular Songs and Broadsides in the English Drama 1559–1642', *Harvard University Graduate School of Arts and Sciences. Summary of Theses* (Cambridge, Mass., 1935), pp. 341–3.

Ward, A. W. and Waller, A. R. (eds.), *The Cambridge History of English Literature*, vol. IV: *Prose and Poetry. Sir Thomas North to Michael Drayton* (Cambridge, 1909).

Wehse, R., *Schwanklied und Flugblatt in Grossbritannien*, Artes populares. Studia ethnographica et folkloristica, ed. L. Röhrich, vol. 3 (Bern, 1979).

Weimann, R., *Shakespeare und die Tradition des Volkstheaters. Soziologie. Dramaturgie. Gestaltung* (Berlin, 1967).

Weiss, W., 'Das elisabethanische Zeitalter', *Shakespeare Handbuch. Die Zeit, der Mensch, das Werk, die Nachwelt*, I. Schabert, ed. (Stuttgart, 1972), pp. 2–35.

'Der Refrain in der elisabethanischen Lyrik. Studien zur Entwicklungsgeschichte eines literarischen Formelements (thesis, Munich, 1964).

Wellek, R. and Warren, A., 'Literature and Society', *Theory of Literature* (New York, 1956), pp. 82–98.

Welte, W., *Moderne Linguistik: Terminologie/Bibliographie*, 2 vols. (Munich, 1974).

Wienold, G., *Semiotik der Literatur* (Frankfurt, 1972).

Wilson, F. P., *The English Drama 1485–1585* (Oxford, 1969).

(ed.), *The Oxford Dictionary of English Proverbs* (Oxford, 1970).

Wimsatt, W. K. Jr. and C. Brooks, *Literary Criticism. A Short History* (New York, 1966).

Wolpers, T., 'Kürze im Erzählen. Überlegungen zu einer Poetik und Geschichte kurzen Erzählens und zur angloamerikanischen short story im 19. und 20. Jh.', *Anglia*, 89 (1971), pp. 48–86.

Wright, L. B., *Middle Class Culture in Elizabethan England* (London, 1925, 2nd edn, 1964).

Wunderlich, D., 'Die Rolle der Pragmatik in der Linguistik', *DU*, 22, 4 (1970), pp. 5–41.

(ed.), *Linguistische Pragmatik* (Frankfurt, 1972).

'Pragmatik, Sprechsituation, Deixis', *LiLi*, 1 (1971), pp. 153–90.

'Probleme einer linguistischen Pragmatik', *Papiere zu Linguistik* 4, J. Bechert *et al.*, eds. (Munich, 1973), pp. 1–19.

'Unterricht als Dialog', *STZ*, 32 (1969), pp. 263–87.

Würzbach, N., 'An approach to a context-oriented genre theory in application to the history of the ballad: traditional ballad – street ballad – literary ballad', *Poetics* 12 (1983), pp. 35–70.

'Die englische Strassenballade: eine schaustellerische literaturform im Umfeld volkstümlicher Literatur', *Balladenforschung*, ed. W. Müller-Seidel; Neue Wissenschaftliche Bibliothek 108: Literaturwissenschaft (Königstein/Ts., 1980), pp. 134–53.

'Die Sprechsituation in der englischen Strassenballade, in der ersten Hälfte des 17. Jahrhunderts. Textkonstitution und sozio-kulturelle Bedingungskomponenten', *GRM*, n.s. 31 (1981), pp. 390–403.

'Fiktion, Fiktionalität', *Enzyklopädie des Märchens. Handwörterbuch zur historischen und vergleichenden Erzählforschung*, K. Ranke, ed., vol. 4 (Göttingen, 1984), pp. 1105–111.

Zimmermann, H. D., 'Das Vorurteil über die Trivialliteratur, das ein Vorurteil über die Literatur ist', *Akzente*, 19 (1972), pp. 386–408.

Žmegač, V., 'Probleme der Literatursoziologie', *Zur Kritik literaturwissenschaftlicher Methodologie*, Žmegač, ed. (Frankfurt, 1973), pp. 253–82.

Lightning Source UK Ltd.
Milton Keynes UK
17 February 2011

167668UK00001B/143/P